T0385597

A Revolutionary Friendship

A Revolutionary Friendship

Washington, Jefferson, and the American Republic

FRANCIS D. COGLIANO

HARVARD UNIVERSITY PRESS

Cambridge, Massachusetts & London, England

2024

First printing

Publication of this book has been supported through the generous provisions of the Maurice and Lula Bradley Smith Memorial Fund.

Library of Congress Cataloging-in-Publication Data
Names: Cogliano, Francis D., author.
Title: A revolutionary friendship : Washington, Jefferson, and the American
  Republic / Francis D. Cogliano.
Description: Cambridge, Massachusetts : Harvard University Press, 2024. |
  Includes bibliographical references and index.
Identifiers: LCCN 2023027832 | ISBN 9780674292499 (cloth)
Subjects: LCSH: Washington, George, 1732–1799—Friends and associates. |
  Washington, George, 1732–1799—Adversaries. | Jefferson, Thomas,
  1743–1826—Friends and associates. | Jefferson, Thomas,
  1743–1826—Adversaries. | United States—Politics and government—To
  1775. | United States—Politics and government—1775–1783. | United
  States—Politics and government—1783–1809.
Classification: LCC E312.17 .C64 2024 | DDC 973.4—dc23/eng/20230717
LC record available at https://lccn.loc.gov/2023027832

To my siblings—

those I was born with, and those I acquired along the way

Contents

A Revolutionary Friendship

Introduction

We begin with a fish tale.

In early June 1790, President George Washington invited Secretary of State Thomas Jefferson to go fishing with him. Washington was recovering from a bout of pneumonia that had threatened his life. A few weeks earlier, Senator William Maclay of Pennsylvania had visited the president and noted, "Every Eye full of tears, his life despaired of."[1] By the end of the month, the crisis had passed, and the president was recovering. He had always enjoyed outdoor activities—especially hunting, fishing, and riding—and a fishing trip would allow him to get out of New York (then the nation's capital) for a few days. He invited Jefferson, only recently arrived in the city as a member of Washington's cabinet, to join him.

Jefferson had been beset by his own health problems at the time, suffering from a prolonged migraine headache. On June 6 he wrote to his daughter Patsy, "I am going tomorrow on a sailing party of three or four days with the President. Should we meet sea enough to make me sick I shall hope it will carry off my headach."[2] Jefferson seemed to be trying to make the best of the situation. That he hoped that seasickness might cure him is testimony to how debilitating he found his headache.

Some historians and biographers have made much of the outing. According to Ron Chernow, biographer of both Washington and Alexander Hamilton, Hamilton joined the president and secretary of state on the trip.

Dumas Malone, one of Jefferson's most sympathetic biographers, claims it was a turning point for Jefferson. Malone wrote, "Jefferson went as a harmonious co-adjutor and in some hope of beneficial physical effects," but by the time he returned from the outing, "Jefferson had learned what Washington expected of one of his executive heads, and what his own public business really was. To sum it up, he was to be an assistant to the President, presumably the most intimate one, and it was the President, not Congress, that he had to please." According to this reading, the fishing trip was a crucial moment in the relationship between Washington and Jefferson that had profound political implications. The problem with this analysis is that the fishing trip likely did not happen.[3]

We know that Washington went fishing between June 7 and 9. The *Gazette of the United States* reported on June 12 that the president had "returned from Sandy Hook and the fishing banks, where he has been for the benefit of the sea air, and to amuse himself in the delightful recreation of fishing." The paper observed that the president caught "great numbers" of sea bass and blackfish but failed to mention the presence of the secretary of state. For his part, Jefferson noted in his Memorandum Book, a daily record of his expenses and other notable events, that he had seen a whippoorwill on June 8 (while also making payments for various household expenses on June 7 and 9, including providing the enslaved Robert Hemings with £8 to relocate to Fredericksburg, Virginia). Jefferson confirmed the bird sighting, which he was unlikely to have made while at sea, also noting, in a letter to his daughter Polly on the June 8, that the first peas and strawberries of the season had arrived. All this suggests that while Washington was enjoying "remarkably fine" weather and fishing off Sandy Hook, Jefferson, never a keen sailor, had begged off the trip, presumably citing his migraine, and remained in New York City.[4]

The belief that Washington and Jefferson went fishing together seems to be based on Jefferson's statements that he planned to accompany the president on the trip as well as an early twentieth-century work that suggested that the men might have used a sloop owned by Alexander Hamilton (who may have joined the party).[5] It remains possible, though unlikely, that Jefferson did make the trip. Whether Jefferson accompanied Washington on his fishing trip is less important than the fact that Washington extended the invitation to him. We know, as this book will show, that the two men came to have significant political differences that resulted in a personal rift between them that was unhealed when Washington died in 1799. We know, too, that Jefferson and Hamilton became bitter enemies and their antipathy helped engender the partisan strife of the 1790s. Set against these factors, the fishing trip, especially if Hamilton was there, assumes a powerful political significance. It is a small, compelling moment of human drama seemingly pregnant with implications for subsequent American political development.

To see the trip in such a light is to misread it, revealing one of the challenges this book seeks to address. In June 1790 Jefferson had only recently arrived in New York to join Washington's cabinet. Though he was skeptical about aspects of the recently ratified federal constitution, he had not yet had any meaningful disagreements with Washington. Indeed, he and Hamilton still had a cordial relationship at that point. Washington had no need yet to effect a reconciliation between Jefferson and Hamilton. On the contrary, Washington's invitation to Jefferson to join him on the fishing trip is best seen as evidence of the strength and depth of their friendship in spring of 1790. Having suffered a near-fatal health crisis and needing exercise and recreation during his convalescence, Washington invited an old friend to go fishing with him. This is not how we usually think about the interactions between the two men. Because Jefferson and Washington came to have substantial political differences during and after Washington's presidency, and because they never reconciled, historians have tended to project their estrangement back in time. Such was not the case in the late spring of 1790.

Washington and Jefferson had a thirty-year relationship. For most of those three decades, the two Virginians enjoyed a productive and positive relationship that blossomed into a friendship before deteriorating at the end of Washington's life. The fishing trip is proof of that friendship at its closest rather than a portentous encounter that anticipated future discord. It suggests that we should trace the development of the relationship between Washington and Jefferson over three decades without committing the error of anachronism, interpreting what happened in earlier years through the lens of what happened thereafter. This book seeks to do that.[6]

In January 1814 Jefferson, seventy years old and living in retirement, sat at his desk and wrote a lengthy letter to an old friend and political ally, Walter

Jones. Jones had studied at William & Mary with Jefferson in the early 1760s. He had served in Congress during Jefferson's presidency as a member of the president's Republican Party. Jones had written to the former president the previous November asking for feedback on a draft essay he had written in which he traced the rise of political partisanship in the United States. Jefferson presented his former classmate with a detailed account of the partisan battles of the 1790s. In his response to Jones, Jefferson wrote at length about Washington. He concluded by outlining the long arc of their relationship:

> These are my opinions of General Washington, which I would vouch at the judgment seat of god, having been formed on an acquaintance of 30. years. I served with him in the Virginia legislature from 1769. to the revolutionary war, and again a short time in Congress until he left us to take command of the army. during the war and after it we corresponded occasionally, and in the 4. years of my continuance in the office of Secretary of state, our intercourse was daily, confidential and cordial. after I retired from that office great and malignant pains were taken by our Federal-monarchists and not entirely without effect, to make him view me as a theorist, holding French principles of government which would lead infallibly to licentiousness and anarchy.[7]

Jefferson neatly summarized the main phases of his relationship with Washington. For the first half of their relationship, roughly from 1769 until 1783, they worked together, playing different roles in the revolutionary cause, though they weren't especially close. They were in broad agreement about the main issues at stake between Britain and the colonies and how the colonists should seek redress of their grievances. When Jefferson became governor of Virginia in 1779 (while Washington was serving as commander of the Continental Army), the two men enjoyed a productive collaboration that lasted through the War of Independence (including repeated British invasions of Virginia). This laid the foundation for their friendship, which flourished from 1783, when Washington gave up command of the Continental Army, until the end of 1793. After Jefferson resigned from Washington's cabinet with effect from January 1, 1794, until Washington's death in 1799, the two men became increasingly estranged. The animus between the former friends was deep, as each came to believe that the views of the other constituted a mortal threat to America's experiment with republican government. Their differences became political, ideological, and personal. However, after Washington's death, Jefferson (who lived until 1826) sought to make a posthumous peace with Washington and to reconcile their apparently conflicting views.

———

The bitter estrangement between Washington and Jefferson at the end of Washington's life has distorted our understanding of their relationship. Hindsight, with the rift between the two men in mind, has led historians and biographers to miss the productive collaboration that grew into a warm friendship between the two men over the quarter century before their split.[8] Aware of the breakdown of the Washington-Jefferson friendship, historians have been tempted to read into their dispute an explanation for the broader, bitter partisan differences that characterized American politics during the 1790s and the early years of the nineteenth century (a period that coincided with the presidencies of Washington and Jefferson). Washington and Jefferson have come to represent the ideological choices that confronted the new American republic in the aftermath of independence.[9] There is some merit to this interpretation—Washington and Jefferson *did* come to have profound political differences, and these fueled the breakdown of their friendship between 1794 and Washington's death in 1799. Nonetheless, emphasizing these differences obscures the broad agreement between the two men on fundamental issues. That agreement was borne of their common background as members of Virginia's elite and their decades of cooperation in the same cause.

As members of the Creole elite of the largest, most populous, and wealthiest mainland colony in British North America, Washington and Jefferson shared a similar outlook at the outset of the revolution. They believed that the efforts of imperial administrators and politicians in London to reform the British Empire in the aftermath of the Seven Years' War endangered liberty in the colonies. They accepted that political protests and economic pressure were the best means for the colonists to seek redress of their grievances. When these failed and the British deployed military force to uphold parliamentary sovereignty, they accepted that the colonists should resort to arms in defense of their liberty and, eventually, declare independence.

The Declaration of Independence clarified and raised the stakes at issue between the colonies and Britain. When Congress adopted Jefferson's declaration with its assertion of equality grounded in natural rights (implicitly circumscribed by race and gender), overthrowing monarchy in the colonies and creating a confederation of independent republics, the conflict in America became a revolution. Congress charged Washington with commanding the army that waged a lengthy eight-year war that would make independence a reality. To win popular support for the effort, the leading revolutionaries, including Jefferson and Washington, were compelled to extend greater rights and liberties to common white men than they had enjoyed under their colonial governments. In so doing these men transformed themselves from subjects into citizens from whom the new republic's sovereignty was derived.

Washington and Jefferson agreed about the revolution and its aims during the War of Independence. Jefferson, who had done so much to define those aims in the Declaration of Independence, was more comfortable than Washington with the egalitarian impulse at the heart of the revolution. After Congress declared independence, he sought to enact constitutional and legal reform in Virginia that would remove the vestiges of feudalism in the Old Dominion and extend the rights of its citizens. Washington, on the other hand, had practical experience commanding the men who won independence, and this persuaded him that those men had earned their rights by their sacrifices on the battlefield.

The colonists, having won their independence, were now citizens. They were compelled to draft new constitutions to govern themselves and their new republics. This is where the views of Washington and Jefferson began to diverge. Both men were republicans in the sense that they believed that sovereignty in the United States was derived from the people. They recognized that American independence had been won thanks to the efforts, sacrifices, and blood of the American people. Although they knew that Americans of all sorts had fought for (as well as against) independence, they, like many of their peers, agreed that the political community of active citizens should be limited by race and gender—it should be all-white and male. They disagreed over who should exercise power in the new republic. Washington favored a more elite-oriented political system in which the common people exercised their (limited) franchise and allowed their social betters—men like himself and Jefferson—to govern. Jefferson had a much more capacious and democratic conception of the American political community. He favored a more open political system in which common white men, at least those who owned property, exercised more political power.

Most historians, focused on the internal development of the new United States after the revolution, have emphasized and exaggerated the differences between Washington and Jefferson. In their view Washington favored a strong union at the expense of republican liberty, and Jefferson prioritized liberty at the expense of the union. Washington thought in terms of the United States as a single nation. He supported the creation of a strong federal government and the consolidation of power at the expense of the states as the best way to promote and protect liberty and maintain the independence of the United States. Jefferson, by contrast, saw Virginia, with its vast land farmed by free (white) self-governing farmers, as the model for America's republican future. He believed sovereignty should reside in the states, as their citizens were best qualified to govern themselves and safeguard their own liberty. In his mind the new nation should be Virginia writ large. He believed that power should be vested in the states, as a consolidated federal government would, ultimately, endanger liberty in the United States, just as the British government in London had.[10]

This conventional interpretation presents a false dichotomy. Washington and Jefferson had much more in common than what divided them. They came of age on the edge of an empire, and each played a key role in creating an independent republic among the rebellious former British colonies in North America. For all their differences about the internal workings of that republic, they agreed that it must be strong enough to survive in a world of hostile empires actively seeking to destroy it. Otherwise, the former colonies would simply become, in Washington's words, the "insignificant & wretched fragments of Empire" and fall prey to one of several hostile regimes intent on the failure of their experiment with republic government. Rather, Jefferson and Washington were committed to creating what Jefferson called "our new empire," a republican empire that could withstand its enemies while guaranteeing the liberty of its citizens. They believed that they were creating a new type of empire that would be different from the regimes of Europe.[11]

Historians generally acknowledge that one of the paradoxes of the American War of Independence was that the rebels in North America had to create a standing army, an institution usually associated with tyrannical

European empires, to win their independence. Less widely recognized is that the American revolutionaries also created a new form of empire—a republican empire that Jefferson termed an "Empire of Liberty"—to sustain their independence. This was the impetus behind both the creation of a stronger union under the federal constitution and the westward expansion of that union. It also helps to explain why both Washington and Jefferson failed to take meaningful action against slavery, an institution that threatened to fracture the union, and favored the displacement of Native peoples, whose land they viewed as essential if the American republic were to survive. They were not compelled to make a choice between a strong union and a weak republic. The survival of the United States as a republic was paramount. To achieve this the United States should become a republican empire, able to compete with and defend itself against the monarchical imperial regimes of the Old World. To be sure, there were important differences between the two men over how the republican empire should be structured and operate. Nonetheless, taking a broad perspective and reading the Washington-Jefferson relationship forward in the order that it unfolded, rather than backward after it collapsed in rancor, one sees the common purpose that united the two men.[12]

This book considers the relationship between Washington and Jefferson from their first meeting in 1769 until Washington's death in 1799. It also considers Jefferson's efforts after Washington's death to shape how posterity viewed their relationship. It considers their interaction, collaboration, and conflicts as well as their engagement with the major issues they confronted in their public and private lives. When we view the Washington-Jefferson relationship as it unfolded over time rather than backward, with the knowledge that it ended in acrimony, we see its gradual and natural development. We can see that theirs was a story of convergence and divergence. Washington and Jefferson were products of the same culture and place. The book first examines this background and the circumstances that shaped both men before they met in the late 1760s. After that, it considers the long history of their relationship, when their interests converged before politics and miscommunication caused them to diverge prior to Washington's death in 1799. The main argument is that Washington and Jefferson agreed on much more than they disagreed over—and on much more than subsequent generations have appreciated. This becomes apparent when we consider their views and actions with respect to slavery and the treatment of Native Americans. These are treated in thematic chapters that punctuate the largely chronological treatment of the Washington-Jefferson relationship.

———

The language of families and family relations suffuses study of the American Revolution. Contemporary critics of British rule in America called themselves Sons and Daughters of Liberty. The leaders of the revolution have, for more than a century, been referred to as "Founding Fathers" (and Founding Mothers). More recently they've been described as "Founding Brothers."[13] Those familial relationships don't really help us when it comes to Washington and Jefferson. Although Washington was the older of the two men, he was only eleven years Jefferson's senior. The patriarchal image of father and son does not capture their relationship. Owing to this significant, but narrow, age gap between the two, and to the fact that for most of the three decades each knew Washington was superior in wealth, power, and social standing, fraternal imagery does not suffice either. It is better to think of Washington and Jefferson as cousins.

George Washington and Thomas Jefferson shared a distant kinsman. Sir Ralph Neville was born around 1364 in northern England to an elite family. When he was twenty-four, he inherited his father's title as Baron Neville. He served successive English monarchs—Richard II, Henry IV (Neville's brother-in-law), and Henry V—mainly by securing the English-Scottish border and by suppressing rebellions. In 1397 Richard rewarded Neville's loyalty by naming him first Earl of Westmorland. By the time of his death in 1425, Neville had fathered twenty-two children by two wives. Unsurprisingly, his descendants number in the many thousands, including the two Virginia revolutionaries who were descended from Neville and his second wife, Joan Beaufort. Shakespeare immortalized Neville, as Earl of Westmorland, in three of his history plays. It is ironic that a border warlord who advanced his interests by suppressing rebellions and upholding royal authority could count among his descendants two men who became famous for overthrowing monarchy and establishing a republic.[14]

It is highly unlikely that Washington and Jefferson were aware of their common ancestry. Both men claimed to be indifferent to genealogical research. When Sir Isaac Heard, of the College of Arms in London, wrote to

Washington in 1792 to inquire about his ancestry, the president demurred, writing, "This is a subject to which I confess I have paid very little attention." He told Heard, "I have often heard others of the family, older than myself, say that our ancestor who first settled in this Country came from some one of the Northern Counties of England, but whether from Lancashire, Yorkshire or one still more northerly I do not precisely remember."[15] Jefferson also claimed to be indifferent to genealogy. In his 1821 autobiography, he noted that his father's family came from Wales. About his mother, Jane Randolph, descended from one of Virginia's most prominent families, he wrote, "They trace their pedigree far back in England & Scotland, to which let every one scribe the faith and merit he chooses."[16]

Despite their claims to the contrary, both Washington and Jefferson were interested in their lineages. In his reply to Heard, Washington enclosed a detailed account of his family genealogy, which extended as far back as his family's arrival in Virginia in 1657.[17] In 1771 Jefferson, contemplating marriage to a wealthy widow, Martha Wayles Skelton, wrote to a friend in London asking him to "search the Herald's office for the arms of my family. I have what I have been told were the family arms, but on what authority, I know not. It is possible there may be none." If necessary, Jefferson wanted his friend to buy a coat of arms for him. As if to downplay his vanity, Jefferson softened his request with a humorous reference to his favorite author, Laurence Sterne, "I would with your assistance become a purchaser, having Sterne's word for it that a coat of arms may be purchased as cheap as any other coat."[18] That Washington and Jefferson shared an interest in their families' lineages is not that surprising. As ambitious members of Virginia's landed gentry—an elite that carefully recorded the births among the enslaved persons they held in bondage and traced the bloodlines of its horses—they were aware that wealth was transmitted across the generations through inheritance. Owing to the often-complex family structures in the colony, they knew how important it was to record their antecedents and descendants and to have these recognized by law.

Which brings us back to Ralph Neville. Although Washington and Jefferson were unaware of their distant consanguinity (they were eleventh cousins), it offers us a way to understand their relationship. In modern Western culture, we tend to think of first cousins—that is, the children of siblings—when we think of cousins. Such was not the case in the world that Washington and Jefferson were born into. Samuel Johnson, the eighteenth-century English lexicographer, defined a cousin as "any one collaterally related more remote than a brother or sister." In this usage any distant relative beyond immediate family was a cousin. Johnson offered a second, social and political, definition of the term: "a title given by a king to a nobleman, particularly to those of a council."[19] In this usage a cousin is a friendly political ally. In *Henry V,* Shakespeare's eponymous king addresses his famous St. Crispin's Day speech before the Battle of Agincourt to the Earl of Westmorland, the kinsman of Washington and Jefferson, whom he calls "my cousin, Westmorland." *Cousin* here is a term of affection between unrelated or distantly related social equals. In *Henry VI part 1,* the king refers to the dukes of York and Somerset, who are descended from the same great-grandfather, as "good cousins both."[20] This is a usage that Washington and Jefferson, as lovers of the theater, would have appreciated and understood.

Describing the relationship between Washington and Jefferson as one of cousinage allows us to understand them on their own terms while also appreciating the evolution of their relationship over time. They were cousins in the sense that they shared a very distant family connection. Much more important, they came from the same relatively small social and political class in late colonial Virginia. They were like modern cousins in that they shared a relationship for a long period that ebbed and flowed over time. They began as political allies before becoming friends. Indeed, as this book shows, they became friends *because* they were political allies.

Samuel Johnson defined *friendship* as "the state of minds united by mutual benevolence." Johnson elaborated by adding several other definitions: "highest degree of intimacy," "favour; personal kindness," "assistance; help," and "conformity; affinity; correspondence; aptness to unite."[21] Each of these captures aspects of the Washington-Jefferson relationship, and friendship as they would have understood the concept. Johnson's first and final definitions are particularly apt, as they capture the political quality of the Washington-Jefferson relationship, and of friendship for eighteenth-century Americans, at least those of Washington's and Jefferson's class. Washington and Jefferson became friends because they were united in a common political cause. As this book shows, they had much in common as elite Virginians, but they only became friends when politics—first, resistance to British imperial policy and then, support for independence—bound them. Friendship for them was, in Johnson's formulation, an affinity that connected Washington and Jefferson across time and space. They formed a political attachment that became personal. For them the personal and the political were one and the same. That is why, when they diverged politically in the mid-1790s, their friendship deteriorated. It was only after Washington's death in 1799 and with his own election to the presidency in 1800–1801 that Jefferson came to believe that their differences had not been as severe as he had believed and he sought to restore his friendship with Washington in the eyes of the American people and posterity.[22]

— *1* —

Never Did Nature and Fortune Combine More Perfectly

I have often heard others of the family, older than myself, say that our ancestors who first settled in the Country came from some one of the Northern Counties of England, but whether from Lancashire, Yorkshire or one still more northerly I do not precisely remember.

—George Washington to Isaac Heard, May 2, 1792

We don't know exactly when George Washington and Thomas Jefferson met for the first time. They may have encountered each other on May 2, 1768, when they both attended the Old Theatre in Williamsburg. In his diary, Washington recorded, "Went to Williamsburg with Colo. Bassett, Colo. Lewis & Mr. Dick. Dind with Mrs. Dawson & went to the Play." Jefferson's account is even more concise. In his Memorandum Book on the same day, he noted simply, "Pd. At play house 5/."[1] The play in question was put on by the Virginia Company, run by David Verling, the company's actor-director, at a theater on Waller Street behind the colony's capitol. We know little else about that evening. We don't know which play Jefferson and Washington saw. The Virginia Company offered a broad repertoire that included Shakespeare and Restoration tragedies, comedies, and farces.[2] Nor do we know whether Washington and Jefferson met each other at the theater. Nonetheless, that evening is important because it is the first time that we can definitively place the two Virginians in the same room at the same time.

Jefferson later wrote that colonial Virginia "had no towns of consequence," observing that Williamsburg, the provincial capital, "never contained above 1800 inhabitants." He conceded that the most notable public
buildings in the colony—the capitol, the governor's palace, and William &
Mary (where he had been a student just a few years before)—were all
located in Williamsburg, but even by the standards of colonial America,
Virginia's capital was modest.[3] During court sessions and meetings of the
assembly, the town's population might have doubled, but it would have
been difficult for members of the gentry to avoid each other, particularly in
the town's rather small playhouse. It is hard to believe that Washington and
Jefferson didn't meet each other on that evening in 1768, though neither
mentioned it. Jefferson would certainly have been aware of Washington's
presence. To Washington, an encounter with Jefferson might have been
unremarkable.

In 1768 Washington was thirty-six years old and had established a reputation as a soldier and planter. He was a great landholder well-known on
both sides of the Atlantic because of his exploits during the Seven Years'
War. The Virginia Company had started a run in Williamsburg to coincide
with the session of the House of Burgesses, the colony's representative assembly, of which Washington was a member, a mark of esteem and responsibility expected of a great planter. Jefferson, by contrast, was just twenty-
five in the spring of 1768. Having inherited land from his father and been
educated at William & Mary, he was establishing himself as a lawyer and
had yet to marry. He was an ambitious young man, but his fame and most
important achievements lay in the future. Did Washington, older, more famous, and powerful, take notice of the younger, better-educated planter
from the piedmont? Did they exchange greetings as fellow members of the
provincial gentry? We don't know. We do know that their lives would become intertwined over the subsequent three decades in ways neither could
foresee that evening. They shared a love of theater—both men attended
plays and performances throughout their lives—and they found themselves playing starring roles in an unfolding drama over the course of the
next thirty years.

It does not really matter whether Washington and Jefferson met at the
theater in 1768 or, as is generally accepted, in the House of Burgesses the
following year. Theirs was a small society where the elite—and those who
aspired to elite status—encountered each other regularly at church, militia

musters, elections, public balls, dances, private dinners, horse races, and myriad other social, cultural, and political events. They asserted themselves and demonstrated their status through displays of wealth, with their clothes and behavior. The actors on the stage at the theater on Waller Street were not the only ones performing that evening. Washington and Jefferson would have recognized each other that evening whether they had met or not. To some extent, as ambitious members of the Virginia gentry, still young men keen to achieve wealth, status, and fame, they already knew each other.[4]

The English first explored the land they dubbed "Virginia" in the 1580s. They had been preceded in the region by the Spanish several decades before. Of course, these Europeans did not "discover" that land, as it had long been inhabited by numerous Indigenous peoples when the English established their first permanent settlement at Jamestown in 1607. The "Virginia" where George Washington and Thomas Jefferson were born in the first half of the eighteenth century was carved out of land stolen from Native peoples. There were three main language groups that inhabited the territory that the English colonized. Iroquoian-speaking people inhabited the region south of modern Richmond, below the fall line in what became the extreme southeast and southwest of the colony. Algonquian speakers were the most numerous people and inhabited the territory along the tidewater that came to be the focus of English settlement and expansion during the seventeenth century. They dominated the area that the English came to call Virginia but which they knew as Tsenacomoco. This included Pope's Creek, in Westmoreland County, where George Washington was born in 1732, and Mount Vernon, which was his home for most of his adult life. Siouan speakers inhabited the land to the north and west of the fall line in the piedmont region—including the site of Shadwell, where Jefferson was born in 1743, and Monticello, where he later made his home. Like all wealthy Virginians, Washington and Jefferson were the beneficiaries of the displacement of Indigenous peoples.[5] Indeed, both had a direct personal connection with that colonization. Washington worked as a land surveyor as a young man, helping to map western (Native) lands for sale and settlement. He later came to fame as a soldier in the early 1750s, serving British, and Virginian, efforts to expropriate Native lands in the Ohio country. Thomas Jefferson's father, Peter Jefferson, was a noted surveyor who completed a map of Virginia in 1753 with Joshua Fry that was both an accurate rendering of the colony and a statement of British imperial ambition the year twenty-one-year-old George Washington first asserted Virginia's claim to Ohio.

In its early years Virginia struggled to survive. The colony was run as a private entity by the Virginia Company, based in London. Disease, Indigenous resistance, and famine all took a heavy toll, and the settlement appeared to be failing. It wasn't until 1612 when the settlers began cultivating Spanish tobacco that the colony showed any economic promise. Tobacco cultivation quickly spread; Virginians had found a crop that they could export across the Atlantic. The mortality rate among settlers remained high, and in 1623 the Crown took direct control of the colony. Despite the colony's high mortality rate, the lure of the riches to be gained from tobacco proved powerful, and thousands of migrants from around Britain and Ireland emigrated to Virginia during the subsequent decades. Most of the migrants were poor and unskilled, and they were predominantly male. They came as indentured servants, exchanging their labor for passage across the Atlantic and the promise of land after they completed their indentures (usually between four and seven years). Tobacco was a labor-intensive crop, and the demand for servants appeared to be limitless. By the middle of the seventeenth century, mortality rates began to improve and the population in Virginia stabilized. Life expectancy increased and the gender imbalance improved thanks to the emigration of more female servants and natural increase. Paradoxically, as the standard of living and life expectancy in the colony improved, opportunities for servants and former servants diminished. In the second half of the seventeenth century, tobacco prices plateaued and much of the best land in the colony was occupied by successful planters who'd emerged from the hardscrabble competition of previous decades. In 1676 restive and fearful servants and small landholders rose up, attacking Indigenous people before turning their ire on the colonial government, burning Jamestown.[6]

Bacon's Rebellion, as the rising was known (after its leader, Nathaniel Bacon), was a turning point in the history of colonial Virginia. The unrest demonstrated to wealthy Virginians that they could not rely on an endless supply of indentured servants to meet the seemingly insatiable labor demands of tobacco production. Servants expected to become free landholders and to earn their own fortunes. Social and political chaos resulted when their expectations went unmet. In the wake of Bacon's Rebellion, wealthy Virginians sought an alternative labor source. They found it by enslaving Africans.

The first enslaved people arrived in Virginia in 1619 when Dutch slavers brought approximately twenty African slaves to the colony from the West Indies. Throughout most of the seventeenth century, enslaved Africans and their descendants made up a small proportion of Virginia's workforce. Their lives and status weren't all that different from those of the white servants they worked beside—with the crucial distinction that slaves did not become free. In 1662 the Virginia assembly adopted a law which stipulated that enslavement was heritable and that the children of enslaved mothers would themselves be enslaved for life. Thanks to improving mortality rates later in the century, it increasingly made sense for masters to pay more for enslaved laborers they would own for life rather than for servants whose labor they had for a limited time and who might, as Bacon's Rebellion demonstrated, pose a danger to the colony. After Bacon's Rebellion, Virginia planters began to import large numbers of enslaved persons from Africa to meet their labor demands. By the end of the century, Virginians imported their slaves directly from West Africa rather than from the Caribbean.[7]

By the turn of the eighteenth century, Virginia had become more stable demographically. The colony was dominated by a relatively small number of large planters, concentrated in the tidewater, who owned large tracts of land and made their fortunes exploiting enslaved labor to raise tobacco. These were the "First Families of Virginia," many of whose antecedents had emigrated to the colony in the middle of the seventeenth century.[8] This elite sold its tobacco in London and built larger, more stylish homes than their predecessors in the middle of the seventeenth century had and decorated them with the latest goods imported from Britain. They did so to express their authority and convey stolidity. However, the political and social culture of eighteenth-century Virginia remained embryonic and fluid. The colony's elite remained small. The "First Families" called themselves such to give the impression that their society was rigid (and they sat at its apex), but many were only a generation or two removed from more modest beginnings. The elite sought to give the impression that the Virginia gentry was as stable and well established as the English gentry. They imitated

English manners in the style they built their homes, the ways they dressed, the books they read, and in their modes of worship. They did so, in part, because they knew that Virginia was not stable. It was not England. Their obsessive attention to family and genealogy, which both Washington and Jefferson partook in while affecting to disdain it, was largely aspirational. Washington and Jefferson were born on the periphery of Virginia's elite. They were certainly wealthy by almost any measure, but they were not, yet, at the absolute pinnacle of their society. However, they understood that they could achieve that through the acquisition of land and slaves and by marrying well and establishing successful families.

Below the large planters was a large cohort of small and middling planters who owned smaller plots of land and who raised tobacco for sale and livestock, wheat, and other grains for domestic consumption. They often enslaved small numbers of persons or employed one or two indentured servants to supplement the labor provided by family members. These smallholders frequently migrated, seeking land, and pushed the boundaries of the colony ever westward. Below those Virginians who owned land were those, enslaved and free—most of the population—who did not own land but provided most of the colony's labor.

There was a limited degree of social mobility in eighteenth-century Virginia. Social advancement was limited by gender, race, and class. White men with property were more likely to acquire more property, in the form of land and persons, and to climb the social ladder. These opportunities were denied to Native Americans and enslaved Africans. (There were a small number of free Black people in colonial Virginia, but their opportunities were extremely limited.) Middling planters who were industrious and lucky might acquire enough land and slaves to establish themselves as members of the provincial gentry. Those with capital might speculate in Native lands. Another route to advancement for ambitious men was marriage—a strategic match with a widow with property could bring social and economic benefits, as both Washington and Jefferson would come to learn.[9]

Race and wealth conditioned social relations in eighteenth-century Virginia. A strict hierarchy was enforced by custom and law. Non-white people were expected to defer to white people, and those with property could expect deference from those with less (or no) property. Women should defer to men and were expected to live in households under the

authority of a male head. While propertied white men could expect deference from those without social and political power, they were expected to
serve their communities. White men who met property requirements voted
and chose local officer holders. Members of the gentry held a variety of
local and colonial offices, in the militia, the local government, and the
church. George Washington, for example, served as a colonel in the Virginia militia and was a church warden and a vestryman as well as a member
of the House of Burgesses. Thomas Jefferson was also elected to the House
of Burgesses and was a colonel in the Albemarle County militia, but, unlike
Washington, he never saw active service and declined to use the title.

While politics in eighteenth-century Virginia had some democratic features, notably the election of men to the House of Burgesses, and that assembly acted to represent the interests of the men and women of the colony,
these were limited, even by the standards of British America. Only white
men who met property requirements to vote could participate in elections.
Wealthy planters like Washington and Jefferson dominated the House of
Burgesses, whose power was limited. Virginia's governor usually resided in
Britain and dispatched a deputy to act in his place—denoting the colony's
subordinate status within the British Empire.

While Virginia was the largest and most populous of Britain's colonies
in North America, it was one of twenty-six such colonies in the region and
its primary purpose was to serve the economic and strategic needs of the
empire. Although the great planters of Virginia were big men in their
colony, when viewed from London, they lived on the periphery of the
world, at the far edge of civilization. Therein lay a paradox for men like
Washington and Jefferson. They dominated their society and held sway
over the lives of hundreds of persons, Black and white, male and female.
They expected, and received, deference and respect (and fear) from those
who they saw as below them in the colony's rigid social hierarchy. At the same
time, they felt their subordination—political, economic, and cultural—to
the imperial center more than three thousand miles away. They owed allegiance to the king. They were expected to obey laws adopted by the Parliament at Westminster. The priests in their Anglican parishes had to go to
England for ordination. They depended on the British army and the Royal
Navy to protect their trade and defend their frontiers. They sold their tobacco to merchants in London and Glasgow. They borrowed money and
purchased goods, both luxury items and the necessaries of day-to-day life,

from many of the same merchants. They styled themselves as aristocrats, but they were not, with few exceptions, actual aristocrats, that is to say noblemen with inherited titles that could be transferred to their posterity. Some elite Virginians, like Washington and Jefferson, chafed against their subordinate status, but there was little they could do to change it before 1776.

————

In 1814 Jefferson provided a detailed description of Washington. It is probably the fullest and most perceptive account he left of Washington. According to Jefferson, Washington "was indeed, in every sense of the words, a wise, a good, & a great man. his temper was naturally irritable and high toned; but reflection & resolution had obtained a firm and habitual ascendancy over it. if ever however it broke it's bonds he was most tremendous in his wrath. . . . his person, you know, was fine, his stature exactly what one would wish, his deportment easy, erect, and noble; the best horseman of his age, and the most graceful figure that could be seen on horseback." Jefferson captures Washington's physical presence and his personality well. Washington was a man who learned to master his emotions. He could be thin-skinned and had a powerful, sometimes fearful, temper, but he struggled to control it. He was acutely aware of his reputation and realized that excessive displays of emotion might threaten it. He was also, as Jefferson notes, an impressive physical specimen, well aware of the power that conveyed in a society where physical presence mattered. Jefferson continued, "Altho' in the circle of his friends, where he might be unreserved with safety, he took a free share in conversation, his colloquial talents were not above mediocrity, possessing neither copiousness of ideas, nor fluency of words. in public when called on for a sudden opinion, he was unready, short, and embarrassed. yet he wrote readily, rather diffusely, in an easy & correct style. this he had acquired by conversation with the world for his education was merely reading, writing, and common arithmetic, to which he added surveying at a later day. his time was employed in action chiefly, reading little, and that only in Agriculture and English history. his correspondence became necessarily extensive, and, with journalising his agricultural proceedings, occupied most of his leisure hours within doors." Jefferson concluded, "On the whole, his character was, in it's mass perfect, in nothing bad, in few points indifferent; and it may truly be said that never did nature and fortune combine more perfectly to make a man great, and to place him in the same constellation with whatever worthies have merited from man an everlasting remembrance."[10]

George Washington was born on February 22, 1732, at Pope's Creek farm in Westmoreland County, Virginia. Pope's Creek was located on the Northern Neck, a peninsula bounded to the north by the Potomac River and to the south by the Rappahannock River. His father, Augustine Washington, was a third-generation English colonist who, owning nearly three thousand acres of tobacco land, was firmly ensconced in the middle ranks of the colony's gentry. George's mother, Mary Ball Washington, was Augustine's second wife. George had two older half brothers, Lawrence and Augustine, and, after George's birth, Mary Ball Washington gave birth to five additional children (four of whom, three brothers and a sister, survived to adulthood). When George was six years old, Augustine moved his family to Ferry Farm, across the Rappahannock River from Fredericksburg. In 1743, when George was just eleven years old, his father died. Augustine Washington left Ferry Farm to George, who lived there with his mother and siblings.[11]

George's prospects were limited because his older half brothers had inherited most of their father's land. They had also been sent to England to complete their educations. Augustine's death meant that George did not enjoy the benefits of an English education. Rather, as Jefferson notes, he received rudimentary schooling locally, which ended when he was fifteen. At the urging of his older half brother Lawrence, George considered joining the Royal Navy, but his mother opposed the idea. Instead, George trained as a land surveyor. He enjoyed the patronage of the Fairfax family, genuine British aristocrats who owned millions of acres in Virginia from the Northern Neck to the Shenandoah Valley. Lawrence Washington married Ann Fairfax, the eldest daughter of the family's patriarch in America, Colonel William Fairfax. In 1748 George, just sixteen, went on an expedition to survey Fairfax lands in the Shenandoah Valley with George William Fairfax, the colonel's eldest son. This expedition was a formative experience for Washington. It gave him an understanding of what it took to live and work in frontier conditions. It also gave him a taste for Native land that he never lost. He began to speculate in western lands, acquiring 9,000 acres within the next few years.

The expedition confirmed his own connection to the Fairfax family: George William Fairfax would be an important friend and ally for George Washington. In 1755 Washington, who was by then living at the Mount Vernon estate, which adjoined the Fairfaxes' Belvoir plantation, wrote to his younger brother, Jack, "I should be glad to hear that you live in perfect Harmony and good fellowship with the family at Belvoir, as it is in their power to be very serviceable upon many ocassion's to us as young beginner's." George acknowledged, "To that Family I am under many obligation[s]."[12] George William Fairfax and his wife, Sally, entertained George and Martha Washington at their home frequently. When they left Virginia for England in 1773 to attend to legal matters, the Fairfaxes gave George Washington power of attorney to look after their affairs. (The Fairfaxes never returned to Virginia.)

In 1751 George Washington made his one trip beyond the North American mainland, traveling to Barbados with his half brother Lawrence. Lawrence was suffering from tuberculosis and believed he might find relief from his condition in the tropics. The brothers spent six weeks on the island in November and December. The visit did nothing to improve Lawrence's health, and George contracted smallpox. George was fortunate in that his case of smallpox was relatively mild and gave him immunity to the disease, which was a scourge of eighteenth-century armies. While George carried the telltale pockmarks left by the disease on his face for the rest of his life, his survival, and subsequent resistance to the malady, made his military career possible.[13] Lawrence Washington enjoyed no such good fortune. His health continued to deteriorate, and he died from tuberculosis in July 1752. Upon Lawrence's death, his infant daughter, Sarah, inherited the Mount Vernon estate on the banks of the Potomac River. When Sarah died soon after, her mother, Lawrence's widow, Anne Fairfax Washington, inherited the estate. She eventually remarried and leased the estate to George Washington. George inherited the estate outright when Anne died in 1761. Mount Vernon remained Washington's home until his death in 1799.

In 1752 Robert Dinwiddie, the lieutenant governor of Virginia, with the support of William Fairfax, appointed Washington as a major in the Virginia militia. The next year Dinwiddie dispatched Major Washington, just twenty-one at the time, to the headwaters of the Ohio River. At the time the Ohio country was contested ground, inhabited by Native Americans but claimed by both the French and British. The French had recently expanded their military activities south of the Great Lakes into the Ohio country (particularly the borderland between the modern states of Pennsylvania and Ohio). Ohio was coveted by settlers and speculators from Virginia (including competing claims from rival companies involving Lawrence and Augustine Washington and Peter Jefferson). Dinwiddie sent Major George Washington to the disputed region with a letter to the French that asserted that the territory was British and enjoining them to cease building forts and roads in the region.

Washington took half a dozen men with him to warn the French off and to assert Virginia's claims to the contested ground. Between October 1753 and January 1754, Washington and his small band, including fellow surveyor Christopher Gist; Jacob Van Braam, who acted as a French translator; and Seneca leader Tanaghrisson (known to Washington as the Half King) journeyed through western Pennsylvania and Ohio, traveling as far as Fort Le Boeuf near Lake Erie. Washington asserted Virginia's claim to the Ohio country, but the French and Natives that he encountered paid him little heed. The 900-mile journey provided Washington with still more experience in coping with wilderness conditions (in the middle of winter) and potentially hostile adversaries. He kept a journal during the expedition that formed the basis of his report to Dinwiddie. Dinwiddie arranged to publish Washington's account in February 1754.[14]

The *Journal of Major George Washington* was reprinted in colonial newspapers and as a pamphlet in London. It was Washington's first major public statement. It provided a coherent and dramatic narrative of the expedition—including Washington's wilderness journey and accounts of his fruitless attempts to negotiate with the French and Native Americans. According to Washington's version of events, he dealt honestly and forthrightly with the Native Americans he encountered, in contrast to the efforts of the French, who treated them with contempt. Washington reported that a French officer dismissed Tanaghrisson, declaring, "I am not afraid of Flies, or Musquitos, for Indians are such as those."[15] Washington, by contrast, addressed the Natives as "brothers," pledging friendship and alliance on behalf of Virginia and the British. Whether Washington, a young officer on this first mission, negotiating through translators and inexperienced in diplomacy, read the situation accurately is doubtful. What is beyond doubt is that his *Journal* presents him as a hardy soldier and an honest defender of

British (and Virginian) interests in the Ohio country. The *Journal* established Washington's transatlantic reputation at the age of twenty-two.

During the summer of 1754, Dinwiddie ordered Washington to return to the Pennsylvania-Ohio borderland with a larger force. This time he led approximately 140 men to the Forks of the Ohio River in western Pennsylvania. Washington's men and their Native allies encountered a force of French soldiers, Canadian militia, and Native Americans. During a brief skirmish on May 28, 1754, the Virginians captured or killed most of the French and Canadian soldiers. It was Washington's first experience of combat. Several days later he wrote to his younger brother Jack, with sangfroid, "I can with truth assure you, I heard Bulletts whistle and believe me there is something charming in the sound." Among the dead was a French officer, Joseph Coulon, de Villiers, Sieur de Jumonville. The circumstances of Jumonville's death remain the subject of controversy. The French claimed that he was killed after surrendering, while the Virginians averred that he was killed in the skirmish. According to Washington's concise account, "The Battle lasted abt 10, or 15 minutes, sharp firing on both sides, when the French gave ground & run, but to no great purpose; there were 12 killed, among which was Monsr De Jumonville the Commandr, & taken 21 prisoners."[16]

The French counterattacked several weeks later, and Washington and his men took refuge in a hastily constructed palisade dubbed Fort Necessity. The Virginians were outnumbered and, after a fierce fight on July 3, 1754, Washington surrendered his command. Before returning to Virginia, Washington signed a capitulation, written in French (a language he could neither read nor speak) that accepted responsibility for the "assassination" of Jumonville. Despite the failure of the expedition, the House of Burgesses voted to thank Washington and his men, for "the gallant Defense of your Country."[17] The skirmishing in western Pennsylvania ignited a wider conflict, the Seven Years' War—known to British North Americans as the French and Indian War. In 1755 the British sent a large army to western Pennsylvania under the command of General Edward Braddock. Washington joined Braddock's staff as a volunteer aide-de-camp. On July 9, 1754, Braddock's army was comprehensively defeated by the French and their Indigenous allies at the Battle of the Monongahela. When Braddock was mortally wounded, Washington helped to rally the British forces and coordinated their retreat. He reported, "I had 4 Bullets through my Coat, and two Horses shot under me yet although death was levelling my companions on every side of me [I] escaped unhurt."[18]

Washington's performance during Braddock's defeat repaired any damage to his reputation he may have suffered because of his defeat and surrender at Fort Necessity the previous year. Lieutenant Governor Dinwiddie gave Washington overall command of Virginia's militia forces in October 1755. Washington, then in his midtwenties, coordinated the defense of his colony's 350-mile western frontier. He oversaw the raising of troops, purchasing of supplies, and building of fortifications. He commanded officers, many of whom were older than himself. He could be a strict disciplinarian. He had deserters flogged, and in some cases executed.[19]

After more than three years in command of Virginia's defenses, Washington unsuccessfully sought a commission in the British army in 1758. By that time the main theater of the war had shifted to the north. His aspirations for a military career seemingly stymied, Washington decided to return to civilian life and build his fortune as a planter. In December 1758 he resigned his command and returned to Mount Vernon. From the time in 1753 when he went to Ohio on behalf of Dinwiddie until he resigned his command six years later, Washington had acquired significant military experience. He had served in combat and negotiated with the French and Native Americans, as well British and colonial officials. He had become experienced in the world of imperial politics—acquiring renown as a soldier on both sides of the Atlantic, while also experiencing frustration as an ambitious provincial whose career prospects seemed limited. He had learned to exercise life-and-death authority over those he commanded. He could be thin-skinned and sometimes struggled to maintain control over this temper, and he was keenly aware of his reputation. He was not yet thirty.

———

In March 1758 George Washington, still in command of the Virginia regiment (Figure 1.1), journeyed to Williamsburg to meet with the colony's leaders who had gathered to attend the House of Burgesses.[20] Traveling from Mount Vernon, Washington stopped at Poplar Grove, the plantation of Richard Chamberlayne, on the Pamunkey River in New Kent County, approximately thirty-five miles from Williamsburg. While dining with the

FIGURE I.I   Charles Willson Peale, *George Washington in the Uniform of a Colonel of the Virginia Militia* (1772). Commissioned by Martha Washington, this is the earliest known portrait of George Washington, Peale's painting shows Washington in his uniform as a colonel of the Virginia regiment, which he commanded between 1755 and 1758. Peale completed the portrait, which celebrated Washington as a loyal British subject, just before the deterioration of colonial-imperial relations compelled Washington to return to military life in 1775.   Reproduction courtesy of Museums at Washington and Lee University, Lexington, Virginia.

Chamberlaynes, Washington met their neighbor, the recently widowed Martha Dandridge Custis (Figure 1.2). Martha's husband, Daniel Parke Custis, one of Virginia's richest men, had died the previous summer. Martha Custis, just twenty-six years old, was among the wealthiest women in Virginia, which made her one of the colony's most attractive widows. Colonel Washington, who had himself just turned twenty-six a couple of weeks

FIGURE 1.2   John Wollaston, *Martha Dandridge Custis in 1757*. Martha Dandridge Custis was twenty-five when she sat for this portrait. She had been married to Daniel Parke Custis, also painted by John Wollaston in 1757, since 1750. Daniel Parke Custis died on July 8, 1757, leaving Martha a widow at twenty-six with two children and a fortune in land and enslaved labor. Reproduction courtesy of Museums at Washington and Lee University, Lexington, Virginia.

earlier, had achieved fame and status as a soldier. He was attracted to Martha Custis and visited her at her plantation, White House, both on his way to Williamsburg on March 16 and again as he returned to the army on March 25. Each time, perhaps trying to impress the young widow with his good manners and largess, he left a generous tip of thirty shillings for her enslaved house servants.[21]

Martha Dandridge was born on June 2, 1731. She was the first of eight children born to John Dandridge, an English migrant to Virginia, and Frances Jones, whose father was a member of the House of Burgesses. John Dandridge was a moderately successful planter who owned approximately 500 acres of land and up to twenty enslaved laborers along the Pamunkey River in New Kent County, Virginia. The Dandridges were minor gentry and although John did not serve in the House of Burgesses he held various local offices—clerk of the New Kent County court, vestryman, and militia colonel—which suggested that his neighbors respected him.[22] Given her family's rather modest wealth, Martha Dandridge might have expected to marry a small planter like her mother had done. Nonetheless, when she was sixteen, Martha attracted the attention of her wealthy New Kent County neighbor, Daniel Parke Custis, whose father, John Custis IV, served on the Governor's Council. Custis was more than twenty years older than Martha Dandridge but had been unlucky in his attempts to find a wife. John Custis IV died in November 1749 and left most of his vast estate, which included 17,500 acres scattered across six counties and nearly 300 enslaved persons, to his son. Daniel Parke Custis married Martha Dandridge on May 15, 1750, a couple of weeks before her nineteenth birthday. Upon her marriage, Martha Dandridge Custis moved to her husband's White House plantation. She had also moved from the ranks of the minor gentry to the very pinnacle of Virginia society.[23]

Upon her marriage to a great planter, Martha Dandridge Custis became a plantation mistress. This entailed managing a large household—particularly enslaved men and women. In the more modest circumstances in which she had grown up, enslaved laborers would likely have worked in the fields, whereas Daniel Parke Custis was wealthy enough to have around a dozen enslaved persons whose main labor maintained his household. Their management would have fallen to his new young bride. Martha would also have coordinated and arranged social events at White House—dinners and dances. In a predominantly rural society, like Virginia in the mid-eighteenth century, these events lay at the heart of the social life for the colony's elite. They promoted social and political cohesion, allowed for the courtships that resulted in marriage alliances between the great families, and provided opportunities to exchange news and conduct business.

As a young Virginia wife, Martha Custis's primary responsibilities revolved around the demands and expectations of motherhood. The family was the primary social unit in colonial Virginia. It was the vehicle by which economic and political power was consolidated, maintained, and transmitted across generations. Many years later Thomas Jefferson explained how Virginia's elite families preserved their power by employing the vestiges of feudalism—primogeniture (inheritance by the firstborn son) and entail (keeping estates intact): "Certain families had risen to splendor by wealth and the preservation of it from generation to generation under the law of entails; some had produced a series of men of talents; families in general had remained stationary on the grounds of their forefathers."[24] While individual families might rise or fall owing to good (or bad) fortune, particularly if they produced "men of talents," the majority maintained their positions by producing children and transmitting wealth in the form of land and slaves to the next generation. In such a culture marriage was an economic and social imperative that had little to do with modern notions of romantic love or the autonomy of young people.

Martha delivered her first child, a boy named after his father, on November 19, 1751. Seventeen months later she gave birth to a girl, Frances Parke Custis. In February 1754 Daniel Parke Custis II died, aged two. In November of the same year Martha gave birth to another son, John Parke Custis, known to his family as Jacky. Jacky's birth was followed by that of another sister, Martha (Patsy) Parke Custis in April 1756. Almost a year after Patsy's birth, Frances, aged three, died. Additionally, Martha's father John Dandridge died in August 1756, followed in death by her husband, Daniel Parke Custis, on July 8, 1757. In the space of almost six years, Martha Dandridge Custis had given birth to four children (Daniel, Frances, Jacky, and Patsy), buried two of them (Daniel and Frances), and lost her father and husband. She was twenty-six years old.

These rapid deaths in quick succession must have taken an emotional toll on Martha. As historian Flora Fraser has written, "This catalogue of deaths when she was in her early twenties must go some way toward explaining an anomaly in Martha's character. All her future life she was to be, for one so capable and strong-minded, exceptionally nervous and fearful about the health of her children and, later, her grandchildren." As we shall see, those fears and anxieties were to prove to be well-founded.[25]

Daniel Parke Custis had died without leaving a will. That meant that the management of his considerable estate—285 enslaved persons and 18,000 acres of land, together valued at approximately £30,000 plus liquid assets

and cash reserves in Virginia, and Britain valued at an additional £10,000—
fell to his young widow. As the widow of a man who had died intestate,
Martha Dandridge Custis inherited outright ownership of one-third of her
late husband's personal property and received a life right to one-third of
his land and enslaved laborers—8,800 acres of land and 126 men, women,
and children. These were "dower" lands and slaves, which, along with the
personal property she inherited, would come under the control of her husband should Martha marry again. Upon her death the dower lands and
slaves would revert to the Custis estate. Daniel Parke Custis's two surviving children, a two-year-old and an infant, were each entitled to one-
third of their father's property. Jacky Custis, as Daniel's sole surviving
son, would inherit all his father's land and slaves, two-thirds vesting immediately and the other third upon the death of his mother. Since Jacky was a
toddler at the time, an executor would manage his share of the estate (as
well as Patsy's inheritance). Martha petitioned to become the administrator
of the Custis estate and was required to post a bond for the full value of the
estate. For nearly eighteen months, she managed the estate—selling surplus produce, negotiating with tenants, exporting tobacco to Britain, or-
dering consumer goods, and making loans.[26] When Colonel Washington
came calling in March 1758, Martha Dandridge Custis had rarely traveled
beyond her native New Kent County. However, she had been married and
widowed, given birth to four children, buried two of them, and was managing one of the largest fortunes in Virginia.

We know little of George Washington's private life before he began
courting Martha Custis. Like many members of the Virginia gentry, he
may have found an outlet for his sexual desires among the enslaved women
at Mount Vernon, or with the young women, free or enslaved, in nearby
Alexandria. Whether he engaged in sexual relations with Native American
women during his frontier service is unknown. His most enduring, and
complicated, relationship with a woman prior to his marriage to Martha
Custis was with his neighbor, Sally Cary Fairfax.

As we have seen, the Fairfax family was an important influence on
young George Washington. His elder brother Lawrence had married into
the aristocratic family when he wed Anne Fairfax, the daughter of Sir William Fairfax—who acted as Washington's patron when he began his
training as a surveyor—and the sister of George William Fairfax, who became a close friend of Washington. In 1748 George William Fairfax

married the beautiful Sally Cary, who came from a wealthy and prominent Virginia family. George Washington was just sixteen when Sally Cary, then eighteen, married George William Fairfax and moved to Belvoir, the plantation neighboring Mount Vernon. Washington frequented Belvoir with his brother Lawrence and his wife. He seems to have become smitten with Sally Fairfax. He encountered her many times at Belvoir, and she introduced him to the ways of the Virginia elite, including polite conversation and dancing.[27]

There is no evidence that Sally Fairfax and George Washington had a sexual relationship. Nonetheless, he seems to have fallen in love with the unattainable Sally. On September 12, 1758, while he was courting Martha Custis, he wrote an extraordinary letter to Sally. Washington began by denying that he was anxious about "the annimating prospect of possessing Mrs. Custis" (the only surviving reference to Martha in his correspondence prior to their marriage). He then wrote a telling, if oblique, passage: "I profess myself a Votary to Love—I acknowledge that a Lady is in the Case—and further I confess that his Lady is known to you. . . . I feel the force of her amiable beauties in the recollection of a thousand tender passages that I coud wish to obliterate, till I am bid to revive them.—but experience alas! sadly reminds me how Impossible this is.—and evinces an Opinion which I have long entertaind, that there is a Destiny, which has the Sovereign controul of our Actions—not to be resisted by the strongest efforts of Human Nature." A few months before marrying Martha Custis, George Washington apparently professed his love for the wife of his neighbor. While little of his correspondence with Martha survives, there is nothing in those letters equivalent to the "thousand tender passages" he associated with Sally Fairfax.[28] These hardly seem the words of a man happy about the prospect of his forthcoming marriage. Given that Sally Fairfax was married, and unattainable, Washington gives the impression that his initial attraction to Martha Dandridge Custis was animated by practical considerations: her wealth and status more than passion. Flora Fraser has argued persuasively that the Washingtons' marriage became a loving and close partnership. This may be so, but it does not seem to have begun as such. Throughout his life George Washington never lost his affection for Sally Fairfax.

As he indicated in his letter to Sally Fairfax, George Washington continued his courtship of Martha Custis, despite his feelings for his neighbor.

George and Martha were married on January 6, 1759, Twelfth Night, the end of the Christmas festive season. On January 23, Francis Fauquier, the lieutenant governor of Virginia, reported, "Colonel Washington has resigned his command of the Virginia Forces (and is married to his agreeable widow)."[29] Fauquier's choice of the word *agreeable* to describe Martha is notable. Washington himself used the same adjective to describe his new bride to his London agent when writing from Mount Vernon several months later: "I have quit a Military Life; and Shortly shall be fixd at this place with an agreable Partner."[30] It suggests that, for George Washington, at least, marriage was as much a pragmatic as a romantic undertaking.

What was in it for Martha Dandridge Custis Washington? Martha, whose origins were arguably more modest than George's, had already scaled Virginia's social heights. During her seven-year marriage, she had experienced happiness and grief—starting a family and losing children and, ultimately, her husband. She inherited vast wealth and responsibility when Daniel Custis died, and she managed it effectively. Martha was a very wealthy widow who had demonstrated business acumen when she met George Washington. It was unlikely that she would remain unmarried for long. She had options. We do not have any letters between Martha and George from this period, but it's possible that she, her financial position secure, did make a choice out of love or attraction. Young George Washington was a war hero and a celebrity. He was reputed to be a striking physical specimen and he was a fine horseman and dancer—two skills that were highly prized among the Virginia elite. He did not bring as much wealth to the marriage as Martha did, but she didn't need his money. Unlike her first husband, who was much older than she and not publicly active, George Washington was her own age, ambitious for fame and wealth, and exciting to be around. They were, in the phrasing of a later age, a power couple, and this seemed to satisfy them both, though possibly from different motives.

With his marriage to Martha Dandridge Custis, George Washington entered a new phase of life. He gave up military life, permanently he believed, and concentrated his efforts on his new family and on managing his and Martha's considerable fortune.[31] While he continued his public service, as befitted a great man in Virginia, he focused on managing his plantation at Mount Vernon, acquiring additional western lands, and administering Martha's inheritance. The family moved from its home in

FIGURES 1.3, 1.4   Charles Willson Peale, *Martha "Patsy" Parke Custis* (1772) and *John "Jacky" Parke Custis* (c. 1774). George and Martha Washington were devoted to Martha's surviving children, Patsy and Jacky. Patsy suffered from epilepsy and died suddenly in 1773, aged seventeen. Jacky was an indifferent student and married Eleanor Calvert in 1774. Custis died, aged twenty-six, in 1781 after contracting "camp fever" (likely typhus) while serving as an aide to his stepfather during the Yorktown campaign. His two youngest children, Eleanor "Nelly" Parke Custis and George Washington "Wash" Parke Custis lived at Mount Vernon with Martha and George Washington. Reproduction courtesy of Mount Vernon Ladies' Association.

New Kent County to Mount Vernon in the spring of 1759. George and Martha set about redecorating and expanding their home. By September Washington reported, "I am now I beleive fixd at this Seat with an agreable Consort for Life and hope to find more happiness in retirement than I ever experiencd amidst the wide and bustling World."[32]

When he married Martha, George Washington acquired a wife but also a new family in her two young children, Jacky and Patsy Custis, then aged four and two. George managed their financial affairs and eventually became their guardian. George and Martha Washington had no children of their own. It is not known if they were unable to have children—though Martha gave birth to four children during her marriage to Daniel Parke Custis. George took a great interest in his Custis stepchildren (and grandchildren) and was a conscientious and supportive stepfather to them. Patsy and Jacky (Figures 1.3 and 1.4) would prove challenging, though in very different ways.

As the children of Daniel Parke Custis, Jacky and Patsy Custis were wealthy heirs whose mother and stepfather doted upon them. Martha, having lost two children, was especially keen that her surviving children should not want for anything (and she worried particularly about their health). Their stepfather spared no expenses on the children. (Though, always a scrupulous bookkeeper, as their guardian he charged expenses to their accounts.) In their annual orders to the London merchants to whom they sold tobacco and from whom they ordered manufactured goods, George and Martha often bought luxury items—fine clothes, jewelry, books, silver plate, a harpsichord, and other items for their children. George even bought from a passing sea captain a pet parrot for young Patsy.[33]

Martha's anxiety for the health of her children was well-founded. As a child Patsy developed epilepsy. Throughout her life she was afflicted with seizures, which George and Martha referred to as "fits," that became more frequent and powerful with adolescence. On August 15, 1770, for example, George Washington reported, "Patcy has been very unwell . . . not only with her old complaint [epilepsy] but also with the Ague [malaria] and fever, but from the latter she has recovered."[34] Washington's comment is instructive. It suggests that Patsy's epilepsy had become persistent. Indeed, during that summer her stepfather made careful notes of her attacks and recorded that she had seizures, sometimes more than one, on twenty-six days between June 29 and September 22. He noted on July 31 that she had a "very bad" attack.[35]

Martha and George Washington sought in vain for an effective treatment to cure Patsy, or at least to alleviate her symptoms.[36] Patsy's condition did not improve; indeed, it worsened as Washington's notations from the summer of 1770 indicate. On June 19, 1773, George Washington made a (typically) concise diary entry: "At home all day. About five oclock poor Patcy Custis Died Suddenly." He wrote a fuller account to his brother-in-law, Burwell Bassett, the following day: "Yesterday removed the Sweet Innocent Girl into a more happy & peaceful abode than any she has met with in the afflicted Path she hitherto has trod. She rose from Dinner about four Oclock, in better health and spirits than she appeared have been in for some time; soon after which she was siezd with one of her usual Fits, & expired in it, in less than two Minutes without uttering a Word, a groan or scarce a Sigh." Patsy was just seventeen years old when she died. Her life had been difficult and short. Her death was a sharp blow to her mother and stepfather. As George Washington wrote to Bassett, "This Sudden, and unexpected blow, I scarce need add has reduced my poor Wife to the lowest ebb of Misery."[37]

While Martha and George Washington struggled in vain to find a way to relieve Patsy's symptoms, Jacky Custis presented them with a very different challenge. During the American Revolution, Thomas Jefferson sought to reform Virginia society by ridding it of what he saw as feudal vestiges—primogeniture and entail—that he thought had created an elite class that was indolent, self-indulgent, and unfit for leadership in a republic. Jefferson did not have Jacky Custis in mind when he advocated these reforms, but he might well have. Custis embodied the limitations of Virginia society, as Washington wrote to Jonathan Boucher, an English-born Anglican minister, who ran schools for the sons of planters in Virginia and Maryland, "He is a promising boy—the last of his Family—& will possess a very large Fortune—add to this my anxiety to make him fit for more useful purposes, than a horse Racer &ca." As Washington added when closing a letter to Boucher after he had taken Jacky on as a student, "Mrs Washington joins me in Complimts to you—& desires her love may be added to her Lazy Son as does dear Sir Yr Most Obedt Serv."[38] Their anxieties would prove well-founded.

Jacky Custis lacked ambition and seemed content to await his majority and live off his considerable inheritance. Owing to the early death of his own father, George Washington had not benefited from an extensive education. He was determined that his stepson should labor under no such disadvantage. When Washington wrote to inquire whether Boucher would take Jacky on as a pupil, he described Jacky: "He is a boy of good genius about 14 years of age, untainted in his Morals & of innocent Manners. Two yrs and upwards he has reading of Virgil, and was . . . entered upon the Greek Testament, tho I presume he has grown not a little rusty in both; having had no benefit of his Tutor since Christmas." In addition to offering to "chearfully pay Ten or Twelve pounds a year" to Boucher, Washington offered the tutor the use of horses and an enslaved boy as inducements.[39]

Custis studied, intermittently, under Boucher from 1768 until 1773, including after Boucher moved his school to Maryland in the summer of 1770. His progress was uneven. Custis would apply himself to his studies before giving in to distractions and temptation. In December 1770 the minister wrote what was hardly the most reassuring school report a parent ever received. "I have observ'd his growing Passions taking this unpleasing Cast without the Power of preventing it," reported Boucher. The reverend identified two main dangers in Custis's personality: "I mean, his Love of Ease, & Love of Pleasure—Pleasure of a Kind exceedingly uncommon at his Years. I must confess to You I never did in my Life know a Youth so exceedingly indolent, or so surprizingly voluptuous; one wd suppose Nature had intended Him for some Asiatic Prince." Boucher lamented that in social situations, Custis, who received invitations it would have been rude or impossible for him to decline, "seldom or never goes abroad without learning Something I cou'd have wish'd Him not to have learn'd." Among the inhabitants of Annapolis, Jacky, "contriv'd to learn a great Deal of Idlness & Dissipation. . . . One inspires Him with a Passion for Dress— Another for Racing, Foxhunting, &c." Predictably, the sixteen-year-old was showing far more interest in young women than books.[40]

The Washingtons despaired over Jacky's prospects. Eventually, they sent him to King's College in New York in the hope that a change of scene might produce different results. He didn't stay in the city very long before dropping out to marry Eleanor "Nelly" Calvert, the sister of one of his classmates at Boucher's school who came from one of Maryland's wealthiest families. Jacky and Nelly were married on February 3, 1774. Martha did not attend her son's wedding, which was held at the bride's estate, Mount Airy, in Maryland, because she was still mourning Patsy's recent death. As Jacky Custis entered marriage and settled into life as a Virginia planter, George Washington must have doubted whether he succeeded in his oft-stated desire to train his stepson to be useful in life.

———

By the time he arrived at the theater in Williamsburg in the spring of 1768, George Washington had established a reputation as a soldier and acquired a fortune as a planter and through marriage and speculation in western lands. He was one of his colony's most important and powerful figures.

The same could not, yet, be said of Thomas Jefferson.

— 2 —

My Great Good Fortune

The tradition in my father's family was that their ancestor came to this country from Wales, and from near the mountain of Snowdown, the highest in Gr. Br. . . . He was born Feb. 29, 1707/8 and intermarried 1739 with Jane Randolph, of the age of 19, daur of Isham Randolph. . . . They trace their pedigree far back in England and Scotland, to which let everyone ascribe the faith & merit he chooses.

—Thomas Jefferson

As an adult, Thomas Jefferson, at six feet, two inches, was slightly taller than George Washington, and thin with red hair. A fellow politician described him as "a slender man; has rather the air of stiffness in his manner; his clothes seem too small for him; he sits in a lounging manner, on one hip commonly, and with one of his shoulders elevated much above the other; his face has a sunny aspect; his whole figure has a loose, shackling air."[1] Jefferson was born at Shadwell, his family's plantation on the outskirts of Charlottesville, on April 13, 1743. Shadwell was named for the parish in London where his mother, Jane Randolph Jefferson, had been born in 1721. His father, Peter Jefferson, was a middling planter and surveyor with limited education who was drawn to the piedmont by the opportunity to acquire land, which was the prerequisite for advancement in colonial Virginia.[2] Jefferson evidently took greater pride in his father's accomplishments, despite his relatively humble origins, than he did of his mother's connection to the Randolphs, one of Virginia's leading families. According to Jefferson his father was a self-made man who valued education. "My father's education had been quite neglected; but being of a strong mind, sound judgment and eager after information, he read much and improved himself." Jefferson took pride in the fact that his self-educated father joined Joshua Fry to survey the boundary between Virginia and North Carolina and draft a map of the colony. Fry was an English-born, Oxford-educated surveyor who had been a professor at William & Mary. He preceded George Washington as commander of the Virginia regiment.[3]

The Fry-Jefferson map (Figures 2.1 and 2.2) is a grand statement of the colony's pretensions and its leaders' ambitions, as it includes the land then claimed by Virginians in modern Kentucky and Ohio as well as all of Maryland and Delaware and parts of North Carolina, Pennsylvania, and New Jersey. It's a Virginia-centered view of the world. Fry and Jefferson completed a draft of their map in 1751. It was published in London in 1753, just as George Washington was heading to Ohio to assert Virginia's claims to the region. The cartouche on the printed edition shows enslaved laborers packing tobacco for export while overseen by a planter sipping madeira. The map is dedicated to the Earl of Halifax and the commissioners of Britain's Board of Trade, responsible for overseeing colonial commerce. The Fry-Jefferson map is an expression of Virginia's importance *and* its subordinate place within the broader British Empire. It is also a visual expression of the space in which both Jefferson and Washington would spend most of their lives and a testimony to the importance of land, its acquisition and exploitation, to their society. That Jefferson's father was a surveyor and mapmaker, and Washington began his career as a surveyor and speculated heavily in land throughout his life, is further testimony to this. Thomas Jefferson took great pride in his father's role in producing the map and included it in published editions of his *Notes on the State of Virginia.*[4]

Peter Jefferson and Jane Randolph Jefferson had ten children, eight of whom, six girls and two sons, survived when Peter died in 1757. Thomas, their third child and oldest son, inherited his father's books and surveying equipment. He also inherited twenty enslaved persons and more than 5,000 acres of land. As the oldest son, Thomas did not face the legal and family obstacles to inheriting wealth that had confronted George Washington when his father died. Peter Jefferson ensured that his son received a superior education to his own. As a boy Thomas boarded with two Anglican clergyman, first William Douglas and then James Maury, who ran small

schools and prepared Thomas to enter William & Mary. Douglas and especially Maury taught Jefferson Latin, Greek, and French. Jefferson went to
Williamsburg to study in 1760 and was a student at William & Mary until
1762. (He did not receive a degree.) While at William & Mary, he encountered two men, William Small and George Wythe, who were important
formative influences. Sixty years later Jefferson recalled, "It was my great
good fortune, and what probably fixed the destinies of my life that Dr.
Wm. Small of Scotland was then professor of Mathematics, a man profound in most of the useful branches of science, with a happy talent of communication, correct and gentlemanly manners, & an enlarged & liberal
mind. He, most happily for me, became soon attached to me & made me
his daily companion when not engaged in the school; and from his conversation I got my first views of the expansion of science & of the system of
things in which we are placed. Fortunately the Philosophical chair became
vacant soon after my arrival at college, and he was appointed to fill it per
interim: and he was the first who ever gave in that college regular lectures
in Ethics, Rhetoric & Belles lettres."[5]

Small returned to Britain in 1762, which might have prompted Jefferson
to conclude his studies at the college. Jefferson did not leave Williamsburg,
however, but rather began to study law with George Wythe, Virginia's
leading jurist, whom Small had introduced to him. Jefferson recalled, "Mr.
Wythe continued to be my faithful and beloved Mentor in youth, and my
most affectionate friend through life. In 1767, he led me into the practice of
the law at the bar of the General court, at which I continued until the revolution shut up the courts of justice." Jefferson spent three years studying
law under Wythe's direction. He was admitted to the bar in 1765 and to the
colony's High Court two years later. He began to build a legal practice,
arguing cases before the colony's highest court.

Jefferson's association with Small and Wythe wasn't simply educational
but also social. During his time at William & Mary, he joined the older men
at the table of Francis Fauquier, then the lieutenant governor of the colony.
The four men—Jefferson, then in his late teens—ate, drank, and played
music together. This experience gave Jefferson a different type of education. In his retirement Jefferson recalled, "With him [Fauquier], and at his
table, Dr. Small & Mr. Wythe, his amici omnium horarum, [friends of all
hours] & myself, formed a partie quarree, & to the habitual conversations
on these occasions I owed much instruction." At the age when Washington

FIGURES 2.1, 2.2   *A Map of the Most Inhabited Part of Virginia Containing the Whole Province of Maryland with Part of Pensilvania, New Jersey and North Carolina.* (London 1755). The "Fry-Jefferson Map"; the map's cartouche was added by the London printer. Joshua Fry and Peter Jefferson completed their draft map in 1751, just before competing British and French claims over the Ohio River valley sparked the Seven Years' War. The map, first published in 1753, was the most complete map of Virginia and its environs published in the mid-eighteenth century and presents an

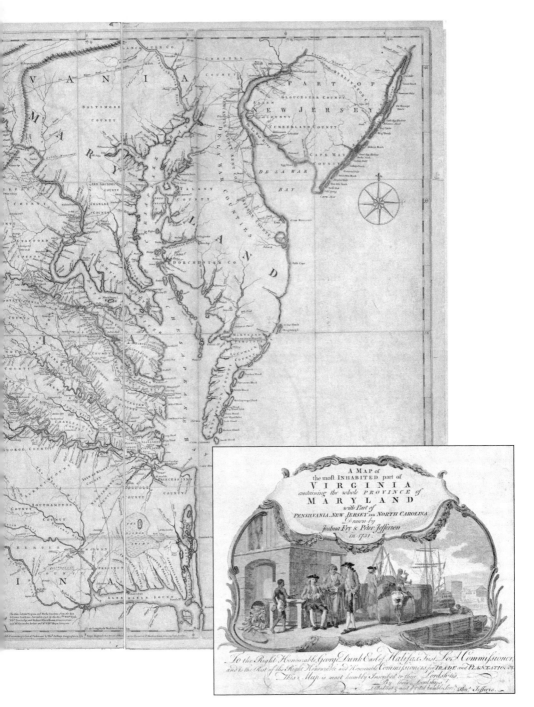

expansive view of Virginia extending to the Ohio River. It shows the extensive river system in the colony that was essential to the plantation economy. The map's cartouche is a visual expression of that economy, showing an enslaved boy serving a planter-merchant a glass of madeira while other slaves load casks of tobacco on board a ship. The map is dedicated to the Earl of Halifax and commissioners of the Board of Trade and Plantations. Library of Congress, Geography and Map Division.

was learning to measure and navigate the wilderness and to negotiate with Native American and French adversaries, Jefferson was learning the genteel sociability that was central to the style of discourse that scholars have described as the Enlightenment: a project through which polite and intellectually curious men and women during the eighteenth century sought to understand and improve the world. He would master the arts of conversation and sociability and use them throughout his future political career. No less than Washington, as a young man Jefferson learned skills that would serve him well for the rest of his life.

———

When he was around fourteen or fifteen, Thomas Jefferson began copying passages from literary works onto sheets of foolscap paper, which he later had bound. This practice, known as commonplacing, had its roots in the Middle Ages and was especially popular among educated men and women from the Renaissance until the nineteenth century. Jefferson copied passages of poetry, prose, and drama in Greek, Latin, and English.[6] Among the passages he transcribed were several from a 1680 play by Thomas Otway called *The Orphan, or The Unhappy Marriage*, a tragedy concerning unrequited love and mistaken identity popular throughout the eighteenth century. Jefferson replicated six passages from *The Orphan*. These are suffused with misogyny. Among them is an extract from the third act of Otway's play:

> I'd leave the World for him that hates a Woman.
> Woman the Fountain of all human Frailty!
> What mighty ills have not been done by Woman?
> Who was't betrayed the Capitol? A Woman.
> Who lost Marc Antony the World? A Woman.
> Who was the Cause of long ten years War,
> And laid at last old Troy in ashes? Woman.
> Destructive, damnable, deceitful Woman![7]

We should be careful about ascribing too much significance to a few passages the adolescent Jefferson chose to commonplace. Nonetheless, he seems to have been threatened by female sexuality. He copied this from the first act of *The Orphan*:

—Your Sex
Was never in the Right; y'are allways false,
Or silly, ev'n your Dresses are not more
Fantastic than your Appetites; you think
Of Nothing Twice; Opinion you have none.
To Day y'are nice, tomorrow not so free;
Now smile, then frown; now sorrowful, then glad;
Virtue you affect, Inconstancy's your Practice;
And when your loose Desires once get Dominion,
No hungry Churl feeds coarser at a Feast;
Ev'ry rank Fool goes down.—

Jefferson may have felt so resentful because he was frustrated by his own sexuality. The very next passage he transcribed reads as follows:

Who'd be that sordid foolish Thing call'd Man,
To cringe thus, fawn, & flatter for a Pleasure,
Which Beasts enjoy so very much above him?
The lusty Bull ranges through all the Field,
And from the Herd singling his Female out,
Enjoys her, & abandons her at Will.[8]

Thomas Jefferson wouldn't have been the first adolescent frustrated and confused by, and resentful of, those to whom he was sexually attracted. His commonplacing reflects that. Still, it suggests an ambivalence toward women that characterized his early years.

In 1763 Jefferson, then twenty, wrote a letter to a college friend, Will Fleming. Jefferson had left William & Mary and was then studying law under George Wythe. He complained about spending time away from Williamsburg at the family home at Shadwell when he wrote the letter: "I do not like the ups and downs of a country life: to day you are frolicking with fine girls and tomorrow you are moping by yourself." This was at odds with Jefferson's later idealization of country life, particularly at his home, Monticello. Jefferson anticipated his imminent return to Williamsburg: "Thank god! I shall shortly be where my happiness will be less interrupted. I shall salute all the girls below in your name, particularly S[ucke]y P[otte]r." While the letter might be read as the lustful boasting of a twenty-year-old to a friend, Jefferson then made a proposal to Fleming: "Dear Will I have thought of the cleverest plan of life that can be imagine. You exchange your land for Edgehill, or I mine for Fairfeilds, you marry S[uke]y P[otte]r, I marry R[ebecc]a B[urwel]l [join] and get a pole chair and pair of keen horses, practise the law in the same courts and drive about to all the dances in the country together. How do you like it?" This is one of the earliest of a series of similar entreaties—inviting male friends to live near him—that Jefferson made throughout his life. It is remarkable because in this instance Jefferson linked the invitation to his (and Fleming's) career and marriage prospects. For Virginians of their class, the two were closely related. Soon after he wrote to Fleming, Jefferson made a somewhat half-hearted attempt to marry.[9]

Rebecca Burwell was a sixteen-year-old orphan whose father had been a member of Virginia's council and served for a time as acting governor of the colony. After her parents' deaths, she was raised by her uncle, William Nelson, himself a councillor and later acting governor of Virginia. Nelson's son, Thomas, was a friend of Jefferson's who later signed the Declaration of Independence and would succeed Jefferson as governor of Virginia in 1781. Thomas Jefferson likely met Rebecca Burwell in Williamsburg when he was studying law with George Wythe. He was smitten with her during the winter of 1763–1764. In October he danced with Rebecca (whom he called "Belinda") at the Apollo Room in the Raleigh Tavern in Williamsburg, later reporting, "I asked no question which would admit of a categorical answer, but assured [Belinda] that such questions would one day be asked." He continued, "My fate depends on [Belinda's] present resolutions, by them I must stand or fall: if they are not favorable to me, it is out of my power to say anything to make them so which I have not said already."[10] Jefferson's language was obtuse: it does not seem that he asked Rebecca to marry him; rather, he hinted that he intended to do so at a later time. Burwell does not seem to have been too impressed by Jefferson's equivocation. Jefferson spent the winter months at Shadwell studying law. When he returned to Williamsburg in spring, he discovered that Burwell was engaged to Jacquelin Ambler.

When Jefferson learned that Burwell intended to marry Ambler, he wrote to Will Fleming, discussing various women in their social circle. "You say you are determined to be married as soon as possible: and advise me to do the same. No thank ye," Jefferson demurred, "I will consider it first." Jefferson then responded to Fleming's arguments in favor of marriage (which don't survive), "Many and great are the comforts of a single state, and neither of the reasons you urge can have any influence with an inhabitant and a young inhabitant too of Wmsburgh." Fleming and Jefferson had, presumably, discussed sex as one of the benefits for marriage, for Jefferson continued, "For St. Paul only says it is better to be married than to burn. Now I presume that if that apostle had known that providence would at an after day be so kind to any particular set of people as to furnish them with other means of extinguishing their fire than those of matrimony, he would have earnestly recommended them to their practice."[11] Jefferson suggests that Williamsburg afforded young men like himself and Fleming with sexual options other than marriage that were unavailable to him when he spent the winter reading law at the family home at Shadwell in the company of his mother. The implication is that Jefferson frequented prostitutes while he was in Williamsburg. While not a large city, as a substantial town and home to a college, as well as the colonial government, Williamsburg would have had several taverns and "disorderly houses" where prostitutes plied their trade. It seems that Jefferson did not just seek pleasure at the theater and in conversation with George Wythe when he was in the colonial capital.

A few months after his quasi-courtship of Rebecca Burwell collapsed, Jefferson attended the wedding of a close boyhood friend, John Walker. John Walker and Jefferson had attended James Maury's school together when they were boys and later went to William & Mary at the same time. Walker recalled, "We had previously grown up together at a private school & our boys['] acquaintance was strengthened at college. We loved (at least I did sincerely) each other." Walker's father, Dr. Thomas Walker, had been one of the executors of Peter Jefferson's will. Walker's bride, Elizabeth Moore, known as Betsy, was the daughter of Colonel Bernard Moore, a planter. Two of her brothers were at William & Mary with Jefferson and Walker. When Walker married Betsy Moore in June 1764, he recalled, "I took Mr. J. with me[,] the friend of my heart to my wedding. He was one of my bridemen."[12]

After they married, the Walkers settled at Belvoir (not to be confused with the Fairfax plantation of the same name neighboring Mount Vernon), a plantation five or six miles from Jefferson's home at Shadwell. In 1768 Walker was named to serve as a clerk for the Virginia delegation, led by his father, charged to negotiate a treaty with the Iroquois at Fort Stanwix in

New York. Anticipating that he would be away for several months, Walker made his will, naming Jefferson one of his executors. "I left my wife & infant daughter at home," he recalled, "relying on Mr. Jefferson as my neighbor & fast friend" to look after them. Walker was away for four months. During his absence, Jefferson made a sexual proposition to Betsy, who rebuffed his advance. John Walker claimed that Jefferson, unbeknownst to him, pursued his wife for more than a decade until 1779. It was only after Jefferson departed for France in 1784 that Betsy, who feared disclosing Jefferson's misbehavior because it might result in a duel in which her husband might be killed, told her husband about "these base transactions."[13] Jefferson admitted that he was inappropriate with Betsy a single time, during John's absence in 1768. Years later Jefferson conceded, "when young & single I offered love to a handsome lady. I acknolege its incorrectness."[14]

Dumas Malone, perhaps Jefferson's most sympathetic biographer, downplayed the significance of what he termed "the Walker affair."[15] He wrote, "Jefferson's incorrect conduct was not reported to the injured husband in 1768, however, or soon afterwards, and the natural supposition is that the lady did not regard the offense as grave. . . . As [John] Walker wrote it all down fifteen or twenty years after he got the report, it was a disgusting tale which bore the marks of gross and willful exaggeration whatever may have been the cause." Malone, who also dismissed the allegation that Jefferson had a sexual relationship with Sally Hemings, was equally dismissive of the significance of Jefferson's encounter with Betsy Walker.[16] He accepted Jefferson's version of events—that he made a single approach to Betsy that she rebuffed and that he accepted her rejection (which, according to Malone's supposition, Betsy did not consider to be a serious offense) and later apologized to John (though not, it seems, to Betsy) for his transgression.[17]

Malone's dismissal of John Walker's account and privileging of Jefferson's version of events rests on assumptions about Jefferson's character—he was sensitive toward women, and a devoted husband and father, while ignoring Jefferson's incentive to downplay what had happened. The scandal was revealed, alongside the Sally Hemings revelations, when Jefferson was president of the United States and his political foes used the information to attack him. If we place Jefferson's approach to Betsy Walker alongside what we know of his attitudes toward women and sex when he was young (during a period of "youthful ardor," as Malone termed it), his actions make sense. He may have become a devoted husband and kind father, but that didn't preclude him from seeing women as outlets for his sexual desire prior to his marriage (and perhaps afterward). His encounters with Williamsburg prostitutes and the wife of his childhood friend certainly place his future relationships with the married Anglo-Italian painter Maria Cosway and the enslaved Sally Hemings in a different, more comprehensible light. Contrary to Malone's assertion, these would seem to be entirely in character for Jefferson.

———

Throughout his adult life, Thomas Jefferson carefully recorded his expenditures in a series of pocket-sized memorandum books. In January 1770 he began a fresh memorandum book for the new year. He wrote a four-line epigram in Latin on the inside cover that translates:

> Entrust a ship to the winds, do not trust your heart to girls,
> For the surge (of the sea) is safer than a woman's loyalty:
> No woman is good; but if a good one has befallen anyone
> I know not by what fate an evil things has become a good one.

He wrote this when he was twenty-seven years old.[18] He may still have been smarting over the Walker affair, or, if John Walker was correct and Jefferson's pursuit of Betsy was ongoing and unsuccessful, he may have been frustrated by her continued rejection of him. Despite this rather pessimistic view of women at the beginning of 1770, Jefferson recorded numerous expenses in his memorandum books for 1770 and 1771 associated with his courtship of the wealthy and attractive widow he would later marry.

Martha Wayles was born on October 30, 1748, at The Forest, the plantation in Charles City County (west of Williamsburg) of John Wayles and Martha Eppes Wayles, who died a week after the birth of her daughter. In his autobiography Jefferson wrote of his father-in-law, "Mr. Wayles was a lawyer of much practice, to which he was introduced more by his great industry, punctuality & practical readiness, than to eminence in the science of his profession. He was a most agreeable companion, full of pleasantry & good humor, and welcomed in every society."[19] John Wayles was born in

Lancaster, England, and emigrated to Virginia in the 1730s. He established himself as a successful lawyer, merchant, and slave trader. He married Martha Eppes in 1746, and they had twins, who did not survive, prior to the birth of Martha in 1748. After the death of his first wife, Wayles married twice more. When his third wife died in 1761, Wayles began a long-term relationship with a woman whom he had enslaved, Elizabeth Hemings. Wayles and Hemings had six children: Robert, James, Peter, Critta, Sally, and Thenia Hemings.[20]

We have no surviving likeness of Martha Wayles. Her great-grand-daughter, Sarah N. Randolph, related family tradition concerning Martha: "She is described as having been very beautiful. A little above middle height, with a lithe and exquisitely formed figure, she was a model of graceful and queenlike carriage. Nature, so lavish with her charms for her, to great personal attractions, added a mind of no ordinary calibre. She was well educated for her day, and a constant reader; she inherited from her father his method and industry."[21] Henry Randall, who interviewed Jefferson's grandchildren in preparing his biography of Jefferson, wrote of Martha, "Her complexion was brilliant—her large expressive eyes of the richest shade of hazel—her luxuriant hair of the finest tinge of auburn."[22] Martha Wayles married a planter, Bathurst Skelton, on November 29, 1766. She gave birth to a son, John Skelton, on November 7, 1767. Bathurst died suddenly on September 30, 1768. Like Martha Washington after the death of her first husband, Martha Wayles Skelton was a young widow and mother of considerable means.

Jefferson likely met the attractive young widow in Williamsburg in the autumn of 1770, and he began courting her soon afterward. Just as Washington tipped Martha Custis's enslaved servants when he was courting her, Jefferson's account book reveals that he gave an enslaved servant at The Forest five shillings on December 10.[23] On its face, making such gifts may have been meant as rewards for favored slaves, but they were also likely meant to impress the widows the men courted. In the small, face-to-face society that characterized colonial Virginia, the gentry were expected to display gentility and good manners through such gestures.

According to Jefferson family tradition, Martha had two other suitors when she was being courted by Thomas Jefferson. They appeared at The Forest seeking to win her hand when they heard Martha and Thomas singing together while she played the harpsichord and he the violin.

The two would-be swains hearing the couple perform together gave up and left.[24] Whether the story is apocryphal or not, the couple shared a passion for music. On June 1, 1771, Jefferson ordered a pianoforte for his presumptive bride-to-be.[25]

Jefferson's family home at Shadwell burned in February 1770. Although no one was hurt in the blaze, Jefferson lost most of his books, papers, and other personal possessions. Soon thereafter he began building a new home at a small mountain nearby, which he dubbed Monticello. Though the loss of Shadwell was devastating, it allowed Jefferson to focus on building his new home, which he came to see as a physical expression of himself. He would later call the house "my essay in architecture."[26] Beginning in the 1730s, members of the Virginia gentry sought to express their authority and assert their status through their homes. They built, and rebuilt, increasingly grand homes that they decorated with furniture, housewares, and artwork imported from Europe. Through their homes the gentry sought to demonstrate their gentility and their connection with Britain. Both Washington at Mount Vernon and Jefferson at Monticello sought to show that they had the wealth and taste to justify places at the pinnacle of Virginia society. Each spent thousands of pounds to build, refurbish, and decorate their homes. Mount Vernon, on the banks of the Potomac River, was typical of the types of gentry homes, most of which fronted Virginia's river system, allowing planters to trade with the wider world. Monticello, built atop a small mountain, was an outlier, which allowed for spectacular views but was impractical.[27]

The fire at Shadwell was a setback to Jefferson's plans to marry Martha Wayles Skelton. He felt that he could not bring Martha and her young son to Monticello to live in its present, partially built state. "I have lately removed to the mountain from whence this is dated," he wrote. "I have here but one room, which like the cobler's, serves me for parlour for kitchen and hall. I may add, for bed chamber and study too."[28] Young John Skelton would never live at Monticello. Martha suffered a grievous blow when her son died suddenly on June 10, 1771, aged three and a half. Like Martha Washington, the future Martha Jefferson experienced the grief of losing her first husband and a child in a relatively short period of time at a very young age.

Thomas Jefferson was a regular visitor to Martha Wayles Skelton while she grieved the loss of her son. His account books reveal that he paid enslaved servants at The Forest on June 9 (the day before John Skelton died), July 11 and 24, October 8, and November 11.[29] Robert Skipwith, who was married to Martha's half sister, Tabitha, wrote to Jefferson on September 20 of his sister-in-law: "My sister Skelton, Jefferson I wish it were, with the greatest fund of good nature has all that sprightliness and sensibility which promises to ensure you the greatest happiness mortals are capable of enjoying. May business and play[,] musick and the merriments of your family companions lighten your hearts, soften your pillows and procure you health, long life and every human felicity!"[30]

Thomas Jefferson married Martha Wayles Skelton on January 1, 1772. His accounts show that he purchased a marriage license and made payments to two ministers (it's not clear whether both officiated at the service), a fiddler, and the enslaved servants at The Forest.[31] The newlywed couple spent two weeks at The Forest before making the midwinter journey to Monticello. In 1772 Monticello was not the grand Palladian mansion familiar to modern visitors (such a building wouldn't exist until the early nineteenth century). It was a building site. The first completed dwelling was a relatively simple two-room structure where Jefferson lived while enslaved workers built the main house. Today the original structure is the south pavilion off the main house. Although dubbed "the Honeymoon Cottage," Martha Jefferson Randolph remembered that her parents said of their first home, "The horrible dreariness of such a house at the end of the journey, I have often heard both relate."[32]

Notwithstanding the inauspicious beginning of their lives together atop Jefferson's "Little Mountain," the marriage of Thomas and Martha Jefferson seems to have been remarkably happy. The young man who disdained marriage and copied misogynistic passages into his commonplace book disappeared. Sarah N. Randolph, their great-granddaughter who preserved the family traditions and memories during the nineteenth century, wrote that "if the attractions of a woman can be measured by the love borne her by her husband, hers must have been great indeed, for never was a wife loved with more passionate devotion than she was by Jefferson."[33] The Jeffersons appeared to enjoy the happiness foretold by their brother-in-law Robert Skipwith, but, unfortunately, Martha did not enjoy good health. This, in part, may have been a result of her pregnancies. During her ten years of marriage to Thomas Jefferson, she gave birth to six children (having, of course, already lost her first child by Bathurst Skelton).

The Jeffersons' first child, a daughter named Martha (known as Patsy to her family) after her mother, was born on September 27, 1772. She was followed by a daughter, Jane Randolph, in April 1774, who died at three years of age; an unnamed son born in 1777, who only lived for a couple of weeks; a daughter, Maria (known as Polly), born in August 1778; and two daughters, both named Lucy Elizabeth, born in November 1780 and May 1782, respectively. The first Lucy died when she was five months old.[34]

———

Washington and Jefferson both enjoyed happy marriages (though Jefferson's was cut short by Martha Jefferson's premature death). To some extent happiness was a fortunate by-product of their unions. Marriage for elite Virginians like Washington and Jefferson was an institution intended to consolidate and transmit wealth across the generations. This was certainly the case for George Washington, whose marriage to Martha Custis made him one of the wealthiest men in Virginia. Jefferson was similarly fortunate, though not on quite so grand a scale. When John Wayles died in 1773, his daughter, by then Martha Jefferson, inherited considerable wealth in land and enslaved persons—including the Hemingses—as well as substantial debt that took Thomas Jefferson and his coexecutors several years to sort out. Nonetheless, Jefferson noted that Wayles had accumulated a "handsome fortune" that "was about equal to my own patrimony, and consequently doubled the ease of our circumstances."[35] Martha Jefferson's inheritance consisted of more than 11,000 acres of land and 135 enslaved persons. To clear John Wayles's debts, Jefferson sold approximately half of the land, retaining 5,500 acres in several counties, including Poplar Forest in Bedford County some eighty miles southwest of Monticello (where he would build a second home as a retreat). This doubled Jefferson's landholdings and more than doubled the number of enslaved laborers he owned. Jefferson was a wealthy man when he married Martha Wayles—his own inheritance made him the fifth-largest landowner in Albemarle County—but his marriage (and Martha's inheritance) made him a very rich man indeed. At the time of her death in 1782, he owned approximately 10,000 acres of land and more than 200 enslaved persons.[36]

The early lives of George Washington and Thomas Jefferson were similar in several ways. They both lost their fathers at relatively young ages.

They each married wealthy widows. By coincidence each married a young widow (with an English-born father) named Martha. Beyond those superficial similarities, both women were wealthy, and the wealth they brought to their marriages enabled the men to pursue the public service for which they are best remembered. Perhaps most important, they both were products of a system of plantation agriculture that gave them the wealth and social status that would make their public careers possible. This system rested on enslaved labor and the cultivation of tobacco. The land and enslaved persons they inherited allowed them to build fortunes that were greatly enhanced by their strategic marriages, which increased their wealth and power considerably. After they married, Washington and Jefferson were among the largest landowners and slaveholders in Virginia.

While there were many similarities between Washington and Jefferson, there were important differences too. Washington traveled much more extensively in North America than Jefferson did. (Jefferson would later travel to Europe, which Washington never did, but he did so when he was middle-aged.) Washington had extensive military and diplomatic experience as a young man; Jefferson had none. Jefferson, who benefited from a much better formal education than Washington did, read French, Italian, Spanish, ancient Greek, Latin, and Anglo-Saxon. Washington, by contrast, was monolingual. Their differences were those that one finds between individuals. Their similarities reflected their class and society. They shared a powerful bond as leading members of the most important colony in British North America. They believed themselves to be great men in an important place.

Both men, as boys, realized that establishing families of their own was the key to their success and was the standard by which they would be judged. As historian Lorri Glover has written about the Virginia gentry, including Washington and Jefferson, "Though at different stages of life and on different paths, they wanted the same thing, which was what all well-to-do men from Virginia wanted: to be respected as patriarchs. Patriarchal power, expressed through mastery of a family, a plantation, and the social order, lay at the center of their identity. Exercising that authority was a duty they inherited from their fathers. If they succeeded in preserving their estates and their family's good name, they could bequeath that legacy to their own sons. . . . A good patriarch—the highest aspiration of a Virginia gentleman—balanced rearing children, building wealth, mastering slaves, protecting kin, leading households, and governing."[37] The fundamental prerequisite for a patriarch was to marry and establish a family—only when they achieved this could men like Washington and Jefferson build their fortunes and become true leaders. Indeed, for both men, marriage and building wealth were closely related. They could not achieve success unless they married well. Both men married wealthy widows and in so doing greatly enhanced their social status and power. It is not too much to say that the public careers Washington and Jefferson enjoyed were made possible by their marriages.

For elite Virginians, "family" often had a more capacious concept than for contemporary Americans. Mount Vernon and Monticello were the homes of not simply Washington and Jefferson and their wives and children but also extended networks of kin—stepchildren, grandchildren, in-laws, and cousins. When Martha Jefferson died, Thomas Jefferson cared for his three surviving daughters but also frequently present at Monticello was his sister, Martha Jefferson Carr, the widow of Jefferson's closest boyhood friend, and her six children. Of course, "family" also encompassed the hundreds of enslaved persons Washington and Jefferson owned during their long lives, whose labor made their achievements possible.

— 3 —

Drivers of Negroes

The unfortunate condition of the persons, whose labour in part I employed, has been the only unavoidable subject of regret. To make the Adults among them as easy & as comfortable in their circumstances as their actual state of ignorance & improvidence would admit; & to lay a foundation to prepare the rising generation for a destiny different from that in which they were born; afforded some satisfaction to my mind, & could not I hope be displeasing to the justice of the Creator.

—George Washington (as told to David Humphreys)

Samuel Johnson was one of eighteenth-century Britain's most famous men of letters. In 1755 he published his *Dictionary of the English Language,* which became a landmark in the history of language and could be found in the libraries of gentlemen on both sides of the Atlantic, including those of Washington and Jefferson. Johnson was also a prolific literary critic, poet, essayist, and novelist. He was known for his caustic wit and trenchant criticism. He was immortalized in James Boswell's 1791 biography, *The Life of Samuel Johnson.* While Boswell dedicated thousands of pages to capturing Johnson's wit, Johnson himself offered a concise self-portrait in his *Dictionary* defining a lexicographer as "a writer of dictionaries; a harmless drudge, that busies himself in tracing the original, and detailing the signification of words."[1] Although Johnson was a Tory (in the British sense) in his politics, he was an outspoken critic of slavery. In 1758 he wrote with reference to Britain's American colonies, "Slavery is now no where more patiently endured, than in countries once inhabited by the zealots of liberty." In a subsequent essay he observed, "Of black men the numbers are too great who are now repining under English cruelty." Johnson's opposition to slavery wasn't simply rhetorical. In 1750 he employed Francis Barber, a man formerly enslaved in Jamaica, as his valet. Barber became a de facto son to the childless Johnson, who eventually named him as his heir.[2]

It is not surprising that Johnson, a Tory, was unsympathetic to Whigs in Britain or America. In 1770 he published a pamphlet, *The False Alarm*, that attacked the English radical John Wilkes and his supporters.[3] In 1775 Johnson published another political tract, *Taxation, No Tyranny*, in which he offered a critique of the resolutions the Continental Congress had adopted in defense of American liberty in 1774. Johnson argued that Parliament's sovereign authority over the colonies could not be divided or challenged. Apart from constitutional issues, Johnson, an opponent of slavery, was enraged by what he believed to be American hypocrisy. Near the end of the pamphlet, Johnson pointedly asked, "How is it we hear the loudest yelps for liberty from the drivers of negroes?"[4]

Johnson had posed a question that underscored an uncomfortable truth. Many of the leaders of the American Revolution, men like Washington and Jefferson, were slaveholders. Indeed, in 1776 when Congress used Jefferson's words to declare the United States independent in the name of universal equality, one-fifth of the population in the new United States was enslaved. Virginia, the largest and most populous of the new states, depended on slavery. The resistance to Britain posed a difficult dilemma for men like Washington and Jefferson—how could they reconcile the egalitarian impulse at the heart of the revolution with slavery? How could they, to paraphrase Johnson, lead a movement for liberty while enslaving hundreds of children, women, and men? This dilemma lies at the heart of all attempts to understand Washington and Jefferson. Before we do that, we must try to understand the experiences of the hundreds of men, women, and children they enslaved.

———

George Washington acquired his first slaves in 1743. Upon the death of his father, Augustine, eleven-year-old George inherited ten enslaved persons as well as a 280-acre farm near Fredericksburg, Virginia. Young George did not offer any reflections about what it was like to gain possession of other human beings as a child. However, more than forty years later,

Thomas Jefferson, born the year Washington inherited his first slaves, claimed that one of slavery's most pernicious effects was its influence on white children. "The whole commerce between master and slave is a perpetual exercise of the most boisterous passions, the most unremitting despotism on the one part, and degrading submissions on the other." White children, Jefferson believed, learned how to interact with enslaved people from their parents: "Our children see this, and learn to imitate it; for man is an imitative animal," he wrote. "The parent storms, the child looks on, catches the lineaments of wrath, puts on the same airs in the circle of smaller slaves, gives a loose to his worst of passions, and thus nursed, educated, and daily exercised in tyranny, cannot but be stamped by it with odious peculiarities. The man must be a prodigy who can retain his manners and morals undepraved by such circumstances."[5] Whether slavery turned George Washington into a despot or a prodigy, he was dependent on the institution throughout his life. From the day his father died in 1743 until his own death fifty-six years later in 1799, George Washington enslaved an increasing number of persons. He inherited a portion of Lawrence Washington's enslaved population when his older half brother died in 1752, and he purchased additional slaves in the 1750s prior to his marriage to Martha Dandridge Custis. Washington enslaved approximately fifty people by the time he married Martha in 1759.

Martha Washington's first husband, Daniel Parke Custis, had been one of the wealthiest men in Virginia and owned 285 slaves at the time of his death in 1757. Two-thirds of these were inherited by his eldest surviving male heir, Jacky Custis, who was only three at the time of his father's death. Martha Washington retained the use of the remaining third of Custis's slaves during her lifetime, after which they would revert to her Custis heirs. These enslaved people were so-called dower slaves Martha brought into her marriage to George Washington. After he married Martha, Washington took on the management of the dower slaves as well as his own enslaved people. He was prohibited by law from selling or manumitting the Custis dower slaves. Over time the two communities merged at Mount Vernon and at Washington's other four plantations. In 1799, a few months before his death, Washington compiled a list of the enslaved persons he employed on his property. All told 317 persons labored for George and Martha Washington. Of these, George owned 124 outright. Custis dower slaves totaled 153, and the balance were enslaved persons whom

Washington hired after he acquired the rights to Dogue Run farm near Mount Vernon in 1786.[6]

In the mid-1760s Washington began to make the transition from tobacco to wheat cultivation. Having completed his service during the Seven Years' War and married (thus substantially increasing the number of enslaved people at his command), he was eager to increase the productivity—and profits—of his holdings. He made the transition to wheat for several reasons. Historically he, like all the great tidewater planters, had raised sweet-leaf tobacco for sale to London merchants. The market for tobacco was in a state of flux: prices (and profits) were declining, and consumers, especially in Europe, came to favor oronoco tobacco (which Jefferson raised and which flourished in the piedmont) over the sweet-leaf tobacco that tidewater planters like Washington cultivated. Ecologically, wheat was less demanding on the soil than tobacco. Wheat was also less labor-intensive than tobacco, which meant that Washington had to consider how to deploy his (increased) workforce as he made the transition. As an avid student of agriculture, he was keen to maximize the efficiency of his plantation operations, and the transition to wheat had important implications for the way he practiced slavery.[7]

During the latter 1760s, Washington employed free white and enslaved Black laborers to harvest his wheat and he carefully measured their productivity. He had mainly used free white laborers as "cradlers" to scythe the wheat before it was raked, bound, and stacked by enslaved laborers. By the summer of 1769, he concluded that it made better sense economically for him to use enslaved laborers for all tasks, particularly if he varied the types of wheat he planted, so that the harvest could be spread over a longer period. He remarked in his diary as the harvest was coming to an end:

> Note—from the Remarks and observations made this year in Harvesting my Wheat, it appeard evidence that 10 and sometimes 9 Cradlers (according as the Wheat was thick or thin) was full suff[icient] to keep the rest of my hands employd—and it likewise appeard that it was evidently to my advantage to employ my own hands to Cradle the Wheat rather than to hire white men to do it—to get Rakers and binders if it be necessary to hire any at all, as these may be got for 2 shill[ings] or half a Crown a day whereas the Wages of the White Cradlers are exorbitantly high—but if Wheat of different kinds are

sowed so as to prevent the Harvest coming on at once it is my opinion that hirelings of all kinds may be dispensed with. Two Rakers in the generality of the Wheat is sufficient to Rake & bind after a Cradle— and the rest of the hands can manage (after the Water Carriers & Cooks are taken out) to get the Wheat into conven[ien]t places & attend the Stackers.[8]

Washington was an exacting taskmaster. His goal was to maximize the labor he could extract from his slaves while minimizing the cost to himself for hiring outside laborers. That was his primary concern when it came to managing enslaved persons.

Washington took pride in the treatment he meted out to those he enslaved. "It has always been my aim to feed & cloath them well & be careful of them in sickness," he wrote. He believed that enslaved persons owed him for his generosity to them; "in return, I expect such labour as they ought to render."[9] He expected his slaves to be productive throughout the year and in all weather. On January 3, 1788, a bitter cold day—Washington recorded the temperature was twenty-one degrees in the morning, thirty degrees at noon, and twenty-five degrees in the evening—Washington toured his farms and observed that enslaved men and women were engaged in a variety of tasks: the women were clearing swamps and cutting trees while the men made fencing and charcoal.[10]

While he conceived of himself as a benign master, Washington was willing to use force to coerce or punish recalcitrant slaves. An English visitor to Virginia reported in 1798 that he had heard that Washington "treated [his slaves] with more severity than any other man."[11] Forty years earlier, in 1758, while Washington was away serving in the Seven Years' War, his plantation manager reported on the building work at Mount Vernon, "As to the Carpent[e]rs, I have minded em all I posably could and has whipt em when I could see a fault[,] old Kit is a very poor hand at any thing."[12] In 1793 Anthony Whitting, then managing Washington's estates, reported that he had whipped Charlotte, a seamstress at Mansion House Farm, for impudence. "I took a hickory Switch," wrote Whitting, "& gave her a very Good Whiping." The following Monday Charlotte informed Whitting that she was unable to work (Whitting had whipped her on a Saturday) and said that she would tell Martha Washington of her mistreatment. Whitting was unapologetic: "I fully expect I shall have to Give her More of it before

She will behave herself for I am determined to lower her Spirit or Skin her Back." The president endorsed Whitting's actions several days later: "Your treatment of Charlotte was very proper—and if she, or any other—of the Servants will not do their duty be fair means—or are impertinent, correction (as the only alternative) must be administered."[13] Charlotte tended to Washington during his final illness and was one of three enslaved persons present when he died in 1799.[14]

In principle, Washington was opposed to selling enslaved persons if it meant breaking up families. Indeed, during the War of Independence, he forbade his cousin Lund, who managed Mount Vernon and surrounding estates during his absence, from selling enslaved persons without their consent.[15] While Washington recognized that slaves might not mind having new masters, they maintained family bonds that were threatened by possible sale: "If these poor wretches are to be held in a state of slavery, I do not see that a change of masters will render it more irksome, provided husband & wife, and Parents and children are not separated from each other, which is not my intention to do."[16] Despite his professed reluctance to do so, occasionally Washington punished slaves by selling them. In 1766 he ordered the sale of Tom, a "Rogue & Runaway," from his River Farm plantation to the West Indies. Washington instructed the ship captain to whom he had consigned Tom to sell the man "for whatever he will fetch" and to purchase, in return, West Indian goods such as hogsheads of molasses and rum and a barrel of limes.[17] Even when punishing enslaved persons, Washington looked after his commercial interests. In 1793 Anthony Whitting reported that he was having ongoing problems with a fifteen-year-old slave named Ben. Ben had fought with others, and Whitting suspected him of theft. Washington advised his manager to try "further correction, accompanied with admonition and advice." If that failed, Washington instructed Whitting, "He, his father & mother (who I dare Say are his receivers [of stolen property]) may be told in explicit language that if a stop is not put to his rogueries, & other villainies by fair means & shortly; that I will ship him off (as I did Waggoner Jack) for the West Indias, where he will have no opportunity of playing such pranks as he is at present engaged in."[18] To coerce his slaves, Washington was willing to use threats, physical punishment, exile to the West Indies, and the threat of breaking up families by sale.

In 1788 a European visitor to Mount Vernon reported that Washington's slaves "are treated with the greatest humanity: well fed, well clothed, and kept to moderate labour; they bless God without ceasing, for having given them so good a master."[19] Several people Washington enslaved disagreed with this view and sought to win their freedom by running away. During the War of Independence, seventeen enslaved persons—fourteen men and three women—sought their freedom aboard HMS *Savage* when the British warship moored in the Potomac near Mount Vernon.[20] Seven of these men and women were recaptured and returned to slavery after the British surrender at Yorktown later in the year.[21]

Perhaps the most famous enslaved person to flee from the Washingtons was Ona Judge. Judge, one of the Custis dower slaves, was born around 1773. She was the mixed-race daughter of an enslaved seamstress at Mount Vernon, Betty, and a free white tailor, Andrew Judge. Ona worked in the mansion house at Mount Vernon and became one of Martha Washington's favorites. The Washingtons brought Ona to New York with them when George became president in 1789. A year later she followed them to Philadelphia when the capital was moved to Pennsylvania. In Philadelphia Ona encountered a large and growing free Black population (in 1780 Pennsylvania had enacted a gradual emancipation law). In 1796, facing the prospect of leaving Pennsylvania and returning to Virginia permanently, Ona fled to New Hampshire, where she lived as a free woman (though legally still enslaved) until her death in 1848. George Washington sought the recapture and reenslavement of most runaways, including Ona Judge, usually by offering rewards for their return. Though he, himself, would come to have serious qualms about slavery as an institution, he could not accept what he believed to be enslaved persons stealing their labor from him.[22]

————

According to family tradition, Thomas Jefferson's earliest memory was of being carried on a pillow by a mounted slave while he was a toddler.[23] Like Washington, Jefferson acquired his first slaves from his father. Peter Jefferson died in 1757 when Thomas was fourteen. When he turned twenty-one in 1764, Thomas inherited around thirty enslaved persons from his father's estate.[24] A decade later, when he married the wealthy widow Martha Wayles Skelton, the daughter of the slave trader John Wayles and sister of Sally Hemings, she brought 135 slaves with her to their marriage. Jefferson eventually purchased an additional twenty enslaved persons (and sold more than one hundred persons).[25] During the five decades between 1776 and 1826, at any one time he enslaved between 165 and 225 people. All told, during his long life, he enslaved at least 607 persons. They were scattered across more than 14,000 acres that he owned in Albemarle and surrounding counties; near his home Monticello and various outlying plantations; and at his second home, Poplar Forest, in Bedford County, eighty miles southwest of Charlottesville.

Jefferson, like Washington, believed that he treated enslaved people in a benign and fair fashion. His granddaughter, Ellen Coolidge, claimed he "was always most considerate of the feelings and the well-being of his slaves." Jefferson wrote in 1792, "My first wish is that the labourers may be well treated, the second that they may enable me to have that treatment continued by making as much as will admit it." Jefferson's awkward circumlocution is instructive. While he stated that he would like to treat enslaved people well, he put the onus on them to ensure good treatment by their behavior and productivity. Through his use of the passive voice, Jefferson absolved himself of responsibility for the treatment of the persons he enslaved.[26]

Most of Jefferson's bondspeople worked in the fields around Monticello or outlying plantations. They raised tobacco as well as wheat, rye, and livestock. A considerable number labored to build and maintain Monticello. During the winter of 1770–1771, for example, enslaved people worked in the cold to dig a well and a cellar at Monticello—which had not yet been built. Jefferson described their efforts in his Memorandum Book. With respect to those digging the cellar he noted the following with the precision that characterized his recordkeeping: "Four good fellows, a lad & two girls of abt. 16. each in 8½ hours dug in my cellar of mountain clay a place 3.f. deep, 8 f. wide & 16½ f. long = 14⅔ cubical yds. under these disadvantages, to wit: a very cold snowy day which obliged them to be very often warming; under a cover of planks, so low, that in about half the work their stroke was not more than ⅔ of a good one; they eat their breakfast in the time which one of them went to cook; they were obliged to keep one or two constantly hawling away the earth to prevent it's rolling in again. From this I think a tolerable midling hand in 12. hours (including his breakfast) would dig & haul away the earth of 4 cubical yds., in the same soil." In the next passage Jefferson noted that other slaves were digging a fourteen-foot well. He remarked that the soil was "a yellow rotten stone with a great many hard stones as large as a man's head and some larger, or else the digger would have had time to spare." In the very next line, Jefferson paraphrased the poet Alexander Pope, "Long life, long health, long pleasures, & a friend."[27]

Because Jefferson was away from Monticello so much between 1775 and his retirement in 1809, most of the day-to-day management of his enslaved laborers fell to overseers (Figure 3.1). At the end of 1792, he entered into negotiations with Samuel Biddle of Elkton, Maryland, who would serve as an overseer at Monticello for a year from late 1793 until November 1794. Jefferson was particularly interested in finding an overseer from that area because he believed that it provided a model for how he might raise crops and manage his labor at Monticello. As he wrote several months after contacting Biddle, "The husbandry about the head of Elk [Elkton] is in wheat and grazing: little corn, and less pork. This I think is what would suit us best, for which reason I turned my attention to that quarter, and also because the labour there being performed by slaves with some mixture of free labourers, the farmers there understand the management of negroes on a rational and humane plan."[28] Jefferson explained to Biddle that he was making the transition from tobacco cultivation (which he never entirely renounced) to wheat and other grains. In this, he was following the example that Washington had set a generation before. "The farm is about 5. or 600. acres of cleared land, very hilly, originally as rich as any highlands in the world, but much worried by Indian corn and tobacco. It is still however very strong, and remarkeably friendly to wheat and rye. These will be my first object. Next will be grasses, cattle, sheep, and the introduction of potatoes for the use of the farm instead of Indian corn in as great a degree as possible." He did this, in part, he hoped, to render slavery more rational and humane—he also did so because, like Washington, he recognized that the profits in tobacco were diminishing. In describing what he expected from an overseer, Jefferson wrote, "You will have from 12 to 15 laborers under you. They will be well clothed, and as well fed as your management of the farm will enable us, for it is chiefly with a view to place them on the comfortable footing of the laborers of other countries."[29]

Jefferson's interest in the "rational and humane" management of his labor and his land arose from several sources. He was opposed to slavery, just as he depended on the institution to maintain his lifestyle. By the 1790s, when he began the transition from tobacco to wheat cultivation, he had

FIGURE 3.1   Benjamin Henry Latrobe, *An Overseer Doing His Duty near Fredericksburg, Virginia* (1798). This watercolor by Benjamin Henry Latrobe, an English-born architect who later designed the US Capitol, shows a white overseer near Fredericksburg, Virginia, supervising two enslaved women who are hoeing a newly cleared field. Such a scene would have been familiar at Mount Vernon, Monticello, and the other properties that Washington and Jefferson owned. Reproduction courtesy of the Maryland Center for History and Culture, Item ID #1960.108.1.3.21.

begun to reconcile himself to the fact that the abolition of slavery in his lifetime was unlikely and sought to make the institution more palatable and humane (at least by his own reckoning). Like Washington, Jefferson found himself with more labor than he believed he required when he made the transition to wheat. To find additional sources of revenue (which he badly needed) and employment for "surplus" hands at Monticello, Jefferson instituted various manufacturing schemes for the enslaved people on his plantation, including nail-making and textile production. Numerous slaves were trained to take on skilled jobs servicing the Monticello community and to provide the labor for Jefferson's near-constant renovation of his home (Figure 3.2). Jefferson's emphasis on making labor more "rational" stemmed from Enlightenment assumptions about efficiency. One can see his desire in an undated passage (likely from the 1790s) from his Farm

FIGURE 3.2   Isaac Granger Jefferson (1775–c.1850). Isaac Granger Jefferson was born at
Monticello. His father, George Granger, was a foreman on the plantation and became the only
enslaved overseer at Monticello. His mother, Ursula Granger, was an enslaved domestic servant who
worked as a laundress and pastry cook. Isaac became a blacksmith and tinsmith and manufactured
nails at Monticello. In 1797, Thomas Jefferson gave Isaac; his wife, Iris, and their two children,
Squire and Joyce, to his daughter Maria and her husband, John Wayles Eppes, as part of their
marriage settlement. Isaac Granger Jefferson became free in the 1820s and later dictated a memoir,
one of the few accounts of life at Monticello provided by an enslaved person. Reproduction © Thomas
Jefferson Foundation at Monticello.

Book, in which he described how he could maximize the productivity of
enslaved children and elderly women:

> build the Negro houses near together that fewer nurses may serve
> & that the children may be more easily attended to by the super
> -annuated women.
> children till 10. years to serve as nurses.
> from 10. to 16. the boys make nails, the girls spin.
> at 16. go into the ground or learn trades.[30]

Putting children between the ages of ten and sixteen to work in manufacturing was certainly rational and efficient. Those children likely disagreed with their master as to whether it was humane.

When searching for a new overseer in 1805, Jefferson declared, "I love industry & abhor severity."[31] Though there is no evidence that Jefferson ever personally whipped enslaved people, the record shows that the overseers and managers he employed routinely used physical coercion against enslaved persons at Monticello and his other holdings. Gabriel Lilly was a brutal overseer at Monticello from 1800 to 1805, during Jefferson's first term as president. Jefferson paid Lilly an annual salary of £50 per year with an additional £10 for managing the nailery on Mulberry Row, the center of slave manufacturing at Monticello. Although the initial reports on Lilly's management were positive, Jefferson's son-in-law, Thomas Mann Randolph, reported in April 1800, "All goes well at Mont'o.: what is under Lillie admirably," Jefferson became concerned about Lilly's use of the whip against the men and boys in the nailery.[32] He wrote to Randolph in January 1801 asking him to "speak to Lilly as to the treatment of the nailers. it would destroy their value in my estimation to degrade them in their own eyes by the whip. this therefore must not be resorted to but in extremities. as they will be again under my government, I chuse they should retain the stimulus of character." Jefferson's choice of language is noteworthy. He asked Randolph as a "favor" to speak to Lilly, and he provided Randolph with arguments to persuade Lilly to stop whipping the slaves in the nailery—suggesting that it would undermine their productivity and would make them unmanageable when Jefferson returned to Monticello.[33] He did not explicitly prohibit Lilly from using the whip. This may have been the result of Jefferson's lifelong aversion to personal conflict, or a recognition that as an absentee plantation-owner, he relied on overseers to manage his interests and he had to give them discretion in managing his slaves (and he likely recognized that he could not enforce his will at a distance). At the end of January, Randolph reported that all was well at the nailery and that he had urged Lilly to refrain from using the whip, "but [on] the small ones for truancy," crediting "the sound sense cleverness & energy of Lillie."[34]

Lilly's forbearance didn't last. In 1804 James Oldham, a free white joiner at Monticello, wrote to Jefferson to complain about Lilly's abuse of the workers in the nailery. Oldham reported that when seventeen-year-old James Hemings was ill for three nights—Oldham feared the boy might die—he informed Lilly that Hemings was unable to work "and Begd him not to punnish him, but this had no affect, he whipd him three times in one day, and the boy was r[e]al[l]y not able to raise his hand to his Head."[35] James Hemings ran away from Monticello to escape the abuse, and he found work as a boatman on the James River, plying the waters between Richmond and Norfolk. He was captured in Richmond, and Oldham, then living in Richmond, acted as an intermediary in negotiations between Jefferson and Hemings. The president assured Oldham, "I can readily excuse the follies of a boy and therefore his return shall ensure him an entire pardon." He promised that he wouldn't force James to return to the nailery but that he could work as a joiner at Monticello. Despite these terms James Hemings fled rather than return to Monticello. It is noteworthy that Jefferson adopted a conciliatory tone and sought to persuade Hemings to return to Monticello rather than to use force. He made no effort to recapture James, acquiescing to his escape. This was likely owing to his favored status as a member of the extended Hemings family and a recognition that he had been mistreated.[36] There were no recriminations for Lilly for driving James Hemings away. In 1805 he sought a huge pay raise, from £60 to £100. Though frustrated with Lilly's salary demands, Jefferson wrote of him as an overseer, "He is as good a one as can be."[37] Jefferson refused to increase Lilly's pay—though not because he whipped the men and boys in the nailery—and Lilly gave his notice and emigrated to Kentucky at the end of 1805.

James Hemings wasn't the only person driven from Monticello by Lilly's abuse. James Hubbard was born in 1783 at Jefferson's Poplar Forest plantation, where his parents were enslaved. In 1794, Jefferson ordered Hubbard, age eleven, to be removed from his parents and brought to Monticello to work in the nailery on Mulberry Row. After some early struggles, James excelled as a nailmaker, producing seven pounds of eight-penny nails in one day at the age of thirteen. He made ninety pounds of nails from every hundred pounds of nail rod, making him among the most productive workers in the nailery. He was also adept at making charcoal, which was essential to fuel the fires in the nailery. This involved chopping and burning 100 to 150 cords of wood per year. Hubbard was so productive at making charcoal that Jefferson gave him a $4 bonus in September 1802.[38] Despite his proficiency Hubbard, like other enslaved workers in the nailery, suffered at Gabriel Lilly's hands. In the summer of 1805, Hubbard planned his escape. He acquired clothing and a forged pass (from Lilly's son) and fled on foot to Washington, DC, where he planned to live as a free man (or to migrate further north). On September 3 he was apprehended by the Fairfax County sheriff and jailed. The sheriff, Daniel Bradley, interrogated Hubbard (presumably using force) and concluded that he was Jefferson's property. Jefferson eventually paid $55 for Hubbard's return.[39]

James Hubbard didn't give up his quest for freedom. He fled again in late 1810 or early 1811, this time going southwest and settling near Lexington, Virginia. Perhaps exasperated, Jefferson sold Hubbard in absentia to his carpenter at Poplar Forest, Reuben Perry. According to the agreement Jefferson made with Perry, Perry should pay Jefferson $500 (in cash or labor) if Hubbard was discovered and returned to Monticello, or $300 if he wasn't.[40] Essentially, Perry was betting that he could recover Hubbard while Jefferson was selling Perry the right to find him—and offloading a perennial problem. Perry took out an advertisement in the *Richmond Enquirer* offering a $40 reward (advanced by Jefferson) for Hubbard's return. Years of swinging hammers and axes to manufacture nails and stoke the kiln at the nailery had transformed Hubbard from a young boy to a formidable man. Perry described Hubbard as "a Nailor by trade, of 27 years of age, about six feet high, stout limbs, and strong made." After Perry reported to Jefferson that he had heard that Hubbard had been seen on the Rivanna River near Charlottesville, Jefferson (who still had a financial stake in Hubbard's return thanks to his deal with Perry) alerted the local slave patrols to be on the lookout for the runaway and offered a reward to a "trusty negro man of my own" for information leading to Hubbard's capture.[41]

James Hubbard lived as a free man for more than a year. It could not have been an easy time for him, as he was in constant danger of capture and reenslavement. In March 1812 Jefferson learned that Hubbard was living in Lexington. He hired a local Albemarle farmer, Isham Chisholm, to apprehend Hubbard and return him to Monticello. Chisholm arrived in Lexington several days after Hubbard, having been accused of theft, had fled. He returned empty-handed, having spent thirteen days searching for Hubbard. Chisholm, encouraged by the promise of a $25 reward from Jefferson (in addition to expenses plus a per diem and the $40 reward offered by Perry), spent an additional nine days tracking Hubbard, finally capturing him in Pendleton County, Virginia (in modern West Virginia). All told, Jefferson had spent $70 to recapture James Hubbard.[42]

Isham Chisholm returned Hubbard to Monticello in chains. Notwithstanding his stated abhorrence of "severity," Jefferson was unflinching when it came to punishing Hubbard. "I had him severely flogged in the presence of his old companions," he told Reuben Perry before committing him to jail in irons. Jefferson told Perry that in his view Hubbard "will never again serve any man as a slave" and advised him to sell him out of state.[43] Although he did not wield the whip himself—presumably overseer Edmund Bacon did so at Jefferson's behest—Jefferson's pursuit and punishment of James Hubbard is testimony to the limits of his "rational and humane" approach to slavery. Faced with persistent defiance—the advertisement in the *Richmond Enquirer* described Hubbard as having a "daring demeanor, bold and harsh feature, dark complexion, apt to drink freely and had even furnished himself with money and probably a free pass," Jefferson resorted to flogging and advocating selling Hubbard away from his family and friends (having first removed him from his parents as a boy). The punishment meted out to Hubbard was done at Jefferson's direct instruction. There was no miscommunication between the benign master and a heavy-handed overseer in this case. When Hubbard sought his independence, Jefferson punished him as severely as he could. (He would have sold him out of state but was unable to do so because Reuben Perry was his legal owner.) Not all Virginians were allowed to pursue happiness in Jefferson's Virginia.[44]

Thomas Jefferson had James Hubbard whipped "in the presence of his old companions" to send a message to the other people that he enslaved at Monticello. That Hubbard had twice run away and had remained at large for a year might be an inspiration to others and was a direct challenge to Jefferson's authority as a master, and Hubbard deserved the harshest treatment that Jefferson could mete out. Dozens of other people that Jefferson held in slavery fled from his various plantations and farms. Jefferson's granddaughter, Ellen Coolidge, recalled that Jefferson allowed "such of his slaves as were sufficiently white to pass for white men, to withdraw quietly from the plantation; it was called running away, but they were never reclaimed." Coolidge noted that four enslaved people achieved their freedom this way. (James Hemings was one of these. Two of the others were among Jefferson's children by Sally Hemings, Beverly and Harriet.)[45] Those four were the exceptions. Jefferson sought to recapture and reclaim other fugitive slaves. He claimed to have lost thirty men, women, and children during the War of Independence alone, mostly during a ten-day period when Cornwallis established his headquarters at Jefferson's Elk Hill plantation in Goochland County. The refugees, fleeing from Jefferson to the British, came from three different plantations scattered over different counties. Cassandra Pybus, the historian who has looked at this issue most closely, argues that "these defections had the hallmarks of well-planned premeditated action."[46] While Jefferson, like Washington, harbored sincere doubts about slavery, his opposition to slavery seems to have taken root sooner and more deeply than Washington's; he did not countenance his own bondswomen and men challenging the institution (except for his own children). Jefferson went to considerable lengths to recover runaways, as we have seen in the case of James Hubbard, and he was willing to use the lash to make an example of him. In this Jefferson was like Washington and thousands of their fellow Virginia slaveholders.

Like Washington, Jefferson reserved the ultimate punishment—exile through sale—for enslaved people that he regarded as persistent malefactors. Late in life he averred that he had "scruples, about selling negroes but for delinquency, or their own request." Longtime Monticello overseer Edmund Bacon recalled that Jefferson's "orders to me were constant: that if there was any servant that could not be got along with the chastising that was customary, to dispose of him."[47] Notwithstanding Ellen Coolidge's claims about her grandfather's beneficence, he punished more enslaved people through sale than he allowed to escape. In May 1803 Cary, an eighteen-year-old man working in the nailery, assaulted Brown Colbert, another enslaved youth, hitting him with a hammer "with his whole strength" and fracturing Colbert's skull. Jefferson responded immediately, informing Thomas Mann Randolph, "It will be necessary for me to make an example of him in terrorem to others, in order to maintain the police so rigorously necessary among the nailboys." Jefferson's solution was to sell Cary: "There are generally negro purchasers from Georgia passing about the state, to one of whom I would rather he should be sold than to any other person. if none such offers, if he be sold in any quarter so distant as never more to be heard among us, it would to the others be as if he were put out of the way by death." Jefferson recognized that Cary's exile would be equivalent to his death as far as his family and friends were concerned and intended the punishment to serve as an example to them. Jefferson was more concerned with punishing Cary and setting an example of him than realizing a profit from his sale. "I should regard price but little in comparison with so distant and exile," he wrote, "as to cut him off compleatly from ever again being heard of."[48]

As slaveholders Washington and Jefferson had much in common. As great planters in Virginia, the two were born into a world and a class that accepted slavery, and the white supremacy upon which it was premised, without question. This should not surprise us. They were outliers in that they enslaved hundreds of men, women, and children when most white Virginians owned few or no slaves. As young men striving to make their fortunes, they benefited from slavery without expressing serious qualms about it. They inherited slaves from their fathers, who died while they were young, and greatly increased their wealth and the numbers of slaves they owned, through marriage to wealthy widows. While they would both come to oppose slavery, especially after the American Revolution, they continued to hold slaves until their deaths (though both increasingly resisted purchasing additional bondsmen and women). They both continued to coerce labor from the men, women, and children whom they owned, and they punished those who resisted enslavement. They did so well after they concluded that slavery was unjust and immoral. Both men concluded that gradual emancipation was the only way to close the gap between the egalitarian ideals of the Declaration of Independence and the reality on the ground in the United States.

While the struggles of Washington and Jefferson with the moral, political, and social challenges posed by slavery were profound and had long-lasting consequences for the United States, it was the enslaved men, women, and children at Mount Vernon and Monticello who paid the highest, most immediate price for those struggles with their liberty, lives, and blood. We see their names in the lists of slaves that Washington and Jefferson meticulously compiled and in the scattered references in their correspondence over the management of their affairs. We must remember names such as Tom, sold in the West Indies for molasses and rum; Old Kit, whipped for his poor carpentry; Charlotte, whipped for impudence; Ben, whipped and possibly sold for his recalcitrance; and Ona Judge, who found freedom by defying the Washingtons and running away. We should also recall James Hemings, whipped because he was too ill to work, and James Hubbard, whipped and sold for seeking his freedom, along with the young boys put to work in Monticello's nailery. Their names cry out against the "rational and humane" slave regime on Jefferson's little mountain. They stand for the millions of enslaved persons whose lives would be shaped by the decisions men like Washington and Jefferson made, and failed to make, as they struggled to live up to the ideals Jefferson articulated so well in the Declaration of Independence. While Washington and Jefferson grappled with moral complexity—seeking to balance their principles and self-interest, others suffered.

Samuel Johnson intended his question, "How is it we year the loudest yelps for liberty from the drivers of negroes?" as a sarcastic jibe. He sought to expose the hypocrisy of Americans who protested about British threats to liberty while themselves denying liberty to hundreds of thousands of enslaved Africans and their descendants. It was a powerful statement that resonated with his contemporaries on both sides of the Atlantic—and has retained its power down through the years. Powerful and biting as Johnson's question is, it somewhat misses the point. Virginia was the most important colony in the resistance movement and provided so many leaders to the revolutionary cause *because* they were slaveholders, not despite their slaveholding. Slavery and plantation agriculture drove the Virginia economy and generated the wealth and power that meant that American independence could not be achieved without Virginia—Jefferson, of course, articulated the meaning of independence, and Washington led the struggle to win that independence.

Washington and Jefferson matter because they helped start a revolution and led the nation that emerged from that struggle. Were it not for the Declaration of Independence and the rebel success in the war, they would likely be little-remembered Creole planters who had made a poor decision to support a failed rebellion—not unlike the aristocrats in the Scottish Highlands who rallied to Bonnie Prince Charlie's standard in 1745. Yet they did succeed and are remembered for their contributions during and after the American Revolution. Their success was made possible *because* they enslaved others. They eventually came to believe that slavery and republicanism were incompatible—though their actions in response to that conclusion were limited. The American Revolution was the turning point in their lives.

— 4 —

Americans Will Never Be Tax'd without Their Own Consent

The god who gave us life, gave us liberty at the same time: the hand of force may destroy, but cannot disjoin them.

—Thomas Jefferson, *Summary View of the Rights of British America* (1774)

On May 8, 1769, the members of the House of Burgesses, including Washington and Jefferson, gathered in Williamsburg. This is the first time that we can be certain Washington and Jefferson met. The burgesses met in the council chamber of the colonial capitol to take their oaths of office before formally meeting Virginia's new royal governor, Lord Botetourt. Unlike his predecessor, Jefferson's patron, Francis Fauquier, who had died in March 1768, Botetourt was the full royal governor of Virginia and not a lieutenant governor deputized to fill the role. Botetourt sought to impress the provincial planters and lawyers assembled before him with his grandeur and authority as befit the king's representative in the colony. He had traveled the short distance from the governor's palace to the capitol in a coach drawn by six white horses bearing the arms of Virginia. The governor instructed the burgesses to go to their chamber and select a speaker. They did so, unanimously electing Peyton Randolph, a forty-seven-year-old planter and lawyer from one of Virginia's grandest families (and a distant kinsman of Thomas Jefferson). Botetourt recognized Randolph's authority and the speaker asserted the rights and privileges of the burgesses: freedom of speech and debate, exemption from arrest, and protection of their estates. The governor agreed to defend their "Just Rights and Privileges" before giving a short speech.[1]

Thomas Jefferson, just twenty-six and among the newest burgesses, was nominated by Edmund Pendleton, a veteran member of the assembly and a prominent planter-lawyer, to draft the House's formal response to Botetourt. This was mundane committee work delegated to a junior member. The new member from Albemarle wrote a series of resolutions to thank the governor. It was the first public paper by a man who would become famous for his pen and facility with words. Jefferson employed traditional language, expressing the gratitude and loyalty of the House to the governor (and the king). Jefferson wrote of the mother country and its oldest North American possession, "that her Interests, and Ours, are inseparably the same: And, finally, offering our Prayers, that Providence, and the Royal Pleasure, may long continue his Lordship the happy Ruler of a free and an happy People."[2] Botetourt and Jefferson (on behalf of the assembly) celebrated the harmony and common interests between Britain and Virginia more in hope than in expectation. Within ten days the governor would dismiss the assembly after George Washington introduced controversial resolutions, endorsed by Jefferson, condemning British taxation.

In May 1769 Washington and Jefferson took their first significant steps on the road that would lead them to become revolutionaries. In 1769 they—as the rhetoric employed by Botetourt and Jefferson suggests— were torn between loyalty to Britain, its institutions, and the constitution they believed was the wellspring of their liberty, and the desire to preserve and protect what they believed were their historic rights. They sought to maintain their (largely imagined) link to a vanishing conception of the British Empire, an empire they believed had guaranteed their rights, all the while coming to believe that the greatest threat to their liberties came from London.

The lives of elite Virginians like Washington and Jefferson were shaped by the contours of their colony and the empire of which it was a part. It is one of the arguments of this book that we cannot understand them without understanding their relationship with Virginia and the ways in which Virginia shaped their understanding of the world. They were both born in Virginia to elite families. They spent their formative years in the colony and married Virginians, establishing and running large plantations.

Although both achieved fame as revolutionary leaders on behalf of the United States, they owed their power and status to their connection to Virginia. They occupied positions of authority and subordination simultaneously. They were great men in Virginia, but provincials from a marginal place within the British Empire. In 1769, when they encountered each other in the House of Burgesses, Washington and Jefferson began to reassess Virginia's place within the empire. They began to push back at their subordination as colonial subjects and would eventually come to believe that Virginia's future lay outside the empire. Eventually they would see Virginia as leading a new, republican empire.

———

At the end of the Seven Years' War in 1763, Britain found itself with a public debt of £137 million. Interest payments on the debt alone amounted to £5 million annually, at a time when the government's total revenue was £8 million. Faced with such fiscal pressure, the government in London was desperate to seek sources of revenue to maintain its newly expanded empire. It looked to its overseas colonies, particularly those in North America, which had benefited from the British victory in the recent war. In February 1765 the prime minister, George Grenville, introduced legislation to impose a stamp duty on Britain's colonies in North America and the Caribbean. An equivalent duty was already in place in Britain. According to its terms, colonists would have to pay tax on almost anything formally written or printed, including wills, deeds, almanacs, advertisements, diplomas, bills, bonds, newspapers, and even dice and playing cards. For the first time, Britain would impose a direct tax on colonists within their colonies (colonists already paid customs duties, which they considered external taxes). Grenville intended that the revenue generated by the tax should be earmarked to support British troops stationed in America, most of whom were stationed north and west of the Ohio River, on land formally claimed by Virginia that King George III had set aside as a Native protectorate by proclamation in 1763. Grenville intended the measure to be an assertion of British authority over the colonies in the wake of Britain's triumph in the Seven Years' War. The legislation made its way through Parliament and received George III's assent on March 22, 1765. The new tax was scheduled to take effect on November 1.[3]

News of the Stamp Act reached America in April 1765. Virginia played a leading role in the unfolding crisis when a young member of the House of Burgesses, Patrick Henry, who had been a member of the house for only nine days, introduced a series of resolutions condemning the Stamp Act on May 29, 1765. Thomas Jefferson, then a twenty-two-year-old law student, was among those who crowded into the back of the chamber to hear Henry condemn the act. Henry, a twenty-nine-year-old lawyer, was renowned for his oratory. Jefferson later remembered, "I attended the debate however at the door of the lobby of the H. of Burgesses, & heard the splendid display of Mr. Henry's talents as a popular orator." Jefferson recalled, "He appeared to me to speak as Homer wrote."[4]

Henry introduced seven resolutions to the House of Burgesses condemning the Stamp Act. These included uncontroversial statements that Virginia's white settlers brought their rights with them when they migrated from Britain, that these rights were confirmed by royal charter, that taxation by consent was an ancient British right, and that Virginians should be governed by laws to which they had given their consent and which the king had approved. The burgesses rejected three, more radical, resolutions that Henry introduced, including one which asserted that only the House of Burgesses could tax Virginians; another which claimed that Virginians were not obliged to pay taxes that had not been adopted by their assembly; and a third which stated that any person who challenged the view that the House of Burgesses had the sole right to tax should be deemed "an enemy of His Majesty's Colony."[5] Although the assembly endorsed only the four mildest of Henry's resolutions (it had adopted the fifth, but then repealed it the following day), some newspapers reported that the burgesses had endorsed all the resolutions—and reprinted them in their entirety—giving the impression that the assembly had made a much stronger stand against the Stamp Act than it actually had.[6]

George Washington was a member of the House of Burgesses in 1765 but he does not seem to have been present when Henry introduced the Virginia Resolves (most members of the assembly had departed by that point). In a September 1765 letter to Martha's uncle Francis Dandridge, who lived in London, Washington observed that the Stamp Act "engrosses the conversation of the Speculative part of the Colonists, who look upon this unconstitutional method of Taxation as a direful attack upon their Liberties, & loudly exclaim against the Violation." Washington's use of language is interesting. He writes of those, like Henry, "the Speculative part of the Colonists," who opposed the act on ideological grounds as though he was not one of them. Washington opposed the act. He described it as "ill judgd," but his objections were largely practical, befitting his business-minded approach to plantation management in the mid-1760s. As he explained the situation to Dandridge, "the advantage accrueing to the Mother Country will fall greatly short of the expectations of the Ministry" because Americans would forgo British manufactures, especially luxury goods, that would do more harm to Britain than the colonies. Washington accurately predicted that the act would fail because colonial courts would refuse to enforce it. Washington's belief that American colonists could do without British manufactures was belied by a lengthy order he placed with his London agent, Robert Cary, on the very day he wrote to Dandridge. That order included tools, fine clothing, housewares, and tea. Although, Washington wrote to Dandridge, "the Eyes of our People—already beginning to open—will perceive, that many Luxuries which we lavish our substance to Great Britain for, can well be dispensd with whilst the necessaries of Life are (mostly) to be had within ourselves," he was not himself ready to dispense with imported luxuries. In the cover letter he sent to Cary with his latest order for British goods, Washington complained about the price for which Cary had sold his last tobacco consignment.[7]

Washington's assessment of the situation in America in 1765 was astute. During the summer, widespread rioting and protests, especially in the port cities, forced most of the men who had been appointed to enforce the Stamp Act to resign. A pan-colonial "Stamp Act Congress" met in New York in October to coordinate the colonial resistance to the act, including a boycott of British manufactured goods. By November 1, when the Stamp Act was meant to take effect, the law was a dead letter throughout Britain's mainland colonies. Courts refused to take action to enforce it. In March 1766 Parliament bowed to reality and repealed the Stamp Act while adopting the Declaratory Act, which asserted it had the right to tax and legislate over the colonies in "all cases whatsoever."[8]

The repeal of the Stamp Act did not address the question of the governance of the colonies—if anything, repeal of the act made the question of governance much more complicated. Since the colonists had objected to the Stamp Act as a direct, internal tax that would have been paid by individuals but had previously paid customs duties, in 1767 the

British chancellor of the exchequer, Charles Townshend, introduced legislation to impose taxes on a long list of goods that Britain exported to the colonies—including wine, porcelain, glass, paint, and tea, among other items.[9] As Washington had anticipated, the introduction of new taxes elicited an immediate response from aggrieved colonists, who had been organizing themselves since the Stamp Act crisis. Although they might have paid such duties in the past, Americans now objected to paying *any* taxes, internal or external, to which they had not given their consent. Consequently, protesters in most of Britain's mainland North American colonies, who dubbed themselves Sons of Liberty, adopted boycotts of British goods. These boycotts were often enforced by violence and threats of violence. Violent protest was so prevalent in Boston that by 1768 the British government sent five regiments of troops to the city to protect customs officers and merchants who sought to sell imported goods. This gave the lie to British claims that the revenue raised in America would be used to defray the cost of protecting Americans. Many colonists, especially in New England, viewed the Townshend Duties as an attempt to tax them without their consent and to use the ensuing revenue to pay for an army that threatened American liberties. In February 1768 the Massachusetts assembly, the Great and General Court, sent a circular letter to the speakers of the other colonial assemblies, urging united resistance to the Townshend Duties. It argued that no colony could enjoy liberty as long as the king controlled the appointments and salaries of colonial officials and asserted that Parliament could not tax the colonies for the purposes of raising revenue.[10] On April 15 the House of Burgesses unanimously praised their counterparts in Massachusetts for defending "American Liberty" while condemning the "fatal Tendency of the Acts of Parliament" and declaring their intention to work with the other colonies to seek redress of their grievances.[11] It was against this backdrop that the House of Burgesses met in the spring of 1769, and why Botetourt and Jefferson offered dubious declarations of common goodwill when the assembly met.

————

Though George Washington had been critical of the Stamp Act—he believed it was counterproductive and ill-judged—he had not taken an active stand against it. By the time he made the familiar trip from Mount Vernon

to Williamsburg in May 1769, he had begun to take a much more momentous ideological journey. The planter who worried more about the price of
tobacco and the possible disruption of Atlantic trade in 1765 was, by 1769,
poised to play a leading role in organizing Virginia's resistance to the
Townshend Duties. The Stamp Act and Townshend Duties had prompted
many colonial Americans, including Washington, to consider, and question, the nature of the colonies' relationship with the British Empire. As a
young man, he had experienced the contempt that British officers and soldiers felt for their colonial counterparts and was frustrated in his efforts to
secure a commission in the British army. Now, in middle age, he had come
to believe that Britain's North American colonists were being denied their
rights as free-born Britons. He believed that Virginians—at least those
who were white, Protestant, and owned property—should enjoy the same
rights as those who resided in Britain and Ireland. Foremost of these was
that they should give their consent to the taxes they paid through their
elected representatives, for if the government could take the property of its
subjects without their consent, it could deny them their rights and liberties
and might well enslave, or even kill, them. They believed they were not,
and could not, be represented in Parliament. Fortunately, Washington and
many other Americans believed they could give their consent through their
local assemblies, such as the House of Burgesses. These ideas were widespread in the British Atlantic world during the eighteenth century, and
their adherents, in both Britain and the colonies, called themselves Whigs.
(As the dispute with Britain intensified, American Whigs would eventually
call themselves Patriots.) By 1769 Washington was well versed in and ad-
hered to Whig ideas. He was guided in his thinking by his Fairfax neighbor
George Mason. Mason, like Washington, was a prominent planter and enslaver. A sometimes politician, Mason was unwilling to leave his large family for the long periods required by public service. Nonetheless, he had a
reputation as a formidable political, legal, and constitutional thinker.

Before the assembly convened in May 1769, Washington consulted
Mason. On April 5 he sent Mason a copy of a nonimportation plan that
merchants in Philadelphia had adopted in March. In his cover letter, Washington wrote: "At a time when our lordly Masters in Great Britain will be
satisfied with nothing less than the deprivation of American freedom, it
seems highly necessary that something shou'd be done to avert the stroke
and maintain the liberty which we have derived from our Ancestors; but

the manner of doing it to answer the purpose effectually is the point in question." By 1769 Washington had become more militant since his earlier, pragmatic condemnation of the Stamp Act as "ill judgd"; he now believed that the government in London intended to take away American liberty. Having petitioned Parliament without success, the colonists had to seek other forms of redress. "[H]ow far then," Washington wrote, "their inattention to our rights & priviledges is to be awakened or alarmed by starving their Trade & manufactures, remains to be tryed."[12] Washington believed that Virginians should join New Englanders and Pennsylvanians in boycotting British goods. If nonimportation failed, Washington told Mason, then Americans should be willing to take up arms to defend their rights.

Nonimportation, Washington argued, would have private as well as public benefits. Beyond putting pressure on Parliament to repeal the Townshend Duties and acknowledge American rights, nonimportation would help Virginians learn fiscal responsibility, weaning them from their dependence on British manufactures and, crucially, British credit. "The extravagant & expensive man," Washington might have been describing himself, "is thereby furnished with a pretext to live within bounds."[13] Washington, whose correspondence with Robert Cary & Co. during the 1760s revealed that he, Martha, and her children were enthusiastic consumers of imported luxury goods, ran up huge debts. In early 1764 Cary wrote to inform Washington that he owed the firm more than £1,800, a debt that increased by 5 percent per year in interest charges.[14] A generation later Jefferson, who also found himself in debt to British creditors, lamented, "The unprofitable condition of Virginia estates in general, leaves it now next to impossible for the holder of one to avoid ruin. . . . if a debt is once contracted by a farmer, it is never paid but by a sale."[15] To clear his debt, Washington sought to control his spending, and from 1766, he made the transition from raising tobacco to wheat on his Mount Vernon estate and outlying farms. In his letter to Mason, he showed acute self-awareness and a perceptive understanding of the psychology of consumption of himself and his fellow planters, "prudence dictated œconomy to him before, but his resolution was too weak to put it in practice; for how can I, says he, who have lived in such & such a manner change my method? I am ashamed to do it: and besides such an alteration in the System of my living, will create suspicions of decay in my fortune, & such a thought the world must not harbour; I will e'en continue my course: till at last the course discontinues the Estate, a

sale of it being the consequence of his perseverance in error."[16] Pledging
not to consume British imports as political protest might help Virginians
secure both their political liberties *and* economic autonomy.

George Mason replied immediately to Washington expressing his support for the creation of a nonimportation association. Mason spent three
days at Mount Vernon with Washington during which time they surveyed
the boundary between their land and, presumably, discussed the nonimportation plan. On April 23 Mason sent Washington a modified version of the
Philadelphia nonimportation plan, which called for the creation of the Virginia nonimportation association. Washington brought this plan to Williamsburg to present it to the House of Burgesses in May.[17]

On May 16, 1769, the burgesses passed a series of resolutions that became known as the Virginia Resolves; the resolutions claimed that they,
with the consent of the governor and his council, had the sole right to tax
Virginians. The burgesses also voted to circulate copies of the resolves to
the assemblies of other colonies and to petition the king.[18] At noon the next
day, just nine days after Botetourt and the assembly had pledged that Britain
and Virginia were bound by common interests and affection, the governor
summoned the burgesses to the council chamber at the capitol and declared, "I have heard of your resolves, and augur ill of their effect. You
have made it my duty to dissolve you; and you are dissolved accordingly."[19]
Undaunted, the burgesses left the capitol and proceeded with "the greatest
Order and Decorum" to the Apollo Room in the nearby Raleigh Tavern
(where Jefferson had once danced with Rebecca Burwell) to continue their
deliberations, without the sanction of the governor. Thomas Jefferson recorded in his expense accounts that he contributed ten shillings "towards
asstg. Doorkeepers of H. Burgesses," presumably for lost income during
the aborted session.[20] Washington introduced Mason's resolutions, and a
committee was formed to draft a plan for the meeting to consider the next
morning. On May 18 the burgesses reconvened and created the Virginia
Association, pledging to cease importing and consuming most manufactured goods from Britain after September 1, 1769, until the Townshend
Duties were repealed. Eighty-eight of the "late representatives" in assembly, including both Washington and Jefferson, signed the pledge. As
testimony to his newfound political militancy, the same day Washington
purchased a copy of John Dickinson's pamphlet *Letters from a Farmer in*

Pennsylvania, which argued that Parliament did not have the authority to tax the colonies for the purpose of raising revenue.[21]

The Virginia nonimportation resolutions that Washington introduced in May 1769 speak to the confused and confusing nature of colonial resistance at that time. They begin with an assertion of the signers' "inviolable and unshaken Fidelity and Loyalty to our most gracious Sovereign," before declaring that they were "deeply affected with the Grievances and Distresses, with which his Majesty's *American* Subjects are oppressed, and dreading the Evils which threaten the Ruin of ourselves and our Posterity, by reducing us from a free and happy People to a wretched and miserable State of Slavery." After endorsing the nonimportation plan, the signers toasted the king and his family as well as Lord Botetourt and "a speedy and lasting Union between *Great-Britain* and her Colonies" and "the constitutional *British* Liberty in *America,* and all true Patriots, the supporters thereof."[22]

Indeed, just two days after Botetourt dissolved the assembly and a day after the former burgesses adopted the Virginia Association, Botetourt "gave a splendid ball and entertainment at the Palace to a very numerous and polite company of Ladies and Gentlemen," in honor of the queen's birthday. Among those in attendance was George Washington.[23] Leading Virginians, including Washington and Jefferson who signed the resolutions *and* offered toasts to the king, sought to defend their liberty by declaring their loyalty to the Crown and to the British constitution. They believed the latter was the source of their rights and the former was their chief protector. Curiously, given that many eighteenth-century Britons believed Parliament was the bulwark of their liberties, the Virginians were directing their ire at Parliament and the government, which they believed were imposing unjust taxes that threatened the normal constitutional and political order in the colonies, disrupting the normal relationship between Britain and its colonies. The Virginians believed they were upholding and defending the traditional British constitution and that government officials in London were the innovators who sought to change the normal order of things and subvert the rights of British colonists in America. As such, at least in the beginning, the early resistance to British rule was conservative and backward-looking. This partially helps to explain why the future leaders of what would become a more radical independence movement were drawn from the top of Virginia society.

While not all colonial Americans supported the resistance against the Town-shend Duties (the protest movement was often enforced by violent intimida-tion), the boycotts were effective. British merchants, whose profits were hit by the colonial nonimportation and nonconsumption agreements, put pres-sure on the government and Parliament to repeal the duties. Faced with the realization that the cost of collecting the duties and protecting the officials charged with doing so outweighed the revenue generated by them, Freder-ick, Lord North, who became prime minister in early 1770, bowed to the inevitable and asked Parliament to repeal all the duties. Just as Parliament had given in to colonial pressure and repealed the Stamp Act in 1766 while asserting in the Declaratory Act that it had the right to govern the colonies, so when it repealed the Townshend Duties, it maintained the duty on tea as a symbolic statement of its right to tax, and thus to govern, the colonies.

After five years of near-constant turmoil, British-American relations entered a period of relative calm after the repeal of the Townshend Duties. In Virginia George Washington and Thomas Jefferson attended to their affairs and served in the House of Burgesses. Both continued to adhere to the Virginia Association, though in June 1771, as he contemplated mar-rying Martha Wayles Skelton, Jefferson placed an order for a pianoforte for Monticello—hoping that his music-loving bride-to-be would be pleased with the purchase—as well as cotton and silk stockings for himself and an umbrella. Jefferson placed his order in anticipation of the "certainty that the restrictions will be taken off everything but the dutied articles." If the association was still in force, Jefferson was content to leave the items in storage under the authority of the committee charged with enforcing the boycott until it was repealed, but he was eager to get the items, "particu-larly the Forte-piano for which I shall be very impatient."[24]

The quietude in British-American relations proved to be something of an illusion. As Jefferson recalled nearly fifty years later, "Nothing of par-ticular excitement occurring for a considerable time our countrymen seemed to fall into a state of insensibility to our situation." In early March 1773, he was among a small group of younger members of the House of Burgesses that met in the evenings at the Raleigh Tavern "to consult on the state of things." According to Jefferson, the group, which included Patrick Henry, Richard Henry Lee, Francis Lightfoot Lee, and his boyhood friend

Dabney Carr, "were all sensible that the most urgent of all measures was that of coming to an understanding with all the other colonies to consider the British claims as a common cause to all, & to produce an unity of action." The Virginians proposed the creation of intercolonial committees of correspondence that would circulate information and coordinate the resistance to any new British initiatives. The committees would soon be called into action.[25]

In May 1773 Parliament adopted an act designed to save the British East India Company from bankruptcy by changing the way tea was sold in the colonies. Under the terms of the Tea Act, the remaining duty on tea would be lowered but tea would be sold, and duty collected, directly by the company, allowing it to undercut competitors, including colonial smugglers. The result would be cheaper tea for Americans, more tax revenue for the government, and greater profits for the East India Company. The Sons of Liberty and committees of correspondence had done their work well. When Americans learned of the Tea Act, many were reminded that the duty on tea—and Parliament's right to tax them—had never been repealed. Rather than view the act as a reform-minded piece of legislation that benefited all concerned, some Americans saw it as a pernicious device that would see Parliament swallow their liberty as they drank their tea. During the summer and autumn of 1773 when ships bearing the East India Company's tea arrived in North American ports, they were met with protests. In most cases protesters prevented the tea from landing and being sold. In Boston members of the Sons of Liberty, crudely disguised as Mohawks, boarded three tea ships and destroyed 342 chests containing more than forty-six tons of tea worth approximately £10,000 on December 16, 1773.[26]

Parliament's response to the "Boston Tea Party" was swift and severe. In March 1774 it adopted four bills that became known in America as the "Coercive Acts," which were intended to punish Boston until the city paid restitution for the destroyed tea. The Boston Port Act closed the city's harbor to trade until the ruined tea was paid for. The Massachusetts Government Act altered the province's charter, curtailing the powers of the assembly and making most major offices appointed directly by the king. The Justice Act provided that a person accused of committing a capital offense while attempting to suppress a riot or enforce the law could be tried outside the colony—thereby subverting the right to trial by jury. The Quartering Act allowed military commanders to house troops in private buildings. Taken together, these acts, a direct response to the destruction of the East India Company's tea that Parliament viewed as a challenge to its authority, were intended to punish Boston and assert parliamentary authority, at the expense of American liberties, once and for all.

————

The House of Burgesses, including Washington and Jefferson, was meeting in Williamsburg when word of the Coercive Acts reached Virginia. On the evening of May 23, Jefferson and a group of younger burgesses met to discuss how the assembly should respond to the acts. According to Jefferson the group "cooked up a resolution" calling for a day of fasting and prayer on June 1, the day the Boston Port Act was to take effect. The house passed the resolution on May 24.[27] The royal governor of Virginia since 1771 was an aristocratic Scotsman, John Murray, Earl of Dunmore. In a replay of the events in the spring of 1769, Dunmore followed the precedent set by his predecessor when faced by recalcitrance from the assembly. Jefferson recalled, "The Governor dissolved us as usual. We retired to the Apollo as before, agreed to an association, and instructed the commee of correspdce to propose to the corresponding commees of the other colonies to appoint deputies to meet in Congress at such place <u>annually</u>, as should be convenient to direct, from time to time, the measures required by the general interest: and we declared an attack on any one colony should be considered an attack on the whole."[28]

Washington, who had spent the evening with the governor on May 25 and had had breakfast with Lord Dunmore the next morning, the day he dissolved the assembly, was surprised by Dunmore's decision. He wrote, "This Dissolution was as sudden as unexpected for th[e]re were other resolves of much more spirited Nature ready to be offerd to the House wch would have been adopted respecting the Boston Port Bill as it is call'd but were withheld till the Important business of the Country could be got through." As befitted the Janus-like attitude of many of the burgesses who resisted British rule but still respected British institutions and power, Washington was among those who attended a ball in honor of Lady Dunmore on May 27, the very day that he and eighty-eight other members of the house signed a renewed association agreeing to boycott tea and other goods imported by the East India Company.[29]

Washington and Jefferson had gradually become more radical on the British question since their first encounter in 1769. Jefferson and a coterie of younger burgesses had taken the lead in calling for the creation of the committees of correspondence in 1773, which prepared the ground for the rapid and coordinated colonial response to the Coercive Acts in the spring of 1774. Washington summed up the growing militancy among leading Virginians in mid-June: "The Ministry may rely on it that Americans will never be tax'd without their own consent[,] that the cause of Boston[, and] the despotick Measures in respect to it . . . ever will be considerd as the cause of America." Washington, always careful about matters relating to private property, did add a parenthetical qualification concerning the behavior of the Bostonians: "(not that we approve their cond[uc]t in destroyg the Tea)."[30]

Washington, Jefferson, and the other former burgesses returned to their homes in early June. They had called for a further meeting, a convention that would meet without the sanction of the governor, to select the colony's delegates to attend the Continental Congress to meet in Philadelphia in September. In most cases the voters selected the former burgesses as delegates to the upcoming Virginia Convention. On Sunday, July 17, Washington's learned neighbor George Mason came to dine with him after church. Over the previous weeks, they had been working on a draft set of twenty-four resolutions that asserted that the rights of Americans derived from British liberty and that Parliament had no right to tax colonial Americans, calling for a boycott of most British imports (including enslaved persons) and endorsing the pan-colonial congress to be held in September. Washington and Mason spent the afternoon and evening editing and polishing the resolutions that Washington presented to a "General Meeting of the Freeholders and other Inhabitants of the County of Fairfax" the next day. The meeting adopted the resolutions, which became known as the Fairfax Resolves. It also named Washington as one of Fairfax's two representatives to the upcoming Virginia Convention and chose him to lead a twenty-five-man committee to enforce whatever measures were deemed necessary by the convention. Washington, who as a young man had led men into battle in defense of the British Empire, had emerged as one of his colony's most important leaders in opposition to British rule twenty years later.[31]

To the west, the freeholders in Albemarle County gathered on July 26. They, like their compatriots in Fairfax, adopted a set of resolutions, which

Jefferson drafted, that asserted that Parliament had no authority over them, condemned the Coercive Acts, and called for a boycott of British imports. The voters elected Jefferson and his old college friend and neighbor, John Walker (the husband of Betsy Walker), as their deputies for the Virginia Convention.[32] One of the main tasks of the upcoming convention would be to select Virginia's delegates to attend the Continental Congress that would begin meeting in Philadelphia on September 5. Jefferson drafted a lengthy set of instructions for the delegates that he intended to submit to the convention for approval. He set out with his enslaved body servant, Jupiter Evans, for Williamsburg in late July but suffered an attack of dysentery that prevented him from continuing. Jefferson was forced to return home to convalesce. He sent Evans on to Williamsburg. It seems likely that he entrusted copies of his draft instructions for the Virginia congressional delegation to the enslaved man.[33] Given that these instructions constituted one of the most radical statements in defense of colonial rights in 1774, it would be ironic if they were delivered by an enslaved man who did not enjoy the rights for which white Virginians contended.

Jefferson sent copies of his draft instructions to Peyton Randolph, the most powerful man in Virginia politics and who he knew would preside over the Virginia Convention, and to Patrick Henry, who he hoped would be sympathetic to their spirit. In his autobiography Jefferson offered an acidulous comment: "Whether Mr. Henry disapproved of the ground taken, or was too lazy to read it (for he was the laziest man in reading I ever knew) I never learned: but he communicated it to nobody." Randolph was more reliable and tabled Jefferson's document before the convention.[34] Some of the delegates in attendance were so impressed by it that they had it anonymously published as a pamphlet with the title *A Summary View of the Rights of British America*.[35] Although Jefferson had not drafted his instructions with the intention of publishing them, his bout of dysentery inadvertently led to the publication of one of the most radical colonial pamphlets during the imperial crisis prior to the appearance of Thomas Paine's *Common Sense* in 1776.

In the *Summary View*, Jefferson reviewed the history of the British-American dispute. He went much further back than the Stamp Act to advance a novel theory of the British Empire. Colonial Americans, he argued, were similar to the ancient Saxons, who emigrated to England in the early Middle Ages but retained the natural rights they brought with them from

Europe. They did not cede their rights when they migrated, nor were they subordinate to the native Britons they encountered.[36] Like the ancient Saxons, the British settlers in America retained their rights. Jefferson argued that the relationship between Britain and the colonies was no different from that between England and Scotland (prior to the 1707 Act of Union)—that is, they had a common executive in the person of the king, but otherwise they had "no other necessary political connection." This was a radical position that completely denied Parliament's authority to govern America. According to Jefferson, in 1774 most of his fellow patriots "stopped at the half-way house of John Dickinson," who had argued in his *Letters from an American Farmer* that Parliament had the right to levy taxes to regulate American trade but not to raise revenue. For Jefferson this position had no basis in reason or history. The *Summary View* was a fundamental challenge to British rule in America.[37]

The Virginia Convention endorsed a revised version of the Virginia Association and selected six delegates to attend the Continental Congress in Philadelphia. Peyton Randolph would lead the delegation (and would be elected to preside over the congress). Among the delegation was George Washington, who purchased a copy of Jefferson's *Summary View* before departing for Philadelphia.[38] The First Continental Congress met from September 5 until October 14, 1774. Washington attended the conclave but added little to its deliberations. In its final Declaration of Rights and Grievances, the congress claimed that Parliament had no authority over the colonies except to regulate commerce and not to raise revenue—Dickinson's halfway house. The congressmen agreed to create a Continental Association, which called for a complete ban on imports from Britain and Ireland beginning December 1, 1774, and a total ban on exports that would begin on September 10, 1775. The colonists resolved to maintain the association until Parliament repealed the Coercive Acts. The congressmen intended to reconvene the following spring.

———

Between 1769 and 1774, Washington and Jefferson were in broad agreement about the aims and objectives of the resistance movement in Virginia and the other colonies. They collaborated as members of the House of Burgesses and signatories to the Virginia Association. They acted as

Virginians in defense of the interests of Virginia. They were not, yet, close personally, though they spent time together in Williamsburg. When Washington, well-known throughout the colonies, went to Philadelphia to attend the First Continental Congress in September 1774, he took his first steps on what would be a journey toward national leadership. Of course, he didn't know that, and the nation he would lead did not exist. He was in Philadelphia to represent Virginia. Jefferson, for his part, did not even attend the convention that elected the Old Dominion's delegates to the Congress (and it's doubtful he was prominent enough to have been selected to go to Philadelphia). Nonetheless, the publication of the *Summary View of the Rights of British America* was an eloquent and powerful statement of what was then the most radical position on American rights. It signaled Jefferson's arrival as an important figure. Jefferson would join Washington as a delegate to the Second Continental Congress in the spring of 1775.

George Washington and Thomas Jefferson began as reluctant revolutionaries. Indeed, in 1769 they were not yet revolutionaries at all. Rather, they were great planters, selected by their humbler (white) neighbors to represent and protect their interests. Andrew Burnaby, an English clergyman who visited Virginia a decade earlier, wrote of the type of men who sat in the House of Burgesses: "[T]hey are haughty and jealous of their liberties, impatient of restraint, and can scarcely bear the thought of being controuled by any superior power." Burnaby visited Virginia before the disputes over taxation resulted in a crisis in British-American relations. He continued, "Many of them consider the colonies as independent states, not connected with Great Britain, otherwise than by having the same common king, and being bound by natural affection."[39] This was exactly the constitutional position that Jefferson laid out in the *Summary View*. When Washington and Jefferson defied British taxes, and thus Parliament's authority, they did not set out to become revolutionaries. On the contrary, they were great men in Virginia seeking to preserve their status, power, and authority. They, like other elite Virginians, believed they could govern themselves with minimal interference from the British state. As they interpreted Virginia's history, their forebears settled the colony with minimal (or no) assistance from the empire and governed themselves, enjoying the rights of free-born Britons who happened to reside on another continent. They believed they owed allegiance to the king, who was represented by the colony's royal governor, but not to Parliament. Their assembly, in which they sat, was the equivalent of Parliament. The system had served Virginia—and Britain—well for more than 150 years. It was only when George III's ministers sought to change the system and aggrandize power at the expense of the colonies that the great men of Virginia were moved to resistance. Theirs began as a conservative attempt to preserve the status quo. They relied on economic coercion and (mainly) nonviolent protests, as well as petitions to the Crown to seek redress of their grievances.

A consistent theme that appears in the writings of colonial Whigs during the crisis was the claim that Britain intended to enslave the colonists. Washington and George Mason claimed in the Fairfax Resolves that parliamentary taxation was "calculated to reduce Us, from a State of Freedom and Happiness, to Slavery and Misery."[40] Perhaps we should dismiss as hypocrisy the claim by a conclave of slaveholders that British taxation was part of a plot to enslave them. To do so is to misunderstand how these particular Virginians—those with political and economic power who between them enslaved thousands of men, women, and children—saw themselves and their place in society. They believed that they were free and enjoyed rights and liberties and that among these it was their right to hold property in enslaved human beings. Their way of life depended on enslaving others. Enslaved persons were a commercial and political weapon to be deployed to gain leverage over Parliament. In 1769 Washington, Jefferson, and the other recalcitrant burgesses who had turned their backs on Governor Botetourt and marched to the Raleigh Tavern declared "that they will not import any Slaves, or purchase any imported, after the First Day of <u>November</u> next, until said acts of Parliament are repealed." In their next resolution, they vowed not to import "any Wines of any Kind whatever."[41] These leading Virginians did not eschew importing slaves out of concern for the rights of enslaved people. On the contrary, they did so out of fear that there was a plot afoot to enslave *them*. They were still committed to slavery and the belief that their way of life, and their own liberty, depended on enslaving others. Indeed, in the definitive published edition of Thomas Jefferson's papers, the next document but one after the nonimportation resolutions, is an advertisement that Jefferson submitted to the *Virginia Gazette* for the recovery of an enslaved man named Sandy, who had fled in search of his own liberty in 1769.[42]

— 5 —

An Immense Misfortune to the Whole Empire

I am sincerely one of those [who] would rather be in dependance on Great Britain properly limited, than on any nation upon earth, or than on no nation. But I am one of those too who rather than submit to the right of legislating for us assumed by the British parliament, and which late experience has shewn they will so cruelly exercise, would lend my hand to sink the whole island in the ocean.

—Thomas Jefferson to John Randolph, August 25, 1775

By the time George Washington arrived in Philadelphia to attend the First Continental Congress on September 4, 1774, he was well versed in the ideological stakes between Britain and the colonies. He was fervently committed to the defense of colonial liberties and willing to use force, if necessary, to defend them. Crucially, he had begun to think about the colonial struggle broadly, encompassing all the British colonies in North America. Thomas Jefferson, as we have seen, had also articulated a more radical position in the *Summary View*. Jefferson's perspective was still, largely, Virginia focused, though he would find common cause with the other colonies. Over the course of the next two years, both men would come to accept the necessity of waging war and declaring independence in order to defend their vision of American liberty.

———

The First Continental Congress adjourned after nearly seven weeks on October 26, 1774. By then most of the Virginia delegation had departed for home, but Washington stayed until the end and did not leave Philadelphia until October 27. He made the 150-mile journey from Philadelphia to Mount Vernon in just under four days, arriving around three in the afternoon on October 30.[1] During the next few months, he managed his plantations, continued to renovate his home at Mount Vernon, and sought to develop and expand his extensive landholdings in Ohio, despite Lord Dunmore having declared his previous surveys of those holdings null and void.[2] He also threw himself into the Patriot cause, playing an increasingly prominent role politically and militarily in the resistance. During the winter and spring of 1774 and 1775, he emerged as one of Virginia's most important revolutionary leaders.

As Virginians began to prepare for war, they looked to their most famous soldier for guidance. On November 13, 1774, three men representing the Prince William Independent Company of Volunteers, one of the first independent militia companies that began training in Virginia in anticipation of a likely war between Britain and the colonies, visited Washington at Mount Vernon to "wait upon Collonel George Washington, and request him to take the command of this Company as their Field Officer." Washington accepted their invitation as well as those of a further four independent companies in Fairfax, Fauquier, Richmond, and Spotsylvania counties over the coming months. The members of the Fairfax Independent Company were required to carry "a good Fire-lock and Bayonet, Sling Cartouche-Box, and Tomahawk" and to wear "regular Uniform of Blue, turn'd up with Bluff," anticipating the buff and blue that the Continental Army would wear. These independent companies were separate from the colonial militia system and were normally organized by the committees of inspection charged with coordinating and enforcing the boycotts, such as the various Virginia and Continental associations that were adopted in the months before the War of Independence. They were the armed wing of the Patriot movement, which was beginning to adopt the trappings and authority of government. Washington seems to have taken his responsibilities as the commander of these units seriously. He periodically inspected the troops and corresponded with their officers. His willingness to lead the independent companies reflected his prior military experience and his political militancy.[3]

Washington also continued to participate in Patriot politics. For several days in January 1775, he attended the meetings of the Fairfax Committee in

Alexandria with responsibility for enforcing the Continental Association and organizing the county's independent company. He was back in Alexandria in February to attend the meeting where he was chosen as one of the county's delegates to attend the Second Virginia Convention, to be held in Richmond the following month. A few days later, he reported from Mount Vernon, "With us here, things wear a disagreeable aspect; and the minds of men are exceedingly disturbed at the measures of the British government." He expressed the hope that "the Ministry would willingly change their ground, from a conviction the forcible measures will be inadequate to the end designed." As far as Washington was concerned, it was the British, "the Ministry," that would need to give ground, not the Patriots in Virginia (or elsewhere) who were preparing for war to protect their liberties. Washington believed that matters were coming to a head. "A little time must now unfold the mystery, as matters are drawing to a point."[4]

Washington was in Richmond on March 20 (as was Jefferson) for the opening of the Second Virginia Convention, which convened in the Henrico Parish Church. The delegates, who acted as a de facto government of the colony in defiance of Governor Dunmore, spent three days discussing the proceedings of the Continental Congress before unanimously endorsing them. On March 23 Patrick Henry gave what would be his most famous speech, calling for Virginians to prepare for war, proposing a resolution "that this Colony be immediately put into a posture of Defence," and giving a fiery oration culminating in the cry, "Give me liberty, or give me death!"[5] Whether Henry said these precise words, for which he is best remembered, is a matter of some debate among historians. What is not in question is the militancy of Henry's position. Several weeks before the outbreak of fighting between the Patriots and the British in Massachusetts, Henry declared that the colonies and Britain were already at war and called for intensive military preparations. Although Washington remained silent during the debate over Henry's motion, Jefferson was reported to have "argued closely, profoundly and warmly" in favor of Henry's resolutions, which narrowly passed the convention.[6]

On March 23 both Washington and Jefferson were named to a committee to "prepare a Plan for embodying, arming and disciplining" force to defend Virginia's liberties in accordance with Henry's resolution. Two days later the committee submitted its report, which called for each county to "form one or more voluntier Companies of Infantry and Troops of

Horse" and stated that each infantryman should be armed with a rifle and a tomahawk and clad "in a hunting Shirt by Way of Uniform."[7] While putting the colony on a war footing, the convention also selected delegates to represent Virginia in the Second Continental Congress, scheduled to meet in Philadelphia in May. Washington received 106 votes out of 108 cast, second only to Peyton Randolph, as befit his stature as the leader of Virginia's revolutionaries. Jefferson, whose prominence was growing thanks to the publication of the *Summary View of the Rights of British America* and his outspoken support of the most radical positions in opposition to British rule, was named as an alternate in the event Randolph could not attend the Congress.

During April and May 1775, both Washington and Jefferson were increasingly preoccupied with the imperial crisis, which became a full-blown war between Britain and the colonies when British forces clashed with Patriot militiamen at Lexington and Concord, near Boston, on April 19. The violence in Massachusetts arose, in part, because the British sought to seize arms and munitions that the Patriots had stockpiled. In a similar move in Virginia, royal marines seized twenty barrels of gunpowder from the colonial magazine in Williamsburg at three in the morning on April 21 and removed them to a Royal Navy vessel at the behest of Lord Dunmore. Independent militia companies mustered in response to Dunmore's action, and the governor placed his family aboard the ship, fearing for their safety.[8] News of the fighting in Massachusetts reached Virginia in early May; according to Jefferson, "This accident has cut off our last hopes of reconciliation, and a phrenzy of revenge seems to have seized all ranks of people."[9] On May 4 Washington departed Mount Vernon to attend the Continental Congress in Philadelphia. He was accompanied by another of the Virginia delegates, Richard Henry Lee. On the road to Baltimore, they encountered other members of Congress from Virginia and North Carolina. As befitted his military reputation—and the tenor of the times—Washington reviewed Baltimore's independent militia companies. The southern delegates arrived in Philadelphia on May 9. That evening they dined with Joseph Reed, a prominent Philadelphia Patriot. Samuel Curwen, a future Loyalist from Salem, Massachusetts, attended the meal and was impressed by Washington's "fine figure and . . . most easy and agreeable address."[10] The fighting in Massachusetts was a turning point. At the end of the month, Washington wrote to his old friend George William Fairfax in London about the bloodshed, "Unhappy it is though to reflect, that a Brother's Sword has been sheathed in in a Brother's breast, and that, the once happy and peaceful plains of America are either to be drenched with Blood, or Inhabited by Slaves. Sad alternative! But can a virtuous Man hesitate by his choice?"[11] Washington had made his choice. When he left for Congress, he had packed his uniform—likely the buff and blue of the Fairfax Independent Company; soon after arriving, he purchased a tomahawk, new coverings for his holsters, and "5 Military Books."[12] The soldier-turned-planter was becoming a soldier again.

After his arrival in Philadelphia on May 9, Washington was heavily engaged in helping Congress respond to the fighting in Massachusetts, serving on four different committees concerned with military matters. He wore his uniform as a silent but unmistakable statement of his commitment to the Patriot cause and as a reminder to his fellow congressmen of his prior military service. On June 14 Congress resolved to raise six companies of riflemen in Pennsylvania, Maryland, and Virginia to support the army near Boston. Congress also created a committee, which included Washington, to draft rules and regulations for the army. Congress was beginning to act as a "national" government (in embryo) for the rebellious colonies. It was also signaling that military conflict might be prolonged. It further resolved that the additional troops should be placed "under the command of the chief Officer in that army," which meant that its next task would be selecting the army's commander.[13]

Washington's diary entry for June 15, 1776, is typically terse and makes no mention of his appointment to command the army. He wrote simply, "Dined at Burns's in the Field. Spent the Eveng. on a Committee."[14] He made no mention that that day Congress had resolved "that a General be appointed to command all the continental forces, raised or to be raised, for the defence of American liberty," nor that after he was nominated by Thomas Johnson of Maryland, Congress voted unanimously to appoint him to the position.[15]

John Adams later claimed that some of his fellow New Englanders had been opposed to appointing Washington, and that even some Virginians were cool to the idea. According to Adams's account, when Congress decided to raise troops to support the siege of Boston and appoint a commander, he, Adams, declared, "a Gentleman from Virginia who was among Us and very well known to all of Us, a Gentleman whose Skill and Experience as an Officer, whose independent fortune, great Talents and excellent universal Character, would command the Approbation of all America, and unite the cordial Exertions of all the Colonies better than any other Person in the Union." Adams recalled that Washington left the room in embarrassment upon hearing his praise. During the succeeding evening, in Adams's telling, "pains were taken out of doors" to ensure that support for Washington's nomination the next day would be unanimous. With the benefit of hindsight, it seemed clear that Washington's appointment as commander in chief of the Continental Army was the most momentous decision made by the Congress apart from the decision to declare independence a year later. Adams's account shows him playing the decisive role in securing Washington's appointment.[16]

Adams's account of Washington's appointment was undoubtedly self-serving, but it speaks to Washington's appeal. Adams praised Washington's character, wealth, and military experience. He also extolled Washington's ability to unite Americans. Adams recorded this version of events in his autobiography, which he began composing during his retirement, several years after Washington's death. When he died, Washington was the most popular man in the United States and a genuine national hero. This may have colored Adams's account of Washington's appeal in 1775. Nonetheless, that Washington came from Virginia was part of his attraction. The fighting at Lexington and Concord and the subsequent siege of Boston had been exclusively New England affairs. For the rebel war effort to succeed, it was important that other colonies support it. The riflemen that Congress intended to recruit in Pennsylvania, Maryland, and Virginia would provide needed manpower, and their presence would testify to the support for the war beyond New England. So, too, would the appointment of a commander of the fledgling army from outside of New England. If Washington was not yet a unifying figure in an incipient nation-to-be, he was one of the few possible candidates for the appointment with a reputation outside his native colony.

Crucially, Washington had military experience, and he looked the part of a soldier. He was forty-three years old in the summer of 1775 and was a commanding presence. The Philadelphia Patriot and physician Benjamin

Rush wrote of Washington, "He has so much martial dignity in his deportment that you would distinguish him to be a general and a soldier from
among ten thousand people." Notwithstanding Adams's claim that Washington was embarrassed by the praise heaped upon him, the Virginian
subtly pushed his own candidacy. He wore his uniform to remind his fellow
congressmen that, as a young man, he had commanded men in battle, winning fame (and notoriety), and that he was prepared to serve again. Silas
Deane, a congressman from Connecticut, noted that the Virginian had "a
very young Look, & an easy Soldier like Air & gesture." Deane concluded
his description by noting that Washington "speaks very Modestly & in cool
but determined Stile & Accent."[17]

On June 16 Washington formally accepted command of the Continental
Army. He stood at his desk and addressed Congress through its president
John Hancock: "Mr, President, Tho' I am truly sensible of the high Honour
done me in this Appointment, yet I feel great distress, from a consciousness
that my abilities & Military experience may not be equal to the extensive &
important Trust: However as the Congress desire i[t] I will enter upon the
momentous duty, & exert every power I Possess In their service & for the
Support of the glorious Cause: I beg they will accept my most cordial
thanks for this distinguished testimony of their Approbation."

While thanking Congress Washington repeated his doubts about his
abilities and the potential danger to his reputation posed by the command:
"But lest some unlucky event should happen unfavourable to my reputation, I beg it may be rememberd by every Gentn in the room, that I this day
declare with utmost sincerity, I do not think my self equal to the Command
I [am] honoured with." Washington then declared that he would serve
without pay and would only ask that Congress cover his expenses.[18]

The members of Congress were impressed by Washington's performance. Eliphalet Dyer of Connecticut wrote of the new commanding general, "He seems discret & Virtuous, no harum Starum ranting Swearing
fellow but Sober, steady & Calm. His modesty will Induce him I dare say
to take & order every step with the best advice possible to be obtained in
the Army." They were especially impressed by Washington's willingness
to serve without pay. This was not simply because Congress's funds were
limited but because such selflessness and disinterested self-sacrifice was
proof of Washington's virtue, which many believed was as important as
military experience in choosing a commander. John Adams made the

connection between Washington's character and his decision to eschew a salary for his service. "There is something charming to me in the conduct of Washington," wrote Adams. "A gentleman of one of the first fortunes upon the continent, leaving his delicious retirement, his family and friends, sacrificing his ease, and hazarding all in the cause of his country! His views are noble and disinterested. He declared, when he accepted the mighty trust, that he would lay before us an exact account of his expenses, and not accept a shilling for pay."[19]

George Washington was an ambitious man. From an early age, he had craved military glory. When a career in the British army had failed to materialize, he threw himself into his life as a planter and a speculator in Native lands. Those endeavors, along with his marriage to a very rich widow, had made him wealthy and powerful. By 1775 he was a great man in Virginia, as his growing fortune and political influence attested. He came from a culture where such men were expected to sacrifice their personal ambitions for the common good. Indeed, excessive ambition was seen as a moral failing. This partially explains the apparent tension between Washington's obvious desire to be appointed commander of the Continental Army—he prepared for war before he left for Philadelphia and subtly, but unmistakably, angled for command of the army—and his repeated protestations that he might not be up to the job. According to Benjamin Rush, Washington had told Patrick Henry "that he was unequal to the station in which his country had placed him, and then added with tears in his eyes, 'Remember, Mr. Henry, what I now tell you: From the day I enter upon the command of the American armies, I date my fall and the ruin of my reputation.'"[20] While Rush wrote this rather melodramatic account years after the war, when Washington's reputation was secure, it is broadly consistent with Washington's own remarks before Congress when appointed to command the army. Washington's ambition (as well as his belief in the Patriot cause, of course) led him to seek command of the army, and his experience seemed to qualify him for the post; however, he had never commanded a unit larger than a regiment and he was concerned that he might not be up to the task. Should he fail, his reputation would suffer. For a Virginian of his class and status, loss of reputation was surpassed only by the fear of bankruptcy or mortality itself.

Washington's ties to Virginia were one of the reasons he was appointed to command the army. Yet, he would not see Mount Vernon again until

1781 when he briefly visited during the Yorktown campaign. He did not
return to his home to live until December 1783, more than eight years after
he had left to attend Congress. He was charged with transforming a group
of New England militiamen, soon to be joined by soldiers from other colonies, into a united fighting force, representing all the rebellious colonies.
Doing so was the only way that the British could be defeated. In so doing,
Washington gradually transformed himself from a Virginian into an American. By leading what became a national struggle for liberation, he became
a national leader. He had long thought of the Patriot struggle for liberty in
pan-colonial terms. Early on he concluded that a threat to liberty in Massachusetts was a threat to liberty in all the colonies and should be seen as
such.[21] As a young surveyor, he had thought in continental terms, admit-
tedly on behalf of Virginia, and he continued to do so throughout the imperial crisis. When he took command of the grandiloquently named "Continental Army"—the name was more an aspiration than a fact—he took
his first step in what would become a national struggle and an exercise in
national self-creation. He, among all his peers, would become synonymous
with the nation that emerged from the revolution and embodied a particular nationalist version of the revolution.

––––––––

Thomas Jefferson was not present when Congress appointed Washington
to command the Continental Army. Jefferson did not depart for Congress
until June 11. He remained in Virginia to attend a meeting of the House of
Burgesses, called by Lord Dunmore and convened by Peyton Randolph
(Randolph opted to remain in Virginia, making it possible for Jefferson to
eventually replace him in Congress). Dunmore called for the meeting of
the burgesses to consider a reconciliation plan that the prime minister, Lord
North, had presented to Parliament in February. According to North's proposal, if any colonial assembly made a grant to Parliament to support the
common defense and civil government, then Parliament would refrain
from taxing that colony. Jefferson attended the bad-tempered meeting of
the burgesses—the representatives were angry about Dunmore's seizure
of the colony's gunpowder and unimpressed by North's proposal. The
governor, fearing for his safety, joined his family aboard a navy warship
rather than remain in the governor's palace. At Randolph's behest Jefferson

took the lead in drafting a set of resolutions rejecting North's proposal. These were formally adopted after Jefferson departed for Philadelphia, but he took the draft resolutions with him to Congress, and they would form the basis for its response to Lord North in July.[22]

Jefferson had only been to Philadelphia once before, in 1766, to be inoculated against smallpox. Indeed, at this point in his life, he hadn't traveled much outside Virginia. It took him ten days to travel from Williamsburg to Philadelphia. The man who would declare all men equal a little more than a year later traveled in style. He rode in a phaeton—a small, expensive carriage—accompanied by two enslaved men, Jesse and Richard. En route he stopped in Fredericksburg, where he purchased a thoroughbred horse, General, for £50. He stopped in Annapolis to buy books, visit the Maryland capitol, and get his phaeton repaired. He arrived in Philadelphia on June 20, just a few days before Washington left for Boston.[23]

Thanks to the publication of the *Summary View* the previous year, Jefferson's reputation preceded him in Philadelphia. Decades later John Adams recalled that Jefferson "brought with him a reputation for literature, science, and a happy talent at composition. Writings of his were handed about remarkable for the peculiar felicity of expression." Several months after his arrival, James Duane of New York described Jefferson as "the greatest Rubber off of Dust" that he had ever met and noted his skill with foreign languages. Like Washington, Jefferson said little while attending congressional sessions. Also like Washington he quickly threw himself into committee work soon after arriving in Philadelphia. "Though a silent member in Congress, he was so prompt, frank, explicit and decisive upon Committees," Adams recalled, "that he soon seized upon my heart."[24]

Owing to his reputation as a writer, Jefferson was given his first important committee assignment a few days after arriving in Philadelphia. A small group had been working on a statement to justify the use of violence in defense of colonial liberties. Jefferson and John Dickinson, the celebrated author of *Letters from a Farmer in Pennsylvania*, were added to the committee to improve the declaration. Jefferson and Dickinson were probably the most celebrated political pamphleteers in Congress at the time. They exchanged drafts before Dickinson, older and better known than Jefferson, prepared the final text that was adopted by Congress on July 6 as the so-called Declaration of the Causes and Necessity of Taking Up Arms. The declaration rehearsed colonial grievances as well as the military actions undertaken by the British in order to justify the use of violence by the colonists in defense of their liberties. It explicitly denied that the rebellious colonists sought independence.[25]

Despite the militant rhetoric in the Declaration of the Causes and Necessity of Taking Up Arms, Dickinson represented the more conservative wing of Congress. At his urging Congress adopted an "Olive Branch Petition" on July 8, which he drafted, imploring George III to intervene in the American conflict, halt the war, and offer redress of colonial grievances. Dickinson's stature and influence was such that Congress, including Jefferson, voted in favor of the petition, though Jefferson later noted, "The disgust against this humility was general; and Mr. Dickinson's delight at its passage was the only circumstance which reconciled them to it."[26]

Several weeks later Jefferson was named to a committee that included Benjamin Franklin, John Adams—this would be the first formal collaboration between Jefferson and Adams—and his fellow Virginian, Richard Henry Lee. Congress charged this group with writing a response to Lord North's reconciliation proposal. Jefferson had already drafted resolutions to that effect for the House of Burgesses and had brought these with him to Philadelphia. Jefferson's resolutions formed the basis of the series of resolutions adopted by Congress on July 31 rejecting North's proposals.[27] In little more than a month, Jefferson had established a reputation as one of Congress's most eloquent and radical voices with a reliable pen.

Having adopted the struggle in New England as the cause of all the seaboard colonies, established an army, justified its actions to the wider world, appealed directly to the king, and rejected Lord North's proposal, Congress went into recess. Jefferson departed for Virginia on August 1. He went to the Virginia Convention, sitting in Richmond, which was now the de facto government of the colony. The convention selected Jefferson to return to Congress when it reconvened in October. Before going home to Monticello, Jefferson arranged a payment of £13 to his distant kinsman and friend John Randolph, for a violin. In 1771 Randolph and Jefferson had reached an agreement seemingly in jest to the effect that if Randolph outlived Jefferson, he should receive £100 worth of books from Jefferson's library. If Jefferson survived Randolph, he would receive Randolph's violin and its music or £60 worth of Randolph's books. Unlike his brother, Peyton, and son Edmund, who were prominent Patriots, John Randolph remained loyal to the Crown. In the summer of 1775, he was preparing to go into exile in Britain and offered to sell his violin to his friend.[28]

After his return to Monticello, Jefferson wrote to Randolph to arrange to collect the violin. He expressed regret that Randolph felt he could not remain in Virginia but expressed the hope that men like Randolph might be able to persuade the British to appreciate the situation in America and effect a just reconciliation between Britain and the colonies. He wrote: "My first wish is a restoration of our just rights; my second a return of the happy period when, consistent with duty, I may withdraw myself totally from the public stage and pass the rest of my days in domestic ease and tranquility, banishing every desire of afterwards even hearing what passes in the world."[29] Throughout his public career, Jefferson evinced the desire to retire from the world and return to his family. He spent a month at home before returning to Congress at the end of September. What should have been a happy family reunion with Martha and his children was marked by grief, as their daughter Jane had died on September 2, aged just seventeen months.

Hopes for the kind of peaceful reconciliation that Jefferson had expressed to Randolph faded as the leaves fell from the trees and summer became autumn. At the end of August, George III rejected the Olive Branch Petition and declared the colonies in rebellion.[30] After Jefferson returned to Congress, the war came to Virginia. British and Loyalist foraging parties raided the coast in October, resulting in skirmishing around Hampton after Patriots burned a British ship that had run aground on October 26, 1775. In response to this, Dunmore issued a proclamation on November 7, 1775, that offered freedom to any enslaved men who fled from rebel masters and enlisted in the British army. Dunmore's proclamation was a limited move—it only applied to the slaves of rebels—made out of desperation; British rule had completely broken down in Virginia by November 1775. Nonetheless, the proclamation signaled to enslaved people throughout Virginia and beyond that the dispute between the British and white Virginians over liberty and rights might offer them a chance to obtain their liberty. It also made impossible the type of reconciliation that Jefferson had hoped men like Randolph might negotiate. Even a limited British offer of freedom to enslaved people was unacceptable to men like Jefferson and Washington. As Dunmore's proclamation offered freedom to Black Virginians, it alienated many white Virginians, driving them to support the Patriot cause.[31]

After his return to Congress, Jefferson served on numerous committees relating to the ongoing war effort. He pined for home and worried about Martha and Patsy. Given the recent death of his daughter, Jane, his concern is understandable. Unlike Washington, who was away from Mount Vernon for eight years during the war, Jefferson was drawn to Monticello as often as his public duties allowed. He was frequently torn between the demands of public service and his private life.

The king's rejection of the Olive Branch Petition, the spread of the war beyond New England, and Dunmore's proclamation had convinced Jefferson that a peaceful and just reconciliation between the colonists and Britain was increasingly unlikely. On November 29 Jefferson wrote to the exiled John Randolph to inform him that his brother Peyton, the stalwart of Virginia politics for the past generation, had died suddenly while attending Congress. He also shared the news of the war with Randolph, including mentioning that Dunmore "has commenced hostilities in Virginia." He informed Randolph about the fighting around Hampton in late October, observing, "It has raised our country into a perfect phrensy."

Having informed Randolph about the war, Jefferson turned to the larger issues at stake. He laid the blame for the war at the feet of George III. "It is an immense misfortune to the whole empire," he wrote, "to have a king of such a disposition at such a time." In Jefferson's view the king had mismanaged the imperial crisis, ignoring colonial petitions for assistance, resulting in a war that threatened the empire itself. "To undo his empire he has but one truth more to learn, that after colonies have drawn the sword there is but one step more they can take. That step is now pressed upon us by the measures adopted as if they were afraid we would not take it." Jefferson averred that no man "more cordially loves a Union with Gr. Britain than I do" but that it would be impossible to maintain the connection under the terms laid down by Parliament and the Crown. "We want neither inducement nor power to declare and assert a separation," he warned. "It is will alone which is wanting and that is growing apace under the fostering hand of our king."[32] Six months earlier in the Declaration of the Causes and Necessity of Taking Up Arms, Jefferson had explicitly rejected the notion that the colonies sought independence. As the end of 1775 approached, he accepted it as a real possibility. Six months later he would begin drafting the Declaration of Independence.

— 6 —

Our Lives, Our Fortunes, Our Sacred Honor

> When forced, therefore, to resort to arms for redress, an appeal to the tribunal of
> the world was deemed proper for our justification. This was the object of the Dec-
> laration of Independence. Not to find out new principles, or new arguments, never
> before thought of, not merely to say things which had never been said before; but
> to place before mankind the common sense of the subject, in terms so plain and firm
> as to command their assent, and to justify ourselves in the independent stand we are
> compelled to take.
>
> —Thomas Jefferson to Henry Lee, May 8, 1825

Washington left Philadelphia to take command of the siege of
Boston on June 23, 1775. He did not arrive at the rebel headquarters in Cambridge until July 2. His journey was "a good deal retarded, principally by the
desire the different Townships through which I traveld, express'd of shewing
respect to the Genl of your armies." When he passed through New York
City, the colony's Provincial Congress presented him with an address that
expressed the weighty expectations that accompanied Washington on his
journey (and throughout the war): "While we deplore the Calamities of this
divided Empire, We rejoice in the Appointment of a Gentleman from whose
Abilities and Virtue we are taught to expect both Security and Peace." Washington's response was telling: "May your warmest wish be realized in the
Success of America at this important and interesting Period; & be assured
that, every Exertion of my worthy Colleagues & myself, will be equally extended to the re establishment of Peace & Harmony between the Mother
Country and the Colonies." He continued, "As to the fatal, but necessary

Operations of War. When we assumed the Soldier, we did not lay aside the Citizen, & we shall most sincerely rejoice with you in that happy Hour, when the Establishment of American Liberty on the most firm, & solid Foundations, shall enable us to return to our private Stations in the bosom of a free, peaceful, & happy Country." Despite averring that he sought a peaceful reconciliation between Britain and the colonies, Washington was thinking of the rebellious colonies as a country united by a common cause even before he formally took command of the army.[1]

Washington made a striking impression when he arrived in camp. An army surgeon wrote of seeing the general soon after his arrival in Cambridge, "His excellency was on horseback in company with several military gentlemen. It was not difficult to distinguish him from all others; his personal appearance is truly noble and majestic, being tall and well proportioned. His dress is a blue coat with buff colored facings, a rich epaulette on each shoulder, buff under dress and an elegant small sword; a black cockade in his hat." The general cut a particularly impressive figure on horseback. Many years later Jefferson wrote of Washington, "His person, you know, was fine, his stature exactly what one would wish, his deportment easy, erect, and noble; the best horseman of his age, and the most graceful figure that could be seen on horseback." Abigail Adms wrote, "I was struck with General Washington." She chided her husband, John, "You had prepaired me to entertain a favorable opinion of him, but I thought the one half was not told me. Dignity with ease, and complacency, the Gentleman and Soldier look agreably blended in him. Modesty marks every line and feture of his face." Abigail Adams wasn't the only New England woman impressed by Washington. At the end of October, Phillis Wheatley, a formerly enslaved and African-born poet living in Boston, sent Washington a copy of an ode she had written to him. In her cover letter accompanying the elegy she wrote, "Your being appointed by the Grand Continental Congress to be Generalissimo of the armies of North America, together with the fame of your virtues, excites sensations not easy to suppress."[2]

Washington formally took command of the army on July 3, 1775. The army, such as it was, consisted mainly of New England militiamen who had undertaken an impromptu siege of Boston after the fighting at Lexington and Concord. They acquitted themselves well at the bloody battle of Bunker Hill on June 17 while Washington was still in Philadelphia. Nonetheless, they were farmers-turned-soldiers who, in the militia tradition, had turned up during a crisis. They had limited enlistments, which were due to expire at the end of the year, and their commitment to the larger Patriot cause was uncertain. Soon after taking command of the army, Washington issued general orders in which he announced that the troops were now under the authority of the Continental Congress, "for the support and defence of the Liberties of America." He added, "It is hoped that all Distinctions of the Colonies will be laid aside; so that one and same spirit may animate the whole, and the only Contest be, who shall render, on this great and trying occasion, the most essential service to the great and common cause in which we are all engaged."[3]

Soon after taking command, Washington became aware of the magnitude of the task that he faced. He had expected that there would be around 20,000 men in the army but discovered that he had only 14,000 men fit for duty. They were a mixed lot. Washington was unimpressed by the lack of cleanliness and good order in the camps around Boston. He believed that his first challenge would be to instill discipline into the army. He feared that this would be difficult to do given the possibility that the British might again attempt to break the siege as they had at Bunker Hill. "The abuses in this army," he wrote soon after taking command, "I fear, are considerable. and the new modelling of it, in the Face of an Enemy, from whom we every hour expect an attack exceedingly difficult, & dangerous."[4] At the end of 1775, their enlistments expired. Strictly speaking, the Continental Army would not come into formal existence until January 1776. Many of the men reenlisted in the new regiments, which comprised the Continental Army and Congress raised regiments in other colonies to join the new army. "It is not in the pages of History, perhaps, to furnish a case like ours, to maintain a post within Musket Shot of the Enemy for Six months together, without [powder]" observed Washington, "and at the same time to disband one Army and recruit another, within that distance of twenty odd British regiments."[5] Despite the danger posed by the transition, Washington was slowly creating a disciplined, albeit small, army with which to confront the British.

Washington was fortunate that the British, under the command of General William Howe, were unwilling to come out of Boston and confront the rebel army. After their pyrrhic victory at Bunker Hill, the British did not make a serious effort to break the siege. After Washington's chief of artillery, Henry Knox, transported sixty tons of cannons and other armaments

300 miles from Lake Champlain to Boston during the winter of 1775–1776, Washington was able to threaten the city with bombardment. The British position became untenable, and they began to abandon the city on March 17, 1776. By the end of the month, the British had completed their evacuation of Boston, seven and a half years after the first British troops arrived in the New England metropolis. Washington had achieved his first major victory of the war.[6]

Washington, despite his misgivings about the strength of his own forces, was disappointed that he had not been able to draw the British into a decisive showdown that might have ended the war. At several moments during the siege, he proposed an assault on the British lines, expressing the hope, as he did in a war council in February 1776, "that a Stroke well aim'd at this critical juncture, might put a final end to the War, and restore peace & tranquility."[7]

Although Washington did not get the opportunity to inflict a war-ending defeat on the British, he had driven them from Boston. Moreover, he had imposed discipline and order on the disparate group of New England militiamen that he had encountered in July 1775. These had been augmented by soldiers from other colonies. While the "continental" nomenclature was never entirely accurate, he had begun to create an institution that represented the opponents of British rule in the thirteen rebellious mainland colonies. During the siege of Boston, Washington sought to instill discipline in the army and pride and authority in its officers. The commander in chief believed that the Patriots would need to create a standing army if they were going to defeat the British and defend their liberties. As he addressed the army at the beginning of 1776, "It is Subordination & Discipline (the Life and Soul of an Army) which next under providence, is to make us formidable to our enemies, honorable in ourselves, and respected in the world." He did so by drilling the soldiers, enforcing strict discipline, punishing soldiers who failed to fulfill their duties, and court-martialing incompetent officers. He also instituted a program of inoculation against smallpox in the army. This would be of enduring importance to the war effort, as the War of Independence coincided with a prolonged smallpox epidemic that ravaged North America, killing up to 100,000 of the continent's inhabitants.[8]

Beyond the creation of a competent military force, perhaps the most important legacy of the early months of Washington's command of the Continental Army was the emergence of an embryonic national identity within the army. In an August 1775 letter to General Thomas Gage, then the commander of the British forces in North America, protesting the mistreatment of Patriot prisoners, Washington referred to his men as "Citizens of America." Washington noted that Gage, alongside whom he had served during the Seven Years' War, refused to recognize his rank because he did not accept the authority of Congress. In response Washington asserted that his authority derived from the American people and, "I cannot conceive any more honourable [source], than that which flows from the uncorrupted Choice of a brave and free People—the purest Source & original Fountain of all Power."⁹ A little more than a month into his tenure as commander in chief of the Continental forces, and eleven months before Congress declared independence, Washington saw the dispute between Britain and the colonies in national terms. He believed the colonists were defending their rights as a people in opposition to Britain, which he saw as a separate country. Washington came to see the war as a national struggle, and the army he led helped create the nation.

Washington became a nationalist, and a national leader, gradually. The day after he wrote to Gage, Washington wrote to his kinsman Lund Washington, who was managing Mount Vernon in his absence. He described the officers of the army—then mostly from New England—as "indifferent," and characterized the enlisted men, also mostly New Englanders, as "an exceeding dirty & nasty people."¹⁰ Command of the Continental Army encouraged Washington to see the war against Britain as a national struggle and the soldiers he led as Americans. He came to see the "United Colonies," as he termed them during those early months of command, as a single entity. The war compelled him to think in national terms. During the war the army would be the most important national institution, and he was its most visible representative. Washington and the army were, in many ways ahead of Congress and the American people in seeing the struggle in national terms. It was not until the summer of 1776 that Congress finally, and formally, declared the colonies independent. The task of drafting the declaration fell to Thomas Jefferson.

———

In late December 1775, Thomas Jefferson settled his accounts in Philadelphia and began the journey to Monticello. He was desperate to see Martha and Patsy. In early November, on the very day that Lord Dunmore issued his proclamation offering freedom to some enslaved Virginians, Jefferson wrote a plaintive letter to his brother-in-law, Francis Eppes. While Jefferson was away in Philadelphia, Martha Jefferson had taken Patsy to stay with her sister, Elizabeth, and her husband at their plantation, Eppington, in Chesterfield County. Jefferson complained to Francis, "I have never received the scrip of a pen from any mortal in Virginia since I left it, nor been able by any enquiries I could make to hear of my family." He continued, "The suspense under which I am is too terrible to be endured. If any thing has happened, for god's sake let me know it." He was back in Charlottesville and reunited with his wife and daughter around the tenth of January and spent the winter and early spring of 1776 at home.[11]

Jefferson was thrilled to be reunited with Martha and Patsy. He did not ignore the rebellion while he was home. Sometime in late January, he compiled notes for a possible essay on the history of the settlement of Virginia. He did so in response to remarks that George III had made to Parliament the previous October. The king had explained that he was determined to retain colonies that Britain had "planted with great industry, nursed with great tenderness, encouraged with many commercial advantages and protected and defended at much expense and treasure." The claim rankled Jefferson, who set out to draft a "Refutation of the Argument that the Colonies were Established at the Expense of the British Nation." The draft essay amplified and expanded the recitation of early Virginia history that Jefferson had first laid out in the *Summary View* in which he claimed that the colony was settled without material support from England. Jefferson did not complete the essay. This may have been because in early February he received a copy of Thomas Paine's pamphlet, *Common Sense,* first published in Philadelphia in January, which made a powerful case that the colonies should declare independence as soon as possible. Paine's pamphlet had moved the debate in the rebellious colonies beyond rather dry recitations of historical precedent, and Jefferson set his draft "Refutation" aside, though he would return to some of its arguments and evidence a few months later when drafting the Declaration of Independence.[12]

While Jefferson was at home, his mother, Jane Randolph Jefferson, died suddenly on March 31, 1776. Jefferson said little about his mother's death. Only a single mention of her passing survives in his vast correspondence. The following June he wrote to Jane's brother, a merchant in England,

"The death of my mother, you have probably not heard of. This happened on the last day of March after an illness of not more than an hour. We suppose it to have been apoplectic [stroke]." Because Jefferson had little to say about his mother in his correspondence, some historians and biographers have assumed that he disliked her. However, as the historian Virginia Scharff has pointed out, Jefferson's surviving papers are often silent when concerning some of his most important relationships—either through accident or a deliberate effort to hide these links from posterity. He burned his correspondence with Martha after her death in 1782 and only made passing reference to the enslaved Sally Hemings, with whom he had six children. The absence of evidence does not allow historians to draw any firm conclusions about the nature of Jefferson's relationship with his mother. According to her tombstone, Jane Jefferson died at Monticello. Presumably, she had been visiting with her son, daughter-in-law, and granddaughter at the time of her sudden death. Jefferson's account books reveal numerous payments for doctors to treat his mother. We do know that after her death, he was severely incapacitated by a severe migraine headache that lasted for more than five weeks.[13]

Jefferson was well enough to travel by early May. On the seventh he set out to return to Congress in the company of an enslaved personal servant, Bob. The two men took a week to get to Philadelphia. Waiting for him when he arrived were letters from two Virginia friends. Dr. James McClurg reported from Williamsburg, "The Notion of Indepency seems to spread fast in this Colony, and will be adopted, I dare say, by a Majority of [the] next Convention." Jefferson's old friend, John Page, also writing from the Virginia capital, was more direct, imploring Jefferson, "For God's sake declare the Colonies independant at once, and save us from ruin." Jefferson was aware of the strength of opinion in Virginia on the independence question. Before he departed and while he traveled, Jefferson solicited opinions on the matter. By his estimation nine out of ten people he spoke to in northern Virginia favored independence.[14]

Although Jefferson was in Philadelphia, his mind, and heart, remained in Virginia. Martha was too ill to travel, and he was concerned about her health and keenly felt her absence. Just two days after arriving, he confessed to one of his oldest friends, "I am here in the same uneasy anxious state in which I was the last fall without Mrs. Jefferson who could not come with me." He was also worried that he was in the wrong place, since he would miss the action in Williamsburg, where yet another revolutionary convention was meeting. On May 15 the convention unanimously resolved that the colony's representatives in Congress should call on that body to issue a declaration of independence. The convention also created a committee to prepare "such a plan of government as will be the most likely to maintain peace and order in this colony, and secure substantial and equal liberty to the people."[15] Jefferson anticipated that the convention would need to draft a constitution for Virginia if the colony became an independent state. He desperately wanted to contribute to drafting the constitution. Jefferson believed that creating a new system of government for Virginia was so important that he spent several weeks in May and June 1776 drafting a proposed constitution. Meanwhile, the convention in Williamsburg did its work without Jefferson's assistance, preparing a constitution (largely the work of George Mason). Jefferson forwarded his own draft, but it arrived after the convention had completed its work.[16]

Jefferson's wish to be in Williamsburg, not Philadelphia, during the summer of 1776 wasn't simply a matter of homesickness. He believed that the rebellion in America was reaching a climax and the most important actions would be taken in the individual colonies as they became states and created new legal and political systems. It was, he wrote, "the whole object of the present controversy."[17] For Jefferson the American Revolution was first and foremost a Virginia Revolution. He appreciated that there was a common cause between and among the rebellious colonies, but he believed the real work of creating a new, more equitable society must happen within the new states themselves. Washington, who spent the spring of 1776 shifting the Continental Army, composed of men from throughout the colonies, was coming to see the struggle in pan-colonial terms. He recognized that independence could not be won without the support of all the colonies, and the Continental Army was both the manifestation of the Patriot struggle and the means by which it would be achieved. For Jefferson the real action of the revolution would occur within the states, and he believed Virginia would be the revolution's center of gravity. He wanted to return to Virginia and sought unsuccessfully to prevent the Virginia Convention from electing him to return to Congress for another year beginning in August. On July 1 he wrote to his old college friend Will Fleming. He was distressed because he had heard that his revolutionary credentials had been called into question because of his unwillingness to return to Congress.

"It is a painful situation to be 300 miles from one's country," he wrote, "and thereby open to secret assassination without a possibility of self-defence." He assured Fleming, "If any doubt has arisen as to me, my country will have my political creed in the form of a 'Declaration &c.' which I was lately directed to draw."[18] Even on the eve of Congress adopting the Declaration of Independence, arguably Jefferson's most important achievement, he was thinking about Virginia as his country.

On June 7 Richard Henry Lee, speaking at the behest of the Virginia Convention, introduced a series of resolutions calling for Congress to declare the colonies independent, seek foreign alliances, and create a plan of confederation to replace the ad hoc system by which Congress had been acting as national government and managing the war effort since the spring of 1775.[19] According to John Adams, Lee, rather than Jefferson, was chosen to speak on behalf of the Virginia delegation because, "Mr. Jefferson could stand no competition with him or any one else in Elocution and public debate."[20] While a majority of the delegates in Congress supported the independence resolution, there was still significant reluctance to take the step, particularly in the mid-Atlantic colonies. Recognizing that such a momentous decision should be unanimous, the radicals in Congress decided to delay the final vote on independence by several weeks. In the meantime Congress created three committees to deal with the issues raised by Lee's resolutions: one to prepare the Articles of Confederation, which would perfect the union of the independent states; another to draft a model treaty between the states and foreign powers; and a committee to prepare a draft Declaration of Independence.

Jefferson and Adams, along with Roger Sherman of Connecticut, Robert Livingston of New York, and Pennsylvania's Benjamin Franklin, were named to the Committee of Five to prepare a draft Declaration of Independence. Jefferson, thirty-three, was the youngest and least experienced member of the committee. Almost five decades later, Adams described Jefferson's attributes while claiming that he played a decisive role in persuading his fellow congressmen to appoint Jefferson to the committee: "Mr Jefferson came into Congress in June 1775. and brought with him a reputation for literature, science, and a happy talent at composition. Writings of his were handed about remarkable for the peculiar felicity of expression. Though a silent member in Congress, he was so prompt, frank, explicit and decisive upon Committees, not even Saml Adams was more so, that he soon seized upon my heart, and upon this occasion I gave him my vote and did all in my power to procure the votes of others."[21] Although Jefferson's attendance in Congress had been patchy at best, and when he was present he was reticent—throughout his life he was a reluctant and indifferent public speaker—thanks to the *Summary View*, he had acquired a reputation as one of the finer writers in that body.

Jefferson and Adams left the fullest accounts we have of the drafting of the Declaration of Independence. Unfortunately, they contradict each other on important details and the sequence of events.[22] Nonetheless, we do know that Congress appointed the Committee of Five on June 11. Soon thereafter, probably on the June 12, the committee met and discussed the main headings for the declaration before charging Jefferson with preparing the draft. They did so because of Jefferson's reputation as a writer and because they were all quite busy during that momentous month. (Jefferson served on thirty-four congressional committees in 1775 and 1776, several of which were sitting while he composed the draft declaration.[23]) Moreover, as is the way of committees throughout history, someone had to undertake the main task at hand on behalf of the group, and Jefferson was its most junior member. In his notes Jefferson simply (and obliquely) wrote, "The committee for drawing the declaration of Independance desired me to do it."[24] Adams provided more detail, claiming that Jefferson wanted him to prepare the first draft. He stated, "This I declined and gave several reasons for declining. 1. That he was a Virginian and I a Massachusettensian. 2. that he was a southern Man and I a northern one. 3. That I had been so obnoxious for my early and constant Zeal in promoting the Measure, that any draught of mine, would undergo a more severe Scrutiny and Criticism in Congress, than one of his composition. 4thly and lastly and that would be reason enough if there were no other, I had a great Opinion of the Elegance of his pen and none at all of my own. I therefore insisted that no hesitation should be made on his part."[25] Adams believed that Jefferson's Virginia origins were important in explaining his appointment to the Committee of Five and in that group's decision to ask Jefferson to prepare the draft declaration. For Adams it was a question of politics; Virginia needed representation on the committee, and the draft declaration would receive less scrutiny from Congress if it came from the pen of a Virginian rather than from a New Englander. Adams was correct that the Virginia connection was important. He may not have realized the degree to which

Virginia would be central to Jefferson's thinking when he composed the declaration.

Jefferson later recalled how he drafted the Declaration, "I turned to neither book or pamphlet while writing it. I did not consider it as any part of my charge to invent new ideas altogether & to offer no sentiment which had ever been expressed before." Rather, the object of the Declaration was "not to find out new principles, or new arguments, never before thought of, not merely to say things which had never been said before; but to place before mankind the common sense of the subject; [in] terms so plain and firm, as to command their assent, and to justify ourselves in the independant stand we [were] compelled to take." While "neither aiming at originality of principle or sentiment, nor yet copied from any particular and previous writing," according to Jefferson the Declaration's "authority rests . . . on the harmonising sentiments of the day, whether expressed, in conversns in letters, printed essays or in the elementary books of public right, as Aristotle, Cicero, Locke, Sidney E'c." Jefferson did not consult any books or pamphlets; neither time nor circumstances allowed for such research. Rather, he drew on a lifetime of reading and thinking to give voice to what "was intended to be an expression of the American mind."[26]

Although Jefferson may not have consulted any books or published pamphlets when he drafted his version of the Declaration of Independence, he did have important resources at hand that shaped the document. The first of these was his own draft constitution for Virginia, which he had been working on in May and June 1776. Although Jefferson's draft constitution arrived too late to influence the deliberations of the convention in Williamsburg, he incorporated key elements of that document into his draft Declaration of Independence. He was further influenced by the events in Williamsburg via an important statement, the Virginian Declaration of Rights, which was adopted by the Virginia Convention. Drafted by Washington's neighbor, George Mason, the Virginia Declaration of Rights laid out a radical justification for independence and revolution. *The Pennsylvania Gazette* published the Virginia declaration on June 12, just as Jefferson started to work on his draft Declaration of Independence. Jefferson may have been seeking to give expression to the American mind in 1776, but that expression had a particularly Virginian cast to it. That is fitting as, for Jefferson, the Virginia mind and the American mind were one and the same.[27]

According to Adams's recollection, he and Jefferson met to discuss the structure and content of a possible declaration and who would write the first draft. After they agreed that Jefferson should take the lead, the Virginian "accordingly took the Minutes and in a day or two produced to me his Draught."[28] Whether Jefferson produced his draft that quickly is impossible to determine, but it is possible. There were sixteen days between the likely meeting between Jefferson and Adams on June 12 and June 28, when Jefferson presented the draft, lightly edited by the Committee of Five, before Congress. During that period Jefferson was involved in other committee work, including helping to draft a report on the rebels' failed invasion of Canada and efforts to negotiate a prisoner exchange after that defeat.[29] According to Jefferson he prepared his draft and then showed it to Adams and Franklin, "because they were the two members of whose judgments and amendments I wished most to have the benefit," before submitting it to the Committee of Five. The committee then vetted the document before Jefferson presented it to Congress.[30] Given the press of business and the number of persons involved, Jefferson was certainly writing under a great deal of time pressure and may well have produced his rough draft of the Declaration of Independence in a couple of days. Jefferson submitted his draft to Congress on June 28, 1776. His notes are cryptic, "I reported it to the house on Friday the 28th of June when it was read and ordered to lie on the table."[31] It is not clear whether Jefferson, a reluctant public speaker, read his text to Congress or someone else undertook the task. Nonetheless, the draft submitted to Congress was definitely Jefferson's version of the Declaration of Independence.

Jefferson's draft declaration began with a plain statement that the representatives of the United States of America, not the United Colonies, were issuing the declaration to inform humanity why it was necessary for them to separate from Britain. The second paragraph, which owed much to the Virginia Declaration of Rights, asserted the following:

> We hold these truths to be self evident: that all men are created equal; that they are endowed by their creator with inherent and inalienable rights; that among these are life, liberty & the pursuit of happiness: that to secure these rights, governments are instituted among men, deriving their just powers from the consent of the governed; that whenever any form of government becomes destructive of these

ends, it is the right of the people to alter or abolish it, & to institute new government, laying it's foundation on such principles, & organising it's powers in such form, as to them shall seem most likely to effect their safety and happiness.[32]

Premising independence and self-government on equality and popular sovereignty, this clause would transform the declaration from what might have been a narrow statement about colonial taxation and governance into a revolutionary manifesto.

The bulk of Jefferson's declaration consisted of a long list of "unremitting injuries and usurpations" committed by George III against his loyal subjects in North America. This list, which often befuddles modern readers, was at the heart of the declaration because Jefferson and Congress had to persuade the American people to sever their ties with the British monarchy. American Patriots had long ago challenged Parliament's authority, arguing persuasively (for many) that Parliament had no power to tax or even govern the colonies. Many colonists retained loyalty and affection for the monarch. To make the case for independence, Jefferson had to make a case against the king. To do this he turned to his draft constitution for Virginia. In the preamble to that document, Jefferson had included a list of charges against the king to justify Virginia's independence. Jefferson repurposed this list for the Declaration of Independence. He later explained the similarities between the two lists by saying, "Both having the same object, of justifying our separation from Great Britain, they used necessarily the same materials of justification: and hence their similitude." The list itself was strongly grounded in Virginia's colonial history, which Jefferson had rehearsed in the *Summary View* as well as in his rough notes from earlier in 1776 for his unfinished essay refuting the claim that Britain had subsidized the settlement of the colonies. The list of charges against George III was, in Jefferson's draft at least, a selective interpretation of Virginia's history.[33]

On Monday, July 1, Congress spent the entire day debating Virginia's independence resolution before voting on the matter on July 2. In the end twelve of the thirteen delegations voted in favor of declaring independence. (New York, which had not received authorization from its revolutionary government, abstained.) Congress then spent three days, July 2, 3, and 4, editing Jefferson's declaration. Jefferson, as was often his tendency, observed the debate in silence, recalling, "I thought it a duty to be, on that occasion, a passive auditor of the opinions of others. more impartial judges than I could be, of it's merits or demerits." He credited John Adams for supporting the draft declaration "with zeal & ability, fighting fearlessly for every word of it." Jefferson sat with Benjamin Franklin while Congress edited his work. When Franklin observed Jefferson "writhing a little under the acrimonious criticisms" of the declaration, he told him an amusing anecdote about a hatter who faced editorial criticism when he sought to create a sign for his shop and ended up with a wordless image of a hat.[34] All told Congress cut about 25 percent of Jefferson's text and suggested cosmetic changes. Most of these were improvements. For example, Congress altered Jefferson's claim that humanity had "inherent and inalienable rights" to "certain inalienable rights." Jefferson grudgingly accepted the changes. The Declaration of Independence was, after all, intended to be a statement by Congress on behalf of the people of the United States, not an expression of Jefferson's personal views. Still, he took the care and time to make copies of his original draft, which he circulated among his friends. On July 8 he sent copies of the congressional declaration and his draft to Richard Henry Lee, observing, "You will judge whether it is better or worse for the Critics."[35]

Congress made one substantive change to Jefferson's draft. Jefferson had included a lengthy passage concerning the slave trade to the list of crimes and misdeeds it attributed to George III. It read as follows:

> he has waged cruel war against human nature itself, violating it's most sacred rights of life & liberty in the persons of a distant people who never offended him, captivating & carrying them into slavery in another hemisphere, or to incur miserable death in their transportation thither. this piratical warfare, the opprobrium of INFIDEL powers, is the warfare of the CHRISTIAN king of Great Britain. determined to keep open a market where MEN should be bought & sold, he has prostituted his negative for suppressing every legislative attempt to prohibit or to restrain this execrable commerce.[36]

According to Jefferson Congress cut this passage "in complaisance to South Carolina and Georgia, who had never attempted to restrain the importation of slaves, and who on the contrary wished to continue it," while noting the sensitivity of Northerners who had been "pretty considerable carriers of them [enslaved persons] to others."[37]

Such a view conveniently ignored Virginia's participation in the slave trade. When Jefferson wrote this passage, 40 percent of Virginians were enslaved, and he alone enslaved two hundred men, women, and children. His indictment of George III is consistent with the view Jefferson had expressed in the *Summary View*, that the colonists favored abolishing the slave trade and the king had prevented them from doing so. We know that Jefferson labored over every word and phrase in his draft declaration. His comments on the slave trade were not merely rhetorical. Slavery was on Jefferson's mind during the summer of 1776. He had included a clause in his draft constitution for Virginia, "No person hereafter coming into this country shall be held within the same in slavery under any pretext whatever," which would have prohibited the state's participation in the slave trade.[38] He was a relatively young man at the height of a moment of revolutionary fervor. He saw an opportunity to strike a blow against an institution that he knew to be wrong, though Jefferson's condemnation of and efforts to eliminate the slave trade would not have led to the abolition of slavery within Virginia.

Jefferson's deleted passage, though perhaps politically inexpedient (and historically inaccurate), when read in the broader context of the Declaration of Independence, emerges as his most powerful condemnation of slavery. It begins with an assertion that the Africans victimized by the slave trade were a people whose rights of life and liberty had been violated, contrary to human nature. Had this passage remained in the Declaration of Independence, its assertion of human equality would have taken on a much more universal, powerful, and radical cast. Jefferson's draft declaration used similar language of rights and liberties to describe the parallel plights of enslaved Africans in America and British Americans resisting British rule. Indeed, Jefferson, no doubt with Dunmore's proclamation in mind, condemned George III for encouraging enslaved Africans to risk their lives helping to suppress the rebellion in America in order to win their own freedom: "He is now exciting those very people to rise in arms among us, and to purchase that liberty of which he has deprived them, & murdering the people upon whom he also obtruded them; thus paying off former crimes committed against the LIBERTIES of one people, with crimes which he urges them to commit against the LIVES of another."[39]

Unlike Jefferson's private condemnation, not originally intended for the public, of slavery in the *Summary View*, the Declaration of Independence, premised on "a decent respect to the opinions of mankind," was meant for the widest possible audience. Had Congress retained the passage condemning the slave trade in language that made a direct connection to the Declaration's assertion of universal equality, it would have been a truly radical statement, both antislavery and anti-imperial. It would have been a clear, unambiguous statement that Africans possessed the same rights and liberties that British Americans were fighting for. Had such a statement been included in the Declaration, slavery *might* have been impossible to reconcile with republicanism in the new United States. In 1776 Jefferson was briefly willing to contemplate such a statement. Congress was unwilling to go that far.[40]

————

The relatively brief period from April 1775 until July 1776 was momentous for both Washington and Jefferson. From the outbreak of war in Massachusetts until the adoption of the Declaration of Independence, each man made key contributions to the Patriot cause. Washington left Congress, and civilian life, to take control of the rebel war effort. He successfully prosecuted the siege of Boston and began to mold the Continental Army into a national institution that could wage a sustained campaign for independence. Jefferson, torn between Virginia and Philadelphia, was the main author of the Declaration of Independence, which transformed a dispute over taxation and political authority into a revolutionary movement. Washington and Jefferson were in broad agreement about what was at stake in 1775 and 1776. Both supported the resort to arms to defend liberty, and both supported the Declaration of Independence. While they very briefly served in Congress together in the spring of 1775 (and had served together in the House of Burgesses and the various Virginia revolutionary conventions), they had relatively little personal interaction with each other during this period. They made their main contributions to the Patriot cause in relative isolation from each other. Nonetheless, the basis for their future friendship was laid during this critical period when they both committed themselves completely to the Patriot cause. The two men did not begin to correspond with each other until 1777 and did not do so on a regular basis until 1779. Their collaboration, and friendship, did not blossom until the British threatened their native Virginia.

— 7 —

That Service to the Cause of Liberty

I hope it will not be unacceptable to your Excellency to receive the congratulations of a private individual on your return to your native country, and above all things on the important success which has attended it. Great as this has been however, it can scarcely add to the affection with which we had looked up to you.

—Thomas Jefferson to George Washington, October 28, 1781

At the end of December 1778, George Washington wrote a lengthy letter to Benjamin Harrison, a leading Virginia politician. It was a rare letter in which Washington vented his frustration over the course of the war and criticized members of Congress. The general lamented, "Our Affairs are in a more distressed, ruinous—& deplorable condition than they have been in Since the commencement of the War." He described himself as "a faithful labourer then in the cause. . . . a Man who is daily injuring his private Estate without even the smallest earthly advantage. . . . one who wishes the prosperity of America most devoutly and sees or thinks he sees it, on the brink of ruin." He drew a contrast between himself and the men who served in Congress. The states, Virginia included, no longer sent their "ablest & best Men to Congress." According to Washington, "These characters must not slumber, nor sleep at home, in such times of pressing danger—they must not content themselves in the enjoyment of places of honor or profit in their own Country while the common interests of America are mouldering & sinking into irretrievable (if a remedy is not soon applied) ruin." He called out several prominent Virginians by name: "Where is

Mason—Wythe—Jefferson [—] Nicholas—Pendleton—Nelson—& another I could name [presumably Harrison]?"[1]

Washington wrote this letter six months before Thomas Jefferson became governor of Virginia. Jefferson's tenure as governor coincided exactly with a prolonged period of conflict in the state. The "pressing danger" Washington had warned about had arrived in Virginia. That fighting brought Jefferson and Washington together and laid the foundation for their friendship. Washington and Jefferson saw each other regularly during the period from 1769 until June 1775. They were not particularly close, personally, during that period, but they served in the cramped quarters of the House of Burgesses, various Virginia conventions, and the Continental Congress, where they undoubtedly socialized together. They agreed with each other on the major political issues of the day. Their experiences, skills, and temperaments meant they had different contributions to make to the revolutionary cause. They were separated during the War of Independence. Indeed, the two men would not meet in person again until 1783. Nonetheless, seemingly counterintuitively, they became closer during the war years as their prewar acquaintanceship blossomed into a productive partnership that served as a foundation for their postwar friendship. It might be said that their wartime collaboration marked the beginning of the friendship that flourished after the conflict. This was especially so during the period from 1779 to 1781 when Jefferson served as governor of Virginia and the main theater of the war shifted to the South.

———

On July 9, 1776, George Washington ordered the brigades of the Continental Army in New York to assemble "in their respective Parades" at six in the evening to hear the Declaration of Independence "read with an audible voice." No longer would the soldiers of the army find themselves in the anomalous position of fighting the king's soldiers while proclaiming their loyalty to the monarch. According to one of Washington's aides, Samuel Blachley Webb, the soldiers gave "three Huzzas" in response to the Declaration, "every one seemingly highly pleased that we are separated from a King who was endeavouring to enslave his once loyal subjects." The soldiers were so pleased with the Declaration that they, perhaps after toasting the independence of the United States, joined a crowd of New Yorkers who pulled down and decapitated a statue of King George III on the Bowling Green in lower Manhattan. "The troops," reported Webb, "having long had an inclination so to do, tho't this time of publishing a Declaration of Independence to be a favorable opportunity" to destroy the statue. Their commanding officer disagreed. In his general orders on July 10, Washington stated, "Tho the General doubts not the persons, who pulled down and mutilated the Statue, in the Broadway, last night, were actuated by Zeal in the public cause; yet it has so much the appearance of riot and want of order, in the Army, that he disapproves the manner, and directs that in future these things shall be avoided by the Soldiery, and left to be executed by proper authority." The destruction of the statue, and Washington's reaction to it, suggested that the revolution might lead Americans to challenge "proper authority" should they win their independence. This would become a major concern of Washington's throughout the war and its aftermath.[2]

While the Continental Army celebrated the Declaration of Independence in Manhattan by symbolically executing the king, thousands of the king's soldiers were disembarking and establishing camps on nearby Staten Island. On July 2 General William Howe had arrived at the head of a 30,000-man expeditionary force, the largest army the British had ever sent to North America, with orders to end the rebellion either through force or negotiation. The Declaration of Independence clarified the issues at stake in the war. Washington hoped, "This important Event will serve as a fresh incentive to every officer, and soldier, to act with Fidelity and Courage, as knowing that now the peace and safety of his Country depends (under God) solely on the success of our arms: And that he is now in the service of a State, possessed of sufficient power to reward his merit, and advance him to the highest Honors of a free Country."[3] There could be no easy reconciliation after Congress declared independence. However, the advent of Howe's army was a stark reminder that declaring independence and winning independence were very different things. Neither Washington nor the troops under his command could have expected that the War of Independence would last another seven years.

New York and its environs presented William Howe with several advantages. Washington had around 17,000 troops to defend the city—approximately 10,000 Continental soldiers supplemented by 7,000 militiamen.

Geography compelled him to divide these between Manhattan, Long Island, and the mainland. Howe had a larger, better-equipped army at his command. Thanks to the Royal Navy, under the command of his brother, Admiral Richard Howe, General Howe could move his forces between and among the various islands that comprised the city and its environs. On August 27 British forces confronted the Continental forces in Brooklyn at the Battle of Long Island. The British routed the rebels, though, thanks to General Howe's caution; Washington was able to salvage the battered remnants of his forces, which escaped to Manhattan. Howe captured New York City on September 15—the British would occupy the city until 1783—and pursued Washington north into Westchester County before the rebels turned and made a long, slow, fighting retreat southwest across New Jersey. By late 1776 the Continental Army had dwindled to 3,000 men. "[Y]our immagination can scarce extend to a situation more distressing than mine," Washington wrote to his kinsman, Lund. Without an infusion of new Continental enlistments for the 1777 campaign, Washington continued, "I think the game will be pretty well up."[4]

Washington had always been an aggressive commander; he had wanted to attack the British to break the siege of Boston, and he was not ready to give the game up quite yet. Although his men's enlistments were due to expire on December 31, he persuaded enough of them to remain in the army that he was able to turn and fight. In a daring surprise attack on December 26, he captured a Hessian garrison (one-third of Howe's forces were German mercenaries) at Trenton. A week later he followed this up with another successful attack on the British at Princeton on January 3, 1777. The twin victories at Trenton and Princeton, while not important from a tactical standpoint, were hugely important strategic triumphs. They convinced many Americans that the rebellion might not yet be a lost cause. They provided an important boost to Patriot morale and persuaded men to enlist in the army. They were the last victories that Washington would command until the Yorktown campaign in 1781. Prior to the battles at Trenton and Princeton, Washington wrote a lengthy letter to John Hancock, the president of the Continental Congress. He outlined the desperate plight of the army and the uneven performance of rebel militias during the campaigns in New York and New Jersey, informing Hancock that it was necessary "to get a large Standing army, sufficient of itself to oppose the Enemy." Washington recognized that such an army might seem to contradict the ideals for which the rebels were fighting. He wrote, "It may be said, that this is an application for powers, that are too dangerous to be intrusted." He continued, "I can only add, that desperate diseases, require desperate remedies, and with truth declare, that I have no lust after power but wish with as much fervency as any man upon this wide extended Continent for an Opportunity of turning the Sword into a ploughshare; But my feelings as an Officer and a man, have been such, as to force me to say, that no person ever had a greater choice of difficulties to contend with than I have. It is needless to add, that short inlistments, and a mistaken dependance upon Militia, have been the Origin of all our misfortunes, and the great accumulation of our Debt." Congress authorized the creation of a standing army, and Washington and his subordinates concentrated on training the force and instilling esprit de corps in the army. The army became an important national institution, dedicated to its commander. Washington came to believe that the survival of the army was crucial to the success of the revolution. He would learn that preventing the British from annihilating the army was more important than defeating the British on the battlefield.[5]

After the battles of Trenton and Princeton, Washington went into winter quarters at Morristown, New Jersey, where he could keep an eye on the British in New York City. For the remainder of the war, driving the British from New York remained one of Washington's main objectives. He hoped to draw Howe (and his successors) into a decisive battle for control of the city. As she did each winter during the war, Martha journeyed from Mount Vernon to spend the winter with George. During the 1777 campaign, the British undertook two separate, uncoordinated campaigns. General John Burgoyne led a combined force of British regulars, Canadian militia, and Indigenous warriors south from Montreal, intending to march down the Champlain-Hudson corridor to New York, cutting off and isolating New England from the rest of the rebellious colonies. Meanwhile, William Howe set his sights on Philadelphia. Howe took his army on a circuitous sea journey to the rebel capital. Washington confronted him twice near Philadelphia, at Brandywine on September 11 and at Germantown on October 4. Both battles were British victories, and Howe captured and occupied Philadelphia. The loss of Philadelphia was cushioned by news from the north. Continental forces and New England militiamen defeated Burgoyne's army in a series of engagements. Burgoyne surrendered his army to General Horatio Gates at Saratoga on October 17, 1777.

Washington and the main body of the Continental Army spent the winter of 1777–1778 at an encampment at Valley Forge, Pennsylvania. The army experienced extreme privation during that winter. The army was desperately short of supplies, including winter clothes, shoes, and food. Nonetheless, after nearly three years of fighting, the army had developed a strong institutional identity and a loyalty to its commander. The soldiers spent the winter at Valley Forge drilling and training.[6] By the spring of 1778, Washington would have the standing army he believed he needed to win the war. When British forces under Henry Clinton (who had succeeded Howe) abandoned Philadelphia in June and attempted to march overland back to New York City, Washington and the Continental Army confronted them in a bloody battle at Monmouth Courthouse in New Jersey on June 28. Although the battle was a nominal British victory, the Continentals acquitted themselves well and demonstrated they had the mettle to fight the British army. Washington demonstrated physical bravery during the battle, risking his life to reverse a rebel retreat.

Clinton abandoned Philadelphia because the British had adopted a new strategy. In the aftermath of the rebel victory at Saratoga, France entered the war as a formal ally of the United States in February 1778. Facing a wider war—Britain would have to defend its empire in the Caribbean as well as the home islands in the war with France (and later Spain)—and a seemingly intractable conflict in North America in which winning battles did not result in defeating the rebellion, the British decided to abandon the north and focus on the lucrative southern colonies. They planned to use New York as a base of operations, taking advantage of the Royal Navy to launch a series of campaigns to recapture the southern plantation colonies. Because the bulk of British forces continued to occupy New York City, Washington and the main body of the Continental Army maintained positions around New York, awaiting an opportunity to strike a decisive blow. A cat-and-mouse war of raid and counterraid took place around New York as the British and rebels foraged for supplies in New York, New Jersey, and Connecticut. Clinton, meanwhile, launched a series of attacks on Georgia, the Carolinas, and Virginia in 1778, 1779, and 1780. The southern strategy coincided with Thomas Jefferson's election to governor of Virginia and fostered a closer relationship between the governor and the general who commanded the rebel forces.[7]

Jefferson left Congress in September 1776, just before the British captured New York City. He believed that he could make his most important contribution to the revolutionary cause by returning to Virginia. Decades later he recalled, "Our delegation [to the Continental Congress] had been renewed for the ensuing year commencing Aug. 11 but the new government [of Virginia] was now organized, a meeting of the legislature was to be held in Oct. and I had been elected a member by my county." Jefferson believed that the deliberations of the House of Delegates (the successor to the pre-independence House of Burgesses) were of greater importance than those of Congress. "I knew that our legislation under the regal government had many very vicious points which urgently required reformation, and I thought I could be of more use in forwarding that work."[8] For Jefferson, the most important work of the revolution would be accomplished within the states. Independence required drafting new constitutions and reforming the legal and political systems of the new states. These activities would remake society and would transform the war for independence into a truly revolutionary event.

Jefferson entered the House of Delegates in October 1776. Although he had missed out on drafting Virginia's new constitution, he joined the legislature just as it undertook a wholesale reformation of the new state's legal system.[9] For the next three years, he served on the committee charged with revising Virginia's laws. It was arduous, painstaking work that suited Jefferson's precise mind—and his predilection for grand schemes. All told, he drafted 126 separate bills. Among these were bills to abolish primogeniture and entail, disestablish the Anglican Church, revise the penal code, and propose the creation of a system for universal, state-supported education. The House of Delegates did not enact all these measures, but Jefferson had outlined a program of revolutionary reform that he saw as the essential prerequisite if Virginia were to begin to realize the egalitarian principles that Jefferson had laid out in the Declaration of Independence.[10]

Jefferson was most proud of the bills he proposed that abolished primogeniture and entail and removed state support for the Anglican Church in Virginia. According to the laws of primogeniture and entail, large estates and landholding would be passed undivided to first sons. According to

Jefferson, "The transmission of this property from generation to generation in the same name raised up a distinct set of families who, being privi-
leged by the law in the perpetuation of their wealth were thus formed into
a Patrician order, distinguished by the splendor and luxury of their estab-
lishments." Jefferson believed that primogeniture and entail were vestiges
of feudalism, which had to be removed—despite having inherited land and
wealth from his father. "To annul this privilege," he wrote, "and instead of
an aristocracy of wealth, of more harm and danger, than benefit to society,
to make an opening for the aristocracy of virtue and talent, which nature
has wisely provided for the direction of the interests of society & scattered
with equal hand through all it's conditions, was deemed essential to a well
ordered republic." To remove the vestiges of feudalism and place the republic on a sound foundation, Jefferson believed it was necessary to remove state support for the Anglican Church, a pillar of the aristocracy. The
House of Delegates did not adopt his bill calling for the separation of
church and state in Virginia—the first in the history of the United States—
until 1786.[11]

When read beside his draft of the Declaration of Independence, as well
as his proposed constitution for Virginia, Jefferson's proposals to revise the
laws of Virginia outlined a coherent program of revolutionary reform. He
sought to strike at the traditional sources of power, inherited land, wealth,
and privilege, to create a new, more equitable republic in Virginia. Jefferson sought to create a republic in which an aristocracy of "virtue and
talent" would replace the aristocracy of landed wealth that had dominated
colonial Virginia. Talented men would be identified by a state-supported
education system. In his draft constitution, Jefferson called for the redistri-
bution of public land to poorer adult white males so that they could meet
the requirements to vote—effectively extending suffrage to all white men,
and striking at the political power of the gentry, like himself. In seeking to
reform Virginia, Jefferson outlined a radical republican vision that would
help to make real the Declaration of Independence's assertions of human
equality. For him, the revolution was first and foremost about reforming
Virginia.[12]

Despite its radicalism, Jefferson's program of reform was limited. It
largely excluded women. Girls were included in Jefferson's education
bill—they would receive a rudimentary education alongside boys during
the early years of schooling, but they would not enjoy the full rights of

citizens. Despite the antislavery sentiments Jefferson expressed in his draft Declaration of Independence, he made no effort to abolish slavery when he helped to revise the laws of Virginia. Although he sought to strike at some of the sources of aristocratic power and privilege, notably inherited wealth in land, he did not take meaningful action against slavery, a crucial source of gentry wealth and power—and the most egregious challenge to claims that Virginia could be a place where all men were created equal. The land that would be redistributed to poorer white male Virginians to give them economic autonomy and political power would come at the expense of Indigenous people. Moreover, there were serious political obstacles to Jefferson's vision. The House of Delegates, fearing the cost, refused to fund Jefferson's education plan, the key element to his program of reform. Throughout his long public career, Jefferson believed that Virginia should be the seat of reform in the United States, and an example to the world, but it frequently disappointed him.

Jefferson's disappointment in his fellow Virginians would deepen during his tenure as the state's governor. He was elected by the House of Delegates on June 1, 1779. Jefferson faced several formidable challenges when he became governor. First, he lacked executive experience. Although he had a decade of experience as a public servant by 1779, Jefferson's contributions had been as a legislator. Second, the governor's powers were severely limited. The framers of Virginia's 1776 constitution sought to diffuse and limit executive power. They drafted their constitution considering their experiences as subjects of a powerful monarch who, they believed, had ignored constitutional limits and safeguards. They sought to create an executive office that could govern but not threaten the liberty of Virginians. According to the Constitution, the House of Delegates would elect the governor annually. The governor could be reelected but was limited to serving a total of three terms. The governor would work with an eight-man Council of State, whose members served at the pleasure of the assembly. The Constitution vested executive power in the council rather than the governor, who could not call out the militia, make appointments, or grant pardons without consulting the council. The governor and council should exercise their military authority through a Board of War appointed by the House of Delegates. Third, Jefferson was unlucky that his tenure as governor coincided with repeated invasions of the state by the British. These would reveal his lack of experience and weakness of the Constitution.

Jefferson's tenure as governor of Virginia was the low point of his five decades in public service.

By the time Jefferson became governor of Virginia in June 1779, Washington had commanded the Continental Army for nearly four years. Since the two men had parted in 1775, they'd seen each other only once, in Philadelphia in 1776, and had exchanged a handful of routine letters concerning the war. Jefferson's election, combined with the adoption of the southern strategy by the British, would lead to prolonged contact between the men, resulting in the development of a productive relationship that laid the foundation for their genuine postwar friendship.

———

Soon after he became governor, Jefferson was confronted by an issue that required him to consult with George Washington and initiated a period of close collaboration between the two men. On June 7 the new governor of Virginia received a letter addressed to his predecessor, Patrick Henry, containing an appeal from Major General William Phillips. Phillips was a British officer captured at Saratoga, along with nearly 6,000 soldiers. The men who surrendered were known as the Convention Army, because the British commander, John Burgoyne, had signed a convention for the prisoners under the terms of which they would be held by the rebels until they were paroled or exchanged. The prisoners were first held in Cambridge, Massachusetts, before being marched to Charlottesville in late 1778. When the prisoners, whose numbers had dwindled to around 4,000 British and German soldiers, arrived in Virginia, the enlisted men were housed in barracks and their officers lived in the community. Jefferson entertained many of the officers at Monticello, including Phillips, the senior officer among the captives. Phillips had appealed to Governor Henry through an intermediary concerning the fate of another British prisoner, Henry Hamilton, the lieutenant governor of Detroit.

Henry Hamilton was born around 1734 in Dublin. He was the younger son of a member of the Irish parliament. He joined the British army in 1755, serving in North America and the Caribbean during the Seven Years' War. He left the army in 1775 but remained in North America, having been appointed as lieutenant governor of Detroit that year, just as the American war started. He struggled to establish British rule in the territory (which had previously been claimed by the French and was inhabited by a mix of Indigenous peoples and francophone settlers, both Creoles and mixed race), all the while seeking to prevent incursions by soldiers and militias sympathetic to the rebellious Anglo-Americans to the east. Virginians, particularly, coveted land in the greater Ohio Valley.[13]

As George Washington's earliest forays into the trans-Appalachian west in the early 1750s demonstrated, Virginians had a long-standing interest in Indigenous lands in the West. Wealthy men, like Washington, sought to purchase and speculate in Native lands (unusually for a wealthy Virginian, Jefferson was not heavily involved in western land speculation), while poorer Virginians saw opportunity to acquire land of their own—either through purchase or squatting. While the British and the rebels were fighting in the east, settlers from Virginia colonized modern Kentucky and Ohio. The early settlement of Kentucky by Virginians effectively made the territory Virginia's colony. The settlers sought to displace and dispossess Indigenous peoples, including the Cherokees, Shawnees, Yuchis, and Delawares. Even before the War of Independence commenced, Virginia militia and settlers fought Native peoples in the Ohio Valley in Dunmore's War. Henry Hamilton's arrival in Detroit coincided with the war between the British and the rebels in the east, while conflict between settlers and Native Americans continued in the West. In June 1777 Hamilton, who had been making diplomatic overtures to Native Americans, received orders "to assemble as many of the Indians of his district as he conveniently can . . . [and] employ them in making a Diversion and exciting an alarm upon the frontiers of Virginia and Pennsylvania."[14]

The revolutionary government in Virginia, like its royal predecessor, believed that Kentucky, and the wider territory northwest of the Ohio River, was its domain. In early 1778 a Virginia army under the command of George Rogers Clark invaded the Illinois territory, capturing Kaskaskia and Vincennes. In response, Hamilton led a combined force of British soldiers, Canadian militia, and Indigenous fighters and reoccupied Vincennes. In February 1779 Clark counterattacked, capturing Vincennes and numerous prisoners, including Henry Hamilton and several of his officers.[15]

By the time Clark had captured him, Hamilton had acquired a notorious reputation among Virginians. Hamilton had, allegedly, paid bounties to his Indigenous allies for the scalps of Virginia settlers in Kentucky and Ohio. Clark, himself a rather ruthless figure in the bloody racial warfare in the Northwest, described Hamilton as "the Famous Hair Buyer General."[16] Owing to this reputation, and the fact that, unlike Burgoyne, Hamilton had not stipulated the treatment he and his men should receive when he surrendered, Hamilton and several of his officers were roughly handled as they were transported from Vincennes to Virginia between March and June 1779. It was this treatment that caused William Phillips to inquire about Hamilton's well-being through an intermediary in early June. The outgoing governor was undoubtedly happy to pass the query, and the problem of what to do with Hamilton, to his successor, Thomas Jefferson.

If Phillips hoped that the new governor, with whom he had dined and socialized at Monticello, would show similar courtesy to Henry Hamilton, he was to be disappointed. Jefferson reported that he and the Governor's Council had discussed the Hamilton situation on June 7. He wrote, "The indiscriminate murther of men, Women and children with the usual circumstances of barbarity practised by the Indian savages, was the particular task of Governor Hamilton's employment." Jefferson felt that Hamilton's enthusiasm for such warfare against civilians was especially egregious, "if any thing could . . . have made him personally answerable in a high degree it was that eager Spirit with which he is said to have executed it and which if the representations before the Council are to be credited seems to have shewn that his own feelings and disposition were in union with his employment." Jefferson promised that "the truth of these representations will be the subject of their inquiry shortly, and the treatment of Governor Hamilton will be mild or otherwise as his conduct shall appear to merit."[17] The star witness during the council's investigation into Hamilton's actions was one John Dodge. Dodge, a notorious figure in the Northwest, was sympathetic to the American rebels and was captured and imprisoned by Hamilton in Detroit in 1776 before being sent to Quebec, where he escaped. Dodge boasted that after his testimony Hamilton and his senior officers "will all be hanged without redemption, and the Lord have mercy on their Souls."[18] He wrote a sensationalist memoir about his captivity, published in 1779, that likely closely followed his testimony. Dodge was severely critical of Hamilton and alleged that he was the instigator of all the alleged atrocities committed by Native Americans against settlers in the Northwest. Dodge confirmed the popular animus for Hamilton in Virginia, including the views of the governor.

On June 15, 1779, a Virginia officer collected Hamilton and Captain William La Mothe (who had also been captured at Vincennes), who were being held in Chesterfield, Virginia. Hamilton and La Mothe had traveled approximately 1,200 miles under guard from Vincennes. According to Hamilton the officer who met them "behaved very civilly." The captives were placed on horseback and rode the thirty miles from Chesterfield to Williamsburg, arriving on the evening of June 16. The captives and their guard rode to the governor's palace, where, as a young man, Jefferson had played music with Francis Fauquier. Hamilton and La Mothe remained on their horses, threatened and jostled by a hostile crowd. They were kept waiting for thirty minutes before the officer emerged with orders from Governor Jefferson. With the support of the council, Jefferson ordered that Hamilton and La Mothe should be "put in irons, confined in the dungeon of the publick jail, debarred of the use of pen, ink, and papers, and excluded all converse except with their keeper." The men were marched to the "Common prison," placed in shackles, and put in a small cell, which Hamilton estimated was ten square feet, "the only light admitted was thro' the grating of the door," along with Philip Dejean (another of the men captured at Vincennes).[19]

The imprisonment of Henry Hamilton had an unforeseen consequence: it helped give birth to a closer relationship between Jefferson and Washington. Soon after Jefferson had Hamilton jailed, he contacted Washington as the commander in chief of the Continental forces. This was the beginning of correspondence between the two men that would last another decade until Jefferson joined Washington's cabinet. During this second phase of their relationship, they grew to trust each other's opinions and counsel.

Strictly speaking, Jefferson need not have written to Washington about Hamilton's imprisonment. Virginia troops had captured Hamilton, and he was being punished, at the behest of Jefferson as the state's governor, for alleged depredations committed against Virginia settlers by the government of Virginia. Nonetheless, Jefferson recognized that his treatment of Hamilton might have repercussions for rebel prisoners—including Virginians—held by the British. Several days after he had Hamilton confined in the jail in Williamsburg, Jefferson wrote to Washington and sent him a copy of the order for placing Hamilton in irons in close confinement. A few weeks later, Washington gave his approval to Jefferson's action, writing, "I have no

doubt of the propriety of the proceedings against Governor Hamilton, Dejean and Lamothe. Their cruelties to our unhappy people who have fallen
into their hands and the measures they have pursued to excite the savages to
acts of the most wanton barbarity discriminate them from common prisoners, and most fully authorise the treatment decreed in their case."[20]

In early July William Phillips wrote directly to Jefferson to complain
about Hamilton's confinement. Phillips argued that because Hamilton, like
Burgoyne, had signed a document of capitulation when he surrendered, he
should not be subject to close confinement in irons. Rather, like Phillips,
Hamilton should be allowed to live in the community while he awaited a
prisoner exchange. Jefferson again sought Washington's advice, pointing
out that the terms of Hamilton's surrender made no mention of how he
should be treated. Having given the Hamilton matter more thought, and
consulted with some of his senior officers, Washington backed away,
slightly, from his earlier endorsement of Jefferson's decision to imprison
Hamilton in irons. "It seems to be their opinion," he wrote of his officers,
"that Mr. Hamilton could not according to the usage of War after his Capitulation . . . be subjected to any uncommon severity." Washington recognized that the terms of Hamilton's confinement was an issue for Virginia,
and that it depended on public opinion as much as the laws of war. He
wrote, "Whether it may be expedient to continue him in his present confinement from motives of policy and to satisfy our people, is a question I
cannot determine; but if it should, I would take the liberty to suggest that it
may be proper to publish all the Cruelties he has committed or abetted in a
particular manner and the evidence in support of the charges. That the
World, holding his conduct in abhorrence, may feel and approve the justice
of his fate." Washington did not disapprove of Jefferson's treatment of
Hamilton, and he was not, yet, advising that Jefferson should ameliorate
his treatment of the captive. Rather, he was advising Jefferson how he
might justify and win public support for that treatment. Nonetheless, after
receiving Washington's letter, the prisoners' shackles were removed, and
they were allowed out of prison on parole. When the prisoners refused the
terms of their parole—notably a restriction that prohibited them from
saying anything critical of the United States—they were remanded into
custody, though not placed in chains.[21]

Hamilton remained in custody for another year. He refused to accede to
the parole terms stipulated by Jefferson. He became a problem, as Jefferson

learned that the British were treating captive Continental soldiers from Virginia harshly in retaliation for his treatment of Hamilton. When a prisoner exchange was negotiated for British captives in Virginia for Virginians in British custody in September 1780, Washington expressed surprise that Hamilton was not among the prisoners offered for exchange. Jefferson explained that, owing to the tenuous position of Virginia in the Northwest and concern over Hamilton's influence among Native Americans in the region, as well as sensitivity to the views of Virginia settlers in Kentucky, he had resolved to exclude Hamilton from the exchange. Washington, respectful of the state's authority in the matter, and Jefferson's position as the state's governor, accepted the explanation. "I only wanted information on the point," he replied, "that I might know how to conduct myself with propriety and agreable to the views of the State." Jefferson took the hint, however. Two weeks later he wrote to Washington to acknowledge that Hamilton would be sent to New York to await parole in the hopes that "would produce the happiest effect on the situation of our Officers [held prisoner] in Long Island." Washington was satisfied that the saga was over. In November 1780 he wrote to acknowledge the release of Hamilton and another long-term captive, "I am glad to hear that you have permitted Govr. Hamilton and Major Hayes [Hay] to go to New York. While they remain there on parole, they will be less capable of concerting mischief than in Virginia, and it deprive the enemy of a pretext for complaining that they are treated with rigor."[22]

The captivity of Henry Hamilton had little influence on the outcome of the American War of Independence. The saga is revealing about the burgeoning relationship between Washington and Jefferson and their different conceptions of the revolution. When he chained Hamilton and placed him in close confinement, Jefferson sought the advice of Washington, more experienced in military matters. Although Washington supported Jefferson's decision, he eventually counseled him to moderate his position. While doing so Washington acknowledged Jefferson's authority as governor of Virginia. Throughout the war Washington believed that the army must be subordinate to civilian authority. Nonetheless, Jefferson moderated his treatment of Hamilton—removing his irons and offering him parole, in response to Washington's advice. A year later when Washington inquired as to why Jefferson had not allowed Hamilton to go to New York, the general, again, acknowledged the correctness of Jefferson's position, while hinting that it might be best for those Virginians held by the British if Jefferson softened his position and allowed Hamilton to leave. Jefferson acceded to Washington's suggestion. What we see emerging is a constructive relationship between the two. Washington was very much the senior partner at this point—in large part because the questions surrounding Hamilton's captivity were military in nature. Despite this, Washington recognized Jefferson's authority in the matter, even as he subtly suggested the younger man temper his position. Throughout the war Washington recognized the subordination of the military to civilian authority.

The Hamilton affair also reveals the differences between Washington and Jefferson over the revolution. For Jefferson, all the questions relating to Hamilton were oriented around Virginia and its interests. Hamilton's capture was the result of a campaign (undertaken before Jefferson became governor, but which had his support) to advance Virginia's territorial claims in the Northwest. He acted in defense of Virginia's interests and to protect Virginia's settlers in Kentucky and beyond. Hamilton's unforgivable crime, from Jefferson's standpoint, was inciting Indigenous warriors to kill Virginians. This justified his harsh treatment of Hamilton. While Washington was sympathetic to the plight of Virginians and understood the nature of warfare in the Northwest, he took a broader strategic view. His concern was the overall war effort. Although Washington acknowledged that Jefferson's position was correct, he suggested that it might be best if Hamilton's treatment was improved in the interests of the broader Continental war effort, and he gradually convinced Jefferson to accept that view. For Jefferson, the revolution was about Virginia. Washington, acknowledged as the greatest Virginian of the era, had adopted a more expansive view of the revolution and saw it as a national struggle.

It is important not to overstate these differences. In 1779 Jefferson was the governor of Virginia, after all, and defending the state was his paramount responsibility. The relationship between the two men that began in 1779 would deepen in 1780 and 1781 when the British invaded Virginia, resulting in Washington's greatest triumph and Jefferson's most abject failure.

————

Thomas Jefferson served two consecutive one-year terms as governor of Virginia. Unfortunately for him, his tenure as the state's chief executive coincided with the multiple British invasions of the state. Despite its size and importance, Virginia had been spared the brunt of the war. There had been some fighting and raiding along the coast in 1775 and 1776, but between 1779 and 1781, the British invaded the state four times. In the first of these, immediately prior to Jefferson becoming governor, the British briefly occupied the port towns of Portsmouth and Norfolk in May 1779. In October 1780 the British returned to the Virginia coast, again easily occupying Portsmouth and Norfolk before being recalled. A more substantial British force, under the command of Benedict Arnold, who had betrayed the rebel cause in September 1780, arrived off the Virginia coast at the end of that year. Unlike his predecessors Arnold sought to penetrate the interior of the state. His forces ascended the James River, burning and plundering plantations before marching thirty miles overland to capture Richmond. During Jefferson's governorship the capital of Virginia had been moved from Williamsburg to Richmond, which was considered more secure because of its inland location. Arnold's troops, a combination of loyalists, British redcoats, and Hessians, put the government, including the governor, to flight, before plundering and burning several public and private buildings in Richmond. According to Johann von Ewald, a Hessian officer serving with Arnold, the capture of Richmond "resembled those of the freebooters, who sometimes at sea, sometimes ashore, ravaged and laid waste everything. Terrible things happened on this excursion; churches and holy places were plundered." Ewald estimated that two-thirds of his men "were drunk because large stores of wine and beer had been found in the houses. They were so noisy that one could hear us two hours away."[23] Having occupied Richmond for twenty-four hours, Arnold withdrew to Portsmouth for the winter.

In the spring of 1781, a much larger British force, under the command of Lord Charles Cornwallis, entered Virginia from North Carolina. Cornwallis had been one of the most important British commanders in South Carolina and North Carolina. As the southern strategy collapsed in 1781, Cornwallis headed north to link up with the British troops in Virginia. Cornwallis had more than 7,000 troops at his command. Virginia was now the focus of the British war effort in North America. On May 10 the House of Delegates, having learned of the approach of Cornwallis's army, resolved to abandon Richmond and reconvene in two weeks' time in Charlottesville, seventy miles northwest. On May 16 Jefferson left Richmond for Monticello. He intended his return to Charlottesville to be permanent, as his second term as governor was due to expire on June 2. (According to the 1776 Virginia constitution, Jefferson was eligible to serve an additional one-year term but had chosen not to stand for reelection.) Upon learning that Virginia's legislature was reconvening in the west, Cornwallis dispatched Lieutenant Colonel Banastre Tarleton, a British cavalry commander with a fearsome reputation, and 250 dragoons to Charlottesville to capture the governor and members of the assembly. Tarleton reached Charlottesville early on June 4. He sent a detachment of soldiers to Monticello to capture Jefferson. Jefferson remained at his home until the British were just ten minutes away. At that point Jefferson fled. Believing his term as governor had ended, Jefferson went to his vacation home at Poplar Forest, eighty miles south of Monticello near Lynchburg.

Tarleton's arrival in Charlottesville put the House of Delegates to flight again. Before they could elect another governor, the legislators decamped further west, reconvening in Staunton. The assembly was not quorate until June 12, when it elected a popular militia general, Thomas Nelson, as governor. In principle, the state had been left without a governor for the ten days between the expiration of Jefferson's term and Nelson's election. Jefferson's tenure as governor of Virginia had ended in failure. Jefferson's apparent flight in the face of the British and seeming abandonment of his office resulted in accusations of cowardice and incompetence. Indeed, the House of Delegates initiated an inquiry into the former governor's conduct.

If the British invasion of Virginia resulted in humiliation for Jefferson, it provided Washington with a triumphant moment that defined his military career and cemented his reputation as the preeminent leader of the revolutionary cause. After the Battle of Monmouth in June 1778, Washington dedicated most of his efforts to countering the British around New York as the hub of British military power in North America. It was frustrating, painstaking work. Washington was unable to tempt his opposite number, General Henry Clinton, into a decisive battle for New York. Meanwhile, as the overall commander of Continental forces, Washington sought to direct the war in the south from afar while attempting to manage the alliance between the rebels and the French.

Having moved freely around Virginia in the spring and early summer, in August Cornwallis and his army retreated to Yorktown, on a peninsula between the James and York Rivers, to await resupply. Meanwhile, the combined forces of the Continental Army under Washington and the French army under Comte de Rochambeau were marching south for Virginia. On September 5 the French defeated the British in a naval battle off Chesapeake Bay. This victory denied Cornwallis all hope of additional supplies or rescue. On September 9 Washington arrived at Mount Vernon, his first visit to his home since May 1775, when he departed for Congress. He spent several days there planning for the upcoming campaign, while playing host to his military family as well as Rochambeau and his staff. Washington was eager to impress his guests. One of his aides wrote, "All accommodated. An elegant seat and situation, great appearance of opulence and real exhibitions of hospitality and princely entertainment."[24]

By mid-September the combined rebel and French armies, more than 16,000 men, had arrived at Yorktown. They conducted a siege for several weeks in late September and early October, bombarding the British positions while sappers dug trenches bringing the besiegers inexorably closer to the besieged. Out of hope and running low on supplies, on October 17 Cornwallis requested a truce so he could negotiate his surrender. On October 19 he formally surrendered. Washington, with the key assistance of the French navy and army, had secured the victory he had long sought against the British army.[25]

——

During Thomas Jefferson's two terms as governor of Virginia, he and George Washington exchanged more than seventy letters. Almost all concerned wartime matters. The two began their correspondence by discussing the fate of Henry Hamilton but also touched on all manner of issues relating to the overall war effort. Among the themes they returned to were recruiting and supplying Virginia troops for the Continental Army, the military situation in the Northwest, troop movements, the campaigns in the lower South, and, especially, the British invasions of Virginia. The scale and scope of the correspondence is testimony to the productive working relationship that developed between Washington and Jefferson during the war. They came to trust each other's judgment, and this served as the foundation for their postwar friendship.

One can trace the development of the Washington-Jefferson relationship through the tone of the letters. Jefferson signed the first letter he sent to Washington as governor with the traditional and rather formulaic closing, "Your most obedient & most h[um]ble servant." In his response Washington congratulated Jefferson on his election but concluded with a rather impersonal valediction, "I have the Honor &c."[26] By contrast, Washington was effusive when he wrote to Jefferson two years later. He concluded the last letter that he wrote to Jefferson as governor:

> Give me leave before I take leave of your Excellency in your public capacity to Express the obligations I am under for the readiness and Zeal with which you have always forwarded and supported every measure which I have had occasion to recommend thro' you, and to assure you that I shall esteem myself honored by a continuation of your friendship and corrispondence shou'd your country permit you to remain in the private walk of life.
>
> I have the honor to be with every Sentiment of respect & regard Dr Sir Yr. Most Obt. & Hbl Ser[27]

Washington wrote those words just after Jefferson had left office and taken refuge at Poplar Forest, the lowest point of the latter's public career. Washington, of course, was then unaware of the controversial circumstances surrounding the end of Jefferson's tenure as governor. Such was not the case when Jefferson, now a private citizen, wrote to congratulate Washington after Cornwallis's surrender at Yorktown. Jefferson apologized for not visiting Washington at his camp but averred, "I apprehend those visits which are meant by us as marks of our attachment to you must interfere with the regulations of a camp, and be particularly inconvenient to one whose time is too precious to be wasted in ceremony." He may also have been embarrassed about the controversial end of his term of office. (He was awaiting a board of inquiry to be held by the House of Delegates in December, which would vindicate him and pass a resolution of thanks to him.[28]) Jefferson concluded his letter, "I beg you to beleive me among the sincerest of those who subscribe themselves Your Excellency's Most obedt. & most humble servts."[29]

Washington replied to Jefferson from Philadelphia at the end of November. He acknowledged the victory at Yorktown and expressed his hope that it would benefit Virginia and the United States and his gratitude for the contributions of the French to the success of the campaign. At the moment of his greatest personal triumph, Washington was magnanimous and gracious to Jefferson. While Jefferson was suffering his greatest public humiliation, Washington affirmed his friendship to the younger man: "I am most sincerely sorry for the Misfortune which prevented me the pleasure of seeing you in Virginia. Among the Number of my Friends, who made me happy in their Company while I was in that State, it would have afforded me a peculiar Satisfaction to have added you in the List."[30]

———

The War of Independence taught Washington and Jefferson very different lessons about the American Revolution. For Jefferson, the war was a threat to Virginia's experiment with republican government, "the whole object of the present controversy," as he termed it. Jefferson had returned to Virginia in 1776 to continue the work initiated by the Declaration of Independence—an experiment in republican self-government—by committing himself to constitutional and legal reform. During the war Virginia was threatened from without and within. Repeated invasions by the British as well as loyalists and enslaved persons seeking their own freedom threatened Virginia's independence. As governor, Jefferson had come to doubt whether those Virginians who supported independence were virtuous enough to maintain republican government. He drew an unfavorable contrast between the people of Massachusetts and other states, who were able to maintain their republican institutions in the face of British occupation, and Virginians, whose institutions nearly collapsed in the face of the British invasions in 1780 and 1781. According to Jefferson, Virginians were motivated by fear rather than virtue during the war. "In this state alone," he wrote after the conflict, "did there exist so little virtue, that fear was to be fixed in the hearts of people, and to become the motive of their exertions and the principle of their government." Faced with what he believed was the unwillingness of Virginians to enlist in the militia, and the poor performance of that militia when confronted by the British, Jefferson came to accept, grudgingly, the need for his state to create a standing army. "Whether it be practicable to raise and maintain a sufficient number of regulars to carry on the war is a question" he put to the state legislature (which rejected the idea). For Jefferson, the war revealed the weakness of the state's constitution and the flaws of its citizens.[31]

In the spring of 1781, Jefferson, desperate in the face of the British invasion and doubtful of Virginians' ability (and willingness) to fight to defend their state, implored the most famous Virginian to save the state. He beseeched Washington, "Were it possible for this Circumstance to justify in Your Excellency a determination to lend us Your personal aid, it is evident from the universal voice that the presence of their beloved Countryman . . . that your appearance among them I say would restore full confidence of salvation, and would render them equal to whatever is not impossible." Jefferson believed it would be decisive if the tactical situation allowed Washington to leave New York and return to Virginia with the Continental Army (as he would later in the summer). "Should the danger of this State and its consequence to the Union be such as to render it best for the whole that you should repair to it's assistance, the difficulty would then be how to keep men out of the field."[32] Jefferson believed that Washington's presence was necessary to win the war and to preserve the revolution in Virginia.

Washington, who had concluded that the American rebels needed a standing army six years before Jefferson, had learned very different lessons from the war than his younger counterpart. Away from Virginia for more than six years, he was less committed to his native state than he was to the confederation of all states, which he felt was essential to winning the war. When he wrote his "Where is Jefferson?" letter in late 1779, he attributed the danger facing the rebel cause to the unwillingness of the individual states to work together for the common cause. He complained that many of the new states failed to send their ablest leaders to Congress. He might well have been describing Jefferson when he asked, "how little purpose [is it that] the States, individually, are framing constitutions—providing laws— and filling Offices with the abilities of their ablest men?" These efforts would come to nothing if the overall war effort failed, which would happen if "the greatest abilities & the honestest men our (i.e., the American) world affords" did not serve the national effort in Congress or the army. The states, alone, were not up to the task at hand. "[T]he States in their seperate capacities have very inadequate ideas of the present danger," he wrote, "removed (some of them) far distant from the scene of action & seeing, & hearing such publications only as flatter their wishes they conceive that the contest is at an end and that to regulate the government & police of their own State is all that remains to be done—but it is devoutly to be wished that a sad reverse of this may not fall upon them like a thunderclap that is little expected." While he went to pains to point out that he was not singling out any particular state—"I wish to cast no reflections upon any one"—he had accurately described the situation in Virginia, and Jefferson's position, prior to the British invasions.[33]

The war fostered a closer and more productive relationship between Washington and Jefferson. During the years when Jefferson served as governor, he came to appreciate the importance of the war effort that Washington managed. Washington, for his part, came to see Jefferson as a reliable partner upon whom he could depend even as the military situation deteriorated in their home state. Out of that collaboration was born a friendship that flourished for more than a decade.

— 8 —

Yr. Most Obedt. & Very Hble. Servt.

As I have accustomed myself to communicate matters of difficulty to you, and have met forgiveness for it, I will take the liberty, my good Sir, of troubling you with the rehearsal of one more, which has lately occurred to me. . . . and of hearing the sentiments of my friends upon the subject; . . . none would be more acceptable than yours.

—George Washington to Thomas Jefferson, February 25, 1785

Just before noon on Tuesday, December 23, 1783, General George Washington, aged fifty-one and dressed in his buff and blue Continental Army uniform, entered the chamber of the Maryland State House in Annapolis where the US Congress was meeting. The chamber was packed. Women occupied the main gallery "as full as it would hold," while men crowded in below. They had come to witness a historic moment. The general was announced and took a seat opposite Thomas Mifflin, who presided over Congress. At the stroke of noon, the secretary called for silence in the chamber. Washington rose, bowed to the members of Congress, including Thomas Jefferson, and read a short speech. He offered his congratulations on the successful outcome of the war and formally announced his resignation as commander in chief and his wish "to claim the indulgence of retiring from the Service of my Country." He credited Providence and his countrymen for the success and made special mention of the officers of the Continental Army, particularly those who were his closest aides and served with him throughout the war. According to a congressman who witnessed the scene, when Washington spoke of his official family, "he was obliged to support the paper with both hands." The general then commended, "the Interests of our dearest Country to the protection of Almighty God," at which point his voice faltered. Washington paused to recover his composure before saying "in a penetrating manner": "Having now finished the work assigned me, I retire from the great theatre of Action; and bidding an Affectionate farewell to this August body under whose orders I have so long acted, I here offer my Commission, and take my leave of all the employments of public life." At the close of his speech, Washington took his commission from the breast pocket of his coat and presented it to Mifflin. One of the witnesses wrote, "The spectators all wept, and there was hardly a member of Congress who did not drop tears." Mifflin delivered remarks, prepared by Jefferson, to thank Washington for his service. Washington bowed and briefly left the chamber. After the members of the public vacated the chamber, the now-former general returned, "bid every member farewell and rode off from the door, intent upon eating his Christmas dinner at home."[1]

Contemporaries recognized that they had witnessed a moment of profound significance. An immensely popular, triumphant general ceded power and went into retirement without seeking further power or personal recompense. James McHenry, one of the congressmen present, wrote, "It was a solemn and affecting spectacle; such a one as history does not present."[2] Forty years later, when Congress commissioned the artist John Trumbull (a veteran of the Continental Army) to paint four scenes from the revolution to decorate the rotunda of the Capitol building in the city that bears Washington's name, the general's resignation was one of the scenes Trumbull chose to paint (along with the adoption of the Declaration of Independence and the surrenders at Saratoga and Yorktown) (Figure 8.1). Trumbull described Washington's resignation as "one of the highest moral lessons ever given to the world." Another American-born painter of historic scenes, Benjamin West, reported that King George III said that Washington's resignation "placed him in a light the most distinguished of any man living, and that he thought him the greatest character of the age."[3] Thomas Jefferson described Washington's resignation as an "affecting scene" and called Washington's address to Congress "worthy of him."[4] Jefferson was the main author of the Congress's reply to Washington, delivered by Mifflin. Its most salient passage ably summed up the moment: "Having defended the standard of liberty in this new world: having taught

FIGURE 8.1   John Trumbull, *The Resignation of General Washington, December 23, 1783*
(1824–1828) Jefferson, a member of Congress in 1783, is seated facing Washington, third from the
left. Jefferson drafted Thomas Mifflin's response to Washington on behalf of Congress. Trumbull
Collection, Yale University Art Gallery.

a lesson useful to those who inflict and to those who feel oppression, you
retire from the great theatre of action with the blessings of your fellow
citizens—but the glory of your virtues will not terminate with your military Command. It will continue to animate remotest ages."[5]

Washington's resignation at Annapolis also marks the beginning of a
new phase in the relationship between Jefferson and Washington. The two
men did not see each other in person for seven years from May 1776, when
Washington briefly visited Philadelphia to consult with Congress before
the New York campaign, until November 1783. Despite this absence their
relationship had undergone a significant evolution. Their productive collaboration during the latter stages of the war, albeit at a distance, established the foundation for a real friendship between the two men. Their
friendship flourished during the 1780s, culminating in Washington's invitation to Jefferson to join his administration in 1790.

British and American negotiators formally signed the Peace of Paris, ending the war in America, on September 3, 1783. Under its terms the British recognized the independence of the United States and conceded generous borders to the republic—the new nation was bounded by the Mississippi River to the west and extended from the Great Lakes in the north to East and West Florida (controlled by Spain) in the south. When news of the treaty reached the United States, Congress decided to disband the Continental Army whose raison d'être had been achieved. At Princeton, the scene of one of his most important victories, on November 2, Washington issued his final orders to the army. "Who, that was not a witness," he asked, "could imagine that the most violent local prejudices would cease so soon, and that men who came from different parts of the Continent, strongly disposed, by the habits of education, to despise and quarrel with each other, would instantly become one patriotic band of Brothers?" He urged the soldiers to return to civilian life to enjoy "the rights of Citizens and the fruits of their labor," whether they engaged in agriculture, commerce, or the maritime trades in the various regions of the country. He advised the troops to "prove themselves not less virtuous and useful as Citizens, than they have been persevering and victorious as Soldiers." The general added a warning that "unless the principles of the federal government were properly supported and the powers of the union increased, the honour, dignity, and justice of the nation would be lost forever." Washington believed that the army had made American independence possible, and the result was a new nation that should transcend regional differences. That nation had to be sustained by virtuous citizens and a strong national government.[6]

Washington disbanded the army at Princeton because Congress had been meeting in the town since June before moving to Annapolis at the end of November. Jefferson arrived at Princeton to take up his seat in Congress just before the move to Annapolis. He encountered Washington there for the first time since 1776. A few days later, he wrote, "I had the happiness of seeing Genl. Washington the other day after an interval of 7 years. He has more health in countenance than I ever saw in it before."[7] With the war won, and believing he was leaving public service behind once and for all, Washington was likely in an ebullient mood. Having bade farewell to the army, in a few weeks Washington would journey to Annapolis to resign his commission and return permanently, he believed, to Mount Vernon.

During the waning days of the War of Independence, both Washington and Jefferson suffered grievous personal losses. In the immediate aftermath of the siege of Yorktown, Washington's stepson died, aged just twenty-six. Although Jacky Custis had exasperated Washington during his teenage years, he and Washington seemed to have enjoyed a better relationship after Custis married Nelly Calvert in 1773. In 1776 Jacky paid tribute to Washington, declaring, "He best deserves the Name of Father who acts the Part of one." Jacky and Nelly had purchased a plantation, Abingdon, near Mount Vernon and had seven children, four of whom survived. In October 1781 Jacky went to Yorktown to act as a civilian aide to his stepfather. He contracted "camp fever" during the siege and died on November 5. On November 6 Washington wrote from Eltham, Virginia, "I came here in time to see Mr Custis, breathe his last. about Eight o'clock yesterday Evening he expired. The deep and solemn distress of the Mother, and affliction of the Wife of this amiable young Man, requires every comfort in my power to afford them." With the death of Jacky Custis, Martha Washington would bury the last of her children. Jacky's widow placed her two youngest children, Eleanor Parke Custis (aged two) and George Washington Parke Custis (an infant) in the care of their grandparents. These children, known as Nelly and Wash, were raised at Mount Vernon and became de facto stepchildren to Martha and George Washington.[8]

Almost a year later Jefferson suffered a devastating loss when his beloved wife, Martha, aged thirty-three, died on September 6, 1782. After the birth of her last child in May 1782, Martha Jefferson endured a prolonged postpartum illness from which she never recovered. Thomas Jefferson described the summer of 1782 as a "state of dreadful suspence," and he rarely left Martha's bedside.[9] Patsy, who was then ten years old, remembered her father tending to her dying mother: "For four months that she lingered he was never out of Calling. When not at her bed side he was writing in a small room which opened immediately at the head of her bed."[10] During her illness Martha began copying a passage from Laurence Sterne's *Tristram Shandy,* Jefferson's favorite book. It is one of a handful of documents that survive in Martha's hand (Thomas Jefferson burned their letters to each other). She wrote:

Time wastes too fast: every letter
I trace tells me with what rapidity

life follows my pen. The days and hours
of it are flying over our heads like
clouds of windy day never to return—
more every thing presses on . . .

The dying Martha did not complete the passage, but Thomas did:

—and every
time I kiss thy hand to bid adieu, every absence which
follows it, are preludes to that eternal separation
which we are shortly to make![11]

On September 6, 1782, Jefferson entered a brief notation in his memorandum book, "My dear wife died this day at 11H—45' A.M."[12] Patsy recalled, "A moment before the closing scenes he was led from the room almost in a state of insensibility by his sister Mrs. Carr who led with great difficulty got him into his library and remained so long insensible that they feared he would never revive."[13] Jefferson was overcome with grief. Two weeks after Martha's death, a friend reported that Jefferson was inconsolable: "I scarcely supposed that his grief would be so violent, as to justify the circulating report of his swooning away, whenever he sees his children."[14] Almost a month after Martha's death, Jefferson wrote to her half sister, Elizabeth Wayles Eppes. He assured Eppes that he was looking after his daughters, Patsy, Polly, and Lucy; nonetheless, he remained consumed by grief. He wrote:

This miserable kind of existence is really too burthensome to be borne, and were not for the infidelity of deserting the sacred charge left me, I could not wish it's continuance a moment. For what could it be wished? All my plans of comfort and happiness reversed by a single event and nothing answering in prospect before me but a gloom unbrightened with one chearful expectation. The care and instruction of our children indeed affords me some temporary abstractions from wretchedness and nourishes a soothing reflection that if there be beyond the grave any concern for the things of this world there is one angel at least who views these attentions with pleasure and wishes the continuance of them while she must pity the miseries to which they confine me.[15]

Patsy recalled that her father was confined to his room for three weeks. He slept very little. When he finally emerged, he rode incessantly over his land. She remained by her father's side. "In those melancholy rambles," she wrote, "I was his constant companion, a solitary witness to many a violent burst of grief."[16]

Martha Wayles Jefferson was buried in the Monticello graveyard. Jefferson selected a line from Homer as an epitaph for her. It read (in Greek) as follows:

Nay, if even in the house of Hades the dead forget their dead,

Yet will I even there be mindful of my dear comrade.

Below the inscription her tombstone read:

To the memory of
Martha Jefferson,
Daughter of John Wayles;
Born October 19th, 1748, O.S.
Intermarried with
Thomas Jefferson
January 1st, 1772;
Torn from him by death
September 6th, 1782:
This monument of his love is inscribed.

Jefferson's choice of the word *torn* to describe Martha's death speaks to his grief. He was widowed at thirty-nine, the father of three young girls. Overcome by grief and family responsibilities, Jefferson had resolved to quit public life.[17]

To pull Jefferson out of his depression after Martha's death, James Madison sought to orchestrate his friend's return to public service. Madison arranged to have Jefferson appointed to the US delegation negotiating the Peace of Paris. Jefferson eventually declined the appointment but was elected to represent Virginia in Congress with Madison's support in June 1783. He was in Annapolis in December when the commander in chief arrived to resign his commission. Washington arrived in Annapolis on December 19. On December 20 Congress resolved that a "public entertainment" should be given in Washington's honor on Monday, December 22, prior to his attendance at the public meeting of Congress on Tuesday,

December 23. It also created a committee consisting of Jefferson, Elbridge Gerry of Massachusetts, and James McHenry to draft a response to Washington's resignation address. Like its predecessors in 1775 and 1776, the congressional committee looked to Jefferson as its primary draftsman. Gerry and McHenry asked Jefferson to write the response to Washington's resignation message.[18]

To draft a reply to Washington's message, Jefferson needed to see that message in advance. Given the planned events to mark Washington's arrival, Jefferson would have to write his response over the weekend. It is likely that he and Washington met on December 21 or 22. Congress held a public dinner in Washington's honor on December 22 at Mann's Tavern on Main Street in Annapolis. "The feast," according to a congressman from Delaware, James Tilton, who attended the celebration, "was the most extraordinary I ever attended." Tilton claimed that there were between two hundred and three hundred gentlemen in attendance. Jefferson, who dined regularly at Mann's, was likely among those in attendance, along with other congressmen, "The number of cheerful voices, with the clangor of knives and forks made a din of a very extraordinary in nature and most delightful influence," wrote Tilton Thirteen toasts were given in honor of the occasion, and Washington made a pointed political statement when he gave a toast in response, "Competent powers to congress for general purposes." After dinner, the governor of Maryland, William Paca, hosted a ball in Washington's honor at the state house. Tilton, who had been a doctor in the Continental Army during the war and was a great admirer of Washington, confessed that his "villainous awkwardness" prevented him from dancing, but he noted that Washington, who enjoyed dancing, and the company of women, had no such reservations. "The General danced every set, that all the ladies might have the pleasure of dancing with him, or as it has since been handsomely expressed, get a touch of him." Whether the recently widowed Jefferson attended the ball is unknown.[19]

On January 15, 1783, Washington wrote a letter to Bushrod Washington, the son of his brother John Augustine Washington, who was studying law in Philadelphia. Concerned about "the temptation, & vices of Cities," he sought to impart some advice to his nephew. Washington warned Bushrod to avoid gambling, to dress modestly, and to carefully choose those with whom he associated. He wrote of friendship, "Be courteous to all, but intimate with few, and let those few be well tried before you give them your confidence—true friendship is a plant of slow growth, and must undergo & withstand the shocks of adversity before it is entitled to the appellation." Washington likely had Jacky Custis's unfortunate experiences as a student in mind when he wrote to Bushrod, but his analysis of friendship described the evolution of his relationship with Jefferson.[20]

The friendship between Washington and Jefferson had been a plant of slow growth, born of the adversity of revolution and war, by 1783. The meeting between Washington and Jefferson at Annapolis punctuated a new, more intimate phase in the relationship between the two men. They had established a rapport during the war that blossomed into genuine friendship after the war's end. Indeed, the period from Washington's first retirement at the end of 1783 until Jefferson left Washington's cabinet at the end of 1793 was probably the happiest and most harmonious period the two men enjoyed during the three decades they knew each other. Their interests aligned on several issues, and they came to rely on each other for advice. They still did not see each other that often. For most of the period in question, Jefferson served as an American diplomat in France, departing the United States in July 1784 and not returning until November 1789. The distance between them encouraged Washington and Jefferson to correspond on several matters.

Washington had come to hold Jefferson in such high esteem that he sought his advice on a military matter. As the war drew to a close, a group of officers in the Continental Army created a fraternal organization intended "to preserve inviolate those exalted rights and liberties of human nature, for which they have fought and bled" and "to promote and cherish, between the respective states, that union of national honor so essentially necessary to their happiness, and to the future dignity of the American empire," as well as "to render permanent the cordial affection subsisting among the officers." The organization, the Society of Cincinnati, named in honor of Cincinnatus, the Roman consul who assumed power during a crisis but relinquished it after the crisis passed and retired to his farm, was formally created in May 1783 when its founding members adopted a constitution drafted by Henry Knox, one of Washington's most loyal and effective lieutenants. On its face the society, which elected

Washington—who was often likened to Cincinnatus—to serve as its president, was a patriotic fraternal organization for army veterans who had served for at least three years during the war. It was organized into thirteen separate state chapters (eventually a French chapter was created for allied officers) that would meet annually on July 4. Membership in the society was hereditary, passing to firstborn sons according to the principle of primogeniture. Because the society was hereditary and elitist—it was only open to former officers; enlisted men and those who served in the state militias were excluded—opponents criticized it as an attempt to create an aristocracy in the new American republic.[21]

Washington had not been directly involved in the creation of the society, although he was extremely loyal to the officers who had served with him during the war and was especially fond of Knox, his former chief of artillery. As the society prepared for its first general meeting in Philadelphia in May 1784, Washington, sensitive to the criticism it was receiving, wrote to Jefferson, still serving in Congress at Annapolis, seeking his advice. "It is with frankness, and the fullest latitude of a friend," wrote Washington, "you will give me your opinion of the Institution of the Society of Cincinnati, it would confer an acceptable favor upon me." Washington enclosed all the papers he had on the society so that Jefferson might "form a judgment." He asked Jefferson to retain the papers until he passed through Annapolis en route to the society's general meeting two weeks later. Washington did not want to wait to hear Jefferson's opinion until they met, however. He wrote, "The sooner I could receive your Sentiments on this subject the more pleasing they would be to me."[22]

Why did Washington solicit advice about the society from Jefferson, who had no military experience? "You may be assured Sir," he explained, "that to the good opinion alone, which I entertain of your abilities and candor, this liberty is to be attributed." Washington sought Jefferson's counsel *because* he was not part of his military family. The younger man was someone whose judgment Washington had come to respect. He turned to Jefferson as a friend who might provide him with independent advice on a matter that was troubling him. Given that he was beginning to have his own doubts about the society, Washington may have contacted Jefferson expecting him to reinforce the public criticism it was receiving. What is remarkable is that Washington sought Jefferson's views on a sensitive matter and trusted him with confidential papers. Washington's request speaks to the enhanced esteem in which he held his younger counterpart.

If Washington expected that Jefferson would criticize the Society of Cincinnati, he was not disappointed. On April 16 Jefferson wrote a lengthy reply to Washington's letter. Perceptively, he appealed to Washington's concern for his reputation, warning him to avoid the society, "I have wished to see you stand on ground separated from it; and that the character which will be handed to future ages at the head of our revolution may in no instance be compromitted in subordinate altercations." Jefferson acknowledged the society's origins, arising from the desire of men who had served together in the face of hardship and danger to continue to associate and perpetuate their friendships after the army disbanded, might be innocent, but he feared the long-term social and political consequences of a hereditary society based on military service. He, like other critics of the society, feared that it might form the basis of a new aristocracy that would undermine America's republican experiment. Jefferson wrote, "Experience has shewn that the hereditary branches of modern governments are the patrons of privilege and prerogative, and not of the natural rights of the people, whose oppressors they generally are." Jefferson paid tribute to Washington's unique place in the United States. "[T]he moderation and virtue of a single character has probably prevented this revolution from being closed as most others have been by a subversion of that liberty it was intended to establish," he wrote. Jefferson was not concerned that Washington would use his position as the president of the Cincinnati to subvert the republic, but "he is not immortal, and his successor or some one of his successors at the head of this institution may adopt a more mistaken road to glory." Jefferson then outlined the objections of his fellow members of Congress to the society. He concluded by recommending that if the society went ahead, it should abolish inherited membership. Two years later Jefferson, writing from France, was more forthright in describing the threat posed by the society, "A single fiber left of this institution, will produce an hereditary aristocracy which will change the form of our governments from the best to worst in the world."[23]

Washington stopped at Annapolis en route to the first meeting of the society in Philadelphia to speak with Jefferson in May 1784. The two men continued the discussion about the society they had begun in their correspondence. Jefferson's influence on Washington was apparent when the former general arrived in Philadelphia for the inaugural meeting of the society. In a series of speeches at the meeting, Washington called for the abolition of the society. Failing that, he advocated for wholesale reform of its constitution. Among the changes he recommended the following:

> Strike out every word, sentence, and clause which has a political tendency.

> Discontinue the hereditary part in all its connexions, *absolutely*.

Washington sought to allay the concerns of critics, like Jefferson, that the society would be a quasi-aristocratic institution exercising a baneful political influence on the new republic. The members of the society could hardly oppose its president, and after prolonged debate, they agreed to the changes, subject to the approval of the society's member branches.[24]

The debate over the Society of Cincinnati revealed the deepening friendship between Washington and Jefferson in the immediate aftermath of the War of Independence. During the early years of their relationship, Washington, older and more famous and powerful than Jefferson, was very much the senior of the two. They did not encounter each other, nor did they interact, as equals. Prior to the war, they had relatively little interaction with each other apart from both supporting the growing resistance to British rule in Virginia. They collaborated during the later years of the War of Independence, but Washington took the lead, advising Jefferson on the defense of Virginia and Virginia's role in the wider war effort and gradually bringing him round on the question of how to treat Henry Hamilton. Jefferson had won Washington's respect, and the older man came to value the younger man's counsel. Aware of the criticism of the Society of Cincinnati, Washington sought Jefferson's advice on the matter, rather than that of his former officers, undoubtedly because he knew Jefferson was skeptical about the society. Prior to seeking Jefferson's views, Washington extended a warm invitation to Jefferson to visit him at Mount Vernon. "It is unnecessary," he closed a letter on March 3, 1783, "I hope, to repeat to you the assurances of the pleasure I should feel at seeing you at this retreat, or of the sincere esteem & regard with which I am Dear sir Yr. Most Obedt. & very Hble Servt." For a man so notably reserved as Washington, this was an effusive display of affection.[25]

Jefferson was thrilled to receive an invitation to Mount Vernon. He replied, "I shall certainly pay my respects there to Mrs. Washington and yourself with great pleasure whenever it shall be in my power."²⁶ Indeed, he was not able to visit the Washingtons at their home until September 1790 (after his return from France). Nonetheless, he reciprocated Washington's affection and respect during the 1780s. When he was governor of Virginia, he began to draft a lengthy response to a questionnaire from the French legation in Philadelphia seeking information about the various states that comprised the United States. Jefferson extensively revised his remarks over several years, and the resulting text, which he published privately in Paris in 1785 as *The Notes on the State of Virginia,* was, among other things, a passionate defense of the new republic. Jefferson intended the text to be a refutation of the claims of French intellectuals that European species degenerated in the western hemisphere. In defending the United States, Jefferson held up Washington as an example of American genius:

> In war we have produced a Washington, whose memory will be adored while liberty shall have votaries, whose name will triumph over time, and will in future ages assume its just station among the most celebrated worthies of the world, when that wretched philosophy shall be forgotten which would have arranged him among the degeneracies of nature.²⁷

Although Jefferson left the United States for France in July 1784 and would not return to the country for more than five years, distance was not an obstacle in the growing friendship between him and Washington. The two men exchanged twenty-two letters during Jefferson's absence.²⁸

In his first letter to Washington after his arrival in Paris, Jefferson mentioned that the government of Virginia had commissioned a statue of Washington "as a mark of their gratitude to you," to be displayed in the Virginia state house. The governor of Virginia, Benjamin Harrison, charged Jefferson and Benjamin Franklin with making the arrangements to produce the statue. The men discussed the options and decided that Jean-Antoine Houdon whom Jefferson described to Washington as possessing "the reputation of being the first statuary in the world," should sculpt Washington. Jefferson met with the sculptor, who insisted that he must travel to Virginia and meet Washington so that he could make a life mask of his face in order to complete his statue. All told, Houdon estimated that he would need three weeks to make the mask and a further three years after his return to France to complete the statue—which would feature a standing image of Washington. Houdon was so eager to sculpt Washington, which he described to Jefferson as "promising the brightest chapter of his history," that he postponed a commitment to sculpt Catherine the Great and agreed to accept a reduced fee of 25,000 livres.[29]

At around eleven on the evening of October 2, 1785, George and Martha Washington were roused from their bed at Mount Vernon by the arrival of Houdon and three of his assistants, who had arrived from France. Houdon spent more than two weeks at Mount Vernon. Washington sat for him over the course of several days and allowed Houdon to apply plaster of paris to his face in order to create a life mask. This was an arduous, unpleasant process that required the artist to apply wet plaster with a brush which then set to create an impression of the sitter's face. Houdon then created two terracotta busts of the fifty-three-year-old Washington. He presented one to Washington and took the other with him back to Paris to reproduce in marble and to use when he created his statue of Washington. By early

FIGURES 8.2, 8.3   Jean-Antoine Houdon busts of *George Washington* (1786) and *Thomas Jefferson* (1789). Jefferson arranged for Houdon, France's leading sculptor, to create a statue of Washington. Houdon arrived at Mount Vernon in October 1785 and stayed for two weeks creating a life mask and taking measurements of Washington. He returned to Paris and sculpted a bust of Washington as well as a full statue for the Virginia State Capitol in Richmond. Several years later, Houdon also sculpted a bust of Jefferson. Reproduction courtesy of Mount Vernon Ladies' Association; Reproduction © Thomas Jefferson Foundation at Monticello.

January 1786, Jefferson reported that Houdon had safely returned to Paris with the mold of Washington's face. They discussed how Washington should be dressed in Houdon's statue. Washington, Jefferson, and Houdon all agreed that Washington should appear in contemporary rather than classical dress. As Jefferson wrote, "I think a modern in antique dress as just an object of ridicule as an Hercules or Marius with a periwig and chapeau bras."[30] That Jefferson arranged for Europe's foremost sculptor to capture Washington's image for posterity is testimony to the esteem in which he held the older man. Jefferson, himself, sat for Houdon in 1789 (Figure 8.3), and before he left France, he obtained a copy of the Washington bust (Figure 8.2) as well as some other of Houdon's most notable busts, including Franklin, John Paul Jones, Lafayette, Voltaire, and Turgot, for display at Monticello.[31]

––––––

After the war Washington and Jefferson became political confidants. According to Jefferson when he met Washington in November 1783, "Among other political conversations he entered earnestly into one respecting the Western cession of Virginia, and the late vote of Congress accepting it." In January 1781 (when Jefferson was governor), the Virginia legislature agreed to cede its claims to land northwest of the Ohio River to the United States, subject to negotiations with Congress. On September 13, 1783, Congress passed an act authorizing the transfer of the land to the United States, subject to certain conditions—the most controversial among these was a repudiation of the claims of several land companies. According to Jefferson, "[Washington] thinks the conditions annexed by Virginia [protecting the land companies' claims] and not acceded to by Congress altogether unimportant, at least much less important than the consequences which would result from the state's adhering to these conditions. He thinks that a friendly and immediate settling of the matter can alone give us that political happiness and quiet which we must all wish for: and that besides other disagreeable consequences the land will be lost to both as a source of revenue by the settlement of adventurers on it who will not pay anything." In December 1783 the Virginia House of Delegates agreed to Congress's terms and formally voted to cede the territory to the United States.[32]

That first postwar conversation focused on what was probably the most important theme of the Washington-Jefferson relationship during the 1780s—western territory and its place in the new republic. Both Washington and Jefferson had an abiding interest in the development of the trans-Appalachian west, believing it to be essential to the future of Virginia and the United States. During the mid-1780s they corresponded at length about how the West should best be developed and exploited. On this issue, perhaps more than any other, they agreed.

Washington had a long-standing interest in acquiring Native land in the West. He had begun his career as a surveyor and then became a soldier who sought to consolidate and advance Virginia's, Britain's, and, later, the United States' claims to western territory. He had a strong personal interest in western lands, which he assiduously sought to amass. He acquired land through a variety of means—in the form of bounties for military service during the Seven Years' War; he also speculated in western land, purchasing tens of thousands of acres. In 1772 Lord Dunmore approved his patents for more than 20,000 acres along the Great Kanawha and Ohio Rivers in modern West Virginia. After the war Washington continued to purchase western lands. By the time he died in 1799, he owned more than 52,000 acres of land in the West as well as a further 8,000 acres around Mount Vernon. For Washington, western land was essential to the future of the United States as well as to his own fortune.[33]

Thomas Jefferson had less of a personal stake in western land than Washington. He did not engage in widespread land speculation. Perhaps befitting the son of a man who mapped the western reaches of Virginia, Jefferson had a lifelong belief in western land as the source of future wealth, prosperity, social harmony, and political stability for Virginia and the United States. In the *Notes on the State of Virginia*, he idealized yeoman farmers, small landholders, as the ideal citizens in a republic. Thanks to their independence and virtue (if properly educated), they could sustain republican government. He wrote, "Those who labour in the earth are the chosen people of God, if ever he had a chosen people, whose breasts he has made his peculiar deposit for substantial and genuine virtue. It is the focus in which he keeps alive that sacred fire, which otherwise might escape from the face of the earth. Corruption of morals in the mass of cultivators is a phaenomenon of which no age not nation has furnished an example."[34] According to Jefferson, if the United States was to be a successful republic, then most of its citizens should be small farmers. During his brief service in Congress before his departure for France, Jefferson was the prime mover behind a series of land ordinances that culminated in the Northwest Ordinance of 1787. These established a system whereby new territories might join the United States as states, provided they met constitutional and population requirements. In so doing Jefferson laid the foundation for the geographic expansion of the United States.[35]

Land had little value to either Washington or Jefferson if its potential— economic, political, and social—could not be exploited. This was the major theme of their discussions about western land during the 1780s. In March 1784 Jefferson wrote a lengthy letter to Washington, mainly concerned with the West. "All the world is becoming commercial," he wrote from Annapolis. "Was it practicable to keep our new empire separated from them we might indulge ourselves in speculating whether commerce contributes to the happiness of mankind. But we cannot separate ourselves from them. Our citizens have had too full a taste of the comforts furnished by the arts and manufactures to be debarred the use of them. We must then in our own defence endeavor to share as large a portion as we can of this modern source of wealth and power." Rivers were essential to unlocking the commercial wealth of the West, which Americans demanded. As far as Jefferson was concerned, the wealth of the West would be shipped by one of three rivers: the Mississippi, the Hudson, or the Potomac. Although the Ohio River was the most important river in the trans-Appalachian west, it flowed from east to west into the Mississippi. Jefferson felt that the heavy goods—such as lumber and flour—produced in the West would be shipped down the Ohio and Mississippi to the Gulf of Mexico but that it would be "difficult and tedious" to ship manufactured goods up the Mississippi. "There will therefore be a rivalship," he continued, "between the Hudson and Patowmac for the residue of the commerce of all the country Westward of L. Erie, on the waters of the lakes, of the Ohio and upper parts of the Missisipi." Although Washington and Jefferson would come to have different views about the relationship between the federal government and the states, they were in complete agreement that the Potomac (which flowed past Mount Vernon), and thus Virginia, should become the gateway to the West. This would require the building of canals to connect the headwaters of the Potomac with those of the Ohio, and both Washington and Jefferson became keen supporters of a series of projects to do just that.[36]

Washington replied to Jefferson's letter immediately. "My opinion coincides perfectly with yours respecting the practicability of an easy and short communication between the waters of the Ohio and Potomack, of the advantages of that communication and the preference it has over <u>all</u> others." Because of his vast land holdings in the West, Washington stood to profit from any improvements that would link the Potomac and the Ohio. He conceded and contrasted his personal interest in the project with Jefferson's, "I am not so disinterested in this matter as you are; but I am made very happy to find a man of discernment and liberality (who has no particular interest in the plan) thinks as I do, who have Lands in that Country the value of which would be enhanced by the adoption of such a scheme."[37]

Washington had a better understanding about what life was like in the trans-Appalachian west than Jefferson did. He traveled extensively there as a young man as a surveyor, diplomat, and soldier. Having returned to Mount Vernon by Christmas 1783, he spent nine months trying to restore his home and plantation after his eight-year absence. In September 1784 Washington, then fifty-two years old, set out on a journey accompanied by several enslaved men; his nephew Bushrod; and his friend and personal physician, James Craik (and Craik's son, also named James) to explore his landholdings in western Virginia and Pennsylvania as well as his bounty lands on the Ohio and Kanawha Rivers. Washington intended to attend to his business interests in the region, which he had neglected during the war, as well as to explore the feasibility of establishing a water route between the Potomac and the Ohio. The party spent more than a month traveling in the West (the last time Washington would travel in the region). Washington sought to collect rent from tenants on his land who had fallen into arrears. In mid-September Washington encountered settlers who were squatting on one of his tracts of land on Miller's Run in Washington County, Pennsylvania. The state had named the county in Washington's honor in 1781. The settlers along Miller's Run were less willing to honor the retired general. They contested his title to the land on which they lived. Washington met with the settlers and told them they could purchase their land at twenty-five shillings per acre paid over three annual installments (with interest), or they could become his tenants at an annual rent of £10 per year. When the settlers asked Washington if he would extend them credit to buy their land without interest over a longer time frame, he refused. Washington, unlike Jefferson, did not idealize small farmers in the West, and he always drove a hard bargain as a businessman. The settlers refused, and the two parties went to court to settle their differences. Notwithstanding these difficulties, at the conclusion of the trip Washington declared, "I am well pleased with my journey," and he wrote a lengthy analysis concerning the political and commercial potential of the West and making the case—using the arguments that he and Jefferson had rehearsed—in favor of making the improvements necessary to connect the Potomac and the Ohio watersheds.[38]

When Washington returned from the West, he began his return to public life, putting himself at the head of the movement to create a company to link the Potomac and the Ohio.[39] Such a project would require the cooperation of the governments of Virginia, Maryland, and Pennsylvania, which Washington recognized would be a challenge. He continued to consult with Jefferson, who had gone to Paris, on the matter. Indeed, just as he consulted Jefferson about the Society of Cincinnati, he also sought his advice on a delicate matter relating to the Potomac project. In February 1785 Washington wrote to Jefferson about it. He gave him the good news that the legislatures in both Virginia and Maryland had chartered the Potomac Company, with Washington as its president, which would undertake to create roads, canals, and locks; clear rivers; and make other improvements to link the Potomac and the Ohio river systems. Washington acknowledged that considerable financial and political challenges lay ahead. He informed Jefferson that the Virginia assembly had purchased fifty shares in the company for Washington, which would be vested in him and his heirs forever in gratitude for this service to the nation. "It has ever been my wish, and it is yet my intention," he wrote, "never to receive any thing from the United States, or any individual State for any Services I have hitherto rendered, . . . as it is not my design to accept of any appointment from the public, which might make emoluments necessary." He then explained his dilemma, "how to decline this act of generosity without incurring the imputation of disrespect to my Country, and a slight of her favors on the one hand, or that of pride, and an ostentatious display of disinterestedness on the other, is the difficulty." He feared that rejecting the offer might insult the legislature and make it appear that he was attempting to make a grand gesture of selflessness that, itself, might be seen as an act of vanity.[40]

Jefferson assured Washington that accepting the shares would not negatively affect his reputation, "But I must own that the declining them will add to that reputation, as it will shew that your motives have been pure and without any alloy. . . . I must therefore repeat that I think the receiving them will not in the least lessen the respect of the world if from any circumstances they would be convenient to you." Eventually, Washington decided to put the shares in a trust to establish charity schools, "for the Education and support of poor Children: especially the descendants of those who have fallen in defence of their Country." In the mid-1780s, as he struggled to make Mount Vernon profitable after years of relative neglect, Washington needed money and he could be ruthless about getting it, as his dealing with the tenants and squatters on his land suggests. He was more concerned about his reputation than his finances and had an unerring instinct for protecting it. The man who eschewed payment for his wartime service was not going to barter his reputation for canal stock. That Jefferson was among those Washington consulted about the stock is revealing. As Washington wrote, "As I have accustomed myself to communicate matters of difficulty to you, and have met forgiveness for it, I will take the liberty, my good Sir, of troubling you with the rehearsal of one more, which has lately occurred to me." Just as in 1783 when he sought Jefferson's advice about the Society of Cincinnati, Washington sought Jefferson's counsel about a delicate matter pertaining to his reputation.[41]

In the end little came of the Potomac Company's efforts. It did succeed in building some locks and improving aspects of the Potomac watershed, but it did not benefit Virginia in the ways that Jefferson and Washington had hoped. Alexandria did not supplant New York as the great East Coast entrepôt for western trade as they had prophesied. Ultimately, the most important consequence of the effort would be political. The Potomac scheme required Virginia, Maryland, and Pennsylvania to work together. The effort to achieve this was a mixed success and helped convince Washington to call for a meeting of political leaders from the states, which was the catalyst for a larger movement for constitutional reform in the new republic.

The friendship between Washington and Jefferson continued to blossom during Jefferson's absence in France. They continued to correspond about a variety of matters—including their ongoing common interest in the West. Their schemes for westward settlement were premised on the acquisition of land. Both men were aware that that land was occupied by Indigenous peoples, whom they believed would have to be removed to allow the American republic to flourish.

— 9 —

The Same World Will Scarcely Do for Them and Us

> He has endeavoured to bring on the inhabitants of our frontiers the merciless Indian savages whose known rule of warfare is an undistinguished destruction of all ages, sexes & conditions.
>
> —Thomas Jefferson, Declaration of Independence

In the middle of 1776, around the time that Congress was debating Jefferson's draft Declaration of Independence and Washington was preparing the Continental Army to defend New York City, Native delegates from the Mohawk, Ottawa, Shawnee, Nanticoke, and Delaware Nations visited the Cherokee capital at Chota in eastern Tennessee. The Indigenous diplomats sought to persuade the Cherokees to join a coalition in defense of Native lands. At the meeting an unnamed Shawnee diplomat spoke. According to a British official who witnessed the scene:

> He began with pathetically enumerating the distresses of his own and other Nations. He complained particularly of *the Virginians* who after having taken away all their Lands and cruelly and treacherously treated some of their people, had unjustly brought war upon their Nation and destroyed many of their people; that in a very few years their Nation from being a great people were now reduced to a handful; . . . that the red people who were once Masters of the whole Country hardly possessed ground enough to stand on . . .

The Shawnee spokesman provided a passionate summary of the history of European encroachment on his nation's lands in Pennsylvania, Ohio, Kentucky, and elsewhere during the seventeenth and eighteenth centuries. His choice of language is revealing. For many Indigenous people, especially in the Ohio River valley, "Virginian" was a shorthand to describe all land-hungry European settlers.[1] As we have seen, George Washington and Thomas Jefferson were very much Virginians in their origins and outlook. They were also Virginians in the sense that the Shawnee spokesman used the term. When it came to the place of Native Americans, they held remarkably similar views. They were united in the opinion that the future of the American republic lay in the West, "our new empire," as Jefferson described it to Washington, and that it would have little room for Native peoples.

Virginia, of course, was Native land before it was Virginia. In the early seventeenth century, English settlers were vastly outnumbered by the Indigenous members of the Powhatan Confederacy, which had around 14,000 inhabitants living in approximately 150 villages along Virginia's coastal plain. The very earliest English settlers depended on Natives for food to survive. Only when the settlers began cultivating tobacco (a plant of Indigenous origin) did their colony become viable. Tobacco exhausted the soil, and the settlers, their population growing, demanded more and more Native land. Over the course of the seventeenth century, as English (and African) numbers grew owing to natural increase and migration (both voluntary and forced), the settlers came into increasing conflict with Indigenous people. Settlers acquired Native lands through violence and (often coerced) negotiation. By 1700 around 1,450 Native Americans lived in Virginia east of the Blue Ridge Mountains, approximately 10 percent of their numbers a century before. When George Washington was born in 1732, these numbers had dwindled still further to around 1,000. They were vastly outnumbered by more than 100,000 white settlers and almost 50,000 enslaved Africans. While the population of Virginia at the time of Washington's birth (and Jefferson's eleven years later) was predominantly European (and African), the historian Colin Calloway reminds us that "it existed on the outskirts of a vast Indian continent." Most of the population of North America was Indigenous. Nonetheless, the small world of the Virginia elite that shaped both men was one in which it appeared that Indigenous people were vanishing. Both men erroneously believed that

Indigenous Americans were on their way to extinction and that their dwindling numbers must give way to guarantee the success of the American republic. During the War of Independence and while serving as president, each took steps to hasten that outcome. They were fully committed to expansion of the United States and the expropriation of Indigenous lands.[2]

————

Both Jefferson and Washington were familiar with Native Americans from a young age. Washington, as we have seen, made his start in life as a surveyor of Native lands in Virginia and beyond. In the spring of 1748, aged sixteen, he joined a party with his neighbor, George William Fairfax, charged with surveying Fairfax lands in the Shenandoah Valley. It was his first foray to the West, beyond the mountains. The Fairfax surveying party encountered a group of more than thirty Natives at the mouth of the south branch of the Potomac (the area that Washington and Jefferson would later seek to connect to the Ohio River system) in western Maryland. According to Washington they were a war party bearing a scalp. They may have been warriors from one of the Six Nations of the Iroquois (or Haudenosaunee) Confederacy who traveled through the Shenandoah Valley to attack the Catawba to the south. According to Washington, his party shared some of their liquor with the warriors, "it elevating there Spirits it put them in the Humour of Dauncing of whom we had a War Daunce." The teenager soon lost interest in the Natives, who camped with his party for a couple of days. He wrote two days after their arrival, "Nothing remarkable on Thursday but only being with the Indians all day so shall slip it."[3]

While Washington had relatively little interest in the lives or cultures of the people who inhabited the West, he was very interested in their land. Before becoming a soldier, he spent several years as a surveyor, returning repeatedly to the lands that Virginia claimed beyond the Blue Ridge Mountains. Although he earned an income from his efforts, the real benefit of surveying for Washington was the access it gave him to western—that is, Native—land. He made his first western land purchase in 1750, acquiring 2,315 acres in the Shenandoah Valley. By the time he died in 1799, Washington had acquired more than 52,000 acres of western land in the states of New York, Pennsylvania, Maryland, Virginia, and Kentucky as well as in the Ohio Territory. Almost all was territory inhabited and claimed by

Native people when he undertook his first surveying expedition in 1748. George Washington had a considerable personal stake in displacing Native Americans.[4]

Washington only spent a few years working as a surveyor before he pursued his next calling as a soldier. The two roles were closely related, as Virginia's (and Britain's) claims to western lands frequently brought it into conflict with Indigenous peoples (or the French, who also sought to lay claim to the same land). We have seen how Washington's naivety and inexperience with Native diplomacy contributed to the events that led to the outbreak of the Seven Years' War. On his first trip as a soldier to the Ohio country in 1753, when he was charged with warning the French to vacate the region, he encountered Tanaghrisson, a Seneca leader who was a key diplomatic and military power broker. Washington later claimed that during his negotiations with the Seneca, Tanaghrisson dubbed him "Conotocaurious," which translated as "Town Taker" or "Town Destroyer." This was a name that the Susquehannock had given to Washington's great-grandfather, John Washington. As a militia officer during the 1670s, John Washington earned the sobriquet when he participated in the murder of five Susquehannock chiefs while besieging their village in Maryland. In the younger Washington's telling, the memory of the killings was powerful enough that the name persisted among Native Americans, and Tanaghrisson bestowed it on him eight decades later. It seems highly unlikely, the historian Colin Calloway argues, that Tanaghrisson, a Seneca, would have known about a nickname bestowed by the Susquehannock decades earlier, or made the connection between John Washington and the inexperienced young soldier before him. More likely, Washington embraced his forebear's Indigenous name in a bid to give himself a bit of gravitas and enhance his reputation. He seems to have taken pride in the name. He used it in his negotiations with Tanaghrisson the next year (during the expedition that led to the killing of Jumonville and the skirmish at Fort Necessity) and in a 1755 letter to Andrew Montour, an Oneida who acted as an intermediary between Virginians and Native Americans in Ohio. As we shall see, Washington did much to earn the name of his own accord during the War of Independence.[5]

Washington's early experiences as a surveyor and soldier with Native Americans gave him valuable firsthand experience of the "vast Indian continent" that lay beyond Virginia. He acquired a taste for Indigenous land

and experience with Indigenous diplomacy and warfare. He does not seem to have developed much of an interest in or affinity for Native culture. His Indigenous encounters during his youth and early adulthood would serve him well throughout the remainder of his public career. Diplomacy, trade, and conflicts with Native Americans were constants throughout his life, especially as a military leader during the War of Independence and as president of the United States.

Thomas Jefferson's first encounters with Indigenous people were a step removed from George Washington's. Where Washington began his life as a surveyor, Thomas Jefferson's father was a surveyor. Peter Jefferson helped to create one of the most famous and important maps of eighteenth-century Virginia and surveyed and parceled the land in Virginia and beyond, facilitating the displacement of Native peoples and their replacement by white settlers (and enslaved Africans). Under the terms of the 1722 Treaty of Albany, the Haudenosaunee sold Virginia much of the territory to the east of the Shenandoah Valley, including the foothills of the Blue Ridge Mountains, which Virginians dubbed the Piedmont. According to the terms of the treaty, the Iroquois retained the right to traverse the valley as a north-south corridor, which is likely how Washington came to encounter the war party in 1748. This purchase opened the Piedmont to white settlement. Among the earliest European settlers in the region was Peter Jefferson, who acquired 1,000 acres of land, expropriated from the Monacan people, along the Rivanna River in 1735 and established a plantation called Shadwell where his son Thomas was born on April 13, 1743.[6]

When Peter Jefferson established his home at Shadwell, it was a frontier community.[7] In the middle of the eighteenth century, the Piedmont was a cultural and geographic crossroads. Although Washington seems to have had more direct contact with Native Americans as a young man than Jefferson, he had little interest in their cultures. Jefferson, by contrast, developed a lifelong fascination with Indigenous Americans. During his retirement Thomas Jefferson wrote of Native Americans as "a people with whom, in the very early part of my life, I was very familiar, and acquired impressions of attachments & commiseration for them which have never been obliterated." Throughout his life he sought to acquire Indigenous artifacts, some of which he displayed in the Entrance Hall at Monticello, as well as information on Native languages and culture (Figure 9.1). Indeed,

FIGURE 9.1   The Entrance Hall at Monticello. Jefferson, incorrectly believing that the Native peoples of North America were dying out, displayed Indigenous artifacts in Monticello's Entrance Hall. Jefferson intended the Entrance Hall to serve as a museum for visitors. © Thomas Jefferson Foundation at Monticello.

he recalled his early interest in Native Americans in a lengthy letter to John Adams on Native culture and religion.[8]

During Jefferson's youth, traveling Native diplomatic parties often stopped and spent a day or two visiting with Peter Jefferson en route to the colonial capital at Williamsburg. Thomas Jefferson spent time with these Native parties both at Shadwell and, when he was a student, in Williamsburg. One of the most notable of these delegations was a large group of Cherokees led by Ostenaco (also known as Outassetè), who journeyed to Williamsburg in April 1761 as part of the negotiations at the close of the Anglo-Cherokee War (1758–1761), which had devastated the Cherokee population. Ostenaco (Figure 9.2) was received by the governor and his council and was given a banquet at William & Mary, where Jefferson was a student. He was at the beginning of a journey that would take him to London and an audience with George III. Jefferson witnessed Ostenaco's farewell address to his entourage before his departure for England. Fifty years later he described the scene to Adams: "I knew much the great Outassetè, the

FIGURE 9.2   Joshua Reynolds, *Ostenaco* (1762). Ostenaco (c. 1710–1780) was a Cherokee leader.
During the Seven Years' War, Ostenaco led Cherokee warriors who fought alongside troops from
Virginia. In 1762, he and two other Cherokee leaders traveled to London. En route, they stopped in
Williamsburg, where Thomas Jefferson was a student. Jefferson heard Ostenaco's farewell oration
and was impressed by his rhetorical skills (even though Jefferson did not understand Cherokee).
Joshua Reynolds, Britain's leading portraitist, painted Ostenaco while he was in London. Gilcrease
Museum, Tulsa, Oklahoma.

warrior and orator of the Cherokees. he was always the guest of my father,
on his journies to & from Williamsburg. I was in his camp when he made his
great farewell oration to his people, the evening before his departure for
England. the moon was in full splendor, and to her he seemed to address
himself in his prayers for his own safety on the voyage, and that of his people
during his absence. his sounding voice, distinct articulation, animated action, and the solemn silence of his people at their several fires, filled me with
awe & veneration, altho' I did not understand a word he uttered."[9]

Two decades after he witnessed Ostenaco's oration, he asserted in the
Notes on the State of Virginia, "The principles of their [Indians'] society

forbidding all compulsion they are led to duty and to enterprise by personal influence and persuasion. Hence eloquence in council, bravery and address in war, become the foundations of all consequences with them. To these acquirements all their faculties are directed." He offered as an example of Indigenous oratory, which he claimed was equivalent to that of Demosthenes and Cicero, a statement by the Shawnee Tachnechdorus, known to white people as John Logan. Logan had been allied to British-American settlers during the Seven Years' War. Despite this, members of his extended family were murdered by Virginia militia during the Dunmore's War—the bid by Virginians to conquer Ohio in 1774. The killings prompted Logan to take up arms against his former allies. At the end of that conflict, Logan justified his actions in a speech that Jefferson reproduced in *Notes on the State of Virginia*.[10]

Logan's Lament, as the speech was remembered (and memorized) by generations of European Americans during the nineteenth century, can be read as evidence of Jefferson's respect for Native Americans and sympathy for their plight when confronted by an aggressive, expansionist American republic. Jefferson subscribed to a view of history, derived from his reading of the historians prominent during the Scottish Enlightenment, that societies and civilizations went through different stages of civilization. He interpreted Indigenous culture through this "stadial theory" and concluded that Native Americans were at a stage of development akin to that of Europeans north of the Alps prior to the arrival of the Romans. While not inherently inferior to European Americans during the eighteenth century, Native Americans were not at the same stage of development as the settlers who displaced them. As he wrote in the *Notes*, "To form a just estimate of their genius and mental powers, more facts are wanting, and great allowance made for those circumstances of their situation which call for a display of particular talents only. This done, we shall probably find that they are formed in mind as well as in body, on the same module with the Homo sapiens Europæus." In other words, given enough time and a change of environment, Native peoples could achieve the same level of civilization as Americans descended from Europeans (by contrast, Jefferson held that Africans were inferior to Europeans). Nearly forty years later, Jefferson told an English visitor to Monticello that he considered Native Americans "quite on a level, as respects intellectual character, with the Whites." Native physical bravery was beyond question, by including Logan's Lament in the *Notes,* Jefferson sought to demonstrate that Indigenous people were equal to white people "in mind as well as in body."[11]

There is more to Jefferson's inclusion of Logan's Lament (as well as his subsequent efforts to collect and display Indigenous artifacts and to preserve Native languages) than sympathy for Native Americans. Logan's words are an elegy not just for his family but for Native peoples generally. For Jefferson, Logan has no one to grieve for him—not his own relatives, but, by implication, no members of his nation or Native people generally. Jefferson presents this as a lamentable, but inevitable, consequence of white settlement in North America. Despite his subsequent efforts to promote Native assimilation, there would not be enough time for Native peoples to achieve civilization on a par with European Americans. They would die out before they could enjoy the benefits of advanced civilization.

There are two problems with Jefferson's elegiac portrayal of Native Americans. First, it was not true. Natives were *not* on the verge of extinction in 1774 when Logan delivered his oration, nor in the early 1780s when Jefferson included it in the *Notes on Virginia,* nor in 1812 when he wrote to Adams about Ostenaco. Indeed, despite the best efforts of the United States, including the administrations of George Washington and Thomas Jefferson, the Indigenous population of the United States, east of the Mississippi River, actually increased between the 1780s and 1830s.[12] Second, in presenting the eventual extinction of Native peoples as inevitable, Jefferson denied the agency and responsibility of white people, particularly the political and military leaders of the early republic, like himself and Washington, for Indigenous displacement. As historian Andrew Cayton observed, "The chief architect of an imperial policy that involved the cultural as well as the territorial dispossession of Native Americans, Thomas Jefferson taught his fellow citizens to think of their conquest of North America as a natural process whose outcome affirmed their superiority by confirming the unworthiness of the people they displaced."[13] The process of Native displacement was not inevitable. Rather, it was the result of deliberate choices, actions, and policies of soldiers, politicians, and settlers during and after the American Revolution. As prominent leaders of the revolutionary movement, both Washington and Jefferson played key roles in the process.

The War of Independence was at least two conflicts: an anticolonial war of national liberation between the American rebels and their allies against the British and their allies; and an imperial struggle between white people and Native Americans for control over Native lands. The former conflict was fought predominantly east of the Appalachian Mountains, and the Native war was mainly (though not completely) fought in the West. Naturally, there was some overlap between these two concurrent conflicts—Indigenous people often allied with the British against their common foes. They received arms and supplies for doing so but also incurred the wrath of Patriot forces. Patriots adeptly exploited Indigenous alliances with the British to attract support for their cause and to justify the conquest and displacement of Native peoples.[14] In his draft of the Declaration of Independence, Jefferson included a clause concerning Indigenous people to his long list of crimes allegedly committed by George III. "He," Jefferson wrote, "has endeavored to bring on the inhabitants of our frontiers the merciless Indian savages, whose known rule of warfare is an undistinguished destruction of all ages, sexes & conditions."[15] In this political statement, intended to engender popular support, Jefferson expressed none of his supposed lifelong "commiseration" for Native people who were reduced to merciless savages in the foundational document of the new republic. That war against Native Americans was not just rhetorical.

When the War of Independence began, Native Americans had to choose between supporting the rebels, the British, or attempting to maintain their neutrality. Most sought to remain neutral in the conflict or, eventually, sided with the British, recognizing the threat posed to their autonomy by a possible rebel victory. The rhetoric in the Declaration of Independence made clear that there would be little place for Indigenous people in the newly independent American republic should the rebels prevail. Although most Native peoples would have preferred to avoid the conflict altogether, many were eventually drawn into the fighting. As leaders during the war, Washington, as a military commander, and Jefferson, as a state governor, were responsible for significant campaigns directed against Native peoples.

When the War of Independence broke out, one of the most formidable Native polities was the confederacy of the Haudenosaunee—the Six Nations of the Iroquois—the Mohawk, Oneida, Onondaga, Cayuga, Tuscarora, and Seneca—who inhabited a region stretching across central and western New York into the Ohio country. Historically, the Haudenosaunee had maintained a successful policy of armed neutrality for much of the eighteenth century, playing various European powers and groups of settlers off against each other while maintaining their autonomy. Confronted by rebel encroachments on their land after the Patriot victory at Saratoga in October 1777, many Haudenosaunee gave up their neutrality and fought with the British and their Loyalist allies. (The Oneida were an exception, as many in that nation had sided with the rebels early in the conflict.) In July 1778 a combined force of Haudenosaunee and British soldiers attacked Patriot forces in the Wyoming Valley in northern Pennsylvania, killing 300 people and burning numerous homes. In retaliation for what they dubbed "the Wyoming Massacre" (although few noncombatants were targeted), the rebels attacked the Haudenosaunee town of Oquaqua, burning forty houses and killing civilians, including children. In response, in November a British-Haudenosaunee force attacked a white settlement at Cherry Valley, New York, in November, killing thirty-two settlers, many of whom were women and children.[16]

In February 1779 Congress resolved that Washington should launch a campaign against the Six Nations in retaliation for the attacks on the Wyoming Valley and Cherry Valley. Washington selected Major General John Sullivan of New Hampshire to command the expedition. Sullivan was an experienced soldier who had been at the siege of Boston, participated in the invasion of Canada, and fought at Long Island, where he was captured. After three months' captivity, he rejoined the Continental Army in time to fight at the Battle of Trenton. He served in the campaign around Philadelphia in the autumn of 1777 and was blamed, in part, for the rebel defeat at the Battle of Brandywine. Sullivan arrived at headquarters and attended a council of war to plan for the expedition against the Iroquois on April 15.[17] Washington believed the campaign against the Six Nations was so important that he allocated 4,500 troops to Sullivan. (The total population of the Six Nations in 1779 was 9,000.[18])

Washington issued detailed orders to Sullivan for the campaign. He began with a clear statement of the campaign's purpose: "The expedition you are appointed to command is to be directed against the hostile tribes of the six nations of Indians, with their associates and adherents. The immediate objects are the total destruction and devastation of their settlements and the capture of as many prisoners of every age and sex as possible. It will be essential to ruin their crops now in the ground and prevent their planting more." Washington instructed how Sullivan should organize his forces and the route for his invasion of Iroquoia. He then gave Sullivan clear instructions regarding the terms under which he should negotiate with the Haudenosaunee should they sue for peace: "After you have very thoroughly completed the destruction of their settlements; if the Indians should show a disposition for peace, I would have you to encourage it, on condition that they will give some decisive evidence of their sincerity," Washington wrote. Possible evidence of Native goodwill, according to Washington, might be the surrender of the leaders involved in the attacks on Wyoming Valley and Cherry Valley or assistance in capturing the British post at Niagara. "This may be demanded as a condition of our friendship and would be a most important point gained—If they can render a service of this kind." Washington authorized Sullivan to provide the Iroquois with supplies "to assist them in their distress" and replace those destroyed by Sullivan's troops.

Washington prohibited Sullivan from entering into negotiations with the Haudenosaunee before he completed attacking their towns. "But you will not by any means listen to any overture of peace before the total ruin of their settlements is effected. . . . Our future security will be in their inability to injure us the distance to which they are driven and in the terror with which the severity of the chastisement they receive will inspire [them]. Peace without this would be fallacious and temporary." Washington instructed Sullivan to destroy Haudenosaunee towns and crops as part of a deliberate strategy to terrorize the Iroquois into submission. Only then could Sullivan negotiate with them. "When we have effectually chastised them," he continued, "we may then listen to peace and endeavour to draw further advantages from their fears." Even when the Iroquois sued for peace, they could not be trusted. Washington, who had experienced frustration negotiating with Native peoples early in his life, cautioned Sullivan against trusting the pledges made by the Haudenosaunee. "They must be explicit in their promises, give substantial pledges for their performance and execute their engagements with decision and dispatch. Hostages are the only kind of security to be depended on."[19]

Sullivan gathered his forces in June and July 1779 and entered Iroquoia in August. He defeated a combined Native and Loyalist force at the battle of Newton on August 29, which left the Haudenosaunee heartland open to the depredations of his troops. Faced with Sullivan's substantial force, the

Haudenosaunee strategy was to withdraw in order to avoid large numbers of casualties, both for combatants and noncombatants. According to a Seneca leader, Sayengeraghata, "We lost our country, it is true, but this was to secure our Women & Children."[20] Sullivan described the response of his troops when they found an abandoned Native town: "This Town of Konadahee consisted of 20 houses, very neatly built and finished, which we reduced to ashes; and the army spent near a day in destroying the corn and fruit trees, of which there was great abundance; many of the trees appeared to be of great age." Sullivan's troops repeated this behavior in the coming weeks. He boasted to Washington, "Every creek & river has been traced and the whole Country explored in search of Indian settlements, & I am persuaded except one Town situated near the allegany about 57 Miles from Chenessee [Genesee]—there is not a single Town left in the Country of the five nations." Sullivan estimated that his troops had plundered and destroyed forty towns, burning at least 160,000 bushels of corn, devastating orchards, and spoiling vegetables.[21] Washington had intended that Sullivan should terrorize noncombatants and drive the Haudenosaunee from their homes to undermine their will to fight and to put pressure on the British at Niagara. He wrote that he expected that one consequence of the campaign would be "the Indian[s,] Men—women & children, flying before him [Sullivan] to Niagara (distant more than 100 miles) in the utmost consternation—distress—& confusion."[22] By the end of September, more than 5,000 refugees had gathered at the fort, seeking succor. They faced starvation and disease during an especially harsh winter in 1779–1780. Between 1,000 and 1,500 Haudenosaunee died at the hands of Sullivan's troops or from privation because of their campaign. (By contrast, Sullivan's force lost only forty men.) A further 1,500 to 2,000 refugees did not return to their previous homes and migrated to Canada. All told, the Haudenosaunee population in central New York declined by a third, from 9,000 to 6,000, between 1775 and 1783.[23]

The destruction of the Iroquois towns and crops was not an unfortunate, unforeseen consequence of Sullivan's campaign; it was its main object, as Washington's orders had stipulated. As Washington wrote of Sullivan during the expedition, "He had advanced to & destroyed 14 Towns, large & most flourishing Crops of Corn, pulse &ca. He was proceeding in his plan of chastisement & will convince them it is to be hopd of two things—first, that their cruelties are not to pass with impunity—&

secondly that they have been instigated to arms, & acts of Barbarizm by a Nation which is unable to protect them & of consequence has left them to that correction which is due to their villainy."[24] Washington's hope that Sullivan's "chastisement" of the Iroquois would drive them from the war were unfounded. For the next two years, Haudenosaunee war parties continued to attack Patriot settlements alongside their British and Loyalist allies.

One consequence of the Sullivan campaign was that Washington earned his Indigenous name of Town Destroyer. Twenty-five years earlier, as a callow officer inexperienced in Indian diplomacy, he claimed his great-grandfather's nickname as an act of bravado. As a mature military commander, he deliberately sought to persecute the Haudenosaunee, punishing them for their attacks on white settlers while undermining their will to continue to wage war. Although he failed to knock the Iroquois out of the war, he did succeed in terrorizing them. In 1790, when Washington was serving as president, he welcomed a delegation of Seneca leaders for diplomatic talks. Among the Seneca was Cornplanter, a war chief who had fought Sullivan at the Battle of Newton. Cornplanter testified to the trauma Washington had inflicted on his people, "When your army entered the Country of the Six Nations, we called you the Town-destroyer and to this day, when that name is heard, our women look behind them and turn pale, and our children cling close to the neck of their mothers."[25]

———

One continuity between Virginia's prerevolutionary royal and revolutionary governments was that they laid claims on behalf of the colony-cum-state to the vast territory north and west of the Ohio River and south of the Great Lakes. The Old Dominion had imperial aspirations from its inception. We have seen that George Washington made his first foray as a soldier in that region on behalf of Virginia (and its land speculators). During the War of Independence, the state's revolutionary government maintained the same claim. George Rogers Clark sought to drive the British from the Illinois territory in 1778 and 1779 (resulting in the capture of Henry Hamilton). When Clark captured Vincennes in February 1779, he declared that the settlers (but not Natives) in the area were now "citizens of the Republic of Virginia." After Thomas Jefferson was elected governor of

Virginia in June 1779, just as the Sullivan expedition was preparing to enter Iroquoia, he assumed responsibility for the state's military campaigns in the Northwest. The Indigenous people of the Northwest, particularly Ohio, had mounted a vigorous defense of their land and attacked back-country settlers in Virginia and Kentucky.[26]

On January 1, 1780, Jefferson wrote to Clark about the upcoming campaign. As Jefferson viewed the situation, Clark had two options in the Northwest: he could attack the British at Detroit or the Natives of Ohio and Illinois. Jefferson clearly favored the second option. He felt that Detroit was too heavily fortified for Clark's lightly armed forces to capture. Besides, Jefferson believed, even if Clark succeeded in capturing Detroit, the British would continue to support and encourage Native attacks against Virginia settlers in Ohio and Kentucky. The Shawnee, Mingoes, Munsee, and Wyandots in Ohio, Jefferson wrote, "have harassed us with eternal hostilities and whom experience has shewn to be incapable of reconciliation." The governor acknowledged that he was too far from the scene to advise Clark on what course of action to take but, "if against these Indians," he wrote, "the end proposed should be their extermination, or their removal beyond the lakes or Illinois river. The same world will scarcely do for them and us." Several weeks later Jefferson wrote to Washington about Clark's proposed campaign to coordinate the Virginia effort with a possible campaign in Ohio by Continental forces. He reiterated that Clark might choose the option of "giving rigorous chastisement to those tribes of Indians whose eternal hostilities have proved them incapable of living on friendly terms with us."[27]

Jefferson occasionally indulged in rhetorical flights of fancy, employing bloody imagery that was not intended to be taken literally. Infamously, he wrote of the French Revolution, "rather than it should have failed, I would have seen half the earth desolated. Were there but an Adam and an Eve left in every country, and left free, it would be better than as it now is."[28] His orders to Clark cannot be dismissed as such. Jefferson removed any ambiguity in his instructions in March. Owing to "want of men, want of money, scarcity of provisions" and other unspecified reasons, "which cannot be trusted to a letter," Jefferson ordered Clark to forgo attacking Detroit and to make "chastising the hostile Indians as the business of this summer."[29] Jefferson's orders to Clark are similar in spirit or tone to Washington's orders to James Sullivan.

When Jefferson, writing in his capacity as governor of Virginia, gave Clark the option of exterminating Natives in the Northwest, he did so in the knowledge that Clark had the capacity to carry out the order. While he was besieging Vincennes in February 1779, Clark's men captured six Native Americans, whom they murdered at Clark's behest (Clark may have killed one of the captives himself), "a testimony," Henry Hamilton wrote, "of the courage and Humanity of Colonel Clarke."[30] In early August 1780, Clark led around 1,000 Virginia and Kentucky militiamen into Ohio—at a moment when those men were sorely needed to defend Virginia itself. They burned several towns that the Shawnee had abandoned before confronting a combined force of Shawnee, Delaware, Wyandots, and Mingoes at Picqua on the Mad River (near modern Springfield, Ohio) on August 8. Picqua was a large, well-defended Indigenous settlement. After a battle lasting several hours, Clark's men used three cannons to overwhelm the town's fortified blockhouse, forcing most of the defenders to flee. Clark's men killed around forty Natives, including several prisoners they captured after overrunning the town. The attackers lost fourteen dead and a similar number of wounded. Clark's men burned the town as well as the surrounding fields, destroying crops needed for the coming winter. In a scene reminiscent of the flight of Haudenosaunee refugees to Niagara in 1779, many Shawnee sought shelter and food from the British at Detroit.[31]

For all of Jefferson's professed interest in Native culture and sympathy for Indigenous people, there was little difference between his actions as governor of Virginia and Washington's as commander in chief of the Continental Army during the War of Independence. Both men viewed Native Americans as threats to the Patriot war effort. Although some Native people might ally with the Patriots these were likely to be a minority, those that did not, "merciless Indian savages" in Jefferson's phrasing, should be treated as enemies. When waging war against Natives, burning towns and destroying crops—attacking and endangering noncombatants as well as Native soldiers—were acceptable tactics. Indeed, as Sullivan and Clark demonstrated, acting at the behest of Washington and Jefferson, such tactics were believed necessary to make it impossible for Indigenous people to attack white settlers. They did not advocate the use of such tactics against their British and Loyalist enemies.

As the War of Independence ended, both Washington and Jefferson turned their thoughts to the place of the West in the new American republic. Washington suggested that western territory should be settled by former soldiers. He explained the advantages of such a scheme, "It would connect our Government with the frontiers—extend our Settlements progressively—and plant a brave, a hardy [&] respectable Race of People, as our [advanced Post,] who would be always ready & willing (in case [of] hostility) to combat the Savages, and check their incursions." According to Washington, the veterans would benefit from access to land and they would help to protect the United States: "A Settlement formed by such Men would give security to our frontiers—the very name of it would awe the Indians, and more than probably prevent the murder of many innocent Families, which frequently, in the usual mode of extending our Settlements & Encroachments on the hunting grounds of the Natives, fall the hapless Victims to savage barbarity." Washington primarily viewed Native peoples as a threat to white settlers. Establishing colonies of soldier-settlers in the West would keep Natives in check and facilitate the acquisition of additional Native territory. "The appearance of so formidable a Settlement in the vicinity of their Towns . . . would be the most likely means to enable us to purchase upon equitable terms of the Aborigines their right of [preoccupancy and to] induce them to relinquish our Territories, and to remove into the illimitable regions of the West."[32]

While Washington hoped that the United States would acquire Indigenous lands through negotiation rather than war, he did not envision the new republic as a place where Natives and settlers might live together. Rather, because most Native Americans had sided with the British during the war, they had forfeited their right to live among the republican citizens of the United States. Washington addressed a lengthy disquisition on US-Native relations to James Duane, who chaired the congressional committee charged with developing the new nation's Indigenous policy. Washington wrote to Duane in September 1783, just as American and British diplomats were agreeing to terms to end the War of Independence in Paris. He stipulated several nonnegotiable principles. These were that Native Americans should immediately release all prisoners they held, "of whatever age or Sex"; that Natives should be informed that Britain had ceded sovereignty of all lands within the United States (including, by implication, lands still occupied by Native people); and that because Native Americans "were

determined to join their Arms to those of G. Britain and to share their fortune," they, too, might be expelled from the United States. Although such
an expulsion would be justified, the Americans were a generous and
peaceful people and would be indulgent toward their former enemies.
Washington wrote:

> But as we prefer Peace to a state of Warfare, as we consider them as a
> deluded People; as we perswade ourselves that they are convinced,
> from experience, of their error in taking up the Hatchet against us,
> and that their true Interest and safety must now depend upon <u>our</u>
> friendship. As the Country, is large enough to contain us all; and as
> we are disposed to be kind to them and to partake of their Trade, we
> will from these considerations and from motives of Comp[assio]n,
> draw a veil over what is past and establish a boundary line between
> them and us beyond which we will <u>endeavor</u> to restrain our People
> from Hunting or Settling, and within which they shall not come, but
> for the purposes of Trading, Treating, or other business unexcep-
> tionable in its nature.

Indigenous people, in Washington's view, might remain within the United
States *if* they remained separate from most white settlers, except when they
were partaking of carefully defined activities. Their ability to do so depended on American benevolence—and was contingent on good behavior
of Indigenous people as deemed by the United States. In drawing the line
of separation in the West between settlers and Natives, Washington observed, "Care should be taken neither to yield nor to grasp at too much.
But to endeavor to impress the Indians with an idea of the generosity of our
disposition to accommodate them, . . . and if they should make a point of it,
or appear dissatisfied at the line we may find it necessary to establish, compensation should be made them for their claims within it." As someone
who chafed at (and ignored) the British Proclamation Line of 1763, Washington was surely aware of the similarity between what he was proposing
and the earlier British policy.[33]

In his letter to Duane, Washington suggested that Congress should
create two new states in the Northwest. Jefferson, who was then serving in
Congress, was thinking along similar lines. In December 1783 the Virginia
assembly, with Jefferson's support, voted to cede its claims to territory in
the Northwest to the United States, thus helping to consolidate what the

new nation claimed as its national domain. Congress created a committee to draft a plan for organizing and governing western territory, with Jefferson as its chair. Of course, Native relations and western settlement went hand in hand. Washington acknowledged "the line of Conduct proper to be observed not only towards the Indians, but for the government of the Citizens of America, in their Settlement of the Western Country (. . . is intimately connected therewith)."[34] In February 1784 Jefferson prepared a draft Plan for Government of the Western Territory, which he presented to Congress. In the plan Jefferson outlined his vision of the place of the West in the future of the American republic and described the mechanisms whereby western territory could be subdivided and governed by the United States until the individual territories acquired enough settlers and could draft republican constitutions and apply for admission to the United States as new states. Jefferson's report called for the creation of at least fourteen news states in the West. The new states would enter the union on an equal basis with the original states, testimony that Jefferson believed the future of the republic lay in western expansion and settlement (at the expense of Native Americans). The key features of Jefferson's proposal were incorporated into the Ordinance of 1784, the Land Ordinance of 1785, and the Northwest Ordinance of 1787—each of which refined US policy in the west. Jefferson had laid the foundation for the creation of a republican empire in the West.[35]

The diplomats in Paris in 1783 did not consult Native peoples when the British ceded the territory between the Appalachian Mountains and the Mississippi River to the United States. Neither were Indigenous views considered when Virginia relinquished its claims to the Northwest nor when Congress implemented Jefferson's plans to carve up and settle western territory. Despite Washington's vision of settling the West with veterans or Jefferson's dream of creating new states, Native Americans sought to defend their land from encroachment by settlers, both legal and illegal, from the United States. In the decade after the Peace of Paris, Natives in the Northwest offered armed resistance to encroachments on their land. During Washington's presidency the Natives of the region—among them Shawnee, Delaware, Miami, Chippewa, Ottawa, and Potawatomi—formed an alliance, the Western Confederacy, to resist US expansion. After the Confederacy defeated an American army in October 1790, the Washington administration prepared to send another force to the region in 1791.

Washington explained to Jefferson, who was then serving as his secretary of state, the rationale for the campaign: "The United States have no other view in prosecuting the present war against the Indians, than . . . to procure by arms, peace and safety to the inhabitants of their frontier."

Jefferson endorsed the policy. "I hope we shall give the Indians a thorough drubbing this summer," he wrote. Having defeated the Western Confederacy, Jefferson believed that the United States should provide trade goods to the Indians to keep the peace. He wrote, "I should think it better afterwards to take up the plan of liberal and repeated presents to them. This would produce a spirit of peace and friendship between us."[36] Washington's and Jefferson's hopes that peace and amity would follow military victory were dashed in early November when the Western Confederacy inflicted another humiliating defeat on the United States, routing an army commanded by General Arthur St. Clair (killing and wounding nearly 900 of St. Clair's 1,400 soldiers). The United States did not finally defeat the Western Confederacy until 1794. The next year the Washington administration compelled its members to sign the Treaty of Greenville by the terms of which they ceded most of the territory in modern Ohio to the United States. More than forty years after Washington's first foray into the territory, white settlers could finally claim sovereignty in Ohio (which became a state during Jefferson's presidency in 1803).[37]

Washington and Jefferson were not without sympathy for Native Americans. Washington had a soldier's respect for Native military prowess. He had learned hard lessons as a young man when he first experienced Native warfare in Pennsylvania in 1754, which were reinforced when the US army was humiliated in Ohio during his presidency. Jefferson's interest in Indigenous culture and desire to preserve Indigenous languages and artifacts seems to have been sincere (though predicated on the assumption that Native culture would soon disappear). While both men believed that the United States should attempt to deal fairly with Native nations, their top priority was always the interest of western settlers.

During their presidencies, both Washington and Jefferson pursued remarkably similar Indian policies. In 1803 Jefferson provided a detailed outline of US Native American policy in a letter to his fellow Virginian (and future president) William Henry Harrison, who was then serving as a governor of Indiana Territory. It serves as a cogent summary of the policies pursued by the Washington and Jefferson administrations. "[O]ur system is to live in perpetual peace with the Indians," wrote Jefferson, "to cultivate an affectionate attachment from them, by every thing just & liberal which we can do for them within the bounds of reason, and by giving them effectual protection against wrongs from our own people." Owing to the decrease in game, Native Americans could no longer rely on hunting for their subsistence but would be compelled to turn to agriculture, spinning, and weaving. This would require a renegotiation of traditional gender roles, since Indigenous women in the eastern woodlands were responsible for providing agricultural labor. Native men should take up agriculture and move indoors to engage in spinning and weaving, as was expected of white women. Having eschewed hunting in favor of farming, Natives would perceive "how useless to them are their extensive forests, and will be willing to pare them off from time to time in exchange for necessaries for their farms & families." The United States should encourage trade with Native Americans to put them in debt, which would compel them to sell their land. "[W]hen they withdraw themselves to the culture of a small piece of land," wrote Jefferson, "they will percieve to promote this disposition to exchange lands which they have to spare & we want, for necessaries, which we have to spare & they want, we shall push our trading houses, and be glad to see the good & influential individuals among them run in debt, because we observe that when these debts get beyond what the individuals can pay, they become willing to lop th[em off] by a cession of lands." Though farming, in Jefferson's thinking, would guarantee the independence of white small farmers, it would lead to dependence and the loss of autonomy for Native people.[38]

As Native people who converted to settler-style agriculture went into debt and sold their land, their settlements would be surrounded by those of Euro-Americans (and their enslaved laborers). Jefferson believed they would face a stark choice: "They will in time either incorporate with us as citizens of the US. or remove beyond the Missisipi." While Jefferson held out that it was possible that Indians might become US citizens, such a development would come at a price, "The former is certainly the termination of their history most happy for themselves." His desire to preserve Indian languages and artifacts to display in the Entrance Hall at Monticello originated in Jefferson's belief that to become citizens, Indians would have to forgo their land and their culture. For those who might be reluctant to accept the benefits of American republicanism, a different fate awaited.

"We presume that our strength & their weakness is now so visible that they must see we have only to shut our hand to crush them," he wrote, "& that all our liberalities to them proceed from motives of pure humanity only. should any tribe be fool-hardy enough to take up the hatchet at any time, the seizing the whole country of that tribe & driving them across the Mississipi, as the only condition of peace, would be an example to others, and a furtherance of our final consolidation."[39] Several months later Jefferson wrote to another future president, Andrew Jackson of Tennessee, about the possible impact of the recently negotiated purchase of the Louisiana Territory on Native Americans: "It will . . . open an asylum for these unhappy people, in a country which may suit their habits of life better than what they now occupy, which perhaps they will be willing to exchange with us and to our posterity it opens a noble prospect of provision for ages. the world will here see such an extent of country under a free and moderate government as it has never yet seen."[40] Of course, during his presidency, Jackson would oversee the forced removal of thousands of Native Americans from the east to territory west of the Mississippi. In so doing he was continuing a policy initiated by Washington and Jefferson.

— 10 —

I Like Much the General Idea of Framing a Government

> The business of this Convention is as yet too much in embryo to form any opinion of the result. Much is expected from it by some, but little by others, and nothing by a few.—That something is necessary, all will agree; for the situation of the General Government (if it can be called a government) is shaken to its foundation and liable to be overset by every blast.—In a word, it is at an end, and unless a remedy is soon applied, anarchy and confusion will inevitably ensue.
>
> —George Washington to Thomas Jefferson, May 30, 1787

On June 2, 1784, Washington wrote to Jefferson from Mount Vernon. His brief note was a letter of recommendation for one of his former aides, David Humphreys. Humphreys, a thirty-two-year-old Yale graduate from Connecticut, had served in the Continental Army throughout the war. He became one of Washington's aides, and hence a member of his extended military "family." Along with Alexander Hamilton and Tench Tilghman, Humphreys was one of Washington's favorites and would later serve as his personal secretary—and one of his earliest biographers. At the end of the war, Washington urged Congress to give Humphreys a diplomatic assignment. Adept at staff work, Humphreys was appointed as the secretary to an American delegation charged with negotiating commercial treaties in Europe. Jefferson was one of the members of that delegation, and Washington wrote to recommend Humphreys to Jefferson as "a good scholar, natural and acquired abilities, great integrity, and more than a common share of prudence." Washington also wished Jefferson "a pleasant voyage, the perfect accomplishment of your Mission, and in due time, that you may be restored to your friends in this Country." Washington, undoubtedly considered himself among Jefferson's friends, closed his letter with "Yr. Most Obed. and Affecte. Humble. Servt."[1]

It is one of the ironies of the relationship between Washington and Jefferson that they grew to be close friends during a period when they were largely apart physically. Jefferson departed for France in July 1784 and did not return to the United States until 1789. As we have seen, during that period the two men maintained a warm, wide-ranging, rich correspondence. One of the most important topics they discussed concerned the federal Constitution, which was drafted and adopted in Jefferson's absence. Washington came out of retirement to play a direct role in the creation of the Constitution. Indeed, it proved to be one of the most important contributions in his lengthy career of public service. Jefferson, by contrast, despite an abiding interest in constitution-making and political reform, missed the convention in Philadelphia that produced the Constitution and was absent during the debates over its ratification. Nonetheless, through his extensive correspondence network, including with Washington, he expressed his views (and criticisms) on the plan for a new government from afar.

———

Jefferson went to Paris at the behest of his close friend and political ally, James Madison. Madison, nine years younger than Jefferson and almost twenty years junior to Washington, slight of build and formidable of intellect, was, like Washington and Jefferson, a Virginia planter and slaveholder. Concerned about Jefferson's spiral of depression after the death of his wife, Martha, Madison sought to have him named to the commission that negotiated the 1783 Peace of Paris. He believed that Jefferson, a lifelong Francophile, would welcome a trip to Paris. Unfortunately, the peace treaty was completed before Jefferson could depart for Europe. Undeterred, Madison arranged for Jefferson's appointment to the American diplomatic mission charged with negotiating commercial treaties in Europe. Jefferson (Figure 10.1) sailed for Europe from Boston on July 5, 1784. His oldest daughter, Patsy, then eleven years old, accompanied him. Jefferson left his two youngest daughters—Polly, aged six, and Lucy, aged two—in the care of

FIGURE 10.1   Mather Brown, *Thomas Jefferson* (1786). Mather Brown painted Jefferson while he was representing the United States at the French court at Versailles. Although Jefferson has his hair dressed for the court, his black frock coat and the image of Liberty over his left shoulder are meant to convey republican simplicity. National Portrait Gallery, Smithsonian Institution, Washington, DC.

their aunt and uncle Elizabeth Wayles Eppes and Francis Eppes. Jefferson was initially part of an American delegation that included John Adams and Benjamin Franklin. He became especially close with John and Abigail Adams. In 1785 he succeeded Franklin as the American minister to the court at Versailles (Adams had left to represent the United States in London), a post he held until he returned to the United States at the end of 1789.[2]

In addition to his diplomatic duties, which mainly concerned seeking to promote and protect American commercial interests in Europe and the Mediterranean, Jefferson found time to partake of the cultural and social of Europe, particularly France.[3] He engaged in enlightened discourse in the salons of Paris, went to the theater, visited art galleries, and shopped for everything from books to furniture. He traveled around France and visited

England, Italy, the German states along the Rhine, the Netherlands, and Belgium. An avid student of architecture, he was particularly interested in the public buildings, both ancient and modern, he saw. "Behold me at length on the vaunted scene of Europe!" he exclaimed a year after his arrival. "Were I to proceed to tell you how much I enjoy their architecture, sculpture, painting, music, I should want words. It is in these arts they shine."[4] While in Europe Jefferson established social and intellectual connections that he would maintain for the rest of his life.

James Madison's hope that living in Paris might help Jefferson recover from the loss of his wife seems to have been borne out. Although he treasured the memory of his marriage to Martha Wayles Jefferson for the rest of his life, during his time in France, Jefferson entered into two relationships that helped him overcome his grief over Martha's death. In August 1786 Jefferson, then forty-three years old, was introduced to Maria Cosway (Figure 10.2), a twenty-seven-year-old Anglo-Italian artist whose husband, Richard, was a well-known British portrait painter. Jefferson and Cosway spent the next two months sightseeing and cavorting around Paris. The two were clearly enamored with each other and spent a lot of time together. It's impossible to know whether their relationship was sexual, although we know from Jefferson's earlier advances toward Betsey Walker that he may not have considered Cosway's status as a married woman an obstacle. Annette Gordon-Reed, perhaps the most perceptive and subtle student of Jefferson's personal life, writes, "Jefferson actually fell in love with Cosway, an act that marks his recovery from the body blow of his wife's death." Cosway left Paris in October, prompting Jefferson to write her a lengthy letter in which he presented an internal dialogue between his head and his heart concerning their relationship. Although the two corresponded occasionally over the course of their long lives—Cosway lived, mainly in Italy, until 1838—their initial ardor cooled. Nonetheless, Gordon-Reed observes, Jefferson's "reaction upon meeting her—he seems to have come completely undone—is the clearest evidence of his emotional reawakening in those days in Paris."[5]

The following summer Jefferson's youngest surviving child, Polly, joined him in Paris. Jefferson sought to reunite her with her sister, Patsy, after the death of his youngest daughter, Lucy, from whooping cough several months after he departed for France.[6] It took several years to arrange her passage; Polly did not cross the Atlantic until she was nine

FIGURE 10.2   Francesco Bartolozzi, *Maria Cosway* (1785). Cosway (1760–1838) was a married
Anglo-Italian painter when she met Thomas Jefferson. They had a romantic relationship—which
may or may not have been sexual—for several months in 1786. Cosway was the recipient (and
subject) of Jefferson's famous "Dialogue between the Head and Heart" letter that he wrote on
October 12, 1786. It apparently ended their romantic liaison, though Cosway was confused by the
letter, as evidenced by her bemused response on October 30. They corresponded for decades
afterward, exchanging their last letters in 1820–1821.   Reproduction © Thomas Jefferson Foundation at
Monticello.

years old, in the spring and early summer of 1787. She was accompanied by
an enslaved personal attendant, Sally Hemings. Hemings was fourteen
years old when she accompanied Polly to France. She was the half sister of
Jefferson's deceased wife. Their father was John Wayles, an English-born
slave trader, lawyer, and planter who had migrated to Virginia. When John
Wayles died in 1773, his daughter and son-in-law, Thomas Jefferson, inherited 14,000 acres of land and 135 enslaved men, women, and children.
Among the enslaved persons Jefferson inherited from Wayles were the

members of the extended Hemings family, who would play key roles in the community of people, enslaved and free, at Monticello and beyond. Prior to her arrival in France, Sally Hemings's older brother, James, had accompanied Jefferson to Paris, where he trained as a chef.[7]

Sally Hemings was not, originally, supposed to accompany Polly Jefferson to Europe. Thomas Jefferson had intended that an older white or enslaved woman should make the journey with her. This proved impossible, and Jefferson's sister-in-law, Elizabeth Eppes, chose Hemings, who had been working as Polly's servant, to look after her on the voyage. That decision would have momentous consequences for both Hemings and Jefferson. Hemings spent two and a half years in France. During that period she might have availed herself of a provision in French law that would have resulted in her emancipation. Annette Gordon-Reed has shown that both Sally and James Hemings were aware of this legal option. While in France, Hemings and Jefferson entered into a sexual relationship. According to the account of their son, Madison, Hemings eventually agreed to return to Virginia rather than seek her freedom in France, in exchange for the freedom of her children. Over the course of the next thirty-six years, she and Jefferson had six children, four of whom, Beverly, Harriet, Madison, and Eston Hemings, survived to adulthood and acquired their freedom. Though it is impossible to know the precise nature of their relationship—we have no accounts from Hemings's perspective, and Jefferson only made passing reference to her in the vast corpus of materials he bequeathed to posterity—it was one of the constants in Jefferson's life until his death in 1826 (Sally Hemings lived until 1835).[8]

———

While Jefferson was in Europe, George Washington's retirement was anything but restful. A steady stream of visitors and seemingly endless correspondence requiring his attention took up his time. He complained to his old friend, George William Fairfax, "that at no period of the War have I been obliged myself <u>to</u> go thro' more drudgery in writing, or have suffered so much confinement to effect it, as since what is called my retirement to domestic ease & tranquillity. Strange as it may seem, it is nevertheless true—that I have been able since I came home, to give very little attention to my own concerns, or to those of others, with which I was entrusted."

His personal finances, left in disarray by his prolonged wartime absence, required urgent attention. "My accounts stand as I left them near ten years ago," he told Fairfax, "those who owed me money, a very few instances excepted, availed themselves of what are called the tender Laws, & paid me off with a shilling & sixpence in the pound—Those to whom I owed I have now to pay under heavy taxes with specie, or its equivalent value."[9] Washington restored his finances by increasing his land speculation in the West, pursuing those who owed him money, and improving the productivity of Mount Vernon and his adjacent holdings, eventually building a gristmill and a distillery. He also undertook extensive renovations of the mansion house at Mount Vernon, an expansion that doubled its size, adding wings to the north and south facades and a distinctive two-story "piazza" running the length of the east front of the mansion facing the Potomac River familiar to tourists today. It was an improvement in size and style befitting Washington's wealth and status, but also his intention to spend the remaining years of his life at home managing his considerable business interests.[10]

Washington's postwar financial challenges were exacerbated by the economic challenges that beset the United States during the mid-1780s. The War of Independence had been costly in financial as well as human terms. Congress, which had no authority to tax, had depended on requisitions from the states, foreign gifts and loans, and paper money. Between 1775 and 1780, Congress issued $241 million in paper money and promissory notes to pay for the rebel war effort. The result was runaway inflation and currency depreciation. In mid-1781 the Continental dollar collapsed. The states had also incurred substantial debts during the war. Faced with huge public debts and unstable currencies, the various states were faced with difficult choices— they might raise taxes to retire their debts while requiring that debts were paid with specie, hard currency rather than paper, to reduce inflation, or they could continue to print, and accept, paper money. In his letter to George William Fairfax, Washington complained that his debtors had paid their debts to him with worthless paper money but that he was harmed by new laws that required that he pay his own debts and taxes with specie. The problems arising from public and private debt that entangled Washington in the mid-1780s were widespread and underscored the sense of economic, social, and political crisis that beset the new American republic.

Although he claimed (and sincerely wished) he was retired, Washington found himself slowly drawn back into public life. In March 1785 he hosted a meeting of commissioners from Virginia and Maryland to discuss fishing rights and boundary issues on the Potomac River, an issue that Washington had a particular interest in given his desire to improve the Potomac and access to the Northwest (and his stake in the Potomac Company). This "Mount Vernon Conference" led to an agreement on access to the Potomac, which the commissioners declared a common waterway between the two states, as well as fishing rights and sharing the expense of improving access to the river. Delaware and Pennsylvania were invited to join the agreement.[11]

This compact was the first mutually binding agreement between two of the newly independent American states. One of the Virginia delegates to the conference was Jefferson's friend and protégé James Madison. Madison was just thirty-four in 1785. During the latter stages of the war, he had served in Congress. By the mid-1780s he was a member of Virginia's legislature, the House of Delegates. Madison was convinced that the Articles of Confederation were not fit for purpose and needed reforming or replacing. The Mount Vernon conference marks one of his first collaborations with Washington. The two made an unlikely pair but emerged as allies in the movement for constitutional reform. Washington concluded that he and Madison agreed on the need to strengthen the union. Writing to the younger man concerning the need for the states to have a single commercial policy, Washington declared with exasperation, "We are either a United people, or we are not. If the former, let us, in all matters of general concern act as a nation, which have national objects to promote, and a National character to support—If we are not, let us no longer act a farce by pretending to it."[12]

Madison was among twelve delegates from five states who gathered at Mann's Tavern in Annapolis (where Jefferson and Washington had met in 1783 when Washington resigned his commission) for several days in September 1786 to discuss measures to "remedy the defects of the Federal Government" in the rather grandiloquently named "Annapolis Convention." Although several other states had expressed interest in the meeting, their delegates failed to arrive in time to participate. Recognizing that they were too few to recommend changes to the Articles of Confederation, the men in Annapolis (who included Washington's former aide, Alexander Hamilton, representing New York) issued an appeal to Congress to approve the calling of an additional meeting to be held in Philadelphia in the spring of 1787, "to render the constitution of the Federal Government adequate to the exigencies of the Union."[13]

Although the Annapolis Convention had achieved little, for men like Hamilton, Madison, and Washington, the need for constitutional reform became acute during the autumn of 1786. In response to widespread discontent—violent protests and demonstrations had taken place in several states—seven states began issuing paper money. They also adopted debt relief measures, such as stay laws that suspended debt payments, reducing court fees, and valuation laws that required creditors to give debtors fair value for their property. In Massachusetts, Governor James Bowdoin refused to support such measures. Approximately one-third of the adult males in the state's westernmost county, Hampshire, were sued for debt between 1784 and 1786. When called before the courts, debtors risked jail and the seizure of their property. In 1785, 92 of the 103 men in jail in Worcester County, in the center of the state, were imprisoned for debt. Feeling that the government in Boston was hostile to their interests (and nonresponsive to their pleas for relief) hundreds of farmers in western and central Massachusetts, many of them war veterans, took up arms and closed the courts, halting debt prosecutions.[14]

One of the leaders, among several, of the impromptu rebellion was a Revolutionary War veteran from Pelham, Massachusetts, named Daniel Shays, by whose name the uprising is remembered as Shays's Rebellion. Shays was among the militiamen who besieged Boston in 1775 and fought at the Battle of Bunker Hill. He was among the soldiers absorbed into the Continental Army under Washington's command and rose to the rank of captain in the 5th Massachusetts Regiment. He was wounded and left the army in 1780. He had achieved such distinction that the Marquis de Lafayette, another of Washington's favorites, gave him a ceremonial sword. Shays left the army without pay—he later sold the sword Lafayette had given him—and faced mounting debts. For men like Shays, the American Revolution had failed to live up to its promises. On January 25, 1787, Shays led between 700 and 800 rebellious militiamen who sought to capture the state armory at Springfield, Massachusetts. The armory was defended by 1,200 militia loyal to the state government. The loyalists were better armed than the rebels. They turned artillery on the rebels, killing several, putting the rest to flight. The government in Boston had raised an army under Benjamin Lincoln; over the next several months, Lincoln's men pursued the insurgents, and by the spring of 1787, the rebellion collapsed.[15]

One of Washington's most trusted wartime lieutenants, Henry Knox, a Boston native, wrote to his former chief about the events unfolding in Massachusetts in October 1786. According to Knox the rebellion was a war on private property. The Shaysites' creed, Knox claimed, was "that the property of the United States has been protected from the confiscations of Britain by the joint exertions of all, and therefore ought to be the common property of all. And he that attempts opposition to this creed is an enemy to equity and justice, and ought to be swept from off the face of the earth." Knox continued, "In a word they are determined to annihilate all debts public and private and have agrarian Laws which are easily effected by the means of unfunded paper money which shall be a tender in all cases whatever." Knox believed the United States had reached a crisis point, a moment of "national humiliation" when endless civil war threatened to overwhelm the country unless "friends to the liberties of this country" stepped forward to defend the government. "Unless this is done," Knox warned, "we shall be liable to be ruled by an Arbitrary and Capricious armed tyranny, whose word and will must be law."[16]

Washington shared Knox's concerns. Even before news of Shays's Rebellion reached Virginia, he was worried about the possibility of a counterrevolution. In August 1786 he reported that, a mere ten years after the Declaration of Independence, some Americans were contemplating a return to monarchy. "I am told that even respectable characters speak of a monarchical form of government without horror," he wrote. "From thinking proceeds speaking, thence to acting is often but a single step. But how irrevocable & tremendous! What a triumph for the advocates of despotism to find that we are incapable of governing ourselves, and that systems founded on the basis of equal liberty are merely ideal & falacious!"[17] Later, when he learned of Shays's Rebellion, he feared that popular disorder would threaten the rule of law and private property. At the end of the year, he wrote to David Humphreys in despair, "It is but the other day we were shedding our blood to obtain the Constitutions under which we now live— Constitutions of our own choice and framing—and now we are unsheathing the Sword to overturn them! The thing is so unaccountable, that I hardly know how to realize it, or to persuade my self that I am not under the vision of a dream."[18] In early November he wrote to James Madison, quoting extensively from Knox's account of the rebellion. "What stronger evidence can be given of the want of energy in our governments than these disorders?" asked Washington. He continued, "If there exists not a power to check them, what security has a man of life, liberty, or property? Thirteen Sovereignties pulling against each other, and all tugging at the fœderal head, will soon bring ruin on the whole." He offered a solution, "[A] liberal, and energetic Constitution, well guarded & closely watched, to prevent incroachments, might restore us to that degree of respectability & consequence."[19]

———

As he departed the public stage for what he believed was the last time in 1783, Washington offered a valedictory message to the American people in the form of a circular letter, which he addressed to each of the state governors.

As the War of Independence came to an end, Washington reflected on what the American people had achieved. "The Citizens of America, placed in the most enviable condition," he wrote with particular disregard for Native Americans, "as the sole Lords and Proprietors of a vast Tract of Continent, comprehending all the various soils and climates of the World, and abounding with all the necessaries and conveniences of life, are now by the late satisfactory pacification, acknowledged to be possessed of absolute freedom and Independency." The American people had achieved their independence at an opportune moment, "when the rights of mankind were better understood and more clearly defined, than at any former period . . . [a]t this auspicious period, the United States came into existence as a Nation, and if their Citizens should not be completely free and happy, the fault will be intirely their own." Despite these positive auguries, Washington's circular letter was a warning to the states about the "importance of the present Crisis" confronting the new republic and its people.[20]

Washington feared that the American people were in danger of squandering their hard-fought independence. He wrote, "Such is our situation, and such are our prospects: but notwithstanding the cup of blessing is thus reached out to us, notwithstanding happiness is ours, if we have a disposition to seize the occasion and make it our own; yet, it appears to me there is an option still left to the United States of America, that it is in their choice, and depends on their conduct, whether they will be respectable and prosperous, or contemptable and miserable as a Nation; This is the time of their political probation, this is the moment when the eyes of the whole World are turned upon them, this is the moment to establish or ruin their national Character forever, this is the favorable moment to give such a tone to our Federal Government as will enable it to answer the ends of its institution, or this may be the ill-fated moment for relaxing the powers of the Union, annihilating the cement of the Confederation." Washington feared that if the states did not band more closely together at this point of vulnerability, they would "become the sport of European politics," as the great powers would play the states off against each other, stifling their growth, and undermining the revolution. The stakes could not be higher. "For," Washington continued, "according to the system of Policy the States shall adopt at this moment, they will stand or fall, and by this confirmation of lapse, it is yet to be decided, whether the Revolution must ultimately be considered a blessing or a curse."[21]

When Washington mentioned the "Federal Government," he meant Congress. In 1783 the United States was governed under the terms of the Articles of Confederation. According to the Articles, power in the national government was vested in the unicameral Congress, with each state possessing a single vote. On most issues, decisions were made on a majority basis, but on critical questions relating to war, peace, and finance, a two-thirds majority (nine states) was required. The Confederation government lacked an independent executive or judiciary and the power to levy taxes or raise revenue. Essentially, the Articles of Confederation codified what Congress had been doing since 1775. They created a loose confederation between sovereign states. Washington feared that the Articles had created such a loose confederacy that, without the necessity to band together to wage war, the states would go their own ways and the republic would collapse. Paradoxically, with the war won, the United States faced a moment of great peril.

The circular to the states was one of the clearest statements of Washington's constitutional thinking. He asserted there were four principles that should guide Americans as they sought to govern themselves: there should be an "indissoluble Union of the States under one Federal Head"; there should be a "Sacred regard to Public Justice" as well as "a proper Peace Establishment," and Americans should show a willingness to "forget local prejudices" and "sacrifice their individual advantages" to the interests of the United States as a whole. If Americans failed to adhere to these principles and neglected to give their support to a strong national government, Washington warned, "We may find by our own unhappy experience, that there is a natural and necessary progression, from the extreme of anarchy to the extreme of Tyranny; and that arbitrary power is most easily established on the ruins of Liberty abused to licentiousness." By contrast, if Americans decided to "strengthen the hands of Government," then "every one will reap the fruit of his labours, every one will enjoy his own acquisitions without molestation and without danger."[22]

It is telling that Washington's most important constitutional statement during the period was addressed to the governors of the individual states that comprised the union. Although his circular called for the states to support the Confederation government power was so diffuse under the Articles of Confederation that he had to make his appeal to the chief executive of each state. The War of Independence had taught Washington of the importance and power of the states acting in concert. It gave him a strong sense of the United States as a nation at a time when many, including Jefferson, were still focused on their own states. Washington's ideas about constitutional power and nationalism were closely linked. He believed the revolution could only be secured if the states and their citizens gave their allegiance to a central government that was strong enough to protect the nation from external and internal threats. As he left the army, he hoped this might be achieved under the Articles of Confederation. Within a few years, he would conclude that the Confederation government was too weak to achieve its ends and preserve America's republican experiment, and he came to favor more extensive constitutional reform. By the end of 1785, Washington was much more pessimistic about the prospects of the Confederation. He wrote, "Illiberality, Jealousy, & local policy mix too much in all our public Councils for the good government of the Union. In a word, the Confederation appears to me to be little more than an empty sound, and Congress a nugatory body; the ordinances of it being very little attended to."[23]

By the mid-1780s Washington had come to believe that urgent constitutional reform was necessary. In the spring of 1786, he wrote "that it is necessary to revise, and amend the articles of Confederation, I entertain no doubt; but what may be the consequences of such an attempt is doubtful. Yet, something must be done, or the fabrick must fall. It certainly is tottering! Ignorance & design, are difficult to combat. Out of these proceed illiberality, <u>improper</u> jealousies, and a train of evils which oftentimes, in republican governments, must be sorely felt before they can be removed." Of course, Shays's Rebellion exacerbated the situation for Washington. In March 1787 he despaired that the republic would fail and Americans would be forced to resort to monarchy again. "Among men of reflection few will be found I believe," he wrote, "who are not <u>beginning</u> to think that our system is better in theory than practice—and that, notwithstanding the boasted virtue of America it is more than probable we shall exhibit the last melancholy proof that Mankind are not competent to their own government without the means of coercion in the Sovereign." The upcoming convention in Philadelphia to discuss revising the Articles of Confederation "may be the last peaceable mode of essaying the practicability of the pres[en]t form, without a greater lapse of time than the exigency of our Affairs will admit."[24] As far as Washington was concerned, republican government itself would be at stake in Philadelphia.

Unsurprisingly, Washington was among those selected to represent Virginia at the Federal Convention (now known as the Constitutional Convention) in Philadelphia. For a time in the winter and spring of 1787, he demurred, fearing the risk to his reputation if the convention failed (he also took his 1783 pledge to retire from public life seriously, even if the nation did not). Eventually, his political allies, including Henry Knox, John Jay, and especially James Madison, persuaded Washington to attend the conclave, which met in the same room in the Pennsylvania State House (now known as Independence Hall) where Congress had met for most of the War of Independence. It was the room where Washington had accepted command of the Continental Army in 1775 and where Congress debated Jefferson's draft Declaration of Independence in July 1776. Washington arrived in Philadelphia in time for the start of the convention on May 14, 1787. Unfortunately, most of the other delegates were less punctual than the old soldier. Only two state delegations—Virginia, and the hosts from Pennsylvania—were in attendance. The other delegates trickled in over the next couple of weeks, and the convention did not have a quorum until May 25.[25]

In a letter to John Adams (who, like Jefferson, was absent, as he was in Europe on diplomatic service at the time), Jefferson described the Federal Convention as an "assembly of demigods."[26] Whether semidivine or not, the convention met throughout the summer of 1787. The convention's brief, as sanctioned by Congress, was to discuss possible amendments to the Articles of Confederation, which would be subject to ratification by the states. (Amendments to the Articles required the unanimous agreement of all the states.) The Virginia delegation submitted a plan, mostly the handiwork of James Madison, that called for a new federal constitution that would replace the Articles of Confederation and replace the loose confederation of states with a much stronger, centralized federal government partially modeled on Britain's in which power would be divided between three coequal branches of government: the presidency, Congress (which would consist of a bicameral legislature), and the judiciary. Under Madison's plan the states would be completely subsumed by the federal government— which would exercise a veto over state legislation, for example. Delegates from the smaller states in the union, fearing they would be overwhelmed by larger states, like Virginia and Pennsylvania, resisted this plan. The delegates spent most of the summer debating aspects of Madison's plan: key compromises were struck over the relationship between the states and the federal government, representation, taxation, and slavery. The result was a proposed new constitution that would create a new, much stronger federal government for the United States.

According to historian Joseph J. Ellis, "Washington was simultaneously the most important person at the Constitutional Convention and the least involved in the debate that shaped the document that emerged."[27] Washington was the most admired and popular man in the United States (at least among his white countrymen and women). The members of the convention acknowledged his leadership skills when they elected him to preside over their deliberations on May 25. In his capacity as president of the convention, Washington felt he should not intervene in its debates. Nonetheless, his silent presence gave the convention, and the document that emerged from it, legitimacy in the eyes of many. This would be important in the subsequent debate over the ratification of the document. Although amendments to the Articles of Confederation required unanimous consent from all thirteen states, when the Federal Convention finished its work and submitted the Constitution to Congress in mid-September 1787, it stipulated that the new instrument would take effect when it was ratified by special conventions in nine of the thirteen states. Congress accepted these provisions and called for the Constitution to be submitted to the states for ratification on September 28. Reflecting on the convention's work,

Washington wrote, "I wish the Constitution which is offered had been made more perfect, but I sincerely believe it is the best that could be obtained at this time," and he hoped that any of its deficiencies might be remedied by future amendments, which would be more easily achieved under the new system than under the Articles of Confederation. Unsurprisingly, he supported ratification, writing, "The adoption of it under present circumstances of the Union is in my opinion desirable." He worried for the fate of the country if the proposed constitution failed. "From a variety of concurring accounts," he wrote, "it appears to me that the political concerns of this Country are, in a manner, suspended by a thread."[28]

———

Immediately after the Federal Convention completed its work, Washington sent a copy of the document to Jefferson in Paris. The same day he also sent the Constitution to his former comrade in arms, Lafayette, remarking, "It is the production of four months deliberation. It is now a child of fortune, to be fostered by some and buffeted by others." It is telling that the first people Washington sought to share the proposed constitution with were his young French protégé and his friend. Washington knew that Lafayette, himself committed to reform in France, would be interested in the document. Jefferson and he had discussed constitutional matters previously. "Not doubting but that you have participated in the general anxiety which has agitated the minds of your Countrymen on this interesting occasion," Washington wrote, "I shall be excused I am certain for this endeavor to relieve you from it." Jefferson was, indeed, very interested in the deliberations taking place in Philadelphia. He did not receive Washington's letter until December but had learned about the Constitution from other correspondents. His initial response to the document was not what Washington would have hoped for.[29]

It is one of the many ironies of Jefferson's life that he never played a direct role in creating a state or national constitution. Although he had worked on a draft constitution during the summer of 1776, his absence in Congress that summer meant that he missed the convention that drafted Virginia's first, postindependence, constitution. He was not part of the committee that drafted the Articles of Confederation, and in the summer of 1787, he was in Paris while the Federal Convention met in Philadelphia.

While he had little direct experience with constitution-making, Jefferson was deeply engaged with the topic. As we have seen, he played a key role in the process of reforming and redrafting Virginia's legal code. During his second stint in Congress prior to going to France, he was a major architect of the western land policy of the new nation, which facilitated the acquisition of Indigenous lands and its conversion into new states within the American union. Throughout his life he advocated for constitutional reform in Virginia and, later, in the United States. His main contribution to the drafting of the federal constitution was indirect—he sent hundreds of books on the history of earlier republics from Paris to James Madison while Madison was creating the plan that was at the core of the new constitution.[30]

Jefferson's main constitutional preoccupation was removing the vestiges of aristocracy and monarchical government from the United States. He believed that inherited power without merit was the chief threat to republican government in the new republic. That is why he took particular pride sponsoring the laws that eliminated primogeniture and entail in Virginia. It also explains his opposition to the Society of Cincinnati, the membership of which would be inherited. His sojourn in Europe confirmed his belief in the danger posed by aristocracy. He wrote to Washington concerning his fear that the Society of Cincinnati would evolve into a formal aristocracy, "which will change the form of our governments from the best to the worst in the world." He explained, "To know the mass of evil which flows from this fatal source, a person must be in France, he must see the finest soil, the finest climate, the most compact state, the most benevolent character of people, and every earthly advantage combined, insufficient to prevent this scourge from rendering existence a curse to 24 out of 25 parts of the inhabitants of this country." Monarchy compounded the danger posed by aristocracy. Jefferson was dismayed during the summer of 1787 when he heard that some Americans might consider a return to monarchy—the very consequence that Washington feared in response to the failure of the Articles of Confederation. "I am astonished at some people's considering a kingly government as a refuge." Jefferson continued, "Send them to Europe to see something of the trappings of monarchy, and I will undertake that every man shall go back thoroughly cured. If all the evils which can arise among us from the republican form of our government from this day to the day of judgment could be put into a scale against what this country suffers from it's monarchical form in a week, or England in a month, the latter would preponderate."[31]

When Jefferson wrote about the ills of France under the ancien régime, Shays's Rebellion roiled New England, convincing Washington that America's republican experiment faced a more immediate threat than incipient aristocracy. For his part, and from the comfort of Paris, Jefferson was much less troubled about the unrest in Massachusetts than Washington was. In a lengthy letter to Madison in January 1787, Jefferson gave his opinion on the rebellion. While he acknowledged that the actions of the rebels were "absolutely unjustifiable," he feared the reaction to it more than the disorder itself. According to Jefferson, there were three types of societies: those without government; those "wherein the will of every one has a just influence," as in the United States; and "governments of force," which included all monarchies and many republics. He drew on his experience in Europe noting, "To have an idea of the curse of existence under these last, they must be seen. It is a government of wolves over sheep." Jefferson recognized that governments based on popular sovereignty had advantages and disadvantages—notably, they were prone to popular instability—but he believed their benefits outweighed their flaws. "The second state has a great deal of good in it. The mass of mankind under that enjoys a precious degree of liberty and happiness. It has it's evils too: the principal of which is the turbulence to which it is subject. But weigh this against the oppressions of monarchy, and it becomes nothing. . . . Even this evil is productive of good. It prevents the degeneracy of government, and nourishes a general attention to the public affairs. I hold it that a little rebellion now and then is a good thing, and as necessary in the political world as storms in the physical."[32]

Unlike Washington, Jefferson was sanguine about the long-term prospects of republics, provided their governments did not overreact when faced with misguided popular resistance. Later in the year, he offered a mathematical calculation of the danger posed by popular disorder: "We have had 13. states independant 11. years. There has been one rebellion. That comes to one rebellion in a century and a half for each state. What country before ever existed a century and half without a rebellion?" Indeed, Jefferson held that occasional popular disorders might serve a useful function. "And what country," he asked, "can preserve it's liberties if their rulers are not warned from time to time that their people preserve the spirit of resistance? Let them take arms. The remedy is to set them right as to facts, pardon and pacify them. What signify a few lives lost in a century or two? The tree of liberty must be refreshed from time to time with the blood of patriots and tyrants. It is it's natural manure." These are words Washington could never have written.[33]

Unsurprisingly, Jefferson did not feel there was an urgent need to replace the Articles of Confederation. "But with all the imperfections of our present government," he wrote while the Federal Convention was meeting, "it is without comparison the best existing or that ever did exist." He conceded that there were flaws in the current arrangement but felt that these might be corrected with a few amendments to the existing Articles. As he wrote to Madison prior to the convention, "To make us one nation as to foreign concerns, and keep us distinct in Domestic ones, gives the outline of the proper division of powers between the general and particular governments." He did favor a clearer separation of powers "to enable the Federal head to exercise the powers given it, to best advantage, it should be organised, as the particular ones are, into Legislative, Executive and Judiciary." Jefferson recognized that some reform of the Articles of Confederation was necessary but was concerned that an overly strong central government would threaten liberty in the new republic. He believed the states were the best bulwarks of liberty and should retain as much power as possible.[34]

Perhaps because he was not a member of the "assembly of demigods" that drafted the proposed constitution, Jefferson's initial response to the document when he read it in Paris in the autumn of 1787 was lukewarm at best. "I confess there are things in it which stagger all my dispositions to subscribe to what such an assembly has proposed," he grumbled to John Adams in London. Several weeks later his position had moderated slightly: "As to the new Constitution I find myself nearly a Neutral. There is a great mass of good in it, in a very desireable form: but there is also to me a bitter pill, or two."[35]

Over time Jefferson took a more favorable view of the Constitution. When he wrote to Washington in the spring of 1788, he averred, "I will just observe therefore that according to my ideas there is a great deal of good in it." He repeatedly made the same criticisms of the Constitution, writing, "There are two things however which I dislike strongly. 1. The want of a declaration of rights. . . . [and] 2. The perpetual re-eligibility of the President." He hoped that several states, including Virginia, due to meet the following month, would bring pressure to bear at the ratifying conventions to force for the adoption of a bill of rights: "I am in hopes the opposition of Virginia will remedy this, and produce such a declaration." With respect to the presidency, Jefferson had voiced numerous objections to the power the Constitution vested in the executive. It is noteworthy that he expressed these concerns to Washington, who everyone (including Jefferson) expected would be the first president. He drew a direct connection between his criticism of the presidency and his experiences in Europe. He feared that the president might be a king in all but name, especially as he was eligible for perpetual reelection:

> This I fear will make that an office for life first, and then hereditary. I was much an enemy to monarchy before I came to Europe. I am ten thousand times more so since I have seen what they are. There is scarcely an evil known in these countries which may not be traced to their king as it's source, nor a good which is not derived from the small fibres of republicanism existing among them. I can further say with safety there is not a crowned head in Europe whose talents or merit would entitle him to be elected a vestryman by the people of any parish in America. However I shall hope that before there is danger of this change taking place in the office of President, the good sense and free spirit of our countrymen will make the changes necessary to prevent it. Under this hope I look forward to the general adoption of the new constitution with anxiety, as necessary for us under our present circumstances.[36]

Jefferson did not (then) fear that Washington had monarchical aspirations. Rather, he did not trust that his successors would be able to resist the temptation to remain in office. He sketched a scenario to James Madison whereby a future president, having been defeated for reelection, refused to accept the outcome and civil war threatened, "If once elected, and at a second or third election outvoted by one or two votes, he will pretend false votes, foul play, hold possession of the reins of government, be supported by the states voting for him, especially if they are the central ones lying in a compact body themselves and separating their opponents: and they will be aided by one nation of Europe, while the majority are aided by another." The solution would be to restrict the president to a single term (a stricture Jefferson would ignore in 1804 when he ran for a second presidential term).[37]

When Washington responded to Jefferson's letter at the end of August, he ignored his friend's criticisms of the presidency. Rather, he observed tactfully, "The merits and defects of the proposed Constitution have been largely and ably discussed." For Washington, it was important that a crisis had been averted and the union had been saved. "For myself, I was ready to have embraced any tolerable compromise that was competent to save us from impending ruin." He was happy to accept most of the amendments suggested by the ratifying conventions provided they did not undermine the new government's power to raise revenue. He then reminded his younger friend just how perilous the situation had been prior to the drafting of the Constitution (and, by implication, reminded him that he hadn't been in America then), "It is nearly impossible for any body who has not been on the spot to conceive (from any description) what the delicacy and danger of our situation have been.—Though the peril is not passed entirely; thank God! the prospect is somewhat brightening." He concluded by informing Jefferson that eleven states had ratified the Constitution (only North Carolina and Rhode Island had failed to do so), so the new system would soon take effect. When Jefferson replied to Washington's letter in December, he expressed his "infinite pleasure" that the Constitution had been ratified. He observed that "the minorities" against ratification "have been very respectable, so much so as to render it prudent, were it not otherwise reasonable, to make some sacrifices to them. I am in hopes that the annexation of a bill of rights to the constitution will alone draw over so great a proportion of the minorities, as to leave little danger in the opposition of the residue; and that this annexation may be made ... without calling a convention which might endanger the most valuable parts of the system." He dropped his criticism of the presidency, at least in correspondence with Washington.[38]

Washington and Jefferson differed significantly over the new federal Constitution. Washington favored creating a strong, federal government. Indeed, he believed it was essential to preserving and protecting the American experiment with republican government—preserving it from the threat of excessive democracy that might threaten private property, law, and order as represented by Shays's Rebellion. Only by creating a truly national government (and subordinating the petty interests and rivalries of the states), Washington believed, could the American republic be preserved and flourish. Without it the country threatened to degenerate into anarchy, which would leave it subject to the caprices of European empires. The alternative was that the republic would fail because the new United States would revert to monarchy. Given the options of anarchy and monarchy, a strong centralized republic was the only answer in Washington's mind. While Jefferson recognized that the new republic faced threats from within and without, he had more faith in the common people than Washington did. He believed the greatest danger to the United States came from the residue (as he described it) of aristocratic and monarchical culture in the new republic. A counterrevolutionary return to monarchy was a greater danger, Jefferson believed, than popular unrest. Jefferson believed that the new republic should vest as much power as possible in the common people (excluding women, non-white people, and those without property) who would form its bedrock of independent citizens. They should exercise power at the state level. Though Jefferson recognized that a stronger national government was necessary—his experience representing the United States abroad had taught him that—he felt that the states could best represent the interests of their citizens, and safeguard republicanism. The differences between the two men on constitutional questions were subtle and would only become pronounced over time.

Those differences lay in the future, and we should not overstate their significance. By the spring of 1789, Jefferson had come around on the new federal Constitution. In a letter to David Humphreys in March, shortly before Washington's inauguration as the first president, he described the Constitution as "unquestionably the wisest ever yet presented to men," which echoed his previous description of the Articles of Confederation. Jefferson was still concerned about the absence of a bill of rights and the potential that the president might be perpetually reelected. Nonetheless, having had time to consider the new Constitution, particularly the means by which it was adopted, he had modified his original position considerably. He told Humphreys, "The example of changing a constitution by assembling the wise men of the state, instead of assembling armies, will be worth as much to the world as the former examples we had given them."

Even his concern about the possibility of presidential reelection was tempered by his enthusiasm for Washington. "I would wish it to remain uncorrected," he wrote, "as long as we can avail ourselves of the services of our great leader, whose talents and whose weight of character I consider as peculiarly necessary to get the government so under way as that it may afterwards be carried on by subordinate characters."[39]

— *11* —

I Will Converse with You on the Subject

I consider the successful Administration of the general Government as an object of almost infinite consequence to the present and future happiness of the Citizens of the United States.—I consider the Office of Secretary for the Department of State as <u>very</u> important on many accounts: and I know of no person, who, in my judgment, could better execute the Duties of it than yourself.

—George Washington to Thomas Jefferson, January 21, 1790

George Washington (Figure 11.1) was elected as the first president under the new federal constitution in early 1789. He was inaugurated in New York, then the nation's capital, in April. After his inauguration Washington set about filling his cabinet—the men who would run the departments in the government under his direction. He chose his cabinet secretaries according to ability, seeking men with whom he believed he could work productively. He also took account of geography, seeking, where possible, representation from the different regions of the country. He selected Henry Knox of Massachusetts as his secretary of war. Knox, aged thirty-nine, had been Washington's artillery chief during the war. He turned to a fellow Virginian, Edmund Randolph, just thirty-six, as his attorney general. Randolph had been one of Washington's aides-de-camp during the war. He looked to another of his aides, Alexander Hamilton, for his treasury secretary. Hamilton, just in his early thirties, had served with distinction during the war both as one of Washington's aides and in combat during the Yorktown campaign. After the war he had made a successful career practicing law in New York.[1]

FIGURE II.I   Edward Savage, *The Washington Family* (1789–1796). Edward Savage presents an idealized image of George and Martha Washington during George Washington's presidency. They are pictured with their grandchildren, George Washington "Wash" Parke Custis and Eleanor "Nelly" Parke Custis, whom they raised after Jacky Custis's death. An unidentified enslaved servant on the right reminds the viewer that the Washingtons relied on enslaved labor to maintain their presidential residences in New York and Philadelphia.   Andrew W. Mellon Collection, National Gallery of Art, Washington, DC.

Knox, Randolph, and Hamilton had all served closely with Washington during the war. They were his juniors in age as well as rank. The oldest, Knox, was almost twenty years younger than Washington, who was fifty-seven when he took the presidential oath in April 1789. For his final cabinet appointment, secretary of state, Washington looked beyond his military family and across the Atlantic to his friend Thomas Jefferson. Jefferson, who by then had had five years' experience of European diplomacy, was well-suited for the task. In his midforties, he was closer in age to Washington than the other men in his cabinet. Although the two men hadn't served in the war together, they shared a bond as elite Virginians who had known each other for twenty years and who had worked together to create the American republic. From that common effort, their friendship had blossomed. Theirs was not the relationship between a commander and his subordinates but a more equal bond. Washington later told Jefferson that the job required particular experience, "that mere talents did not suffice for the department of state, but it required a person conversant in foreign affairs, perhaps acquainted with foreign courts, that without this the best talents would be awkward and at a loss." Washington had come to value Jefferson's wise counsel, friendship, and independence, but he also felt that Jefferson had the necessary skills and experience for the role, skills and experiences he himself lacked. In May 1789 James Madison, then serving in Congress, approached Jefferson on Washington's behalf. Madison, who had arranged Jefferson's appointment to go abroad, now sought to tempt him to return to the United States. "I have been asked [presumably by Washington]," wrote Madison, "whether any appointment at home would be agreeable to you. Being unacquainted with your mind I have not ventured an answer." Jefferson, still smarting from the criticism he had received at the end of his tenure as governor of Virginia, demurred. He declared that when his time as an ambassador came to an end, he intended to retire. "Whenever therefore I quit the present [appointment], it will not be to engage in any other office, and most especially any one which would require a constant residence [away] from home." Before Jefferson's rebuff had reached Madison, Washington—a man used to getting what he wanted and assuming Jefferson would accept his offer—formally nominated Jefferson as secretary of state on September 25, 1789. The Senate confirmed his nomination that day.[2]

Jefferson, ignorant that he had been confirmed by the Senate, left France the next day. He had received permission from Congress to return home on leave to attend to his personal affairs at Monticello. Although the traveling party, which included Patsy and Polly as well as the enslaved siblings, James and Sally Hemings, had a prodigious amount of luggage—thirty-eight boxes and trunks filled with clothing, books, papers, prints and paintings, sculptures, furniture, and other personal effects (most of which belonged to Jefferson)—Jefferson intended to return to France after his furlough. The Jefferson entourage was delayed leaving France but eventually landed in Norfolk on November 23. Jefferson learned of his nomination as secretary of state soon after his arrival in Virginia. On December 15 he wrote to Washington informing him of his desire to return to his post in Paris while leaving open the possibility of accepting his appointment, "It is not for an individual to chuse his post. You are to marshal us as may be best for the public good." Jefferson turned the question back on the president, asking him to "be so good only as to signify to me by another line your ultimate wish, and I shall conform to it cordially."[3]

Washington must have been exasperated by Jefferson's indecisiveness. Over the Christmas holidays, Madison visited Monticello and urged Jefferson to accept the appointment. In late January Washington wrote to Jefferson, "I consider the Office of Secretary for the Department of State as very important on many accounts: and I know of no person, who, in my judgment, could better execute the Duties of it than yourself." Washington held Jefferson in such high esteem that he repeatedly entreated him to accept the appointment. Jefferson had tried Washington's patience as few men had done. On February 14 Jefferson finally accepted the role. He remained in Virginia for the marriage of his oldest daughter, Patsy, then seventeen years old, to Thomas Mann Randolph Jr., a planter and distant kinsman, on February 23. (Jefferson gave the couple a thousand acres of land and twenty-seven enslaved persons comprising six separate families.) He did not arrive in New York to join the cabinet until March 21, 1790.[4]

Over the course of the three decades they knew each other, Washington and Jefferson probably enjoyed their closest friendship during Washington's first term as president. By 1789 they had come to have a genuine affection and respect for each other. Despite this, Jefferson was an outsider in the Washington administration. He was the only cabinet secretary who hadn't served in the Continental Army during the war. Moreover, owing to his late arrival in New York, he joined the government six months after his confirmation by the Senate and nearly eleven months after Washington's inauguration; Jefferson had to quickly try to get up to speed both with his own brief as secretary of state and with the general business of the government. Beyond the personal and practical circumstances that rendered Jefferson an outlier in the administration were incipient political and ideological differences. Prior to Washington's presidency, these hadn't been a major obstacle in the relationship between the two men. During the forty-five months Jefferson served as Washington's secretary of state, the political differences between the two men became more pronounced. These differences mirrored (and fueled) the intense partisanship that came to divide the United States during the same period.

Soon after Jefferson's arrival in New York, he and Washington began to consult each other regularly on matters relating to the State Department.

On March 23 the two men discussed the size and scope of the American diplomatic presence in Europe. They returned to the subject several days later. Based on their discussions, Jefferson prepared a plan for Washington to bolster the number of American diplomats abroad and to provide them with greater financial support. He provided the president with three options, ranging in cost from just under $37,000 to a little less than $50,000, which would provide for an American minister plenipotentiary in Paris and chargés des affaires in London, Madrid, and Lisbon with an agent in Amsterdam. The more expensive plan would have put a full minister in London as well. Having represented the United States in Europe's most important capital, Jefferson was aware of just how limited his budget had been, and his plan provided for administrative support as well as a budget for clothing. Washington supported Jefferson's plan—though he objected to providing American diplomats with stationery. After negotiations with congressional leaders, Congress approved most of Jefferson's plan, allocating $40,000 to support US diplomats abroad for the coming year.[5]

In this early exchange, Washington and Jefferson established an amicable working pattern, built on their previous friendship and experience, that would serve them well for most of Jefferson's tenure as secretary of state. When working together on an issue, the two men often exchanged ideas, sometimes in writing, but often in person. Jefferson would submit plans or drafts of letters (especially relating to sensitive diplomatic matters) for Washington's consideration. Washington consulted Jefferson when preparing major addresses such as his annual reports to Congress. The two men would meet, occasionally over breakfast, to discuss the drafts and other matters of importance.[6] For example, on Sunday, August 21, 1791, after the capital had moved from New York to Philadelphia, Washington wrote to invite Jefferson to join him early the next morning for breakfast and then to go and view a new threshing machine at the home of Samuel Powell, the president of Philadelphia's agricultural society. Washington included letters for Jefferson, noting, "When you have read the enclosed letters, I will converse with you on the subject of them," with the implication that Jefferson would have done so by the next morning.[7] The encounter, mixing business and pleasure—the two men shared interests in agriculture and technology, and Washington appreciated that Jefferson would want to see Powell's new thresher—was typical of the encounters that Washington and Jefferson had during Washington's presidency.

With the benefit of hindsight, we can see the fissures in the foundation of the Washington administration. On the very day that Jefferson, at Monticello, wrote to accept his appointment as secretary of state, James Madison wrote to him from New York informing his friend, "The Report of Mr. Hamilton, has been, of late, the principal subject of debate."[8] In January 1790 the Treasury secretary had submitted a *Report on Public Credit* to Congress. Hamilton's report, intended to address the serious debt problem that confronted the new government, was also a statement of Hamilton's political and financial philosophy and his vision for the future political and economic development of the United States. It set him at odds with Jefferson, dividing Washington's cabinet and the nation.

Hamilton, who had married a wealthy heiress, Elizabeth Schuyler, and established a lucrative legal practice in New York after serving with distinction during the war, had long been a proponent of consolidating political power in a strong central government. An early supporter of constitutional reform, he had been one of the few men who attended the Annapolis Convention. The following year at the Constitutional Convention, he gave a lengthy address extolling the virtues of the British constitution and the merits of monarchical rule. During the debates over the ratification of the Constitution he, along with his fellow New Yorker, John Jay, and James Madison collaborated to produce a series of eighty-five newspaper essays (later collected as *The Federalist*, familiar to modern readers as *The Federalist Papers*) supporting and explaining the proposed constitution. As one of Washington's aides, Hamilton had demonstrated a capacity for hard work and intelligence as well as a sharp grasp of financial matters.[9]

Hamilton faced a huge task when he became treasury secretary. In 1789 the new government's debt was more than $50 million. Approximately $11.7 million was owed to creditors in the Netherlands, France, and Spain, who had financed the War of Independence. The balance, around $40 million, was owed to American citizens who held bonds and securities issued by Congress to pay for the war. Many of these had originally been issued to soldiers who, in the face of economic uncertainty during the 1780s, had sold them at drastically reduced rates to speculators. In his *Report on Public Credit*, Hamilton proposed that the whole debt—foreign and domestic (with interest)—should be paid with federal funds derived from taxes and loans from a new national bank (modeled on the Bank of England). Although many in Congress, including his former ally, Madison, criticized the speculators who had purchased public securities after the war, Hamilton felt it was crucial to the success of the new government that it win the loyalty of such men, as they would guarantee the future financial security of the United States. Hamilton believed the new government needed the support of the merchants, lawyers, financiers, and manufacturers who possessed capital and speculated in public securities. These were the men the government would need to borrow from in the future, and he sought to wed their economic interests to those of the new federal government.[10]

One of the most important elements of the *Report on Public Credit* was a proposal that the federal government should not only pay its own debts but also it should assume the outstanding war debts of the various states in the union. Hamilton's proposal was controversial because if the federal government took on the debts of the various states, citizens of those states (mainly in the South) that had already retired their debts would be required to raise taxes to pay off the unpaid debts of other states. This was a crucial feature of Hamilton's plan because the Treasury secretary believed it would strengthen the national government by striking at the roots of state sovereignty and independence. In the *Report on Public Credit*, Hamilton laid the cornerstone for a program that would transform the nation by undermining state sovereignty and marrying the wealthy to the interests of a strong federal government.

Hamilton's fiscal program was anathema to Jefferson, who feared that its social and political consequences would undermine America's republican experiment. Jefferson's experience in Europe had taught him that an economy based on commercial manufacturing (Hamilton believed the United States should emulate Britain and promote manufacturing) was incompatible with republicanism. Manufacturing, Jefferson observed when traveling in France and England, depended on a large class of propertyless laborers who were normally poor and ignorant. Such men and women were not fit to maintain republican government. "The mobs of great cities add just so much to the support of pure government," he wrote in the *Notes on the State of Virginia*, "as sores do to the strength of the human body. It is the manners and spirit of a people which preserve a republic in vigor. A degeneracy in these is a canker which soon eats at the heart of its laws and constitution." While Jefferson accepted that some manufacturing was necessary to service the agricultural economy in the United States, he believed that if the nation was to nurture its fragile republican institutions, then its economy should be based on commercial agriculture. He believed that so long as most of the American citizens (white males, of course; he did not equate the enslaved propertyless laborers in the United States with those poor Europeans laboring in manufacturing) owned their own property, the American republic would flourish. The republic's citizens would thrive, economically and politically, enjoying liberty and prosperity, only so long as they tilled their own land and exported their surpluses to feed hungry Europeans and enslaved laborers in the Caribbean. Jefferson envisioned a nation of independent citizen-farmers who owned their own land. For Jefferson, the American republic could only endure if its economy was predominantly agricultural and power was decentralized. While Jefferson accepted that the Confederation government had been unfit for purpose, he believed that the states should retain as much authority as possible. Republican institutions were strongest when citizens were closest to the loci of power.[11] Given their ideological differences, it is not surprising that Jefferson and Hamilton would find themselves at odds within the Washington administration.

Although Jefferson and Hamilton would come to detest each other, they did manage to collaborate productively (and famously) at the beginning of Jefferson's tenure as secretary of state. One day in mid-June 1790, soon after their possible fishing trip, Jefferson ran into Hamilton outside of Washington's residence in lower Manhattan. According to Jefferson's later account of the encounter, the Treasury secretary looked "sombre, haggard, and dejected beyond description." Jefferson said of the usually stylish Hamilton, "Even his dress [was] uncouth and neglected." The two men stood on Broadway by the president's front door and discussed Hamilton's financial plans, especially his proposal that the federal government should assume the debts of the states. The proposal had met with opposition in the House of Representatives and was dividing the nation along regional lines with the states in the Northeast (which had the largest debts and would most benefit from the federal assumption of their debts) pitted against those from the South (which had largely paid off their war debts). Hamilton told Jefferson that he feared that the union might break up over the issue and appealed to him as a Virginian to "interest my friends from the

South" in supporting the proposal. Jefferson averred that he was unfamiliar with the circumstances concerning the debt assumption because he had only "lately returned" to the country and the "fiscal system being out of my department." Nonetheless, he sought to foster a reconciliation between Hamilton and Madison (who was leading the opposition to Hamilton's program in Congress). "On considering the situation of things," Jefferson recalled, "I thought the first step towards some conciliation of views would be to bring Mr. Madison and Colo. Hamilton to a friendly discussion on the subject." Jefferson invited both men to dine with him the next day at his "indifferent" residence on Maiden Lane, believing "that men of sound heads and honest views needed nothing more than explanation and mutual understanding to enable them to unite in some measures which might enable us to get along."[12]

The debate over the assumption of state debts wasn't the only issue stuck in Congress at the time. The new Constitution called on Congress to identify a permanent "Seat of the Government" for the United States. Various proposals had stalled in Congress as local boosters promoted cities and towns in their states as the possible capital of the new republic. Virginians advocated for a site along the Potomac, near the village of Georgetown. Jefferson and Washington, of course, had long envisioned making Alexandria the major entrepôt for east-west trade in the United States. Shifting the capital south from New York would facilitate such a development, particularly if the Potomac site was chosen. It would also be more convenient to Virginians in the national government such as Jefferson, Washington, and Madison.

Madison and Hamilton joined Jefferson for dinner the next day (Jefferson normally ate dinner, the largest meal of the day, around four in the afternoon). There were no other guests in attendance, though the men might have been attended by Jacob Cooke, a servant employed by Jefferson, and their meal was likely prepared by the enslaved James Hemings, who had trained as chef while he was in Paris with Jefferson.[13] According to Jefferson, over dinner Madison agreed that although he would continue to oppose the bill on the assumption of state debts, "he should not be strenuous" in his opposition, and he would no longer block its progress through Congress. "It was observed," Jefferson wrote, "I forget by which of them, that as the pill was would be a bitter one to the Southern states, something should be done to soothe them; that the removal of the seat of government to the Patowmac was a just measure, and would probably be popular with them, and would be a proper one to follow the assumption."[14] This was the famous "dinner table bargain," according to the terms of which the southern congressmen would agree to the federal assumption of state debts in exchange for the movement of the capital to the south, first to Philadelphia in December 1790, and then to the banks of the Potomac in 1800. The main elements of this compromise had been discussed by several politicians prior to the dinner at Jefferson's. Nonetheless, the agreement, and the means by which it was reached, demonstrated that, at least at the beginning of Jefferson's time as secretary of state, he and Hamilton could work together productively. The deadlock over the assumption of debts and the location of the capital was broken, and Congress passed the relevant legislation in July and August.[15]

With the passage of the assumption act in August, Congress had enacted the key elements of Hamilton's *Report on Public Credit*. This was the first step in Hamilton's plan to marry the federal government to the commercial and manufacturing interests of the United States. In the coming months, he would propose additional elements to that program. In January 1791 he introduced a bill to create a national bank, the Bank of the United States, which would combine public and private investment and hold government funds. The government would not only deposit its funds in the bank but also borrow from it, thereby binding the wealthy who would invest in the bank to the interests of the government. In December 1791 Hamilton issued yet another lengthy paper, the *Report on Manufactures*, which argued that the United States should promote manufacturing by providing protected markets for American products and capital and support for infant American industries. Taken together, the *Report on Public Credit*, the Bank Bill, and the *Report on Manufactures* indicate that Hamilton was attempting to create a union of centralized economic and political power in the United States.[16]

Though Jefferson accepted Hamilton's proposals to establish control over public credit, he would oppose the Bank Bill (which he believed was unconstitutional) and the elements of the *Report on Manufactures* because he distrusted their social and political consequences. He feared that concentrating economic and political power in a class of financiers and manufacturers posed a danger to republican government in the United States. As he later wrote to Washington concerning Hamilton (after he and the Treasury secretary had become completely estranged), "His system flowed from principles adverse to liberty, and was calculated to undermine and demolish the republic." In the same letter he acknowledged that he had cooperated with Hamilton over the assumption of state debts but conceded, "I was duped by the Secretary of the treasury, and made a tool for forwarding his schemes, not then sufficiently understood by me; and of all the errors of my political life, this has occasioned me the deepest regret." Nearly three decades later, after the deaths of both Washington and Hamilton, Jefferson explained that his support for the assumption of state debts was motivated by "the preservation of the union & a concord among the states," but he claimed that supporters of Hamilton's program, "monarchists in principle" that he described as a "mercenary phalanx," were committed to undermining republican principles and undermining the Constitution, "to be warped in practice into all the principles and pollutants of their favorite English model."[17]

<hr>

Although Jefferson came to look back on the dinner table bargain with regret, that meal had, at least in the short term, positive consequences for his relationship with Washington. Both men were enthusiastic supporters of the decision to create a new capital on the banks of the Potomac, and they worked closely together on the project throughout Jefferson's tenure as secretary of state. They consulted each other on myriad matters relating to the design and building of what they called the Federal City, including selecting (and eventually firing) an engineer, former French soldier Pierre Charles L'Enfant, who would create a grand original design for the city, and the commissioners charged with overseeing the project. They exchanged more than forty letters relating to the new capital between June 1790 and the end of December 1793, when Jefferson resigned as secretary of state—more than on any single subject. They discussed everything from the site of the city to its layout and the design of the public buildings and the financing of the project. While there were many vexing aspects of the enterprise—from fundraising to managing difficult personalities—both Washington and Jefferson, keen self-taught architects who had designed and expanded their own homes, relished the project. The design and building of the Federal City, soon to be named after Washington, was an project that Washington and Jefferson undertook together with a shared passion that, in many respects, marked the happiest and most productive collaboration between the two men during the three decades they knew each other. Indeed, in late 1790 and early 1791, the men were acting so closely on the new federal capital that Jefferson often spoke for Washington, writing on his behalf to merchants in Georgetown as well as to L'Enfant and Andrew Ellicott, who would survey the district. Jefferson drafted the proclamation that Washington issued announcing the location of the capital along the Potomac.[18]

Even as they worked together to ensure that the new capital would sit on the banks of the Potomac, we can see hints of the differences between the two men. For Washington, the new city was to be a truly national capital. It would be the physical manifestation of his vision for the new republic, the capital of a united country, a union whose whole was greater than the sum of its parts. The creation of the separate federal district, the District of Columbia, carved out of territory from Virginia and Maryland, but not part of any state, was symbolic of this. When he wrote to Washington seeking the appointment to design the new city (even before the Potomac site was selected), L'Enfant gave voice to Washington's vision for the new city. He described the proposed new city as "the capital of this vast Empire." L'Enfant, a veteran of the Continental Army and a member of the Society of Cincinnati, understood the nationalist vision of the revolution that was central to Washington's thinking and appealed directly to it (which partially explains Washington's desire to retain L'Enfant's services even after he proved troublesome). The new federal city would be convenient for Washington, located as it was only a dozen miles from Mount Vernon, but he convinced himself that the location was best for the national interest (particularly given his hope that the Potomac could be the key to connecting the Ohio River valley to the Atlantic).[19]

For Jefferson, skeptical about Hamilton's desire to centralize power in the new government, the capital should serve a different purpose. He hoped that its location along the Potomac would separate it from the financial interests in New York and Philadelphia and would perpetuate Virginia's political preeminence in the new republic. Indeed, he wished that the new city would enhance Virginia's economic power. He wrote shortly after his dinner with Hamilton and Madison that he hoped relocating the capital to the Potomac "will vivify our agriculture and commerce by circulating thro' our state an additional sum every year of half a million dollars." For Jefferson, the location of the new capital would be a bulwark against Hamilton's consolidating, centralizing tendencies. The differences between Washington and Jefferson with respect to the role and purpose of the new capital manifested themselves in their plans for the city. Washington embraced L'Enfant's ambitious vision of an extensive city of wide boulevards and large public spaces that would make a statement about the nation it served. Jefferson, ambivalent about the moral and political consequences of large cities, initially favored a smaller city that might grow over time.[20] Despite these differences Jefferson and Washington worked together effectively, and happily, on most matters relating to the new capital.

———

The increasing enmity between his two most important aides could not escape Washington's notice. The supporters of Washington and his administration called themselves "Federalists" because they supported the new federal government.[21] Their opponents, who went by various names, were often dubbed "Republicans" and coalesced in opposition to the Federalists in Congress and, in the case of Thomas Jefferson, within the Washington administration itself. It would be wrong to think of the Federalists and Republicans of the early 1790s as formal political parties. Rather, they were uneasy, informal coalitions. Nonetheless, the disputes within the government eventually spread beyond the cabinet and Congress thanks to the power of an increasingly partisan press.[22]

In late February 1792, the president invited Jefferson to speak to him prior to his weekly levee, which he held on Tuesday afternoons, receiving members of the public. Jefferson, delayed by his own work at the State Department, was running late and only had a few minutes to speak to the president. He suggested reform of the post office; ostensibly he wanted to improve the daily speed and distance covered by post riders. His ulterior, but more important, motive was to remove the post office from the control of the Treasury Department and place it under the aegis of the State Department. Jefferson told Washington "that the department of the treasury possessed already such influence as to swallow up the whole Executive powers, and that even future Presidents (not supported by the weight of character which himself possessed) would not be able to make head against this department." Jefferson assured Washington that he was not seeking personal aggrandizement because he would not serve in office much longer, as he expected to retire when Washington left office, which he believed would be when his term of office concluded in early 1793. Before the men could continue their conversation, Washington was called to attend the levee. He invited Jefferson to have breakfast with him the next day to continue their discussion.[23]

Jefferson returned the next day and had breakfast with Washington. After they ate, the two men retired to Washington's office to discuss Jefferson's plans to reform the post office. After listening to Jefferson, Washington asked the secretary of state to present his plans to him in writing. Having dispensed with their formal business, Washington, speaking in "an affectionate tone," asked Jefferson about his intention to leave office when Washington did. According to Jefferson's notes of the conversation, Washington recounted his long years of public service and cited his declining health and stated that his intention had only been "to take part in the new government and get it under way." Ever concerned about his reputation, Washington feared that if he sought to remain in office, "it might give room to say that having tasted the sweets of office he could not do without them." Nonetheless, he hoped that the "great officers of the government" would not demit office when he did, as that "might produce a shock in the public mind of dangerous consequence." Jefferson averred that he had not intended to serve as secretary of state for any longer than Washington's presidential term. Jefferson claimed that he didn't believe that Hamilton intended to give up office. Indeed, according to Jefferson, Hamilton had manipulated his fiscal program to extend his power through corruption while undermining the Constitution. Washington did not agree with Jefferson's characterization of Hamilton, but he expressed concern that "tho' the government had set out with a pretty general good will of the public, yet that symptoms of dissatisfaction had lately shewn themselves far beyond what he could have expected."[24]

Jefferson shared Washington's concerns in the spring of 1792. In late May he wrote to Washington, "The public mind is no longer so confident and serene; and that from causes in which you are in no ways personally mixed." Jefferson was keen to assure the president that he bore no responsibility for the popular dissatisfaction, and he sought to persuade Washington to run for reelection later in the year. Jefferson failed to acknowledge his own responsibility for the increasing partisanship in the country. Rather, he placed the blame at the feet of Hamilton. He repeated the argument he had made earlier that the treasury secretary's fiscal program was corrupting the government. Jefferson explained "that the ultimate object of all this is to prepare the way for a change, from the present republican form of government, to that of a monarchy, of which the English constitution is to be the model." He reminded Washington that unnamed "partisans" (referring to Hamilton) had expressed admiration for the British constitution at the Constitutional Convention. Jefferson feared that the American republic might collapse in the face of the threat. He implored Washington to save the nation: "The confidence of the whole union is centered in you," he wrote. "Your being at the helm, will be more than an answer to every argument which can be used to alarm and lead the people in any quarter to violence or secession."[25]

Washington did not immediately respond to Jefferson's letter. Indeed, his desire to retire after a single term was so strong that he put off discussing the possibility of running for another term (which he would certainly win) "because the subject was painful." The two men didn't discuss whether Washington should extend his presidency by another term until July 10. Washington acknowledged that changed circumstances might require him to remain in office, but, ever concerned about his reputation, he feared "it would be said his former professions of retirement had been mere affectation, and that he was like other men, when once in office he could not quit it." Washington then told Jefferson "that with respect to the existing causes of uneasiness, he thought that there were suspicions against a particular party [Hamilton] which had been carried a great deal too far." He did not believe there was a serious plan to overthrow the American republic and replace it with a monarchy. Although he conceded "that there might be a few who wished it in the higher walks of life, particularly in the great cities. But that the main body of the people in the Eastern [New England] states were as steady for republicanism as in the Southern." The two men discussed Jefferson's assertion that Hamilton's fiscal policies were corrupting the government, but Washington denied this. "Finding him really approving the treasury system," Jefferson recalled, "I avoided entering into an argument with him on those points."[26]

The conversation between Washington and Jefferson on July 10, 1792, hints at the future estrangement between the two men. While Washington took seriously Jefferson's advice as to whether he should stand for a second term, he also pushed back against the secretary of state's assessment of Hamilton's fiscal and political program. Indeed, he endorsed and embraced that program as his own. He conceded that there was discord in the country but blamed those who opposed the administration's policies. He particularly cited "the peices lately published, . . . seemed to have in view exciting opposition to the government." Washington did not accept that distinction that Jefferson and other Republicans attempted to make between Hamilton's policies and his administration. Jefferson recalled, "He considered those papers as attacking him directly, for he must be a fool indeed to swallow the little sugar plumbs here and there thrown out to him. That in condemning the administration of the government they condemned him, for if they thought there were measures pursued contrary to his sentiment, they must conceive him too careless to attend to them or too stupid to understand them. That tho indeed he had signed many acts which he did not approve in all their parts, yet he had never put his name to one which he did not think on the whole was eligible." Washington, aware that Jefferson was sponsoring press attacks on his administration, sent a clear signal to Jefferson that he favored Hamilton.[27]

Washington, nonetheless, took the secretary of state's criticisms of Hamilton seriously. In late July he wrote a letter to Hamilton in which he quoted, nearly verbatim, Jefferson's criticisms of the treasury secretary. Unwilling, perhaps, to fuel the growing antagonism between the two secretaries, Washington didn't name Jefferson as the source of criticisms (rather, he suggested that they originated with his neighbor, George Mason). Hamilton, as was his wont, wrote a very lengthy response to rebut the charges (it takes up thirty pages in the modern edition of Hamilton's writings). Washington seems to have found Hamilton more persuasive than Jefferson (he did not share Hamilton's defense with Jefferson as he had Jefferson's attack with Hamilton), and he wrote to both men urging them to work together for the good of the country. "My earnest wish, and my fondest hope," he wrote to Jefferson, "is, that instead of wounding suspicions, and irritable charges, there may be liberal allowances—mutual forbearances— and temporising yieldings on <u>all sides</u>. Under the exercise of these, matters will go on smoothly, and, if possible, more prosperously. Without them every thing must rub, the wheels of Government will clog—our enemies will triumph—and by throwing their weight into the disaffected Scale, may accomplish the Ruin of the goodly fabric we have been erecting." While Jefferson believed that the American experiment with republican government would fail if Hamilton's program prevailed, Washington feared internal strife was a greater danger.[28]

Despite Washington's injunction, Jefferson and Hamilton continued to wage war in the press. In August 1792 Hamilton published several anonymous essays attacking Jefferson under the pseudonym "An American" in the *Gazette of the United States* (a paper friendly to the administration). On September 9 Jefferson wrote a lengthy response to Washington's call for comity. Jefferson dropped all pretense and mentioned Hamilton explicitly. He addressed Hamilton's charges against him in the "American" essays, "for neither the stile, matter, nor venom of the pieces alluded to can leave a doubt of their author." Jefferson did not pull his punches in offering his critique of Hamilton; he remained convinced that "his system flowed from principles adverse to liberty, and was calculated to undermine and demolish the republic, by creating an influence of his department over the members of legislature." This was the same charge that Jefferson had made repeatedly without effect in conversation and in writing with Washington over the previous months. He mentioned his desire to retire but wrote, "I will not suffer my retirement to be clouded by the slanders of a man whose history, from the moment at which history can stoop to notice him, is a tissue of machinations against the liberty of the country which has not only received and given him bread but heaped it's honors on his head."[29]

By the summer of 1792, Jefferson and Hamilton had come to loathe each other. Each believed the other was a threat to the republic. They agreed on just one thing: that only Washington could keep the nation united in the face of the dangerous designs of their political enemies. They succeeded in persuading the reluctant president to accept another term. Jefferson must have been concerned that he was in danger of losing the president's trust. Although Washington had appealed to both Jefferson and Hamilton to set aside their differences for the good of the country, he expressed a clear preference for Hamilton's policies, which he endorsed, and did not share Jefferson's concern that they endangered the republic. Over the final year of Jefferson's time as secretary of state, the two men would continue to work together productively, especially in the realm of foreign relations, but they did so against the backdrop of increasing strain in their relationship.

Soon after Washington's inauguration in April 1789, the Estates General began meeting at Versailles to discuss tax reform in France. As in British North America during the 1760s and 1770s, questions of taxation eventually led to revolution. In July a crowd stormed the Bastille, a prison in Paris, which was a symbol of the authority of Louis XVI. Jefferson was in Paris at the time and welcomed these events. He collaborated with some of the moderate revolutionaries, including the Marquis de Lafayette, helping to draft the Declaration of the Rights of Man and the Citizen, which the National Assembly adopted in August. Jefferson always believed that the American and French Revolutions were part of a global republican movement. In his 1821 autobiography, he wrote of them as a single event, "As yet we are but in the first chapter of it's history. The appeal to the rights of man, which had been made in the U S. was taken up by France, first of the European nations. From her the spirit has spread over those of the South. The tyrants of the North have allied indeed against it, but it is irresistible."[30] Jefferson spoke for many of his fellow citizens at the beginning of the French Revolution. Many Americans saw in the French Revolution echoes of their own struggle for independence and self-government.

American support for the French Revolution began to splinter in early 1793. The execution of Louis XVI and Marie Antoinette in January followed by the Reign of Terror and the French declaration of war on Britain on February 1 alienated many Federalists who distinguished between the bloody disorder they associated with the events in France, which they contrasted with the American Revolution. Like Hamilton's fiscal program, the French Revolution engendered intense partisan divisions in the United States, and within the Washington administration.

The upsurge in violence in France divided Americans. The Federalist supporters of the Washington administration saw in the bloodshed the results of mob rule and anarchy, which threatened order, the rule of law, and civilization. Even during the early days of the French Revolution, Washington urged caution. "The revolution which has been effected in France is of so wonderful a nature that the mind can hardly realise the fact," he wrote in October 1789. "If it ends as our last accounts to the first of August predict that nation will be the most powerful and happy in Europe; but I fear though it has gone triumphantly through the first paroxysm, it is not the last it has to encounter before matters are finally settled." He continued, "In a word the revolution is of too great magnitude to be effected in so short a space, and with the loss of so little blood," and he urged the National Assembly to exercise "great temperance, firmness, and foresight" to avoid violence. The administration's opponents lamented the violence in France but saw it as a minor distraction and small price to pay for republicanism to triumph in Europe's most powerful nation. In January 1793 Jefferson wrote to his former secretary, William Short, then the American minister in The Hague. In a prior letter Short had informed Jefferson about the "September Massacres" in Paris, during which more than a thousand prisoners had been killed by revolutionary guards. Although the death of innocents was regrettable, Jefferson saw them as necessary sacrifices. "The liberty of the whole earth was depending on the issue of the contest, and was ever such a prize won with so little innocent blood?" he asked. He continued, "My own affections have been deeply wounded by some of the martyrs to this cause, but rather it should have failed, I would have seen half the earth desolated. Were there but an Adam and Eve left in every country, and left free, it would be better than as it now is."[31]

Notwithstanding the ideological and political differences that the French Revolution engendered in the United States, the outbreak of war between Britain and France in early 1793 demanded a diplomatic response from the United States. Unconfirmed rumors of war reached Philadelphia in March, and Jefferson, as the secretary of state, turned his mind to how the United States should respond to the conflict. He gave some indication of his thinking in a letter on March 24, "Amidst the confusions of a general war which seem to be threatening that quarter of the globe [Europe]," he wrote, "we hope to be permitted to preserve the line of neutrality. We wish not to meddle with the internal affairs of any country, nor with the general affairs of Europe. Peace with all nations, and the rights which that gives us with respect to all nations, are our objects." Jefferson believed the United States should remain neutral while still maintaining its treaty obligations to France under the terms of the 1778 alliance between the two countries.[32]

Official confirmation of the war between Britain and France reached Philadelphia in early April. On April 18 Washington sent the members of his cabinet a series of thirteen questions regarding how the United States should respond to the European conflict. This was his standard practice when questions of policy were at stake. The president's questions focused on whether the United States should issue a formal declaration of neutrality and what its obligations to France were under the 1778 treaty. Jefferson believed that Hamilton was behind the questions, which he felt encouraged the members of the cabinet to repudiate the Franco-American alliance. Although the questions had issued from Washington's pen, "the language was Hamilton's and the doubts his alone," complained Jefferson.[33]

Washington met with the cabinet at his home at the corner of Sixth and Market Streets in Philadelphia at nine the next morning. The cabinet unanimously agreed that Washington should issue a proclamation prohibiting American citizens from taking part in any hostilities involving the belligerent European parties. It also agreed unanimously that the administration should accept a minister from the French government. There was a prolonged discussion and disagreement over whether that minister should be accepted without restrictions. That discussion took so long that the cabinet secretaries never got to the issue of whether the United States was obligated to uphold its treaty obligations to France. Jefferson disagreed profoundly with his colleagues over the neutrality proclamation. He argued that since Congress had the authority to declare war, only it could formally issue "a declaration that there should be no war." Hamilton, Henry Knox, and Edmund Randolph all took the view that Washington could issue such a proclamation. Jefferson, hoping to maintain support on the French treaty and accepting a French emissary in the United States, gave ground on the question of the constitutionality of the neutrality proclamation.[34]

The question whether to accept a French minister proved to be a much thornier issue. Accepting an emissary without restrictions could be interpreted as upholding the 1778 treaty between France and the United States, while placing conditions on the envoy might be seen as a repudiation of that pact. Jefferson and Randolph argued in favor of accepting the minister without restrictions while Hamilton and Knox opposed doing so. The cabinet could not resolve its position on the matter, even after it reconvened, and Washington eventually asked its members to submit their views to him in writing on that matter as well as on the treaty with France so he could make a decision. Jefferson submitted a lengthy opinion to the president on April 28. He argued that the 1778 treaty was a compact between two nations and not their governments and that repudiating it would be seen by the French not as an act of neutrality but as a declaration of war. He argued that accepting a French minister without restrictions was irrelevant beside the larger question of honoring the treaty.[35] Hamilton and Knox submitted a joint opinion to the president on March 2. They argued that the overthrow and execution of Louis XVI nullified the 1778 treaty. Upholding the treaty in the absence of what they deemed to be a stable government in France would be tantamount to a declaration of war on Britain. Jefferson complained several days later that Hamilton was "panick struck if we refuse our breach to every kick which G. Brit. may chuse to give it. He is for proclaiming at once the most abject principles, such as would invite and merit habitual insults [from Britain]."[36]

Attorney General Randolph submitted his opinion to Washington on May 6. He argued that the 1778 treaty was still binding and that the United States should accept a French minister without restrictions. Washington weighed the responses from his secretaries and decided that the United States should continue to honor the 1778 treaty and that his administration would receive a French envoy without restriction. Despite Jefferson's fears that Washington was in thrall to Hamilton, the president had sided with him on a key matter relating to foreign policy.

While Washington's cabinet deliberated over whether and how to receive a new French minister, the emissary in question had already arrived in the United States in early April. Edmond Charles Genêt was a charming, handsome thirty-year-old, well connected with the ruling Girondin faction then in power in Paris. The son of an interpreter who had served at Versailles during the old regime, Genêt was fluent in English and had served in the French legation at Saint Petersburg before going to America. Gouverneur Morris, the American minister in Paris, reported to Washington that Genêt had annoyed his Russian hosts as well as other French diplomats in Saint Petersburg because of his outspoken support for the French Revolution and was expelled from the country. Genêt had enough support in Paris that he was allowed to pick his next assignment. "He chose America, *as being the best Harbor during the Storm* and," wrote Morris, "*he will not put to Sea again untill it is fair Weather*, let what will happen."[37]

Morris was speaking metaphorically, but poor weather and contrary winds delayed Genêt's arrival and blew him off course. He arrived in Charleston, South Carolina, rather than Philadelphia on April 8, 1793. The diplomat bore wide-ranging orders from his government instructing him to foment rebellions among settlers in Louisiana, the Floridas, and Quebec to overthrow Spanish and British rule, to raise an army among American settlers and Native people in border areas to attack the Spanish, to seek the full repayment of the US debt to France from the War of Independence, and to commission and outfit French privateers in American ports to attack the British in the West Indies. Despite Washington's intention to declare the United States neutral, Genêt intended to wage war against British territories and interests in North America and the Caribbean, effectively making the United States an ally in France's war against Britain.[38]

Encouraged by a warm welcome in Charleston, Genêt took a leisurely, triumphant journey to Philadelphia, enjoying the adulation of those Americans who still supported the French Revolution. He also commissioned French-flagged privateers with American crews to wage war against British shipping in the West Indies. Genêt did not arrive in Philadelphia until May 16.[39] While Genêt was on the road, Washington had issued his neutrality proclamation and had decided that the minister should be received without restriction. Genêt believed that his actions were in keeping with the spirit of the 1778 treaty between the United States and France (Benjamin Franklin had commissioned and outfitted rebel privateers in France during the War of Independence). Washington's position, which Jefferson supported, was that the United States should honor the 1778 treaty, especially the commercial agreement between the two nations, but that it should take no action to violate its neutrality. The administration's position was that the 1778 military agreement did not apply because it was a defensive treaty and France had declared war on Britain in 1793.

Genêt presented his credentials to President Washington on May 18. Jefferson initially had a positive reaction to the envoy. "He offers every thing and asks nothing," he wrote the next day. Within days the new French minister would bombard the secretary of state with requests: asking the United States to repay some of its outstanding debts to France, proposing to renegotiate the terms of the alliance between the two countries, and asserting that the French might wage war against Britain from American ports. Jefferson informed Genêt that the United States would not make an advance payment on its debt to France.[40] Still, he was sympathetic to the Frenchman and his cause. Although Jefferson believed that the United States should formally remain neutral in the European conflict, he also held that it should assist France in any way it could while maintaining its neutrality. As he wrote to Washington, "I think it is very material myself to keep alive the friendly sentiments of that country as far as can be done without risking war."[41]

Genêt, frustrated at his inability to mobilize the US government to take more robust action in support of the French war effort, threatened to appeal to the American people directly (grossly exaggerating his own influence, particularly in contrast to that of the president). In July, while Washington was visiting Mount Vernon, Genêt sent a French privateer to sea out of Philadelphia against the express wishes of Jefferson. Washington was furious. "What must the World think of such conduct, and of the Government of the U. States in submitting to it?" he fumed. He returned to Philadelphia and convened a cabinet meeting on July 23. Washington decided that Jefferson should write to the French government, forwarding the minister's correspondence with the various members of Washington's administration, "with a temperate but strong representation of his conduct, drawing a clear line between him and his nation, expressing our friendship to the latter but insisting on the recall of Genêt, and in the mean time that we should desire him either to withdraw or cease his functions." Jefferson labored over his letter for several weeks, sharing drafts with president and cabinet as he sought to strike a balance between outlining Genêt's misconduct and asserting American neutrality while declaring abiding American affection and gratitude toward France. On August 23 Jefferson sent the letter, with Genêt's correspondence to Gouverneur Morris. The Girondin government in Paris had been overthrown by the Jacobins in June 1793. The new government promised to recall and punish Genêt, which likely meant that he would be sent to the guillotine. Genêt eventually requested asylum from President Washington, which he received; he then married and lived in New York until his death in 1834.[42]

During the Genêt controversy, the cabinet had worked together productively. Although Jefferson felt that Hamilton and Knox were too inclined to distrust France (they believed that Jefferson was too credulous with Genêt), the president and secretary of state agreed that Genêt had gone too far and that American neutrality must be maintained. Nonetheless, the strain of more than three years' service in an administration in which he increasingly felt at odds had taken a toll on Jefferson. On July 31 he wrote to Washington, revisiting the subject of his retirement. Although he had postponed his resignation when Washington decided (at Jefferson's urging) to serve a second term, Jefferson informed the president that he intended to retire at the end of September, "to scenes of greater tranquility, from those which I am every more and more convinced that neither my talents, tone of mind, nor time of life fit me." A week later Washington visited Jefferson at the home he rented outside of Philadelphia during the summer. According to Jefferson's notes, Washington, undoubtedly frustrated, "expressed his repentance at not having resigned himself, and how much it was increased by seeing that he was to be deserted by those on whose aid he had counted." Washington was further concerned about the rising partisanship in the country, "the fermentation which seemed to be working in the minds of the public, that many descriptions of persons, actuated by different causes appeared to be uniting, what it would end in he knew not."[43]

The president was alarmed at the increasing Republican hostility in the press and in Congress. Jefferson, by contrast, felt that the Federalist supporters of Hamilton's fiscal policies had made life unbearable for him. He explained, "I expressed to him my excessive repugnance to public life, the particular uneasiness of my situation in this place where the laws of society oblige me to move always exactly in the circle which I know to bear me peculiar hatred, that is to say the wealthy Aristocrats, the Merchants connected closely with England, the new created paper fortunes that thus surrounded, my words were caught, multiplied, misconstrued, and even fabricated and spread abroad to my injury, that he saw also that there was such an opposition of views between myself and another part of the administration as to render it peculiarly unpleasing, and to destroy the necessary harmony." Jefferson rather disingenuously claimed to know nothing about the inner workings and deliberations of "the Republican part" in Congress but assured Washington they were devoted to the Constitution.

Washington responded that "he believed the views of the Republican party were perfectly pure, but when men put a machine into motion it is impossible for them to stop it exactly where they would chuse or to say where it will stop. That the constitution we have is an excellent one if we can keep it where it is, that it was indeed supposed there was a party disposed to change it into a monarchical form, but that he could conscientiously declare there was not a man in the US. who would set his face more decidedly against it than himself." Jefferson interrupted Washington, saying, "No rational man in the US. suspects you of any other disposition, but there does not pass a week in which we cannot prove declns. dropping from the monarchical party that our government is good for nothing, it is a milk and water thing which cannot support itself, we must knock it down and set up something of more energy." Washington said, "If that was the case he thought it a proof of their insanity, for that the republican spirit of the Union was so manifest and so solid that it was astonishing how any one could expect to move them."[44]

The conversation revealed the most important difference between Washington and Jefferson. Washington believed that the Constitution consolidated and protected the most important legacy of the American Revolution—republican self-government—by creating a national government that was strong enough to provide order and stability even as the American people exercised sovereignty. The greatest danger came from Republicans, inspired by France, who might subvert the government and the Constitution. In other words, Washington agreed with Hamilton on the big political and constitutional questions. Jefferson, by contrast, felt that a coterie of Federalists around Alexander Hamilton (he excluded Washington from this group) were intent on overthrowing the Constitution and imposing a counterrevolutionary monarchical government in the United States and that they would achieve this by promoting corruption within the government. These positions were irreconcilable. Washington believed that Jefferson and (some) other Republicans were well meaning but that the threat they identified was not real. The two men had had several versions of this conversation in recent months, and Washington, convinced by the sincerity of Jefferson's stated intention to resign (and, likely frustrated by Jefferson's and Hamilton's constant sniping within the cabinet), accepted his resignation, having persuaded Jefferson to stay in post until the end of the year.

Thomas Jefferson served as Washington's secretary of state for nearly four years. Although that period was characterized by increasing partisan strife, as well as serious domestic and international challenges, the two men worked together happily for much of that time. Most of Jefferson's conflicts were with Hamilton, and he excluded Washington from his criticism of Federalism. Washington, for his part, seems to have viewed Jefferson as sincere in his attachment to the Constitution but misguided in his criticism of Hamilton. The two men exchanged warm letters as Jefferson left office. Jefferson told the president, "I now take the liberty of resigning the office into your hands. Be pleased to accept with it my sincere thanks for all the indulgencies which you have been so good as to exercise towards me in the discharge of it's duties. . . . I carry into my retirement a lively sense of your goodness, and shall continue gratefully to remember it. With very sincere prayers for your life, health and tranquility, I pray you to accept the homage of the great & constant respect & attachment." Washington replied the next day: "I cannot suffer you to leave your Station, without assuring you, that the opinion, which I had formed, of your integrity and talents, and which dictated your original nomination, has been confirmed by the fullest experience; and that both have been eminently displayed in the discharge of your duties." He continued, "Let a conviction of my most earnest prayers for your happiness accompany you in your retirement; and while I accept with the warmest thanks your solicitude for my welfare, I beg you to believe, that I always am Dear Sir Your Sincere friend and Affecte. Hble Servant."[45]

The affection between the two men could not survive the political differences that drove Jefferson to retire.

— 12 —

The Sincerity of a Friendship

It would give you a fever were I to name to you the apostates who have gone over to these heresies, men who were Samsons in the field and Solomons in the council, but who have had their heads shorn by the harlot England.

—Thomas Jefferson to Philip Mazzei, April 24, 1796

When Jefferson left Philadelphia for what he professed to be retirement on January 5, 1794, the frequent, sometimes daily, contact between him and Washington ceased, as did their steady stream of correspondence. To some extent this represented a change in their circumstances—Jefferson was returning to private life after more than a decade's service as a diplomat and secretary of state, while Washington continued to bear the heavy workload of the presidency. They now had little cause to see or consult each other as they did when they worked together in the government. Although they had labored closely for nearly four years, political differences between the two men had placed a strain on their friendship. Despite their professions of amity as they parted, the two men had begun to grow apart even before Jefferson left Washington's administration. Over the next few years, they would become completely estranged.

Washington and Jefferson had no contact for more than four months after Jefferson left office. On April 24 Washington forwarded a letter to Jefferson from a Flemish correspondent inquiring about the use of manure in American agriculture. The president closed with an oblique reference to the political situation. He wrote, "We are going in the old way 'Slow,' I hope events will justify me in adding 'and sure' that the proverb may be fulfilled.—'Slow and Sure.'" He signed off with a slightly less effusive and formulaic valediction than he had used in the past, "With very great esteem and regard I am Dr Sir Yr. Obedt. & Affecte. Humble Servt." Jefferson responded several weeks later. Prompted by Washington's letter, Jefferson's focus was on agriculture, particularly the use of manure, and his efforts to restore the productivity of his lands, which, he complained, had deteriorated to "a degree of degradation far beyond what I had expected" after his prolonged absence. He did respond to the president's comment about politics. "[T]he maxim of your letter 'slow and sure' is not less a good one in agriculture than in politics." The former secretary of state concluded (without conviction), "But I cherish tranquility too much to suffer political things to enter my mind at all."[1]

Washington and Jefferson exchanged these letters at a moment of rising tension between the United States and Britain. In early November 1793, the British government authorized British vessels to seize neutral ships carrying supplies to the French West Indies. The edict was intended to disrupt American trade with France's colonies in the Caribbean that helped to sustain the French revolutionary war effort against Britain. In addition to seizing American ships, the British also removed suspected deserters from American vessels, forcing them into service in the Royal Navy, and continued to occupy forts on territory claimed by the United States in the Northwest while supporting Native resistance to American expansion. Over the next few months, British privateers and naval vessels captured more than 250 American merchant vessels. In January 1794 James Madison proposed legislation in the House of Representatives calling for commercial retaliation against Britain. The measures failed on a regional, partisan vote, but Congress authorized adding six new frigates to the US Navy. A second British-American war seemed likely in the spring of 1794. In a last-ditch effort to avoid conflict, or at least to be seen as going as far as possible in pursuit of peace, in May Washington dispatched a minister plenipotentiary, Supreme Court Chief Justice John Jay, to London to seek a negotiated settlement. In this context, Jefferson wrote to Washington, "I sincerely wish it may extricate us from the event of a war, if this can be done saving our faith and our rights. My opinion of the British government is that nothing will force them to do justice but the loud voice of their people, and that this can never be excited but by distressing their commerce."[2]

While Jay traveled to London seeking to prevent a second British-American war, the Washington administration faced a more immediate crisis closer to home. In March 1791, as part of Alexander Hamilton's fiscal program, Congress adopted an excise tax on whiskey. Unlike customs duties, which had been the preferred method of taxation, the whiskey excise was a direct tax on Americans. It hit settlers in the West particularly hard, as they often resorted to distillation as the most efficient and profitable way to transport and market their grain in a region with poor transportation connections. Throughout the Appalachian backcountry—from Georgia to Pennsylvania—hard-pressed farmers protested the tax, sometimes threatening the excise collectors. Washington and Hamilton saw the protests as a direct challenge to the authority of the federal government and feared that disgruntled western settlers might seek to leave the union. The situation was most acute in western Pennsylvania, and in February 1794 Washington issued a proclamation expressing his government's determination to enforce the law. Violent protests continued throughout the summer and led to two deaths as 6,000 armed men gathered in Braddock's Field near Pittsburgh (where Washington had fought in 1755) in defiance of the tax and the government. The protesters, taking inspiration from the American and French Revolutions, erected liberty poles and mock guillotines. On August 7 the president issued another proclamation, calling out the militia to enforce the law and suppress what Federalists dubbed the Whiskey Rebellion, which Attorney General William Bradford described as "a well formed and regular plan for weakening and perhaps overthrowing the General Government."[3]

Given the continued successful resistance of Native people in Ohio, the looming threat of war with Britain, and domestic resistance in Pennsylvania and elsewhere, Washington believed the union itself was in peril in the autumn of 1794. Mindful of both his reputation and the power of his image, he donned a uniform and took nominal command of the nearly 13,000 militiamen from several states who were called out under federal authority to suppress the rebellion with a massive show of force. Washington inspected and directed the organization of the army at Carlisle, but he did not accompany it on its march to western Pennsylvania. By the time the federal militia arrived in Pittsburgh and began making arrests, the rebellion had collapsed.[4]

The Whiskey Rebellion contributed to the estrangement between Washington and Jefferson. In an angry message to Congress in November,

Washington claimed the insurrection had been "fomented by combinations of men, who, careless of consequences, and disregarding the unerring truth that those, who rouse, cannot always appease a civil convulsion, have disseminated, from an ignorance or perversion of facts, suspicions, jealousies, and accusations of the whole Government." He claimed that "certain self-created societies" had orchestrated the rebellion, duping credulous western farmers into taking up arms against their government. He was less circumspect in a private letter he wrote in September, declaring that the "insurrection in the western counties of this State . . . may be considered as the first ripe fruit of the Democratic Societies." Washington was referring to Democratic-Republican societies, a network of around forty clubs around the nation organized by supporters of the French Revolution and, increasingly, the opposition to the Federalist administration in Philadelphia. These clubs, which emerged in 1793, were modeled on the Jacobin clubs in revolutionary France. Washington and other Federalists believed, as the president wrote, that the clubs sought to "poison & discontent the minds of the people against the government; particularly by endeavouring to have it believed that their liberties were assailed, and that all the wicked and abominable measures . . . are practiced to sap the Constitution, and lay the foundation of future Slavery."[5]

Unsurprisingly, Jefferson, ensconced at Monticello in retirement, took a different view of the matter. At the end of December, he interrupted his ruminations on manure to complain at length to James Madison about Washington's criticism: "The denunciation of the democratic societies," he fumed, "is one of the extraordinary acts of boldness of which we have seen so many from the faction of Monocrats," using his preferred term of opprobrium for those Federalists he believed sought to create an all-powerful government at the expense of popular liberty. He was, yet, unwilling to criticize Washington personally. Rather, he claimed that Washington had been duped by others, presumably Hamilton, into condemning the societies, which helped organize the nascent party that he and Madison led. "It is wonderful indeed that the President should have permitted himself to be the organ of such an attack on the freedom of discussion, the freedom of writing, printing and publishing." Jefferson drew a contrast between the Democratic-Republican societies and the Society of Cincinnati, which he believed posed a real threat to the American republic, "carving out for itself hereditary distinctions, lowering over our constitution eternally, meeting together in all parts of the Union periodically, with closed doors, accumulating a capital in their separate treasury, corresponding secretly and regularly, and of which society the very persons denouncing the democrats are themselves the fathers, founders or high officers."[6]

The Whiskey Rebellion revealed the growing political differences between Washington and Jefferson, and the growing rift between the nascent political parties in the United States. For Washington and the Federalists, the rebellion undermined law and order and threatened the nation's fragile experiment with republican government. As the president wrote to the governor of Virginia, Henry Lee, in August 1794, "I see, under popular and fascinating guises, the most diabolical attempts to destroy the best fabric of human government & happiness, that has ever been presented for the acceptance of mankind."[7] Jefferson, by contrast, believed that the Federalists had conjured a threat that didn't exist and used it to consolidate their power. He complained to James Monroe, then serving as the US representative in Paris, that the rebellion "answered the favorite purposes of strengthening government and increasing the public debt; and therefore an insurrection was announced and proclaimed and armed against, and marched against, but could never be found."[8]

When Jefferson departed Washington's administration at the end of 1793, the two men had professed their mutual admiration for each other. By the end of 1794, each believed that the other's political views, and associations, posed a mortal danger to the United States. As Dumas Malone, one of Jefferson's most thorough biographers, has written, "If one need pick the precise point at which he began to question the wisdom of Washington, whose judgment he so generally respected, this seems to be it." The change wasn't instantaneous. Jefferson continued to believe that Washington was being duped by Hamilton into supporting unwise policies. In August 1794 Henry Lee reported to Washington that a visitor to Monticello asked Jefferson whether Washington was "governed by British influence." According to Lee, the former secretary of state replied "that there was no danger of [Washington] being biassed by considerations of that sort so long as [he] was influenced by the wise advisers or advice which [he] at present had." Given that Jefferson didn't trust Washington's advisers, this wasn't exactly a repudiation of the allegation. Washington offered an equivocal response to Lee's unsubstantiated gossip: "With respect to the words said to have been uttered by Mr Jefferson," he wrote, "they would be enigmatical to those who are acquainted with the characters about me, unless supposed to be spoken ironically; & in that case they are too injurious to me, & have too little foundation in truth, to be ascribed to him." Washington claimed that if Jefferson had said he was partial toward Britain, "which I do not believe," then "he has set me down as one of the most deceitful, & uncandid men living; because, not only in private conversations between ourselves on this subject, but in my meetings with the confidential servants of the public, he has heard me often, when occasions presented themselves, express very different sentiments with an energy that could not be mistaken by <u>any one</u> present." For his part, Jefferson was unwilling to blame Washington directly for the power grab behind the Whiskey Rebellion, but he noted it was done "under the sanction of a name which has done too much good not to be sufficient to cover harm also." When Jefferson left the Washington administration at the end of 1793, he and the president professed their friendship and admiration for each other. By the beginning of 1795, such statements were grudging and formulaic. Worse was to come.[9]

On November 19, 1794, the same day that Washington told Congress that the Democratic-Republican societies were responsible for the Whiskey Rebellion, John Jay reached an agreement in London with the British government on the outstanding issues between the United States and Britain. Jay yielded to British restrictions on American trade—conceding the right of Americans to trade with France and its colonies in wartime. In exchange, the British agreed to vacate the forts they occupied on US territory and they removed restrictions on American trade with Britain and Ireland, India, and the British West Indies. Vexing outstanding issues concerning prewar debts owed by Americans to British merchants, compensation for enslaved people liberated or captured by the British during the war, and the border between the United States and Canada were to be settled by future arbitration commissions. Jay had succeeded in averting war between Britain and the United States, and he had gained the United States a close economic relationship with its former colonial master. The agreement seemed to confirm the Federalist position that the United States should align its interests with Britain in response to the French Revolution.[10]

President Washington did not receive a copy of the treaty until early March 1795, while Congress was adjourned. In June the Senate reconvened in a special session to consider the treaty. After a rancorous debate, the Federalists in the Senate narrowly ratified the agreement by twenty votes to ten, just achieving the two-thirds majority required by the Constitution. Republicans in the House of Representatives fought a rearguard action, unsuccessfully seeking to block the implementation of the treaty's provisions by withholding funding. The Jay Treaty crystallized the partisan divisions that had been developing over the previous four years. The agreement was unpopular with Republicans and the public. There was a vigorous, vicious debate over the agreement in the popular press as both newspapers and pamphlets appeared in support of and opposition to the treaty. For the first time, Washington was subject to sustained personal criticism in the Republican press (which previously had concentrated its opprobrium on Hamilton). At the end of August, the *American Mercury* in Hartford, Connecticut, asked, "[D]oes the President fancy himself the grand Lama of this country that we are to approach him with superstitious reverence or religious regard? . . . He has disdained to look down with an eye of complacency from the eminence on which they [Federalists] have placed him. We have been guilty of idolatry for too long."[11] In July Washington complained to Alexander Hamilton, "At present the cry against the Treaty is like that against a mad-dog; and every one, in a manner, seems engaged in running it down."[12]

Jefferson, who first saw a copy of the treaty on July 21, agreed that the public was agitated about the agreement. "From North to South this monument of folly or venality is universally execrated," he wrote to his son-in-law, Thomas Mann Randolph. Whereas Washington believed the public had been misled, and he hoped that "after the paroxysm of the fever is a little abated, what the real temper of the people" toward the treaty could be determined. Jefferson believed the popular clamor was appropriate. According to Jefferson, a set of "rogues" (Federalists) had ignored the will of the people and foisted an unpopular and humiliating treaty on the United States. He wrote, "Our part of the country is in considerable fermentation on what they suspect to be a recent roguery of this kind." Jefferson was, yet, still willing to excuse Washington, blaming those around him, Hamilton especially, for the worst excesses of the Federalists. He employed a maritime metaphor to describe the situation. "They say that while all hands were below deck mending sails, splicing ropes, and every one at his own business, and the captain in the cabbin attending to his log-book and chart, a rogue of a pilot has run them into an enemy's port." In Jefferson's metaphor the dutiful captain was the president and the rogue piloting the ship of state into British waters was Alexander Hamilton. He continued to disclaim any interest in politics. "For my part I consider myself now but as a passenger, leaving the world and its government to those who are likely to live longer in it."[13]

The United States and Britain did not each ratify and exchange the final text of the Jay Treaty (formally known as the Treaty of Amity, Commerce, and Navigation) until the end of October 1795. Washington submitted the final, ratified version of the agreement to Congress on February 29, 1796.[14] Although the pact proved beneficial to the United States economically, the treaty shaped American politics and foreign policy for the foreseeable future. During the ratification controversy, Jefferson provided a Republican-tinged analysis of the political situation for James Monroe in Paris: "Mr. Jay's treaty has at length been made public. So general a burst of dissatisfaction never before appeared against any transaction. Those who understand the particular articles of it, condemn these articles, those who do not understand them minutely, condemn it generally as wearing a hostile face to France. This last is the most numerous class, comprehending the whole body of the people, who have taken a greater interest in this transaction than they were ever known to do in any other. It has, in my opinion, completely demolished the monarchical party here."[15] For Washington, whose second term had been marred by increasingly partisan strife and bruising personal attacks, the debate over the treaty was a disheartening experience.

The announcement that the treaty had been formally adopted did not end the attacks on the president. On June 9, 1796, the Philadelphia *Aurora* published a vitriolic attack on Washington that included the text of the thirteen questions the president had submitted to his cabinet prior to issuing his Neutrality Proclamation in April 1793. The publisher of the *Aurora*, Benjamin Franklin Bache, was a well-connected Republican partisan with a history of obtaining and publishing sensitive material—Bache had published the leaked text of the Jay Treaty the previous summer. The publication of this material was intended to embarrass the president and to prove that he had pursued a pro-British, anti-French policy at the expense of the

United States and its most important ally.[16] The essay in the *Aurora* prompted the last exchange of letters between Jefferson and Washington.

As soon as Jefferson received his copy of the *Aurora* at Monticello, he sat down to write to Washington to deny any suggestion that he had leaked Washington's list of questions to the newspaper. "I cannot be satisfied as to my own part," he wrote, "till I relieve my mind by declaring, and I attest every thing sacred and honorable to the declaration, that it has got there neither thro' me nor the paper confided to me. This has never been from under my own lock and key, or out of my own hands." He allowed that he may have shown the paper to Madison, the "one person who possesses all my confidence," but assured the president, "I take on myself, without fear, any divulgation on [Madison's] part. We both know him incapable of it. From myself then or my paper this publication has never been derived." Jefferson asserted that he had never written for the press. He then shifted his attention away from the material that appeared in the *Aurora* to Henry Lee's malign gossip from two years prior, the purpose of which was "to sow tares between you and me, by representing me as still engaged in the bustle of politics, and in turbulence and intrigue against the government." Jefferson, who did not identify Lee by name, continued, "I never believed for a moment that this could make any impression on you, or that your knolege of me would not overweigh the slander of an intriguer dirtily employed in sifting the conversations of my table." Jefferson ended his letter with a discussion of his efforts to grow peas and clover at Monticello, undoubtedly seeking to turn to a subject of common interest with Washington before offering his "very affectionate compliments" to Martha Washington. He signed his letter with the formulaic valediction, "I have the honor to be with great and sincere esteem and respect Dear Sir Your most obedt. & most humble servt."[17]

Jefferson's letter to Washington reads like a desperate attempt at damage control. There is no evidence that Jefferson leaked the offending, sensitive documents to Bache (Washington suspected that former attorney general Edmund Randolph was the culprit), and he generally avoided participating directly in the partisan newspaper battles of the 1790s. He did, however, indirectly encourage attacks on the administration and the president. When he was secretary of state, he paid editor Philip Freneau (with public funds) to establish a newspaper, *The National Gazette*, to oppose Federalist policies. He encouraged his allies, including Madison, to publish attacks on the

Federalists, especially Hamilton. Increasingly, the Republican press targeted Washington. If Jefferson was not immediately responsible for Bache's attack in the *Aurora,* he certainly helped to foster a climate that was increasingly critical of Washington and his policies. Although his denial of involvement in this case was likely true, his claim that "political conversation I really dislike, and therefore avoid when I can without affectation" was certainly untrue.[18] Whether Henry Lee's specific report that Jefferson had said that Washington had embraced pro-British policies was correct is unknown, and probably unknowable. (Jefferson denied it, and Lee was passing along hearsay from someone who claimed to have heard Jefferson say it.) Nonetheless, the statement is of a piece with the criticisms of Washington that had crept into Jefferson's correspondence, and it is plausible to imagine him making such statements over the dinner table at Monticello with his friends and political allies.

Washington wrote a prompt response to Jefferson on July 6. Ostensibly, Washington accepted Jefferson's denial that he had been involved in leaking the documents. "If I had entertained any suspicions before," the president wrote, "that the queries Which have been published in Bache's Paper proceeded from you, the assurances you have given of the contrary, would have removed them; but the truth is, I harboured none." Washington complained about his treatment in the press and the efforts of unnamed persons who "weaken the confidence of the People" in the government. He then turned to the reports that Jefferson had been attacking him behind his back. "As you have mentioned the subject yourself," he wrote, "it would not be frank, candid, or friendly to conceal, that your conduct has been represented as derogating from that opinion I had conceived you entertained of me." Washington continued, "That to your particular friends and connexions, you have described, and they have announced me, as a person under a dangerous influence; and that, if I would listen <u>more</u> to some <u>other</u> opinions all would be well." He claimed that he did not believe such reports. "My answer invariably has been, that I had never discovered any thing in the conduct of Mr. Jefferson to raise suspicions, in my mind, of his insincerity; that if he would retrace my public conduct while he was in the Administration, abundant proofs would occur to him, that truth and right decisions, were the <u>sole</u> objects of my pursuit; that there were as many instances within his <u>own</u> knowledge of my having decided <u>against</u>, as in <u>favor of</u> the opinions of the person evidently alluded to." Washington apparently misunderstood Jefferson's reference to Henry Lee in his letter and assumed Hamilton was the malevolent intriguer Jefferson was referring to.

Washington then turned to the broader issue of partisanship. He made his usual assertion that he was a man above party: "In short, that I was no party man myself, and the first wish of my heart was, if parties did exist, to reconcile them." He then expressed surprise at the bitterness of the partisan divisions that had emerged over the Jay Treaty. He claimed that he had only sought to keep the nation out of a ruinous second war with Britain while seeking to establish "a national character of our own, independent, as far as our obligations, and justice would permit, of every nation of the earth." Washington was surprised, and hurt, that his efforts were met with criticism and personal attacks. "I should be accused of being the enemy of one Nation, and subject to the influence of another; and to prove it, that every act of my Administration would be tortured, and the grossest, and most insidious misrepresentations of them be made (by giving one side only of a subject, and that too in such exagerated , and indecent terms as could scarcely be applied to a Nero; a notorious defaulter; or even to a common pickpocket). But enough of this; I have already gone farther in the expression of my feelings, than I intended." Washington included several paragraphs on agricultural matters before sharing Martha Washington's best wishes and signing off, "with very great esteem and regard I am, Dear Sir Your obedient and Hble Servt."[19]

This last exchange between Jefferson and Washington reads like an argument between two men whose friendship had crumbled under the weight of their differences. Each seemed more eager to win the argument than to clear up any misunderstandings. Although they seem to be agreeing to disagree, both men were determined to air their grievances with each other. Although they didn't name each other directly, each would have read the other's letter as an attack on his fundamental beliefs. The exchange shows both men at their worst. Jefferson is slippery and somewhat deceitful (in spirit if not fact) and Washington is thin-skinned and deliberately obtuse about the political situation. He claimed to be above partisanship, failing to acknowledge that his positions, which he claimed were for the good of the country only, were as political as Jefferson's. The two men had reached a political impasse that had apparently destroyed their friendship.

George Washington was sixty-four years old in the summer of 1796. He had had several serious health problems during his presidency, including a painful carbuncle on his thigh and a dangerous bout of pneumonia. He suffered from chronic and painful dental problems throughout his life, and by the time he became president, he had only one of his original teeth. He resorted to various sets of painful dentures that made it difficult for him to speak, eat, or smile (which partially accounts for his aloof demeanor as well as his grumpy appearance in many of his presidential portraits).[20] He had been in public service almost continually since he left Mount Vernon for Congress (and then the army) in 1775. He was tired and feeling his age. He had agreed to run for a second term in 1792 at the behest of Jefferson and Hamilton, who had assured him that only he could hold the government and the country together and forestall the worst excesses of partisanship. Both Jefferson (1793) and Hamilton (1795) had left the administration, and the partisan divisions that they each encouraged had only become worse. Indeed, partisanship had become so intense that Washington was regularly attacked in the press. For a man who tended his reputation carefully, the cares of office had become too much. He wanted to take Martha and her grandchildren and return to Mount Vernon and live out his final years managing his vast landholdings. By early 1796 he had decided he would not run for a third term as president.

When Washington had contemplated retirement in 1792, James Madison, then still a political ally, had helped him draft a valedictory address to the nation. During the spring of 1796, he revisited the text, giving it over to Alexander Hamilton, who reworked the draft—evidence that, despite his protestations, Washington had become a partisan Federalist. Washington then carefully edited the statement that was intended to be his final public statement to the nation. Washington's Farewell Address appeared in American newspapers in September 1796. It was a concise summary of Washington's political philosophy as he prepared to vacate the public stage. To the extent that Jefferson, despite his claims to the contrary, had emerged as the leader of the opposition to Washington and the Federalists, the Farewell Address might be read as a public response to Jefferson. Washington was using the power of the presidency and his still-considerable status to make a definitive statement and to discredit his opponents, including Jefferson.

He did so not in a fit of pique but because he believed that partisanship was the "worst enemy" of republican government and had to be suppressed.[21]

Washington developed several themes in the Farewell Address. He exalted the union of the states above all else as the bulwark of liberty. "The Unity of Government which constitutes you one people is also now dear to you. It is justly so; for it is a main Pillar in the Edifice of your real independence, the support of your tranquility at home, your peace abroad; of your safety; of your prosperity; of that very Liberty which you so highly prize." While he acknowledged regional differences, he stressed that Americans had more in common than divided them and that the union must supersede local interests. "Citizens by birth or choice, of a common country, that country has a right to concentrate your affections. The name of AMERICAN, which belongs to you, in your national capacity, must always exalt the just pride of Patriotism, more than any appellation derived from local discriminations. With slight shades of difference, you have the same Religion, Manners, Habits & political Principles. You have in a common cause fought and triumphed together—the independence & Liberty you possess are the work of joint councils, and joint efforts—of common dangers, sufferings and successes."

After asserting the importance of the union, Washington then celebrated the Constitution, "the offspring of our own choice uninfluenced and unawed, adopted upon full investigation and mature deliberation, completely free in its principles, in the distribution of its powers, uniting security with energy, and containing within itself a provision for its own amendment, has a just claim to your confidence and your support." Having established their government after such careful deliberation, American citizens owed their government their allegiance and were obliged to adhere to its laws. "The basis of our political systems is the right of the people to make and to alter their Constitutions of Government. But the Constitution which at any time exists, 'till changed by an explicit and authentic act of the whole People, is sacredly obligatory upon all. The very idea of the power and the right of the People to establish Government presupposes the duty of every Individual to obey the established Government."

In Washington's formulation the revolution created the nation as a union of states and the Constitution created a strong government that guaranteed the liberties of the citizens of that union. He then turned to the international situation. He prophesied a future when the United States would be strong enough to ignore Europe and its wars. "If we remain one People, under an efficient government," he predicted, "the period is not far off, when we may defy material injury from external annoyance; when we may take such an attitude as will cause the neutrality we may at any time resolve upon to be scrupulously respected; when belligerent nations, under the impossibility of making acquisitions upon us, will not lightly hazard the giving us provocation; when we may choose peace or War, as our interest guided by justice shall counsel." He recognized that the United States was not yet strong enough to cut itself off from Europe. He accepted, no doubt with the Jay Treaty in mind, that it might be necessary for the nation to make agreements in response to exigent circumstances, but he declared, "'Tis our true policy to steer clear of permanent Alliances, with any portion of the foreign world—So far, I mean, as we are now at liberty to do it—for let me not be understood as capable of patronising infidility to existing engagements. . . . I repeat it therefore, let those engagements be observed in their genuine sense. But in my opinion, it is unnecessary and would be unwise to extend them."

With its emphasis on the union of American states, the primacy of the federal Constitution and the rule of law, and condemnation of partisanship and international alliances, the Farewell Address was a statement of principle very much at odds with the views of Jefferson and the Republicans. They favored a more decentralized union. Jefferson always believed that liberty would best be protected by the states, not the federal government. They also believed that Americans, as republicans, should make common cause with their French counterparts as part of a transnational republican movement. Although Washington would remain in office until March 1797, the Farewell Address was his final, and most substantive, political statement to the American people. He marshaled the authority of his office and his personal reputation to repudiate and discredit his opponents. As the foremost of these, Jefferson would have read the Farewell Address as a personal rebuke. He did not comment directly in writing on Washington's valedictory except to mention to Madison that he held "a very different picture of our foreign affairs from that presented in the Adieu [Farewell Address]."[22]

The publication of the Farewell Address in September marked the formal start of the 1796 presidential election—the first openly contested election in US history (Washington had run unopposed in 1789 and 1792).

It would be an open contest between the Federalists and Republicans for the first time. The main candidates were Vice President John Adams, of Massachusetts, and Jefferson. Jefferson and Adams had been friends going back to their time in Congress during the War of Independence. That friendship deepened while both men served as diplomats in Europe during the 1780s. Their political differences became more pronounced during Washington's presidency. "The" election of 1796 was actually a series of concurrent electoral contests held at the state level throughout the autumn (as required by the political culture of the day, neither of the main candidates actively campaigned for office). Adams eked out a narrow victory over Jefferson in the electoral college. Adams received seventy-one electoral votes to Jefferson's sixty-eight (according to the Constitution, that meant Jefferson would become Adams's vice president). The election revealed the sectional nature of the partisan division in American politics— precisely what Washington had warned against in his Farewell Address. Adams received just two votes from south of the Potomac and Jefferson only eighteen from north of it.[23]

Thomas Jefferson had some trepidation as he contemplated joining yet another administration dominated by his political rivals. He was also wary of the international consequences of the recent election. The French government, which, correctly, viewed the Jay Treaty as a repudiation of the 1778 treaty of alliance between the United States and France, saw the election as a referendum on the treaty. Viewed from Paris, the American people had rejected the pro-French Republicans in favor of the pro-British Federalists. As a consequence, France was determined to stifle American trade with Britain and its colonies. The danger of British-American war in 1794 was replaced in 1796 by the threat of a Franco-American conflict. Indeed, for most of Adams's presidency, France and the United States waged a "quasi-war" at sea while preparing for the outbreak of a formal war between the two former allies. In early January Jefferson wrote to Madison, "I much fear the issue of the present dispositions of France and Spain. Whether it be in war or in the suppression of our commerce it will be very distressing and our commerce seems to be already sufficiently distressed through the wrongs of the belligerent nations and our own follies." Naturally, Jefferson also blamed Hamilton and his fiscal program for the problems facing the nation, "It was impossible the bank and paper-mania should not produce great and extensive ruin." He also criticized Washington explicitly, "The President is fortunate to get off just as the bubble is bursting, leaving others to hold the bag. Yet, as his departure will mark the moment when the difficulties begin to work, you will see that they will be ascribed to the new administration, and that he will have his usual good fortune of reaping credit from the good acts of others, and leaving to them that of his errors." Usually, Jefferson found ways to excuse Washington for the worst excesses of the Federalists. Now, as Washington prepared to demit office permanently, and Jefferson to return to national office, the breach between the two men seemed more serious than ever.[24]

If the new administration filled Jefferson with trepidation, the prospect of retirement thrilled Washington. Before Adams's inauguration, Henrietta Liston, the wife of the British ambassador in Philadelphia, Robert Liston, encountered the president at one of his last public events. A shrewd observer of the American political scene, Liston wrote, "About ten days before his quitting his situation,—I congratulated him on his approaching happiness.—Yes, said he, like a Child within view of the Holydays, I have counted the Months, then the weeks, & I now reckon the days previous to my release."[25]

John Adams was inaugurated as second president of the United States on Saturday, March 4, 1796. Initially, Thomas Jefferson intended to miss the inauguration. He changed his mind in the face of suggestions that his nonattendance might be construed as sulking over the result of the presidential election. Jefferson made the familiar journey from Monticello to Philadelphia in late February, arriving on March 2. He paid his respects to his old friend, the president-elect, but does not seem to have met the outgoing president. He may have attended a public dinner that the Washingtons hosted on March 3 for "the officers of State, Foreign Ministers, principal Senators, & to their respective Ladies," though he made no mention of it. Adams and Jefferson took their oaths in the Senate chamber. The new president described the scene as well as the demeanor of his predecessor, "A Solenm Scene it was indeed and it was made more affecting to me, by the Presence of the General, whose Countenance was as serene and unclouded as the day. He Seem'd to me to enjoy a Tryumph over me. Methought I heard him think Ay! I am fairly out and you fairly in! see which of Us will be happiest. When the Ceremony was over he came and made me a visit and cordially congratulated me and wished my Administration might be happy Successful and honourable."[26]

On March 6, 1797, as the Washingtons prepared to leave Philadelphia for Mount Vernon, the former president hosted the new president and vice president for dinner. We know almost as little about this, the last meeting between Washington and Jefferson, as we do about their first encounter. Jefferson recorded a single line in notes he jotted down several months later that were more concerned with his relationship with Adams and the state of Franco-American relations. Of the dinner with Washington, he said simply, "I think it was on Monday the 6th. of March, Mr. Adams and myself met at dinner at Genl. Washington's, and we happened in the evening to rise from table and come away together." Washington's diary entry for the day said simply, "The wind Shifted to the No. Wt. and turned Cold M[ercury]: 24." He may well have been describing the atmosphere in the room that evening. Washington and Adams had never been especially close. Jefferson and Adams had been close friends, but over the coming years they would become estranged over their political differences. Although they maintained the outward forms of politeness, Washington and Jefferson hadn't corresponded for eight months. Having dined regularly with each other and enjoyed a close friendship during Washington's presidency, one imagines their last meal consisted of stilted conversation and awkward silences as neither man could quite trust the other anymore. Jefferson added a note to his account of the evening: "The reason Genl. Washington assigned to me for having called such a body of Militia to the siege of Yorktown was, that by doubling with our own forces, the numbers of our French auxiliaries, the honour might more indisputably result to us." This suggests that the three old revolutionaries reminisced about the war, a time when they were united in a common cause before they were divided by postwar politics (though, with war with France in the offing, Jefferson might have interpreted this as evidence of Washington's disloyalty to his ally).[27]

In his final letter to Washington, Jefferson claimed, "[F]rom a very early period in my life, I had laid it down as a rule of conduct never to write a word for the public papers." Jefferson generally stuck to this rule (though he certainly encouraged others to publish attacks on his political rivals). Unfortunately for Jefferson, his reputation, and his relationship with

Washington, he received a sharp reminder of why he should avoid the press in the spring of 1797. On May 2, 1797, the New York *Minerva* published edited extracts from a letter between Jefferson and his former neighbor, Philip Mazzei. Mazzei was an Italian physician who had lived in Charlottesville and became a close friend of Jefferson's. He had returned to Italy and was living in Pisa in the spring of 1796 when Jefferson wrote him a lengthy letter in which, among other things, he discussed the political situation in the United States. This was the notorious "Mazzei Letter" of which one of Jefferson's biographers has written, "No single writing from Jefferson's pen pursued him so remorselessly beyond the grave."[28]

According to the extracts in the *Minerva*, Jefferson wrote the following: "Our political situation is prodigiously changed since you left us. Instead of that noble love of liberty, and that republican government, which carried us triumphantly thro the dangers of the war, an Anglo-Monarchico-Aristocratic party has arisen.—Their avowed object is to impose on us the substance, as they have already given us the form, of the British government." Jefferson's description to Mazzei of the political situation in the latter stages of the Washington administration is consistent with what he had been saying in private for several years: the Federalists were beholden to Britain and sought to undermine America's republican experiment at home and its relationship with revolutionary France abroad. Although most of the country remained true to republican principles, these policies benefited the Federalists, who profited personally from promoting an attachment with Britain. "We have against us (republicans) the *Executive Power*, the *Judiciary Power*, . . . *all the officers of government, all who are seeking offices, all timid men who prefer the calm of despotism to the tempestuous sea of liberty, the British merchants and the Americans who trade on British capitals, the speculators, persons interested in the bank and the public funds.*"[29]

What was new in the letter was the explicit criticism of George Washington. Jefferson made a clear reference to Washington when he wrote, "I should give you a fever, if I should name the apostates who have embraced these heresies; men who were Solomons in council, and Samsons in combat, but whose hair has been cut off by the whore England." The editor of the *Minerva* helpfully explained the biblical reference, "probably alluding to the woman's cutting off the hair of Samson, and his loss of strength thereby."[30] This was a direct attack on Washington that did not allow for confusion or misunderstanding. The recently retired former president may have spit out his hot chocolate, a favorite breakfast drink at Mount Vernon, when he read the words of his former secretary of state.

Jefferson wrote his letter to Mazzei on April 24, 1796, at the height of the furor over the Jay Treaty (and shortly before he wrote to Washington to deny any involvement in leaking material to Benjamin Franklin Bache). Mazzei shared extracts of the letter (copied in English) without Jefferson's permission with several correspondents, and the letter, in the parlance of a later age, went viral. In January 1797 a somewhat garbled translation of the letter was published in French in the *Gazette Nationale ou Le Moniteur Universel* in Paris. These extracts were then retranslated into English and appeared in *Minerva* in May. The letter and unflattering commentary were published widely in the Federalist press. The published extracts differ somewhat from Jefferson's original letter, which was translated from English to French and back to English with added commentary (England is a harlot in Jefferson's original and a whore in the published version). The text that appeared in the *Minerva* is the one that entered the public domain in May 1797. Jefferson wrote to Mazzei during his first "retirement," and he did not intend it for publication, but when the letter was published, he was serving as the vice president in John Adams's "Anglo-Monarchico-Aristocratic" administration.[31]

Several months after the Mazzei Letter appeared in the press, Washington received a letter from a man called John Langhorne from Albemarle County, Virginia. Langhorne expressed sympathy for Washington over the "unmerited calumny" to which he had been subjected. Washington, who did not know Langhorne, sent a noncommittal response. When Washington's reply lay uncollected in the post office, John Nicholas, the county clerk (and a Federalist) wrote to Washington. He intimated that Langhorne was an impostor and the original letter was written by someone "closely connected with some of your greatest and bitterest enemies." Nicholas reminded Washington "that living where I do, immediately in cannon shot of the very head-quarters of *Jacobinism*; knowing how much you have been deceived in the principles and *professions of friendship of certain characters in this quarter*, and my own knowledge of their *real dispositions*; have determined me thus to hint to you some things" which he would make known to him if invited for a personal interview. The real author of the Langhorne letter was Peter Carr, Thomas Jefferson's nephew. Why Carr wrote the pseudonymous letter is unknown, as is whether Jefferson was aware that he had done so. The most charitable interpretation is that he was seeking to effect a reconciliation with Washington on Jefferson's behalf. A less sympathetic interpretation is that Carr sought to tempt Washington into writing something intemperate about Jefferson that could be leaked to the press.[32]

John Nicholas wrote to Washington several times over the coming months and identified Peter Carr as "John Langhorne." In early March 1798, Washington replied, attacking Jefferson. "Nothing short of the Evidence you have adduced," he wrote, "corroborative of intimations which I had received long before, through another channel, could have shaken my belief in the sincerity of a friendship, which I had conceived was possessed for me, by the person to whom you allude." Washington's anger and disappointment was not simply personal. He viewed Jefferson's attacks on him as part of a wider strategy to undermine the Constitution and overthrow the republic. He continued, "But attempts to injure those who are supposed to stand well in the estimation of the People, and are stumbling blocks in their way (by misrepresenting their political tenets) thereby to destroy all confidence in them, is one of the means by which the Government is to be assailed, and the Constitution destroyed. The conduct of this Party is systematized, and every thing that is opposed to its execution, will be sacrificed, without hesitation, or remorse; if the end can be answd by it." Although the attempt by Langhorne/Carr had failed, Washington was in no doubt that Jefferson and his allies would continue their attacks on him, Federalism, and the republic (in his mind these were one and the same). "In what form, the next insidious attempt may appear, remains to be discovered. But as the attempts to explain away the Constitution, & weaken the Government are now become so open; and the desire of placing the Affairs of this Country under the influence & controul of a foreign Nation is so apparant , & strong, it is hardly to be expected that a resort to covert means to effect these objects, will be longer regarded."[33]

Henrietta Liston, who had observed Washington closely during his second term, offered an astute assessment of the president as his term came to an end. "The World gives General Washington more credit for his retirement from publick life than I am disposed to do," she wrote. "He has for eight years sacrificed his natural taste, first habits, & early propensities,— I really believe we may truly say—solely to what he thought the good of his Country." While Liston credited Washington for the sacrifices he had made during two decades of public service, she recognized the strain that political partisanship had taken on him. "But he was become tired of his Situation, fretted by the opposition made to his measures; & his pride revolted against the ingratitude he experienced,—and he was also disgusted by the scurrilous abuse lavished upon him by his political enemies."[34] Rather than viewing Washington walking away from office and giving up power as the final selfless act of an honorable patriot, Liston saw that the president had been worn down by the criticism and abuse he had received from his political rivals and adversaries. Liston recognized that for all his public service and sacrifice, Washington was thin-skinned and hurt by the public and private opprobrium he had received during his second term. Jefferson was foremost among those critics, even if he sought to avoid making direct personal attacks on Washington. Washington, however, had heard rumors that his former secretary of state had betrayed him, and these were confirmed by the Mazzei and Langhorne letters.

For his part, Jefferson did not believe that he had betrayed Washington. Rather, he held that the president had been deceived by men like Hamilton and led off the path of true republicanism. (Jefferson never really accepted that Washington held different views from his own.) Although animus had arisen between the two men, the issues that came to divide them were more than personal pique. They each came to believe that they and their allies were the avatars of the republican legacy of the revolution and that their opponents represented a mortal threat to the new republic. Such a political and ideological divergence, reminiscent of the split between Patriots and Loyalists during the War of Independence, increasingly made compromise difficult to achieve and placed a strain on personal relationships such as that between Washington and Jefferson. The particular personalities of each man—Washington was sensitive to criticism and struggled to manage his temper; Jefferson shrank from personal conflict, tending to tell people what they wanted to hear while using surrogates to carry out political attacks, giving him a reputation for duplicity—meant that the perfervid political struggles of the 1790s predisposed both men to assume, and see, the worst in each other.

During the spring of 1798, Henrietta and Robert Liston visited the Washingtons in retirement at Mount Vernon. Henrietta reported that the former president was "improved by retirement.—He now converses with more ease & less guardedly than when in publick life. His hospitality is no way diminished, though the Splendour of his Table is considerably lessened for towards the magnificence with which he lived, while President." She continued, "Washington's fame appears to have been the peculiar care of Fortune.—From the first Soldier in America he became the first Magistrate. He is now the most extensive Farmer—of his great landed property he holds <u>four</u> thousand acres in his own hands—He has five hundred slaves." Two years later the Listons were back in Virginia. During a trip to see the Natural Bridge, they stopped at Monticello to visit the vice president. In her journal Henrietta described ascending Jefferson's little mountain: "We wound round this Hill for more than three miles, no part of the road <u>steep</u> or <u>bad</u> but rather narrow;—no cultivation appeared till we reached the Gardens & Negro-Houses of Mr. Jefferson,—but on attaining the summit, the scene was truly magnificent." Liston observed, "Nothing could be more kind than the reception given to us by Mr. Jefferson, or more agreeable than our whole entertainment."[35]

Liston's accounts of her visits to Mount Vernon and Monticello reveal that Washington and Jefferson shared a common culture despite their political and personal differences. As members of the Virginia ruling class, they were expected to offer hospitality to elite visitors like the Listons. The Listons had grown close to the Washingtons and made several visits to Mount Vernon. They knew Jefferson but were not as close to him, socially or politically. They declined his invitation to spend the night at Monticello. It is notable that Liston mentioned the enslaved persons in passing at both places. Henrietta Liston was born in Antigua to a Scottish family that had made a fortune from enslaving hundreds of people over several generations, and she was not troubled by the presence of enslaved persons at Mount Vernon and Monticello. Nor did she, like many European visitors to the United States, comment on the obvious disparity between the presence of slavery in a republic premised on liberty and equality. Her remarks are a reminder that slavery continued to shape and make possible the lives of Washington and Jefferson. They each sought, unsuccessfully, to reconcile the institution to the postrevolutionary republican order over which they squabbled. For the hundreds of enslaved persons at Mount Vernon, Monticello, and the various outlying farms and plantations that both men owned, their dispute over the nature of republicanism and how the government might best preserve and protect liberty would have rung hollow.

Cruel War against Human Nature Itself

> I never mean . . . to possess another slave by purchase; it being among my first wishes to see some plan adopted, by the legislature by which slavery in this Country may be abolished by slow, sure, & imperceptable degrees.
>
> —George Washington to John Francis Mercer, September 9, 1786

When the War of Independence broke out in the spring of 1775, Phillis Wheatley, a young African woman living in Boston, had seen more of the world than either George Washington or Thomas Jefferson. Wheatley was born in West Africa, likely in modern Senegal or Gambia, around 1753. She was captured, enslaved, and sold in 1761, eventually arriving in Boston, where she was purchased by John and Susanna Wheatley. The Wheatley family taught Phillis to read and write, and by the age of fourteen she wrote poetry. In 1773 she traveled to London with Nathaniel Wheatley, the son of her enslavers, and published a book of poetry, *Poems on Various Subjects, Religious and Moral.* Her literary prowess had attracted the attention of some of the leading political and religious figures in Massachusetts, who attested to the authenticity of her poems when they were published. For these men, Phillis's achievement was remarkable because of her race and her condition of servitude. She would not be enslaved much longer. During the summer of 1773, the Wheatleys emancipated Phillis and she returned to Boston where she married John Peters, a free Black man. By the age of twenty-one, Wheatley had visited three continents, had become a literary sensation thanks to her book of poems (the first published by a North American of African origin), and had won her freedom.[1]

During the autumn of 1775, Wheatley composed a poem, "To His Excellency, General Washington" that she sent to Washington at his headquarters in Cambridge during the siege of Boston.[2] Several months later
Washington wrote a gracious response to Wheatley, "I thank you most sincerely for your polite notice of me, in the elegant Lines you enclosed; and
however undeserving I may be of such encomium and panegyrick, the
style and manner exhibit a striking proof of your great poetical Talent."
The general added that he would have liked to have published Wheatley's
poem as a testimony to her genius but feared that doing so would make him
appear vain (since the poem was a tribute to his greatness). He invited her
to visit him at his headquarters in Cambridge.[3]

It is not clear whether Wheatley met Washington, but their exchange is
remarkable. Washington's reply to Wheatley is somewhat surprising.
When he took command of the Continental Army in 1775, Washington
was, of course, a large slaveholder who had expressed few reservations
about slavery and had voiced little sympathy for the plight of enslaved or
formerly enslaved persons in America. While the slave system rested on
assumptions of white supremacy, there is little evidence of Washington
giving voice to those views (nor is there evidence for him rejecting them).
Although Washington was an enslaver and benefited from a system of racial inequality and oppression, he seems to have been genuinely moved by
Wheatley's poem and impressed by her talent. That she was an African
(and a woman) likely contributed to the fervor of his response. His recognition of her "genius" may have been tempered by the assumption that he
believed that such genius was rare among persons like Wheatley. In this,
Washington may have been like those Massachusetts luminaries who testified to Wheatley's authorship of her poems. Nonetheless, he was able to see
her as an individual and differentiate her from the mass of enslaved Africans in America.

Washington's response to Wheatley's poetry stands in contrast to
Thomas Jefferson's. In the *Notes on the State of Virginia*, Jefferson expressed skepticism and disdain for Wheatley's writing. He asserted that
"never yet could I find that a black had uttered a thought above the level of
plain narration" before writing of Wheatley, "Misery is often the parent of
the most affecting touches in poetry.—Among the blacks is misery enough,
God knows, but no poetry. . . . Religion indeed has produced a Phyllis
Whately; but it could not produce a poet. The compositions published

under her name are below the dignity of criticism."[4] Jefferson's response to Wheatley's poetry is twofold: first, he questioned whether she wrote the poems published under her name (despite evidence to the contrary—that's why the men who examined Wheatley in Massachusetts attested to her authorship); second, if she was their author, the poems weren't very good. Elsewhere in the *Notes on the State of Virginia,* Jefferson wrote, "I advance it, therefore, as a suspicion only, that the blacks, whether originally a distinct race, or made distinct by time and circumstance, are inferior to the whites in the endowment both of body and mind."[5] His condemnation of Wheatley was consistent with that belief.

While Jefferson dismissed African intellectual abilities, he also condemned slavery. In the *Notes* he decried the influence of slaveholding on white people, asserting that slavery turned white people into despots and declaring, "I tremble for my country when I reflect that God is just: that his justice cannot sleep for ever."[6] Unlike Washington, Jefferson had forthrightly condemned slavery in print. Also, unlike Washington, he explicitly endorsed the white supremacy upon which slavery was premised.

Phillis Wheatley's verse tribute to George Washington indicates that she supported the Patriot cause during the American Revolution. In her poem she describes "Columbia" as "The land of freedom's heaven-defended race!" which was a victim of Britannia's cruelty and "thirst of boundless power." Wheatley wrote those lines as thousands of enslaved African Americans in Virginia fled to the British, seeking their freedom in response to the proclamation of Lord Dunmore, which promised freedom to the slaves of rebels who supported the British cause. For all Americans, particularly the enslaved, the War of Independence offered a range of options, often fraught with peril and moral complexity. Phillis Wheatley, like many enslaved and formerly enslaved people in New England, threw her lot in with her Patriot neighbors. She was on the same side of the issue of American independence as Washington and Jefferson. Their responses to her reveal much about the range of opinions among elite Patriots over the related questions of slavery and equality during the era of the American Revolution.

Both Washington and Jefferson came to believe that it wasn't acceptable for men like themselves to enslave women like Phillis Wheatley. Ultimately, both men came to oppose slavery. Their thinking on the issue evolved over time. Jefferson was an earlier, more fervent, and more eloquent opponent of slavery than Washington, whose evolution on the issue was slower, quieter, and more private. Having concluded that slavery was unjust and incompatible with republican principles, both men reached a similar conclusion: the solution was some form of gradual, compensated emancipation. They differed over the specifics of how and when such an emancipation might be accomplished. Because of their different views over race—Washington does not seem to have harbored the same "suspicions" of Black inferiority that Jefferson held—their views about what a post-emancipation United States should look like were very different. Jefferson, unlike Washington, didn't believe that free white people and free Black people could live together peacefully. Jefferson believed that emancipation must be accompanied by the expatriation of formerly enslaved people. Though both men came to oppose slavery and favored gradual emancipation, they each concluded that such emancipation was unlikely to occur during their lifetimes. Confronted by that fact, each man sought to reach a personal accommodation with slavery. Washington manumitted the people he enslaved in his will. Jefferson, who outlived Washington by a generation, reconciled himself to slavery while hoping that the institution would eventually disappear, but he failed to take any meaningful action to end it.

———

George Washington was a cautious and careful revolutionary and in no area was this more apparent than over the issue of slavery. Washington's antislavery journey was slow and gradual. His was a steady evolution that culminated in the manumission of more than 160 persons after his death in 1799. This was a private act—but was also a powerful statement with implications far beyond Mount Vernon.[7]

Washington first began to have doubts about slavery in the mid-1760s as he made the transition from being a tobacco planter to a wheat farmer. It was as a hard-headed businessman rather than as a revolutionary leader that Washington began to question the place of slavery in Virginia. His concern over slavery before the revolution was largely motivated by self-interest and practical economic considerations. Raising wheat required fewer laborers than raising tobacco, and Washington, generally uncomfortable with separating enslaved families, found himself with more laborers than he needed. Washington was concerned that tobacco, which exhausted the soil and rendered planters dependent on British merchants while yielding diminishing profits, had a deleterious effect on Virginia. It also made great planters like himself overly dependent on enslaved labor. Washington sought to make the transition to wheat for economic reasons—tobacco simply didn't generate enough profit—but also because he believed one of the benefits of making the change from tobacco to wheat would be independence from British merchants, and enslaved labor. Washington embraced the independence that wheat offered just as he and other colonists began to question their political dependence on Britain. However, there is little evidence that Washington made an explicit connection between the political dispute with Britain and the slavery question prior to the War of Independence.[8]

Washington took the next step in his evolution on slavery during the War of Independence. When he took command of the Continental Army during the summer of 1775, he found himself in charge of a multiracial, polyglot force from several rebellious colonies. During the early days of the war, the army was mostly comprised of New England militia whose units were absorbed into the new army. In New England there was a long tradition of enslaved and free Black people serving in the militia. (The number of enslaved persons was relatively small in New England, and the prospect of arming slaves was not as threatening to the social order there as it would have been in the southern colonies.) Soon after arriving in Cambridge, the new general noted the ill-discipline among the Massachusetts troops and observed that "the Number of Boys, Deserters, & Negroes" that made up a substantial proportion of the troops meant that the province was unlikely to supply more men and requested that Congress send soldiers from other colonies.[9] Several months later, still bedeviled by manpower shortages, Washington convened a council of war, made up of his senior officers, to consider whether to allow free and enslaved Black people to enlist (and reenlist) in the Continental Army. The council "agreed unanimously to reject all Slaves & by a great Majority to reject Negroes altogether."[10] At the beginning of the War of Independence, Washington was very much a Virginia planter; he resisted arming enslaved and free Black people, fearing the consequences of such a decision, despite the shortage of men in the Continental Army.

Arming slaves was very much on Washington's mind in the autumn and early winter of 1775. On November 7 John Murray, Earl of Dunmore, the royal governor of Virginia, issued a proclamation that offered freedom to enslaved men who fled rebel masters, enlisted in the British forces, and helped to suppress the rebellion. Dunmore was hardly an abolitionist. He issued his proclamation from a British warship off the coast of Virginia after British authority had broken down in the province. It was a desperate move to undermine rebel control of the colony. Nonetheless, his proclamation struck at the heart of gentry power and social order in Virginia. Washington recognized the danger Dunmore's proclamation posed. He decried Dunmore as "that Arch Traitor to the Rights of Humanity" and likened his army to a rolling snowball, which would gather strength and speed "if some expedient cannot be hit upon to convince the Slaves and Servants of the Impotency of his designs." Events in Virginia, near to Washington's heart, demonstrated how volatile, dangerous, and unpredictable the situation could become if enslaved persons were armed. This was a step Washington was initially unwilling to take.[11]

Eventually, Congress and Washington, recognizing the Continental Army's need for soldiers, relaxed the restrictions on enlisting free Black and enslaved soldiers, and all the rebellious states north of Maryland accepted Black soldiers. Enslaved men were offered freedom in exchange for their service in the Patriot cause.[12] The situation was more complicated in the South where the prospect of arming slaves threatened the basis of plantation society. By early 1778 Washington had come to recognize the need for Black support, even in the South. He wrote to Congress and noted that the British were exploiting Native Americans and African Americans against the Patriots. "The enemy have set every engine at work, against us, and have actually called savages and even our own slaves to their assistance." In response, the general proposed that Congress might recruit up to three hundred Native soldiers for the coming campaign. He also suggested hiring Black teamsters in Maryland, Virginia, and the Carolinas to support the war effort. He believed that they might be more affordable than white wagoners. "They ought however to be freemen," he stipulated, "for slaves could not be sufficiently depended on. It is to be apprehended they would too frequently desert to the enemy to obtain their liberty; and for the profit of it, or to conciliate a more favourable reception would carry off their waggon-horses with them."[13] Washington recognized that Black service in the Patriot cause not only threatened the slave system but also challenged the assumptions many white Patriots made about the extent (and limits) of the rights and liberties for which they fought. Those liberties were limited for free Black people and might need to be expanded if free Black southerners were to support the Patriot war effort. Alternatively, free Black people might, like their enslaved brethren, view the British as more likely to guarantee their liberties.

While Washington was considering enlisting free Black teamsters, others were contemplating arming enslaved southerners. Lieutenant Colonel John Laurens was one of Washington's aides-de-camp. He was the son of Henry Laurens, who served as the president of the Continental Congress, and the scion of one of the most prominent families in South Carolina. The younger Laurens was only twenty-three in early 1778 when he proposed raising a regiment of enslaved men in South Carolina. Although Congress endorsed Laurens's proposal, nothing came of the plan as the South Carolina legislature repeatedly rejected it (and John Laurens was killed in battle in 1782). The younger Laurens reported enthusiastically to his father that Washington supported his proposal. According to John Laurens, his commander "is convinced that the numerous tribes of blacks in the Southern parts of the Continent offer a resource to us that should not be neglected." To the extent that Washington had reservations, they were practical; he feared the impact that the loss of enslaved labor might have on planters. Laurens continued, "With respect to my particular Plan, he only objects to it with the arguments of Pity, for a man who be less rich than he might be."[14] Washington expressed stronger reservations about the proposal than the younger Laurens recognized (or perhaps his young aide had heard what he wanted to when he reported Washington's view to his father). At any rate Washington expressed skepticism about the plan when he wrote to the elder Laurens in March 1779: "The policy of arming slaves is in my opinion a moot point, unless the enemy set the example, for should we begin to form Battalions of them I have not the smallest doubt (if the war is to be prosecuted) of their following us in it, and justifying the measure upon our own ground. The upshot then must be who can Arm the fastest—and where are our Arms?" Washington concluded, rather disingenuously, "As this is a subject that has never employed much of my thoughts, these are no more than the first crude Ideas that have struck me upon the occasion."[15] We know that Washington had contemplated the issue of slave enlistments since 1775. He had moved from a position of outright opposition at the beginning of the war to qualified acceptance by

1779. His evolution on the issue was motivated by practical necessity, just as Lord Dunmore's had been when he sought to attract enslaved men to join the British army. The Continental Army needed men. By 1779 Washington recognized the effectiveness of the Black soldiers who fought in the army. As the focus of the conflict shifted to the South, the question was complicated, as he saw it, by the impact Black enlistments might have on slavery as an institution.

Just as Washington came to accept the value of Black soldiers to the Patriot cause, he continued to question slavery. In an August 1778 letter to his distant kinsman, Lund Washington, who managed Mount Vernon in his absence during the war, Washington wrote those he enslaved as those "of whom I every day long more & more to get clear of." The general's statement came in the form of a lament. He'd wanted to purchase land near Mount Vernon and lacked the cash to do so and mentioned bartering slaves for the land he coveted. Although willing to exchange enslaved people for land, he refused to barter "Breeding Mares and Stock of other kinds," suggesting the relative value he placed upon his slaves.[16] Washington's comment about bartering enslaved people for land was a parenthetical throwaway line in his letter to Lund, and when his manager followed up seeking permission to sell slaves, Washington declared, "It would be a matter of little consequence to me, whether my property is in Negroes, or loan office Certificates" but said that he was unwilling to separate families. Lund sold nine enslaved persons in January 1779, receiving £2,303.19, which disappointed Washington. That was the last known large-scale sale of Washington's slaves.[17]

Washington's desire "to get clear of" his slaves in 1778 was hardly a full-throated endorsement of abolition. Indeed, he made the comment in passing when discussing the business of his plantations. A decade after beginning the transition from tobacco to wheat, and several years after taking command of a multiracial army, Washington expressed a willingness, indeed a preference, for living without slave labor. For a great planter from the tidewater, this represented an important shift in his thinking. He still approached the issue as a practical business question. He had not yet come around to believing that slavery should be abolished, let alone considering a scheme as to how such an end could be accomplished. Nonetheless, his experiences as a planter and general had taught him that slavery might be unsustainable.

When Washington returned to Mount Vernon in 1783, he sought to restore his personal finances and took a more direct hand in managing his land, as well as the labor it required. After Washington returned to civilian life, he came to conclude that slavery was unsustainable. Even before the war had formally ended, another young aide in his military family, the Marquis de Lafayette, wrote to Washington, suggesting an experiment to end slavery. Lafayette proposed that he and Washington should purchase a plantation together and operate it with free Black tenants as an alternative to enslaved labor.[18] Washington's reply to Lafayette was that of a skilled politician: both encouraging and noncommittal, "The scheme my dear Marqs which you propose as a precedent, to encourage the emancipation of the black people of this country from the Bondage in wch they are held," he wrote, "is a striking evidence of the benevolence of your Heart. I shall be happy to join you in so laudable a work; but will defer going into a detail of the business, 'till I have the pleasure of seeing you."[19] Washington discussed Lafayette's scheme with William Gordon, a Boston minister who was one of the earliest historians of the American Revolution. Gordon stayed at Mount Vernon for three weeks during the summer of 1784 while conducting research. After Gordon returned to Boston, he wrote to Washington, "You wished to get rid of all your Negroes, & the Marquis wisht that an end might be put to the slavery of all of them. I should rejoice beyond measure could your joint counsels & influence produce it, & thereby give the finishing stroke & last polish to your political characters."[20] Lafayette and Gordon each appreciated that Washington's support for abolition would influence public opinion in the United States and beyond. Washington was aware of his power, and reluctant to use it without due consideration. One of the reasons he moved so cautiously on the slavery question and kept his feelings on the matter private was because he recognized that his actions would have consequences far beyond Mount Vernon. Gordon astutely appealed to Washington's concern for his reputation. That, as much as practical and ethical considerations, influenced Washington's thinking with respect to slavery.

Washington did not condemn slavery solely for Lafayette's benefit. By the mid-1780s he was committed to gradual emancipation. In April 1786 he wrote to the Philadelphia merchant Robert Morris, "I can only say there is not a man living who wishes more sincerely than I do, to see a plan adopted for the abolition of [slavery]," Washington continued, "but there is only one proper and effectual mode by which it can be accomplished, & that is by Legislative authority."[21] Several months later he wrote to John Francis Mercer, a former Continental Army officer and a fellow Virginia planter, "I never mean (unless some particular circumstances should compel me to it) to possess another slave by purchase; it being among my first wishes to see some plan adopted, by the legislature by which slavery in this Country may be abolished by slow, sure & imperceptible degrees."[22]

By the eve of the Constitutional Convention, Washington's private views on slavery were well established: he was opposed to slavery; reluctant to purchase more humans; and favored gradual emancipation, provided it was achieved by legislative action. He had evolved considerably on the issue since the beginning of the War of Independence when he was reluctant to accept enslaved men into the Continental Army. How do we explain this change? In 1786 Washington was fifty-four years old, yet he had come, relatively late in life, to question the cornerstone of Virginia society and the basis, along with land, for the wealth and power of the gentry in his state, including himself. There is no single reason that explains Washington's embrace of abolition. Washington seems to have been motivated by a combination of factors. He expressed sympathy, which appears to have been genuine, for the plight of enslaved persons, to whom he referred as "unhappy people."[23] He was, as Lafayette and William Gordon recognized, concerned about his reputation, and slaveholding was coming to be seen as morally and ethically problematic as the various northern states in the newly independent American confederation abolished slavery via gradual emancipation laws or judicial decisions. As ever, he was a practical businessman. Well before the American Revolution he had begun to question the economic viability of slavery. He recognized that slavery was incompatible with the principles of the American Revolution. He came to this conclusion just as antislavery feeling was gaining currency on both sides of the Atlantic. We can measure his progress by his reading. By the late 1780s, he acquired numerous antislavery pamphlets that he had bound in a separate volume in his library.[24] Washington's was a gradual, steady evolution on the question, but by the mid-1780s he had moved far from his unquestioning acceptance of the institution when he was an ambitious young planter newly returned from military service in the late 1750s.

Washington's antislavery was, however, limited. It was trumped by other concerns—namely, the creation and maintenance of a strong union.

By the time Washington became president in 1789, he had expressed dis-
taste for slavery and endorsed gradual emancipation on numerous
occasions. He always did so as a private citizen, however, and had never
publicly condemned the institution. His public reticence was political.
While Washington had come to believe that gradual emancipation was the
answer to the slavery question, the United States was grappling with fundamental constitutional questions. As a strong supporter of the proposed
Constitution in 1787 and 1788, Washington did not want to do anything
that would jeopardize the union. This, for him, was the most important ob-
jective. Washington appreciated that his views would influence the public
debate over slavery and was loath to ignite a controversy on the matter that
would threaten the federal project.[25] Rather, he believed that abolition and
manumission should be left to the states to decide, and the issue should not
be allowed to endanger the union.

As president, Washington took no meaningful action against slavery. Yet
he remained convinced that slavery should be abolished. During his retirement he wrote, "I wish from my Soul that the Legislature of this State could
see the policy of a gradual abolition of Slavery; It might prevt much future
mischief."[26] It is notable that Washington, a strong Federalist, still hewed to
the position that he had taken a decade before (prior to the drafting and ratification of the Constitution) that abolition should be left to the states. Given
his concerns about sectionalism and disunion, he likely feared that a national
emancipation, imposed by Congress on behalf of the states that had already
abolished slavery, or were phasing it out, would have threatened the union.
Washington did contemplate what a post-emancipation world would look
like. He thought that free Black people might be paid agricultural workers. In
a lengthy letter to the English agricultural writer and theorist Arthur Young
in December 1793, Washington described his landholdings, and he contemplated subdividing and leasing his lands. He suggested that "many of the
Negroes, male & female, might be hired by the year as labourers" to work
the land. He did note that free white and Black laborers working side by side
might be a challenge: "It deserves consideration how far the mixing of white
& blacks together is advisable; especially where the former are entirely unacquainted with the latter," but he did not share Jefferson's view that it would
be impossible for free Black people and white people to live together.[27]

Fearing for the union, Washington (unlike Jefferson) made no public
statements condemning slavery during his lifetime. He did, however, make

a powerful posthumous statement against the institution. On July 9, 1799, less than six months before his death, Washington drafted his last will and testament. In his will Washington declared, "Upon the decease [of] my wife, it is my Will & desire th[at] all the Slaves which I hold in [my] own right shall receive their free[dom]."[28] Washington was able to take this action because the Virginia government had adopted a manumission law in 1782 that made it possible for slaveholders to free those they enslaved in their wills. Consequently, the state was home to not only the largest enslaved population in the new nation but also the country's largest free Black population. At the time of Washington's death in 1799, 317 enslaved persons worked at Mount Vernon and Washington's outlying farms. Washington owned 124 of them outright. These would be freed according to the terms of his will. The balance were the "dower slaves" that Martha Washington had brought into their marriage (and over which George had no legal claim) as well as a smaller number of enslaved workers that Washington had hired from his neighbors.

Washington appreciated that forty years after he married Martha, the enslaved persons each had brought to their marriage had themselves intermarried and established families and that separating these would "excite the most pa[in]ful sensations, if not disagreeabl[e] [c]onsequences," and he sought to protect Martha from that experience (although he was legally unable to prevent those consequences for the enslaved families facing separation). Washington also recognized that some of the enslaved people he owned might be too old or infirmed to provide for themselves, while others would be too young. He required his heirs to provide clothing, food, and shelter for the aged and infirmed among those he enslaved. Those children and infants without families to provide for them should be bound over to the court to work as servants until the age of twenty-five. "The Negros thus bound are (by their Masters and Mistresses) to be taught to read & write; and to be brought up to some useful occupation." Crucially, Washington "expressly forbid the Sale, or transportation out of the said Commonwealth, of any Slave, I may die possessed of, under any pretence whatsoever."[29]

Washington made one exception to the conditions of his will. He stipulated that one man, William Lee (Figure 13.1), should be given his freedom or, if Lee preferred, he might remain enslaved at Mount Vernon. Whether Lee chose freedom or slavery, he should receive an annual payment of $30

FIGURE 13.1   John Trumbull, *George Washington and William Lee* (1780). Washington purchased Lee in 1768. Lee served as Washington's body servant and valet for decades. Lee was at Washington's side throughout the War of Independence. Lee was the only enslaved person freed immediately upon Washington's death in 1799. He lived at Mount Vernon until his death in 1810. Bequest of Charles Allen Munn, 1924, Metropolitan Museum.

and receive food and clothing rations. According to Washington, "This I give him as a test[im]ony of my sense of his attachment to me, and for his faithful services during the Revolutionary War."[30] Washington purchased William Lee in 1768. Lee acted as Washington's body servant and valet for more than two decades. He served at Washington's side, including in combat, throughout the War of Independence. During the war Lee met and married a free Black woman, Margaret Thomas, in Philadelphia. She worked for the Washingtons as a seamstress and laundress and, after the war, Lee insisted that his wife be allowed to go to Mount Vernon. In the 1780s William Lee suffered a series of accidents, breaking both of his knees, that left him disabled. After Washington's death, he elected to remain at Mount Vernon, where he lived until his death in 1810.[31]

Martha Washington outlived her husband by two and a half years, dying on May 22, 1802. Despite the terms of her husband's will, on January 1, 1801, she freed those he had enslaved.

George Washington's last will and testament made a powerful statement about slavery. Although Washington hoped that the individual states, including his native Virginia, should abolish slavery—and that only the states had the authority to take such action—he took personal action upon his death to manumit his own slaves. This was the only legal course of action available to him according to Virginia law at the time. His will is clear and unambiguous in its terms, particularly his injunction that they be enforced "without evasion, neglect, or delay." By the end of his life, Washington believed that slavery was morally wrong and incompatible with the founding principles of the American republic. Though he had some reservations about whether free Black people and white people could live together in that republic, he sought to provide those he enslaved with the opportunity, and in the case of the children, the means to do so. Washington's had been a slow, gradual journey. His will was his final statement on the matter. As the nineteenth century dawned, Washington told the American people that slavery was incompatible with their republic. This was more of a statement than Thomas Jefferson was able or willing to make at the end of his life.

———

Thomas Jefferson was an earlier and more public critic of slavery than George Washington. As a new member of the House of Burgesses in 1769, the year the two men met for the first time, Jefferson supported a bill to allow for the manumission of slaves. According to an account that Jefferson wrote more than four decades later, "In the first or second session of the legislature after I became a member, I drew to this subject [manumission] the attention of Col. Bland one of the oldest, ablest, & most respected members, and he undertook to move for certain moderate extensions of the protection of the laws to these people." Bland's failed effort showed that

Jefferson was troubled by slavery, but he also learned that opposing the institution could come at a significant social cost: "I seconded his motion, and as a younger member, was more spared in the debate but he was denounced as an enemy of his country, & treated with the grossest indecorum."[32] Five years later, in the *Summary View of the Rights of British America*, he wrote, "The abolition of domestic slavery is the great object of desire in those colonies, where it was unhappily introduced in their infant state." Jefferson acknowledged that a wholesale abolition might not then be possible, but the prohibition of the transatlantic slave trade would be a welcome first step: "But previous to the enfranchisement of the slaves we have, it is necessary to exclude all further importations from Africa." He claimed that George III had blocked all attempts to do so by exercising his royal veto, "yet our repeated attempts to effect this by prohibitions, and by imposing duties which might amount to a prohibition, have been hitherto defeated by his majesty's negative."[33]

Jefferson had not written the *Summary View* for publication but rather as a briefing paper for the Virginia delegates attending the Continental Congress. As such he may not have intended its condemnation of slavery for public circulation. The same could not be said for his most important statement about slavery, which appeared in his draft of the Declaration of Independence.[34]

Jefferson's draft of the Declaration of Independence contained a lengthy condemnation of the Atlantic slave trade, which was deleted by Congress when it debated the final version. The passage appeared in the indictment of George III, which makes up the bulk of the declaration. Had Congress retained the passage condemning the slave trade in language that made a direct connection to the Declaration's assertion of universal equality, it would have been a more radical statement, both antislavery and anti-imperial. It would have been a clear, unambiguous statement that Africans possessed the same rights and liberties that Anglo-Americans were fighting for in 1776. It was a statement that Congress was unwilling to make, but Jefferson was willing to write.[35]

Jefferson did not become widely known as the author of the Declaration of Independence until the 1790s, though he did share copies of his original draft of the declaration with some friends and confidants.[36] One of those he gave a copy to was his neighbor, the Florentine merchant, Philip Mazzei. Mazzei lived in Charlottesville during the American Revolution, and he and Jefferson became close friends. Mazzei later remembered that during the revolution, Jefferson had told him that "he would move for abolishing slavery entirely since both humanity and justice demanded it; that to keep in bondage beings born with rights equal to our own and who differed from us only in color was an injustice not only barbarous and cruel but shameful as well while we were risking everything for our own freedom." It is difficult to precisely date Mazzei's recollection, but the language he attributes to Jefferson closely follows that of the deleted slave-trade clause in the Declaration of Independence. Mazzei's account, published in Italian long after both he and Jefferson had died, confirms the view that Jefferson's antislavery views were strongest during the American Revolution. When he drafted the Declaration of Independence and included language linking slavery to the document's call for universal equality, Jefferson made the most radical antislavery statement of his long public life.[37]

Jefferson left Congress in the autumn of 1776 to help revise his newly independent state's law code. Between 1776 and 1779, he drafted a series of proposed laws with the intention of transforming Virginia's legal code in accordance with the principles of republican government. As we have seen he proposed bills to abolish primogeniture and entail, to separate church and state, and to create a system of state-sponsored education, among other reforms. In June 1779 Jefferson presented "A Bill Concerning Slaves" to the committee of revisors. More than forty years later, in his autobiography, Jefferson claimed that the bill "was a mere digest of the existing laws respecting them, without any intimation of a plan for a future & general emancipation." Rather, Jefferson claimed, it would be better to later add an emancipation plan as an amendment to the Bill Concerning Slaves once it had been adopted by the legislature as "it was found by that the public mind would not yet bear the proposition."[38] Despite Jefferson's claim, he had suggested several amendments to the laws pertaining to slaves. He sought to limit the number of enslaved people in Virginia by stipulating that no additional slaves could be brought into the state except those who were already present as well as those descended from enslaved women in the state. The bill further allowed slaveowners to manumit enslaved persons, provided they left the state within a year. Further, Jefferson's proposed bill required that white women who bore children by Black or mixed-race fathers, regardless of whether they were enslaved or free, should leave the state within a year. The bill also included restrictions on whether enslaved or free Black people could testify in court, own arms, and gather and speak in public.[39]

Absent the amended emancipation plan, Jefferson's Bill Concerning Slaves is a restrictive document. While it seeks to minimize the growth of the enslaved population by limiting future forced migration and importation of new slaves into the commonwealth, and allows slaveholders to manumit their enslaved property, it compels newly freed slaves to leave the state. The gendered aspects of the bill—imposing slavery on the children of enslaved mothers while compelling free white women who had children by Black fathers, free or not, to leave the state—are especially regressive (and ironic given that Jefferson himself would father children by an enslaved woman). Jefferson's proposed bill sought, in a relatively small way, to limit slavery in Virginia while seeking to prevent the emergence of a free Black community within the state. By the time the Virginia assembly enacted the bill in December 1785, it had already adopted a more liberal manumission law (which did not require formerly enslaved persons to leave the state), and it removed the restrictions on free Black people and white women from Jefferson's original bill.[40]

In the aftermath of Virginia's manumission law, Jefferson proposed two measures to limit or eliminate slavery in parts of the new republic. In May 1783 Jefferson had heard that a convention would be called in Virginia to draft a new constitution to replace that which the state had adopted in 1776. He spent four weeks drafting a proposed constitution. In the end, no convention was held, and Virginia failed to adopt a new constitution until 1830. However, the draft constitution that Jefferson prepared for the putative convention contained the following clause: "The General assembly shall not have power to ... permit the introduction of any more slaves to reside in this state, or the continuance of slavery beyond the generation which shall be living on the first 31st day of December 1800; all persons born after that day being hereby declared free."[41] This was a clear plan for gradual emancipation without the racial restrictions found in the Bill Concerning Slaves. Jefferson returned to Congress in 1783, and in the spring of 1784, after Virginia had ceded its claims to the western lands to the national domain, Jefferson was instrumental in proposing a plan for the government of western territory after 1800. That plan included a prohibition of slavery in the territory. The key features of this proposal, including the ban on slavery, were later incorporated into the Northwest Ordinance of 1787.[42]

Jefferson's draft constitution and the plan for the government of western territory represent attempts to reconcile his antislavery views with the principles he articulated in the Declaration of Independence.

What of the plan for general emancipation that Jefferson claimed should be added to the Bill Concerning Slaves after it became law? In the absence of a new constitution, surely such an amendment would be necessary? There is no record of such an amendment in the records of Virginia's House of Delegates. However, in the *Notes on the State of Virginia*, Jefferson explained, "An amendment containing it was prepared, to be offered to the legislature whenever the bill should be taken up." Though he doesn't identify himself as the author of the putative amendment, Jefferson provided a detailed summary of his emancipation plan in the *Notes*. According to Jefferson, all the children of enslaved persons born after the adoption of the act should be freed. The liberated children "should continue with their parents to a certain age, then be brought up, at the public expence, to tillage, arts or sciences, according to their geniuses, till the females should be eighteen, and the males twenty-one years of age, when they should be colonized to such place as the circumstances of the time should render most proper, sending them out with arms, implements of household and of the handicraft arts, feeds, pairs of the useful domestic animals, &c. to declare them a free and independant people, and extend to them our alliance and protection, till they shall have acquired strength." Whether Jefferson prepared his plan as an amendment to the Bill Concerning Slaves is unknown. However, his published account in the *Notes on Virginia* remains his most thorough statement on emancipation. It demonstrates that his antislavery views were closely aligned with his belief in Black inferiority. While Jefferson, at least during and immediately after the American Revolution, sincerely wanted to abolish slavery, he could not conceive of a post-emancipation society in which free Black people and white people lived together.[43]

Jefferson advocated gradually eliminating slavery from Virginia. All those enslaved before the act was adopted would remain in bondage, but their children would be free, and the state would undertake the expense of training and teaching them. When they became adults, the children of the enslaved would receive supplies and would leave the state for an unknown destination (at different times Jefferson speculated about sending formerly enslaved people to Africa, the West, or the Caribbean[44]). Because of Jefferson's plan, Virginia would gradually become freer, within a generation or two there would be no enslaved people in the Commonwealth, and it would become whiter. Though Jefferson's plan would gradually "solve" the slavery problem, it would create a different challenge. Virginia would face a labor shortage. As a solution Jefferson proposed, "To send vessels at the same time to other parts of the world for an equal number of white inhabitants; to induce whom to migrate hither, proper encouragements were to be proposed." In essence, Jefferson proposed to gradually eliminate slavery in Virginia by replacing enslaved Africans and their descendants with free white European laborers.[45]

Jefferson then posited a rather obvious question: "Why not retain and incorporate the blacks into the state, and thus save the expence of supplying, by importation of white settlers, the vacancies they will leave?" (This was Washington's solution.) He felt that it would be impossible for white people and Black people to live alongside each other in freedom. Jefferson averred that there were profound "physical and moral" differences between Africans and Europeans that made it impossible for them to live together peacefully. He then, in the most notorious passage he wrote in a lifetime of writing, enumerated what he believed to be the racial differences between Black people and white people before concluding, "I advance it therefore as a suspicion only, that the blacks, whether originally a distinct race, or made distinct by time and circumstances, are inferior to the whites in the endowments both of body and mind."[46] In the immediate aftermath of the American Revolution, Jefferson believed that slavery should be abolished gradually, but there was no place in his thinking for free Black people and white people to live together in the new American republic.

Despite his racism Jefferson was troubled by slavery and recognized that the institution was incompatible with republican government. He believed that it corrupted the manners and morals of slaveholders and debased the enslaved. Elsewhere in the *Notes,* he wrote: "Indeed I tremble for my country when I reflect that God is just: that his justice cannot sleep for ever: that considering numbers, nature and natural means only, a revolution of the wheel of fortune, an exchange of situation, is among possible events: that it may become probable by supernatural interference! The Almighty has no attribute which can take side with us in such a contest." Jefferson held out hope that change was coming. During and after the revolution, each of the northern states had abolished slavery, and even Virginia had legalized manumission in 1782. He hoped that gradual emancipation coupled with expatriation might avert a violent racial conflict.

Despite, or perhaps because of, his hope that slavery was declining, Jefferson took few concrete steps to eliminate the institution (though as president he supported and signed the legislation that outlawed American participation in the transatlantic slave trade in 1808). As he grew older, and slavery spread and became more entrenched in the United States, he became more pessimistic, fearing that the dispute over slavery might cause a sectional schism or civil war, while retaining his belief that emancipation without expatriation would result in a racial conflict. During the crisis over the admission of Missouri as a state in 1820, Jefferson wrote to Congressman John Holmes of Massachusetts that he feared that the crisis would strike the death knell of the union. With respect to the dispute over slavery that had caused the crisis, he wrote, "A general emancipation and *expatriation* could be effected: and, gradually, and with due sacrifices, I think it might be. but, as it is, we have the wolf by the ear, and we can neither hold him, nor safely let him go. justice is in one scale, and self-preservation in the other."[47] In response to the Missouri crisis, he also suggested that "diffusion," spreading the enslaved population across a wider area but limiting its numbers, might be an interim solution to the challenge of reconciling antislavery and white supremacy. At the end of 1820, he wrote a lengthy and pessimistic letter about the Missouri crisis to his former Treasury secretary, Albert Gallatin. He could see only one positive outcome from the crisis. He told Gallatin, "It has brought the necessity of some plan of general emancipation & deportation more home to the minds of our people than it has ever been before." (Of course, nearly five decades earlier in the *Summary View*, he had written that abolition was "the great object of desire" in the southern colonies.) He mentioned that the governor of Virginia (Jefferson's son-in-law, Thomas Mann Randolph) had prepared a gradual emancipation proposal but that it was unlikely to pass because the cost would be too great. Jefferson, echoing the proposal he had included in the *Notes on the State of Virginia*, outlined a plan whereby all enslaved persons born after a certain date would be freed, become wards of the state, and be sent to Haiti. He believed that the scheme could be paid for by a combination of taxation, land sales, and charitable donations. With respect to the latter, he wrote, "I think Europe, which has forced this evil on us, and the Eastern [New England] states who have been it's chief instruments of importation, would be bound to give largely."[48] As was often the case with respect to slavery, Jefferson overestimated the willingness of others to forgo a labor system that he, himself, couldn't live without.

Jefferson had begun his career as an outspoken idealist who recognized that slavery and republicanism were incompatible. He was an eloquent critic of slavery, but his racism prevented him from conceiving of a post-emancipation world in which Black people and white people could live together peacefully. Although he favored gradual emancipation (and expatriation), he took few meaningful steps to achieve it. When Jefferson died in 1826, he freed only five enslaved people, all members of the extended Hemings family (including his sons Madison and Eston). In January 1827 Monticello, Jefferson's personal effects, and 140 enslaved persons were sold at auction to settle Jefferson's personal debt.

———

Although Washington and Jefferson knew each other for three decades, and their lives depended on enslaved labor, their surviving correspondence (and Jefferson's notes of their conversations) suggests that they rarely discussed slavery. Washington, a serious student of farming, carried out a lengthy correspondence with the English agricultural writer Arthur Young during the 1780s and 1790s. In January 1792 Young sent Washington a list of detailed questions on American farming, including a query about the cost of labor in the United States. Washington shared the letter with Jefferson, who provided calculations to show that enslaved labor was cheaper in the United States than was wage labor in Britain. Jefferson estimated slaves cost their owners £12, 5 shillings per annum (and hiring enslaved labor cost £15–£18) while farm laborers in England cost £24 per year. Jefferson qualified his calculations, noting that "there must be some addition to this to make the labour equal to that of a white man, as I believe the negro does not perform quite as much work, nor with as much intelligence." Washington sent Jefferson's notes to Young, adding his own responses to Young's questions. He made a distinction between the cost of white labor in the United States, which was more expensive than English labor, and enslaved Black labor, which was not. Washington shared Jefferson's disdain for the quality of enslaved labor, writing, "Blacks are capable of much labour, but having (I am speaking generally) no ambition to establish a <u>good</u> name, they are too regardless of a <u>bad</u> one; and of course, require more of the masters eye than the former."[49] It is telling that in one of the few exchanges between Washington and Jefferson on slavery, they did not condemn the institution but rather, as Virginia planters, complained about the poor quality of enslaved labor.

We are left with the paradox that Washington and Jefferson were antislavery slaveholders, who largely failed to act against slavery. Both men expressed their strongest opposition to slavery—though they were by no means leaders on the issue either nationally or in Virginia—during and immediately after the revolution. They came to their antislavery by different routes. Washington's was a cautious evolution on the question, whereas Jefferson seems to have opposed slavery from a young age. They both came to believe that gradual emancipation was the best way to solve the slavery problem while preserving the social and political order in the United States. Washington believed this must happen at the state level. Failing that, individual slave owners might take action, as he did when he manumitted the men and women that he enslaved in his will (the only legal avenue open to him in Virginia), but the issue could not be allowed to endanger the union. Jefferson claimed to have developed various emancipation plans over the course of his long career, but they never came to fruition. The most significant action he took was supporting and signing the bill to outlaw the Atlantic slave trade in 1808.

Why didn't Washington and Jefferson do more about slavery? Both men came to believe that slavery was wrong. As Jefferson wrote to Edward Coles, a young Virginia planter who appealed to him to move to Illinois and free his slaves in 1814 (an invitation Jefferson declined), "The love of justice & the love of country plead equally the cause of these people, and it is a mortal reproach to us that they should have pleaded it so long in vain, and should have produced not a single effort, nay I fear not much serious willingness to relieve them & ourselves from our present condition of moral and political reprobation."[50] Many of their contemporaries agreed, and they took more substantive actions against the institution than the revolution's two most prominent leaders. Many thousands of enslaved women and men—including some that Washington and Jefferson held in bondage—sought their freedom during the War of Independence through flight and by taking up arms. Numerous individuals—Phillis Wheatley, John Laurens, the Marquis de Lafayette, Edward Coles, and others—directly challenged

Washington and Jefferson on the issue, but they refused to act (beyond private expressions of condemnation and Washington's manumission of some of the people enslaved at Mount Vernon). Why?

The convenient answer, which satisfies contemporary sensibilities, is that they were blinded by their racism and self-interest. Unable to see persons of African descent as equals and unwilling to jeopardize their standard of living, they could not countenance ending slavery and extending the equality promised in the Declaration of Independence to Black people in the new American republic. There is considerable merit to this argument. Both men, especially Jefferson, struggled to conceive of a post-emancipation world in which free Black people and white people could live together in peace. While compelling, racism and self-interest do not adequately explain the failure of Washington and Jefferson to act against slavery.

Washington and Jefferson came of age in a world shaped by war, violence, and conflict. The new American republic was created through war and the Constitution was intended to safeguard the republic. "Common danger," wrote Washington, "brought the States into Confederacy, and on their Union our safety & importance depend."[51] Externally, the great powers like Britain, France, and Spain and lesser powers like the Barbary States threatened the United States. Internally, Native Americans waged war to resist US hegemony and slavery, which rested on violence and coercion, posed a twofold threat as the twin specters of sectional conflict and slave rebellion preoccupied many white Americans. Theirs was a world in which war was endemic and posed a constant threat to the existence of the United States.

While we view slavery as a morally unacceptable labor system premised on white supremacy, for Washington and Jefferson slavery was another form of war that posed a danger to the new republic. Jefferson described George III's involvement in the slave trade as "cruel war against human nature itself." When he considered the difficulties Black people and white people would face after emancipation, he used the language of civil war and racial conflict. "Deep rooted prejudices entertained by the whites," he wrote, "ten thousand recollections, by the blacks, of the injuries they have sustained; new provocations; the real distinctions which nature has made; and many other circumstances, will divide us into parties, and produce convulsions which will probably never end but in the extermination of the one or the other race."[52] For Jefferson, premature emancipation might destroy the United States. Slavery was unjust but it was another injustice in a world characterized by violence and war. Containing that threat took precedence over addressing the moral questions raised by slavery. (Conveniently, it also meant that although Jefferson favored gradual emancipation, the time was never right to enact it.)

Washington shared these concerns. Early in his presidency, he and Congress received numerous petitions from Quaker activists attacking the Atlantic slave trade.[53] Congress tabled the petitions, so Washington was not compelled to formally respond to them, but he disdained them as an "ill-judged piece of business." Washington feared that the petitions might prompt a sectional rift between North and South, endangering the republic—a position Jefferson would come to hold during the Missouri crisis of 1819–1821.[54] Given the choice between protecting the union or taking a public stand against slavery, Washington and Jefferson always opted for the union of states. We see slavery as a character test for the American revolutionaries, a test that Washington and Jefferson failed. They would not agree with that framing. They knew slavery was wrong but believed that creating and protecting the American republic was the greater good. In their minds the ethical and moral challenges posed by slavery could only be addressed if the republic survived. That, not abolishing slavery, was their priority. Despite their political and personal differences during the 1790s, on that they agreed and never wavered.

Epilogue

Th: Jefferson presents his compliments to the reverend mr Ogden and thanks him for his pamphlet which he has read with great satisfaction. the example which has been set by the great man who was the subject of it, will be of immense value to mankind if the Buonapartes of this world, & those whose object is fame & glory, will but contemplate & truly calculate the difference between that of a Washington & of a Cromwell.

—Thomas Jefferson to Uzal Ogden, February 12, 1800

In mid-November 1799 Robert and Henrietta Liston, the British ambassador to the United States and his wife, visited Mount Vernon. The Listons had been regular visitors in the past, but they made a lengthier visit this time because they were preparing to return to Britain and, as Henrietta wrote, "We thought it might not be in our power to repeat it." She provided a portrait of the Washingtons in retirement. "General Washington & his amiable Wife received us with much Kindness—The pleasing change in the Generals manners which we had remarked since his resigning the Presidency still continued," she wrote. Liston observed that age and poor health were taking a toll on Washington. "I was sorry to observe that a late fit of illness seemed to have somewhat altered his looks a little. His figure—always noble appeared less, & an approaching deafness had in some degree affected his spirits." Despite this, Washington remained active. "We found him still devoted to his Farm," she noted, and, no doubt anticipating his death, "he had of late busied himself in preparing his family Vault." Henrietta recorded an emotional scene as their visit ended: "At our departure he kissed me, & kindly shaking hands with Mr. Liston, ordered his Horse & escorted us to his own boundaries."[1]

Two weeks after the Listons returned to Philadelphia, they received the news that Washington had died from a throat infection at Mount Vernon on December 14. "Mr. Liston & I greatly esteemed & admired the <u>Man</u>," wrote Henrietta, "& felt grateful for his uniform attention & kindness to us; & it is with satisfaction we reflect on having visited him so lately & parted from him so affectionately." Washington's death stunned the nation, and Liston reported that Congress had invited Washington's former comrade in arms (and Jefferson's enemy) Henry Lee to deliver a eulogy for his former commander at a memorial service. Henrietta Liston described the scene as Lee delivered his tribute on Thursday, December 26, at Philadelphia's German Lutheran church "to a vast concourse of people," reportedly several thousand, "admitted by tickets issued by a Committee appointed to arrange the Ceremony." According to Liston, "The President, Vice President, Senators & House of Representatives,—Foreign Ministers,—The Military, & all the different Trades &c—paraded in proper order. A <u>Bier</u> was placed near the Pulpit—decorated with Military Ensigns—Bishop White read the Prayers (Washington was an Episcopal;) & General Lee delivered his oration—pleasing rather than brilliant." In his eulogy Lee described Washington as "First in war, first in peace, and first in the hearts of his countrymen." As befitted the wife of the British ambassador, Liston was attentive to what Lee had to say about her country. "<u>We</u> were satisfied," she wrote, "by his expressing himself handsomely of the British Nation—for in enumerating great deeds of his <u>Hero</u>, a successful opposition to Great Britain Naturally became the principal theme." Liston observed that the service "was conducted with decency & decorum" and that "the President afterwards gave a publick dinner & certainly the most Sombre of which We have ever partaken."[2]

Liston's account of Washington's memorial service is not entirely accurate. Although she reported that the vice president was among the mourners, Thomas Jefferson was not present for the service. He did not arrive in Philadelphia for the new congressional term until two days after the memorial for Washington. As Robert Troup, a member of the Society of Cincinnati whom Washington had appointed to the federal bench, observed a few days later, "Jefferson has just arrived in Philadelphia. He has taken care to avoid all ceremonies of respect to the memory of General Washington."[3] After all the ill-will engendered by the Mazzei Letter, Jefferson, who shrank from conflict and had been reluctant to attend his own inauguration as vice president, probably thought it best to avoid Washington's funeral.

Henry Lee's oration for Washington was perhaps the most famous of hundreds of such tributes that were delivered and published over the coming months. These, of course, heaped praise on the recently deceased national hero. Jefferson, who was sent numerous published eulogies, found them all a bit too much to take. He did not recognize the increasingly godlike attributes ascribed to Washington by his eulogists. As he wrote in response to one such effort, "Praise, when given within the limits of truth & nature affords us an occasion of exercising some of the most pleasing & virtuous emotions of the mind, of paying by a just tribute a debt of gratitude which we owe to those who have deserved well of their fellowmen. but we have seen some examples lately, which if they do not border on impiety, yet revolt us by their extravagance, and would have revolted no one more than the great man who was the subject of them."[4] In early 1800, as he contemplated another run for the presidency, Jefferson was only capable of giving grudging praise to Washington. The wounds of the recent past were too fresh.

The relationship between Washington and Jefferson need not have ended on such a sour note. One can imagine the two men reconnecting over their shared interest in agriculture as the political concerns of the moment faded from view. A decade after their estrangement in 1801, Jefferson and Adams famously reconciled and enjoyed a happy and lengthy correspondence until their deaths in 1826. Jefferson and Adams had shared the common experience of service together as diplomats in Europe, as well as numerous interests beyond politics. There was genuine affection between the families of the two men. None of these factors characterized the Washington-Jefferson relationship.

There would be no personal reconciliation between Washington and Jefferson. In part this was because of bad luck. The two men simply did not have enough time for their tempers to cool and to forgive or forget previous slights, both real and imagined. Washington's retirement was short—he died less than three years after leaving office—while Jefferson continued to hold national office. Once revolutionary comrades, colleagues, and friends, the two men became estranged because each believed the other was a party to a plot to destroy the American republic. Their relationship had, from the start, been grounded on politics—first the struggle for independence and then to create a functioning republican government. Their relationship flourished when they agreed on the major issues of the day—resistance to British encroachments on American liberties, independence, and the need to create a stable republic. When significant political differences between the two men emerged, particularly over the nature of the federal government and the degree to which the United States should support the French Revolution, the basis of their friendship disappeared. They were not revolutionary brothers bound by a fraternal bond of military service. Nor was theirs the bond between fathers and sons, like that between Washington and his aides, the members of his "military family." Rather, theirs was a bond of distant kinship, best characterized as like that between cousins. Products of the same culture and class, they joined a common struggle and developed a close relationship that eventually collapsed under the weight of their apparent political differences. Had Washington lived longer, might they have reconciled? Perhaps, though given that Jefferson remained politically active, holding national office until 1809, there is reason to doubt such an assumption. Jefferson and Adams did not reconcile until after Jefferson left office and retired permanently.

The estrangement between Washington and Jefferson at the time of Washington's death resulted in an irony for Jefferson. Their differences were political—each had come to believe the other represented a type of politics that posed a mortal danger to the American republic—yet for the remainder of his life (Jefferson outlived Washington by more than twenty-five years), Jefferson sought to reconcile his politics with Washington's. He sought to show that the two men *really* agreed with each other on the most important questions facing the United States. Politics was the basis of the Washington-Jefferson friendship, and differences over politics had caused its end, yet Jefferson spent a generation trying to prove that their political differences weren't all that great. He sought to minimize the political differences between them and, in a sense, to repair his relationship with Washington after all. He was more successful in reckoning with the posthumous image of Washington than he had been with the living Washington during his final years. That rehabilitation, which was slow and uneven, began with Jefferson's election to the presidency.

On January 2, 1801, Thomas Jefferson left Washington, DC. The vice president hired a horse and crossed the Potomac River by ferry at Georgetown. He traveled with a fellow Republican, Senator John Langdon of New Hampshire. (Jefferson and Langdon lodged together at Conrad and McMunn's boarding house on Capitol Hill.) The politicians rode a dozen miles south of the capital to Mount Vernon. Washington had died more than a year earlier in December 1799, and Jefferson sought to visit his grave and to pay his respects to Martha Washington. The vice president met with the widow, then aged sixty-nine, and her twenty-one-year-old granddaughter, Nelly Parke Custis Lewis. Jefferson wrote little about the meeting, merely remarking to his daughter, Polly, "mrs. Washington and mrs. Lewis enquired very kindly after you."[5] Martha Washington had much more to say about the encounter. A year later she told a group of visiting Federalist politicians, who made a similar journey from the capital to see her, that her encounter with Jefferson had been remarkably unpleasant. John Cotton Smith, a representative from Connecticut, reported that the widow declared of Jefferson's visit "next to the loss of her husband, it was the most painful occurrence of her life." Another of the party, Representative Manasseh Cutler of Massachusetts, recalled, "Her remarks were frequently pointed, and sometimes very sarcastic, on the new order of things and the present administration. She spoke of the election of Mr. Jefferson, whom she considered as one of the most detestable of mankind, as the greatest misfortune our country had ever experienced."[6]

What explains Martha Washington's contempt for Thomas Jefferson? In part, she was likely suspicious of his motives for visiting her. In January 1801 Jefferson was in the midst of the confusing and confused aftermath of the election of 1800. The vote in the electoral college was deadlocked between Jefferson and his fellow Republican, Aaron Burr, each of whom received seventy-three votes. The incumbent, John Adams, had finished with sixty-five electoral votes. In February 1801 the outgoing (Federalist-dominated) House of Representatives would have to choose between Burr and Jefferson. Jefferson's visit to Mount Vernon may have been intended to shape the outcome of the election as he sought George Washington's posthumous imprimatur. John Cotton Smith (who voted for Burr during the electoral dispute) objected to Jefferson's behavior, "Think of his visiting the tomb of Washington, and shedding crocodile tears over his remains; a transaction evidently intended, for it was extensively published, to favour his election to the presidency, but which was truly distressing to Mrs. Washington."[7] Apart from her immediate distress over Jefferson's apparent desire to exploit her husband's memory, the animus between Martha Washington and Jefferson went back several years. Both George and Martha Washington never really forgot, nor forgave, what they saw as Jefferson's betrayal.

While Jefferson's visit to Mount Vernon *was* political, perhaps Jefferson was also sincere in his desire to pay his respects to Martha Washington and to the memory of his deceased friend. The two motives were not incompatible. The election of 1800 marked the beginning of Jefferson's attempt to repair his relationship with Washington.

After the bitterly contested election, the House of Representatives selected Jefferson to become the third president of the United States. The Republicans had finally defeated the Federalists, who would never again win a national election. Jefferson was inaugurated on March 4, 1801. In his inaugural address, he struck a conciliatory tone toward his adversaries. If the Farewell Address can be read as Washington's statement of principles to Jefferson, then Jefferson's First Inaugural Address might be read as his public response to Washington. It represents the beginning of Jefferson's effort to reconcile his political vision with Washington's. The new president acknowledged that the election campaign had been fiercely contested but asserted that the "voice of the nation, announced according to the rules of the Constitution," had spoken, and he hoped that "all will, of course, arrange themselves under the will of the law, and unite in common efforts for the common good." He sought to reassure his Federalist opponents, observing that while in a republic, "the will of the majority is in all cases to prevail," but for "that will to be rightful [it] must be reasonable; that the minority possess their equal rights, which equal law must protect, and to violate would be oppression." He then called on all citizens to put aside the rancor of the past: "Let us restore to social intercourse that harmony and affection without which liberty and even life itself are but dreary things. And let us reflect that, . . . we have yet gained little if we countenance a political intolerance as despotic, as wicked, and capable of bitter and bloody persecutions." In language he could not summon a decade earlier, Jefferson reminded his listeners that "every difference of opinion is not a difference of principle. We have been called by different names brethren of the same principle. We are all republicans, we are all federalists," the most famous phrase in the address. In contrast to his early assertions that Federalists sought to subvert the republic, Jefferson said, "If there be any among us who would wish to dissolve this Union or to change its republican form, let them stand undisturbed as monuments of the safety with which error of opinion may be tolerated where reason is left free to combat it."

Jefferson then set out to define the shared principles that bound Republicans and Federalists together, most notably, "our attachment to union and representative government," and "Equal and exact justice to all men, of whatever state or persuasion, religious or political." In language that might have been drawn from Washington's Farewell Address, Jefferson called for "peace, commerce, and honest friendship with all nations, entangling alliances with none." He differed from Washington in calling for "the support of the State governments in all their rights, as the most competent administrations for our domestic concerns and the surest bulwarks against antirepublican tendencies" but followed that with fulsome support for the Federal government, "the preservation of the General Government in its whole constitutional vigor, as the sheet anchor of our peace at home and safety abroad," while calling for

> a jealous care of the right of election by the people . . .; absolute acquiescence in the decisions of the majority, the vital principle of republics, from which is no appeal but to force, the vital principle and immediate parent of despotism; a well-disciplined militia, our best reliance in peace and for the first moments of war till regulars may relieve them; the supremacy of the civil over the military authority; economy in the public expense, that labor may be lightly burthened; the honest payment of our debts and sacred preservation of the public faith; encouragement of agriculture, and of commerce as its handmaid; the diffusion of information and arraignment of all abuses at the bar of the public reason; freedom of religion; freedom of the press, and freedom of person under the protection of the habeas corpus, and trial by juries impartially selected.[8]

Had he lived until 1801, Washington would have found little to object to in Jefferson's First Inaugural Address.

It is tempting to dismiss the conciliatory tone of Jefferson's address, like his visit to Mount Vernon, as insincere rhetoric from a man who occasionally bent the truth to suit his political needs. That was certainly the view that many Federalists took. However, if we take Jefferson at his word, then the address takes on a different character. After the partisan strife of the 1790s (which he played no small part in fomenting), culminating in the election of 1800, which for a time threatened the union during the winter of 1800–1801, Jefferson sought to step back from the political abyss and identify the principles that united the two parties. As he concluded his inaugural address, Jefferson called Washington "our first and greatest revolutionary character, whose preeminent services had entitled him to the first place in his country's love and destined him for the fairest page in the volume of faithful history."[9] In praising his predecessor and former friend, Jefferson began his presidency by striking a Washingtonian pose, as a man above party serving the nation. As in Washington's case, such a position could never be entirely convincing; both men were partisans, but faced with the burdens of office and with the passage of time after his retirement, Jefferson came to sincerely believe that he and Washington agreed on much more than they disagreed over.

Jefferson's assertion that Federalists and Republicans had more in common than divided them rang hollow to many Federalists who remembered Jefferson's partisan attacks during the 1790s and doubted his sincerity. Washington, from beyond the grave, became a weapon to attack Jefferson during his presidency. In 1802 Jefferson became concerned when he learned that the chief justice of the Supreme Court, John Marshall (yet another distant Virginia kinsman), was writing a biography of Washington. Marshall was an ardent Federalist and a Continental Army veteran, who had served under Washington.[10]

Over five volumes published between 1804 and 1807, Marshall offered a panoramic overview from the colonial origins of the United States until Washington's death. His fifth volume, published in 1807, dealt with the history of the postindependence United States, particularly the Constitution and Washington's presidency, and was the most problematic from Jefferson's perspective. According to Marshall's interpretation, the Federalists were enlightened and reasonable nationalists who sought to create a competent, credible, and stable government in the face of the selfish, local parochialism of Republicans who promoted disorder and anarchy at the expense of good government. Marshall drew an unfavorable contrast between Washington and Hamilton on one hand, who favored creating a government "which should possess in itself sufficient resources to maintain the character and defend the integrity of the nation" and Jefferson on the other, who "seems to have entertained no apprehensions from the debility of government; no jealousy of the state sovereignties; and no suspicion of their encroachments." Rather, according to Marshall, "His fears took a different direction, and all precautions were used to check and limit the exercise of the authorities claimed by the government of the United States. Neither could he perceive danger to liberty except from the constituted authorities, and especially from the executive."[11] Marshall's Jefferson, infected by his sympathy for the French Revolution, "did not feel so sensibly as those who had continued in the United States the necessity of adopting the constitution," and, by implication, the revolution, which it had safeguarded. This was the standard Federalist critique of Jefferson and the Republicans, and Marshall used Washington's life as a vehicle to attack them and to record the Federalist interpretation for posterity.

Jefferson feared the long-term impact of Marshall's biography of Washington. He recognized the political implications of historical writing. As Joanne Freeman has written, "To Jefferson, it was a critical fight, for Marshall's false history threatened to corrupt the future by misinterpreting the past." Jefferson was correct to be concerned. Marshall's interpretation found a wide audience. More than 7,000 copies of the first American edition of *The Life of Washington* were sold, and it was followed by editions published in Britain as well as translations into French, German, and Dutch. An abridged edition for schools was published in 1838.[12]

Jefferson attempted to make page-by-page corrections to Marshall's fifth volume, but he gave up because of the magnitude of the task after making three extensive corrections. In April 1811 he wrote to Joel Barlow, a writer from Connecticut, asking him to write a history to counter Marshall's account. "What is to become of our Post-revolutionary history?" Jefferson asked Barlow, urging him to supply "antidotes of truth to misrepresentations of Marshall."[13] Barlow had been appointed by James Madison to represent the United States in Paris and declined Jefferson's invitation. Frustrated by his inability to secure someone to write a history to counter Marshall, between 1809 and 1818, Jefferson edited and compiled a collection of his papers as secretary of state. Most of the items in the collection

were public papers and official documents, but these were supplemented by
Jefferson's contemporaneous notes and memoranda, which contained detailed, and often critical, accounts of his conversations with key figures,
including Washington and Hamilton. By February 1818 Jefferson had edited and arranged the selections of his public and private papers in three
large bound manuscript volumes that he intended for publication after his
death. These are often referred to as "the Anas" (Latin for "table talk" or
gossip, though this wasn't a title Jefferson used).[14]

According to the Anas, the Federalists, especially Hamilton, were incipient monarchists intent on subverting the American republic for their
own benefit. Hamilton sought, through his fiscal program, to foster corruption that would allow the Treasury secretary to control the government
and promote monarchy. For Jefferson, the Republican opposition sought
"to restrain the administration to republican forms and principles, and not
permit the constitution to be construed into a monarchy, and to be warped,
in practice, into all the principles and pollutions of their favorite English
model."[15] In this reading the Republicans weren't would-be Jacobins
seeking to overthrow the Constitution but rather true defenders of the revolution and its legacy.

Prompted by Marshall and the attacks of other Federalists (which included the disclosure of his relationship with Sally Hemings), Jefferson
moved away from the conciliatory tone of his First Inaugural to defend the
Republican position, all the while seeking to establish retrospective, posthumous comity with Washington. He made a careful distinction between
the efforts of Hamilton and other extreme Federalists on one hand and
Washington on the other. The Republicans (including Jefferson) were not
opposed to Washington. He wrote of the president, "He was true to the
republican charge confided to him; and has solemnly and repeatedly protested to me, in our conversations, that he would lose the last drop of his
blood in support of it; and he did this oftener and with the more earnest-
ness, because he knew my suspicions of Hamilton's designs against it, and
he wished to quiet them."[16] For Jefferson, Washington remained true to the
principles of the revolution, but his fault was in trusting Hamilton too
much. This was a different, more generous view of Washington than he
had expressed in his letter to Mazzei.

Jefferson's relationship with Washington is one of the major themes of
the Anas. Jefferson sought to present himself as a loyal servant and friend

of Washington's who struggled to protect the president from the threat posed by Hamilton. Jefferson recorded a conversation that he had with Washington before the men had breakfast at Mount Vernon on October 1, 1792. According to Jefferson, Washington sought to convince him to remain as secretary of state, "to preserve the check of my opinions in the Administration in order to keep things in their proper channel and to prevent them from going too far." The two men then discussed Hamilton and his fiscal program. Washington sought to reassure Jefferson "that as to the idea of transforming this Government into a monarchy, he did not believe there were ten men in the United States, whose opinions were worth attention, who entertained such a thought." Jefferson disagreed, and he told Washington there were more monarchists than he suspected and that Hamilton had told him that the Constitution "was a shilly shally thing, of mere milk and water, which could not last, and was only a step to something better."[17]

This conversation is typical of the notes and memoranda that Jefferson inserted into his documentary history of the Washington administration. It advanced the overall theme of the work—that Jefferson fought to maintain republican values in the face of Hamilton's incipient monarchism, and it made a distinction between Hamilton's schemes and Washington's honest adherence to republican principles. Washington, according to this view, had no sympathy for Hamilton's pro-British, promonarchical plotting and corruption. It also demonstrated that the president had trusted Jefferson. Jefferson hoped that such contemporaneous evidence would convince the public and posterity that the accounts of Marshall and other Federalists were unmerited.

Jefferson (Figure E.1) faced a huge challenge when he compiled the Anas: Washington generally agreed with Alexander Hamilton. Although Washington saw himself as a statesman above party, he was a partisan Federalist who supported Hamilton's program. (Put another way, Hamilton's fiscal program served Washington's vision of a consolidated, powerful federal government.) Ultimately, as we have seen, Washington and Jefferson became estranged owing to the significant political differences between them. Jefferson worked around this, both when he was in Washington's cabinet and when he created his history of the administration, by claiming that Washington had been duped by Hamilton because of his age and declining health. In late February 1792, shortly after Washington's sixtieth

FIGURE E.I   Thomas Sully, *Thomas Jefferson* (1821). Thomas Sully painted this portrait during
the period when Jefferson was writing his autobiography and compiling the Anas. Jefferson was
nearly eighty years old and reflecting on his life and legacy. Looking back, Jefferson sought to prove
that he and Washington had agreed on the major issues that had come to divide them during the
1790s. American Philosophical Society.

birthday, the two men discussed whether Washington would seek a second
term. According to Jefferson's account, Washington told him "that he
really felt himself growing old, his bodily health less firm, his memory, always bad, becoming worse, and perhaps the other faculties of his mind
shewing a decay to the others of which he was insensible himself, that this
apprehension particularly oppressed him, that he found moreover his ac-
tivity lessened, business therefore more irksome, and tranquility and retirement become an irresistible passion."[18] In Jefferson's account Washington
was a fading hero who had been easily fooled by Hamilton. Under these
circumstances, by his presence in the cabinet, Jefferson helped protect

Washington from himself even as he protected the republic from extreme Federalists bent on overthrowing the revolution and reinstating a monarchy in America.

Jefferson's carefully constructed history of the Washington administration did not have the impact he had intended. After Jefferson's death on July 4, 1826, his grandson, Thomas Jefferson Randolph, became the executor of his grandfather's estate, inheriting his grandfather's papers. Working with his sisters, Randolph brought out an edited four-volume selection of the papers, *Memoir, Correspondence, and Miscellanies from the Papers of Thomas Jefferson*. Randolph broke up Jefferson's carefully constructed three-volume documentary history of the Washington administration, separating Jefferson's autobiography, which he wrote in 1820–1821 and served as an introduction to the work, from the other documents, and the various notes and memoranda from the public papers. He published the memoranda (redacted to remove some of the more controversial material) as "the Anas" as an appendix to the fourth volume. The result meant that Jefferson's carefully constructed history, meant to rebut Marshall's biography of Washington and answer the criticism, persistent since the publication of the Mazzei Letter, that he was disloyal and dishonest in his dealings with Washington, went unpublished. While eight editions of Marshall's *Life of Washington* were published during the nineteenth century, Jefferson's account of the events wasn't reassembled and presented in full until the relevant documents were published in the modern edition of Jefferson's papers in the late twentieth and early twenty-first centuries. To the extent that Jefferson's three-volume documentary history was intended to prove to posterity that he and Washington agreed on the crucial questions facing the United States, it appears to have been a complete failure.

Viewed another way, Jeff Randolph may have inadvertently done his grandfather a favor by disrupting his history of the Washington administration. The Anas and supporting documents presented a highly partisan account of the disputes at the heart of Washington's presidency. In seeking to rebut Marshall's Federalist account, Jefferson revisited and refought the partisan battles of the early 1790s, reopening old wounds. His argument that Washington *really* agreed with him during this period doesn't stand up to scrutiny. By disrupting (and censoring) Jefferson's account, Randolph diluted its impact. Jefferson didn't need to relitigate old disputes. Rather, he came to believe during his presidency and retirement that those disputes weren't as important as he once believed (even if he couldn't resist responding to Marshall).

———

If Jefferson failed to change posterity's view of his relationship with Washington, he seems to have made his own peace with Washington during his retirement (Figure E.2). In November 1813 Dr. Walter Jones, a former William & Mary classmate and longtime friend and political ally of Jefferson's, sent him a copy of a manuscript essay he had written that sought to explain the emergence of political parties during the 1790s. Jones observed, "I have encountered two perilous Topics, one in Shewing that our own party is not impeccable & immaculate, the other in taking Gen¹ Washington on my Shoulders, to bear him harmless through the federal Coalition."[19] Jones, like Jefferson, sought to separate Washington from Federalism. On January 2, 1814, Jefferson wrote a lengthy reply to Jones. The body of the letter is a 1,200-word character portrait of Washington and Jefferson's relationship with him. It is the most sustained piece of writing that either man left about the other.

FIGURE E.2   Jane Braddick Peticolas, *View of the West Front of Monticello and Garden* (1825). Monticello as it appeared at the end of Jefferson's life. Reproduction © Thomas Jefferson Foundation at Monticello.

Jefferson praised Jones for his account of Washington. He began by asserting, "I think I knew General Washington intimately and thoroughly" and set out "to delineate his character" for Jones. He provided a detailed portrait of Washington, asserting, "It may truly be said that never did nature and fortune combine more perfectly to make a man great . . . [F]or his was the singular destiny & merit of leading the armies of his country succesfully thro' an arduous war for the establishment of it's independance, of conducting it's councils thro' the birth of a government, new in it's forms and principles, until it had settled down into a quiet and orderly train, and of scrupulously obeying the laws, thro' the whole of his career, civil and military, of which the history of the world furnishes no other example."

Having described Washington's character and established his greatness, Jefferson turned to politics. He attempted to demonstrate that Washington belonged to Republicans as well as Federalists. "I am satisfied the great body of republicans thinks of him as I do." He acknowledged that they had had their differences, particularly over the Jay Treaty: "We were indeed dissatisfied with him on his ratification of the British treaty. but this was short lived." But he claimed that Republicans, by implication himself first among them, better understood and revered Washington than Federalists: "We knew his honesty, the wiles with which he was encompassed, and that age had already begun to relax the firmness of his purposes: and I am convinced he is more deeply seated in the love and gratitude of the republicans, than in the Pharisaical homage of the Federal monarchists. for he was no monarchist from preference of his judgment. the soundness of that gave him correct views of the rights of man, and his severe justice devoted him to them. he has often declared to me that he considered our new constitution as an experiment on the practicability of republican government, and with what dose of liberty man could be trusted for his own good: that he was determined the experiment should have a fair trial, and would lose the last drop of his blood in support of it."

Jefferson concluded his character study of Washington with a description of his own relationship with him. He noted that they had known each other for thirty years, from the Virginia assembly through Congress and the war, culminating in his nearly four years as secretary of state when "our intercourse was daily, confidential and cordial." He explained that after his retirement, "great and malignant pains were taken by our Federal-monarchists and not entirely without effect, to make him view me as a

theorist, holding French principles of government which would lead infal-
libly to licentiousness and anarchy. and to this he listened the more easily
from my known disapprobation of the British treaty." He ended on a melancholy note, observing, "I never saw him afterwards, or these malignant
insinuations should have been dissipated before his just judgment as mists
before the sun. I felt on his death, with my countrymen, that 'verily a great
man hath fallen this day in Israel.'"[20]

————

In his letter to Walter Jones, Jefferson provided an astute assessment of
Washington and his relationship with him. It was a more balanced and so-
phisticated account than that which he compiled in his three-volume unpublished documentary history of Washington's administration. In part the
passage of time had healed old wounds, and Jefferson was able to appreciate Washington's achievements in a different, more positive light. He had
made his most caustic comments about Washington (in a private communication) in the aftermath of the furor over the Jay Treaty, which seemed less
important two decades later (when the United States was at war with Britain again). Indeed, the dangers that each man believed he saw in the
other—a turn to monarchical tyranny or an American version of Jacobin-
style anarchy—had lost their potency. Jefferson's change in tone wasn't
simply the product of the passage of time. After two terms as president
himself, during which, like Washington, he was subject to intense attacks in
the press, Jefferson had come to see Washington in a different, more sympathetic light. He also came to appreciate some of the Federalist doctrines
and practices that he had previously criticized, including aspects of the
Hamiltonian fiscal system, a strong federal government and a powerful
presidency. He may have been loath to admit it, but Jefferson had moved in
Washington's direction in important ways by 1814.

   Despite its ugliness, Jefferson came to believe that the election of 1800
was an epochal event. In 1819 he referred to it as "the Revolution of
1800," claiming it "was as real a revolution in the principles of our government as that of 76 was in it's form; not effected indeed by the sword, as
that, but by rational and peaceable instrument of reform, the suffrage of
the people. The nation declared it's will by dismissing functionaries
of one principle, and electing those of another, in the two branches,

executive and legislative, submitted to their election."[21] Jefferson believed that the first peaceful transfer of power between different political parties in the United States in 1801 was as important an event as declaring independence in 1776. In drawing a line between the revolutions of 1776 and 1800, Jefferson hewed back to a time when he and Washington had agreed on the principles at stake in the American Revolution and worked together to achieve them. To draw a line between the revolutions of 1776 and 1800, Jefferson implicitly asserted a connection between himself (the key figure in 1800) and Washington (the hero of 1776). Doing so required him to ignore or dismiss the partisan battles of the 1790s.

On June 24, 1826, Jefferson, then eighty-three years old and in failing health, wrote one of his final letters. He wrote to decline an invitation to go to Washington, DC, to celebrate the fiftieth anniversary of the Declaration of Independence. He expressed regret that he would be unable to join, "with the small band, the remnant of that host of worthies, who joined with us on that day." Looking back with the perspective of fifty years, he summed up what the revolutionaries had achieved and what the Fourth of July should mean for the United States and the wider world: "May it be to the world, what I believe it will be, (to some parts sooner, to others later, but finally to all,) the signal of arousing men to burst the chains under which monkish ignorance and superstition had persuaded them to bind themselves, and to assume the blessings and security of self-government. That form which we have substituted, restores the free right to the unbounded exercise of reason and freedom of opinion. All eyes are opened, or opening, to the rights of man. The general spread of the light of science has already laid open to every view the palpable truth, that the mass of mankind has not been born with saddles on their backs, nor a favored few booted and spurred, ready to ride them legitimately, by the grace of God. These are grounds of hope for others. For ourselves, let the annual return of this day forever refresh our recollections of these rights, and an undiminished devotion to them."[22] Facing his own imminent death, Jefferson sought to express the principles that had animated his life and his foremost achievements. George Washington, dead for a generation, the foremost of the "host of worthies" who made the American Revolution, would have agreed with this sentiment. In death the men achieved the reconciliation that had eluded them in life.

Abbreviations

AA	Abigail Adams
GW	George Washington
GWD	George Washington, *Diaries*, Digital Edition, https://rotunda -upress-virginia-edu.tjportal.idm.oclc.org/founders/default.xqy? keys=GEWN-print-01&mode=TOC
JCC	*Journals of the Continental Congress*, Worthington C. Ford et al. eds., 34 vols. (Washington, DC: Government Printing Office, 1904–1937)
JM	James Madison
Malone, *Jefferson and His Time*	Dumas Malone, *Jefferson and His Time*, 6 vols. (Boston: Little Brown, 1948–1981)
MJ	Martha Wayles Jefferson
MJR	Martha Jefferson Randolph
MW	Martha Washington
PGWDE	*Papers of George Washington*, Digital Edition, https://rotunda -upress-virginia-edu.tjportal.idm.oclc.org/founders/GEWN.html
PTJDE	*Papers of Thomas Jefferson*, Digital Edition, https://rotunda-upress -virginia-edu.tjportal.idm.oclc.org/founders/TSJN.html
TJ	Thomas Jefferson
TJA	Notes on Early Career (the so-called Autobiography), January 6–July 29, 1821, J. Jefferson Looney, ed., *Papers of Thomas Jefferson: Retirement Series*, 20 vols. to date (Princeton, NJ: Princeton University Press, 2004), 17:309–380. https://rotunda-upress-virginia -edu.tjportal.idm.oclc.org/founders/default.xqy?keys=TSJN-search -1-2&expandNote=on#match1

TJMB   Thomas Jefferson, *Memorandum Books*, Digital Edition, https://
          rotunda-upress-virginia-edu.tjportal.idm.oclc.org/founders/
          default.xqy?keys=TSJN-print-02-00-02
TJW   Merrill D. Peterson, ed., *Thomas Jefferson: Writings* (New York:
          Library of America, 1984)

Notes

Introduction

1. Kenneth R. Bowling and Helen E. Veit, eds., *The Diary of William Maclay and Other Notes on Senate Debates* (Baltimore, MD: Johns Hopkins University Press, 1988), 269 (entry for May 15, 1790).

2. TJ to Martha Jefferson Randolph, June 6, 1790, PTJDE. TJ expressed similar sentiments in a letter to William Short that he wrote the same day. TJ to William Short, June 6, 1790, PTJDE.

3. Ron Chernow, *Washington: A Life* (New York: Penguin, 2010), 627; Malone, *Jefferson and His Time*, 2:268.

4. *Gazette of the United States* (New York), June 12, 1790; TJMB entries for June 7, 8, and 9, 1790; TJ to Mary Jefferson, June 13, 1790, PTJDE.

5. Stephen Decatur Jr., *Private Affairs of George Washington: From the Records and Accounts of Tobias Lear, Esquire, His Secretary* (Boston: Houghton Mifflin, 1933), 133.

6. Biographers of Washington and Jefferson have, of necessity, addressed the relationship. Several scholars have analyzed the relationship in essays or as part of larger scholarly works. See, for example, Don Higginbotham, "Virginia's Trinity of Immortals: Washington, Jefferson, and Henry, and the Story of Their Fractured Relationships," *Journal of the Early Republic* 23 (2003): 521–543; Joseph J. Ellis, *Founding Brothers: The Revolutionary Generation* (New York: Alfred A. Knopf, 2000); Peter Henriques, *Realistic Visionary: A Portrait of George Washington* (Charlottesville: University of Virginia Press, 2008), ch. 6. Thomas Fleming's *The Great Divide: The Conflict between Washington and Jefferson That Defined America, Then and Now* (New York: Da Capo, 2016), as its title indicates, stresses the rift between the two men but does not really consider the quarter century when they were allies and friends.

7. TJ to Walter Jones, January 2, 1814, PTJDE.

8. See, for example, Fleming, *Great Divide.*

9. Henriques, *Realistic Visionary,* ch. 6, esp. 110–111; Joseph J. Ellis, *His Excellency: George Washington* (New York: Random House, 2004), 217–220.

10. See, for example, Henriques, *Realistic Visionary,* ch. 6, esp. 111–112, and the contrasting portraits of the two men Joseph J. Ellis presents in *American Sphinx: The Character of Thomas Jefferson* (New York: Knopf, 1997) and *His Excellency: George Washington* (New York: Knopf, 2004). Also see Stanley Elkins and Erick McKitrick, *The Age of Federalism: The Early American Republic, 1788–1800* (New York: Oxford University Press, 1994), chs. 1 and 4. Alan Taylor neatly summarizes the differences between the postindependence Federalists, led by Washington, and the Republicans, led by Jefferson, in *American Revolutions: A Continental History* (New York: Norton, 2016), 408–414.

11. GW to Henry Lee Jr., September 22, 1788, PGWDE; TJ to GW, March 29, 1784, PTJDE.

12. I have written about the relationship between republicanism and empire and Jefferson's conception of an "Empire of Liberty," a phrase he only used twice, in Francis D. Cogliano, *Emperor of Liberty: Thomas Jefferson's Foreign Policy* (New Haven, CT: Yale University Press, 2014), esp. 1–10. My thinking on Washington, Jefferson, and empire is influenced by Peter S. Onuf, *Jefferson and the Virginians: Democracy, Constitutions, and Empire* (Baton Rouge: Louisiana State University Press, 2018), ch. 4.

13. R. B. Bernstein, *The Founding Fathers: A Very Short Introduction* (New York: Oxford University Press, 2015); Cokie Roberts, *Founding Mothers: The Women Who Raised Our Nation* (New York: Harper, 2005); Ellis, *Founding Brothers*; Tom Chaffin, *Revolutionary Brothers: Thomas Jefferson, the Marquis de Lafayette and the Friendship That Helped to Forge Two Nations* (New York: St. Martin's Press, 2019). Senator (future president) Warren Harding coined the phrase "Founding Fathers" in 1916. See Bernstein, *Founding Fathers,* 1–3.

14. Anthony Tuck, "Neville, Ralph, first earl of Westmorland (c. 1364–1425)," *Oxford Dictionary of National Biography,* online edition, 2004, https://doi-org.ezproxy.is.ed.ac.uk/10.1093/ref:odnb/19951, accessed June 16, 2020.

15. GW to Isaac Heard, May 2, 1792, PGWDE 10:333.

16. TJ, Autobiography, January 6, 1821, TJW, 3.

17. GW to Isaac Heard, enc., Washington Genealogy, May 2, 1792, PGWDE. Karin Wulf has recently discovered an earlier genealogy that Washington likely compiled in the 1750s. See Karin Wulf, "This Long-Ignored Document, Written by George Washington, Lays Bare the Legal Power of Genealogy," Smithsonianmag.com, June 18, 2019, https://www.smithsonianmag.com/history/what-george-washingtons-efforts-genealogist-reveal-about-power-family-early-america-180972433/, accessed June 16, 2020.

18. TJ to Thomas Adams, February 20, 1771, PTJDE.

19. "cousin, n.s.1755." Samuel Johnson, *A Dictionary of the English Language,* 1755. https://johnsonsdictionaryonline.com/1755/cousin_ns, accessed May 1, 2023.

20. William Shakespeare, *Henry V,* Act IV, scene 3, lines 21–22; *Henry VI part 1,* Act IV, scene 1, line 114.

21. "friendship, n.s.1755." Johnson, *Dictionary of the English Language,* 1755. https://johnsonsdictionaryonline.com/1755/friendship_ns, accessed May 1, 2023.

22. My understanding of the political nature of friendship owes much to Joanne B. Freeman's *Affairs of Honor: National Politics in the New Republic* (New Haven, CT: Yale University Press, 2001), esp. ch. 5.

1. Never Did Nature and Fortune Combine More Perfectly

Epigraph: PGWDE.

1. GWD, May 2, 1768, PGWDE; TJMB, May 2, 1768, PTJDE. I am grateful to Maurizio Valsania for calling my attention to the fact that Washington and Jefferson attended the theater at the same time in 1768. Washington and Jefferson attended the theater at the same time on at least another seven occasions: June 16, 18, 19, and 29, 1770; May 2 and 3, 1771, and October 30, 1771. See GWD, PGWDE; TJMB, 254, 263. Also see Odai Johnson, "Thomas Jefferson and the Colonial Stage," *Virginia Magazine of History and Biography*, 108 (2000), 139–154, esp. 152–153, and Odai Johnson, *London in a Box: Englishness and Theatre in Revolutionary America* (Iowa City: Iowa University Press, 2017). An English actor, John Bernard, claimed to have discussed the theater with Washington in 1798. According to Bernard, Washington extolled the theater as an "exhibition of manners" and an "agent of good." Bernard also claimed that Washington said, "My friend, Mr. Jefferson, has time and taste; he goes always to the play, and I'll introduce you to him," further claiming that Washington made the introduction. This is untrue since Washington and Jefferson were no longer speaking to each other in 1798. John Bernard, *Retrospections of America, 1797–1811* (New York: Harper, 1887), 92.

2. On April 4, 1768, the Virginia Company performed *Douglas*, a 1756 Scottish tragedy by John Home, along with *The Honest Yorkshireman*, a farce written by Henry Carey in 1736. On May 18 the same company performed *The Constant Couple*, a popular 1699 comedy written by George Farquhar, along with Robert Dodsley's 1737 *The King and the Miller of Mansfield*. *Virginia Gazette*, March 31 and May 12, 1768.

3. TJW, 233, 278.

4. Rhys Isaac, *The Transformation of Virginia, 1740–1790* (Chapel Hill: University of North Carolina Press, 1982).

5. Keith Egloff and Deborah Woodward, *First People: The Early Indians of Virginia* (Charlottesville: University of Virginia Press, 2006); Frederic W. Gleach, *Powhatan's World and Colonial Virginia: A Conflict of Cultures* (Lincoln: University of Nebraska Press, 1997); Helen C. Rountree, *Pocahontas, Powhatan, Opechancanough: Three Indian Lives Changed by Jamestown* (Charlottesville: University of Virginia Press, 2005).

6. Alan Taylor, *American Colonies* (New York: Viking Penguin, 2001), chs. 6–7; Edmund S. Morgan, *American Slavery, American Freedom: The Ordeal of Colonial Virginia* (New York: W. W. Norton, 1975).

7. Morgan, *American Slavery*, chs. 15–16; Ira Berlin, *Many Thousands Gone: The First Two Centuries of Slavery in North America* (Cambridge, MA: Belknap Press of Harvard University Press, 1998), ch. 5.

8. David Hackett Fischer, *Albion's Seed: Four British Folkways in America* (New York: Oxford University Press, 1989), 212–229.

9. Taylor, *American Colonies*, ch. 7; Allan Kulikoff, *Tobacco and Slaves: The Development of Southern Culture in the Chesapeake, 1680–1800* (Chapel Hill: University of North Carolina Press, 1986); Rhys Isaac, *The Transformation of Virginia, 1740–1790* (Chapel Hill: University of North Carolina Press, 1982); T. H. Breen, *Tobacco Culture: The Mentality of the Great Tidewater Planters on the Eve of the Revolution* (Princeton, NJ: Princeton University Press, 1985).

10. TJ to Walter Jones, January 2, 1814, PTJDE. For Washington's efforts to fashion his image, see Maurizio Valsania, *First Among Men: George Washington and the Myth of American Masculinity* (Baltimore, MD: Johns Hopkins University Press, 2022).

11. For Washington's life down to the revolution, see Ron Chernow, *Washington: A Life* (New York: Penguin, 2010), chs. 1–15; James Thomas Flexner, *George Washington: The Forge of Experience (1732–1775)* (Boston: Little Brown, 1965).

12. GW to John Augustine Washington, May 28, 1755, PGWDE.

13. Alicia K. Anderson and Lynn A. Price, eds., *George Washington's Barbados Diary, 1751–52* (Charlottesville: University of Virginia Press, 2018).

14. *The Journal of Major Washington* (Williamsburg, VA: William Hunter, 1754). See also Colin Calloway, *The Indian World of George Washington: The First President, the First Americans, and the Birth of the Nation* (New York: Oxford University Press, 2018), chs. 1–3. For Washington's early life and military career, see Stephen Brumwell, *George Washington: Gentleman Warrior* (New York: Quercus, 2012), chs. 1–4.

15. *Journal of Major Washington*, 8.

16. GW to John Augustine Washington, May 31, 1754, PGWDE. A version of this letter was published in the London Magazine, August 1754. Along with the publication of the *Journal* of his 1753 reconnaissance in London, the appearance of this letter guaranteed that Washington had achieved a remarkable level of notoriety in Britain for a young provincial. King George II was reputed to have said in response to Washington's claim that the sound of bullets was charming: "He would not say so, if he had been used to hear many." Horace Walpole, *Memoirs of the Reign of King George II,* ed. Henry Richard Vassall Holland, 3 vols. (London: Henry Colburn, 1847) 1:400. Also see [Expedition to the Ohio, 1754: Narrative], PGWDE, n59, for the controversy surrounding Jumonville's death.

17. The Capitulation for Fort Necessity, July 3, 1754, PGWDE; John Robinson to GW, September 15, 1754, PGWDE.

18. GW to John Augustine Washington, July 18, 1755, PGWDE. For Washington's early experiences as a soldier in the Ohio country, see Brumwell, *George Washington*, and Calloway, *Indian World of George Washington*, chs. 3–5.

19. Orders, May 18, 1756, PGWDE; Court Martial, May 18, 1756, PGW:CS 3:152–153; GW to Robert Dinwiddie, May 23, 1756, PGWDE; Robert Dinwiddie to GW, May 27, 1756, PGWDE.

20. GW to John Stanwix, March 4, 1758, PGWDE.

21. Ledger A, 1750–1772, 39, The George Washington Financial Papers Project, http://financial.gwpapers.org/?q=content/ledger-1750-1772-pg38, accessed May 26, 2019.

22. Wilson Miles Cary, "The Dandridges of Virginia," *WMQ* 1st ser., 5 (1896–1897), 30–39.

23. Flora Fraser, *The Washingtons: George and Martha, 'Join'd by Friendship, Crown'd by Love* (New York: Alfred A. Knopf, 2015), ch. 2.

24. TJ to William Wirt, August 5, 1815, PTJDE.

25. Fraser, *Washingtons*, 21.

26. Settlement of the Daniel Parke Custis Estate, PGWDE, especially Editorial Note.

27. Fraser, *Washingtons*, ch. 1.

28. GW to Sarah Cary Fairfax, September 12, 1758, PGWDE.

29. Robert Stewart to GW, December 29, 1758, PGWDE, n.5.

30. GW to Richard Washington, May 7, 1759, PGWDE.

31. GW to Robert Cary, May 1, 1759, PGWDE.

32. GW to Richard Washington, September 20, 1759, PGWDE.

33. See, for example, MW to Mrs. Shelbury, August 10, 1764, PGWDE. For the purchase of the pet parrot for Patsy, see GWD, April 5, 1773, n. PGWDE.

34. GW to Jonathan Boucher, August 15, 1770, PGWDE.

35. GWD, July 31, 1770, PGWDE.

36. GWD, March 12, 1768; March 31, 1768; June 11, 1768; November 9, 1768; January 6, 1769; January 31, 1769; February 16, 1769; April 14, 1769; January 2, 1771; February 23, 1771; June 12, 1772; GWD, July 31, 1769; August 6, 1769; August 23, 1769; September 15, 1769; GW to Burwell Bassett, June 18, 1769, PGWDE.

37. GWD, June 19, 1773, PGWDE; GW to Burwell Bassett, June 20, 1773, PGWDE.

38. GW to Jonathan Boucher, May 30, 1768; GW to Jonathan Boucher, August 15, 1770, PGWDE.

39. GW to Jonathan Boucher, May 30, 1768, PGWDE.

40. Jonathan Boucher to GW, December 18, 1770, PGWDE.

2. *My Great Good Fortune*

Epigraph: TJA, 309.

1. Edgar S. Maclay, ed., *Journal of William Maclay* (New York: Appleton, 1890), 272.

2. TJA. For Jefferson's youth and early adulthood, see Dumas Malone, *Jefferson the Virginian* (Boston: Little Brown, 1948), chs. 1–12.

3. TJA, 309.

4. Verner Coolie, "The Fry and Jefferson Map," *Imago Mundi* 21 (1967): 70–94.

5. TJA, 310.

6. Robert Darnton, "Extraordinary Commonplaces," *New York Review of Books*, December 21, 2000, https://www.nybooks.com/articles/2000/12/21/extraordinary-common places/#fn-2, accessed October 14, 2019. For Jefferson's commonplacing, see Douglas L. Wilson, "Thomas Jefferson's Early Notebooks," *William and Mary Quarterly* 42 (1985): 442–445, and Kenneth A. Lockridge, *On the Sources of Patriarchal Rage: The Commonplace Books of William Byrd and Thomas Jefferson and the Gendering of Power in the Eighteenth Century* (New York: New York University Press, 1993).

7. Douglas L. Wilson, ed., *Jefferson's Literary Commonplace Book. PTJ: Second Series* (Princeton, NJ: Princeton University Press, 1989), 118–119. Jefferson also commonplaced misogynistic passages from Euripides and Milton among others at this time; see *Literary Commonplace Book*, 70–71, 98–99, 126–127.

8. *Literary Commonplace Book*, 117–118.

9. TJ to William Fleming [ca. October 1763], PTJDE.

10. TJ to John Page, January 19, 1764, PTJDE.

11. TJ to William Fleming, March 20, 1764, PTJDE.

12. Henry Lee, The Walker Affair, 1805, TJP, LoC, reproduced in Malone, 1:449–50, quotations 449.

13. Henry Lee, The Walker Affair, 1805, TJP, Malone, 1:449.

14. TJ to Robert Smith, July 1, 1805, Founders Online, accessed January 13, 2020.

15. The story of the "Walker Affair" is complicated. It did not come to light until 1802 when James Thomson Callender published in the Richmond *Recorder* the accusation that now-president Jefferson had been inappropriate with Betsey Walker (in the same story, Callender accused Jefferson of having a sexual relationship with Sally Hemings). The story gained wide currency, especially among the Federalist opposition to Jefferson (which included John Walker). Jefferson did not respond to the allegation concerning his relationship with Hemings but did acknowledge he had been inappropriate toward Betsey Walker a single time. Through intermediaries he offered an apology to John Walker. See Malone, *Jefferson and His Time* 1:153–155, 447–451 [appendix III].

16. Malone, *Jefferson and His Time*, 4:494–498.

17. Malone, *Jefferson and His Time*, 1:155.

18. TJMB 1:154 n 41. The origins of this verse are unknown.

19. TJA, 311.

20. See Malone, *Jefferson and His Time*, 1:432–433.

21. Sarah N. Randolph, *The Domestic Life of Thomas Jefferson* (New York: Harper, 1871, repr Charlottesville: University of Virginia Press, 1985), 43–44.

22. Henry S. Randall, *The Life of Thomas Jefferson*, 3 vols. (New York: Derby & Jackson, 1858), 1:63–64.

23. TJMB, December 10, 1770. Jefferson gave another enslaved servant at The Forest two shillings and six pence on December 20, 1770, TJMB.

24. Randolph, *Domestic Life*, 44; Randall, *Life of Thomas Jefferson*, 1:64.

25. TJ to Thomas Adams, June 1, 1771, PTJDE.

26. TJ to Benjamin Henry Latrobe, October 10, 1809, PTJDE.

27. Susan R. Stein, *The Worlds of Thomas Jefferson at Monticello* (New York: Harry Abrams, 1993); Leslie Greene Bowman and Charlotte Moss, eds., *Thomas Jefferson at Monticello* (New York: Rizzoli, 2021); Camille Wells, *Material Witnesses: Domestic Architecture and Plantation Landscapes in Early Virginia* (Charlottesville: University of Virginia Press, 2018).

28. TJ to James Ogilvie, February 20, 1771, PTJDE.

29. TJMB.

30. Robert Skipwith to TJ, September 20, 1771, PTJDE.

31. TJMB.

32. Randall, *Life of Jefferson,* 1:64.

33. Sarah N. Randolph, "Mrs. T. M. Randolph," in *Worthy Women of Our First Century,* ed. Sarah Butler Wister and Agnes Irwin (Philadelphia: Lippincott, 1877), 10.

34. Malone, *Jefferson and His Time,* 1:434, appendix I, E.

35. TJA, 5.

36. See Malone, *Jefferson and His Time,* 1, appendix II, 435–446. Although Jefferson had considerable wealth in land and enslaved people, the two markers most important to elite Virginians, he was often in debt. This was owing to a variety of factors: bad luck, the vagaries of the agricultural economy, excessive spending, and poor judgment (he guaranteed several loans for friends and family that failed). Upon his death in 1826, his estate—including 130 enslaved people—was sold to clear his debts of more than $107,000. See Herbert E. Sloan, *Principle and Interest: Thomas Jefferson and the Problem of Debt* (New York: Oxford University Press, 1995).

37. Lorri Glover, *Founders as Fathers: The Private Lives and Politics of the American Revolutionaries* (New Haven, CT: Yale University Press, 2014), 7.

3. Drivers of Negroes

Epigraph: David Humphreys, *Life of George Washington with George Washington's Remarks,* ed. Rosemarie Zagarri (Athens: University of Georgia Press, 1991), 78.

1. Samuel Johnson, *A Dictionary of the English Language,* 2 vols. (London, 1755), 1195. Washington and Jefferson each owned copies of Johnson's *Dictionary.* Washington had an edition published in London in 1786 and Jefferson an edition published in Dublin in 1775. E. Millicent Sowerby, *Catalogue of the Library of Thomas Jefferson,* 5 vols. (Washington, DC: Library of Congress, 1952–1959), 5:134. Jefferson was critical of Johnson's skills as a lexicographer, writing in 1798, "Johnson besides the want of precision in his definitions, and an accurate distinction in passing from one shade of meaning to another of the same word, is most objectionable in his derivations." TJ to Sir Herbert Croft, October 30, 1798, PTJDE. For Johnson, see Peter Martin, *Samuel Johnson: A Biography* (London: Hachette, 2012).

2. Johnson wrote a series of 103 essays as "The Idler" for the London *Universal Chronicle.* Quotations from #11 (June 24, 1758) and #87 (December 15, 1759) reprinted in Samuel Johnson, *The Idler,* 2 vols. (Philadelphia: Tesson and Lee, 1803), 35, 116. For Francis Barber, see Michael Bundock, *The Fortunes of Francis Barber: The True Story of the Jamaican Slave Who Became Samuel Johnson's Heir* (New Haven, CT: Yale University Press, 2015).

3. Samuel Johnson, *The False Alarm* (London: T. Cadell, 1770). Jefferson owned a copy of *The False Alarm,* Sowerby, *Catalogue,* 3:138.

4. Samuel Johnson, *Taxation No Tyranny* (London, 1775), 89.

5. Notes on the State of Virginia, in TJW, 288.

6. "Washington's Slave List [June 1799]," PGWDE. For earlier listings of Washington's slaves (including his inheritance from Lawrence Washington), see "Division of

Slaves, 10 December 1754," PGWDE; and "Memorandum: Division of Slaves [1762]," PGWDE.

7. Bruce A. Ragsdale, *Washington at the Plow: The Founding Farmer and the Question of Slavery* (Cambridge, MA: Belknap Press of Harvard University Press, 2021), chs. 1–2; Bruce A. Ragsdale, "George Washington, the British Tobacco Trade and Economic Opportunity in Prerevolutionary Virginia," *Virginia Magazine of History and Biography* 97 (1989): 132–162.

8. GWD, entry for July 15, 1769.

9. GW to James Anderson, February 20, 1797, as quoted in Peter Henriques, *Realistic Visionary: A Portrait of George Washington* (Charlottesville: University of Virginia Press, 2006), 148.

10. GWD, entries for January 3–4, 1788.

11. Richard Parkinson, *A Tour in America, in 1798, 1799, and 1800* (London: J. Harding and J. Murray, 1805), 420.

12. Humphrey Knight to GW, September 2, 1758, PGWDE.

13. Anthony Whitting to GW, January 16, 1793; GW to Anthony Whitting, January 20, 1793, PGWDE.

14. Tobias Lear's Narrative Accounts of the Death of George Washington, II, December 14, 1799, PGWDE.

15. Lund Washington to GW, April 8, 1778, PGWDE.

16. GW to Lund Washington, February 24[–26], 1779, PGWDE.

17. GW to Joseph Thompson, July 2, 1766, PGWDE.

18. GW to Anthony Whitting, March 3, 1793, PGWDE. Also see GW to Anthony Whitting, February 24, 1793, PGWDE.

19. J. P. Brissot de Warville, *New Travels in the United States of America, Performed in 1788* (Dublin: W. Corbet, 1792), 289–290.

20. Lund Washington, List of Runaways, April 1781, in John C. Fitzpatrick, ed., *The Writings of George Washington*, 39 vols. (Washington, DC: Government Printing Office, 1931–1944), 22:14n; Lafayette to GW, April 23, 1781, Founders Online, accessed August 8, 2018; GW to Lund Washington, April 30, 1781, Founders Online, accessed August 8, 2018; George Grieve, "Notes on a Conversation with Lund Washington," in Howard C. Rice Jr., ed., *Travels in North America in the Years 1780, 1781 and 1782 by the Marquis de Chastellux*, 2 vols. (Chapel Hill: University of North Carolina Press, 1963), 2:597–598.

21. Cassandra Pybus, *Epic Journeys of Freedom: Runaway Slaves of the American Revolution and Their Global Quest for Liberty* (Boston, MA: Beacon, 2006), 281.

22. Erica Armstrong Dunbar, *Never Caught: The Washingtons' Relentless Pursuit of Their Runaway Slave, Ona Judge* (New York: Simon & Schuster, 2017). Ona Judge provided two newspaper interviews late in her life, and these provide us with a rare insight from the perspective of an enslaved owned by the Washingtons. See Rev. T. H. Adams, "Washington's Runaway Slave and How Portsmouth Freed Her," *Granite Freeman* (Concord, NH), May 22, 1845; Rev. Benjamin Chase, "Letter to the Editor," *Liberator* (Boston), January 1, 1847.

23. Henry S. Randall, *The Life of Thomas Jefferson*, 3 vols. (New York: Derby & Jackson, 1858), 1:11.

24. Will of Peter Jefferson, November 10, 1757, *Family Letters*, http://tjrs.monticello .org/letter/1797, accessed August 24, 2018; Lucia C. Stanton, *Those Who Labor for My*

Happiness: Slavery at Thomas Jefferson's Monticello (Charlottesville: University of Virginia Press, 2012), 56. The best studies of Jefferson and slavery are Stanton, *Those Who Labor for My Happiness*, and Annette Gordon-Reed, *The Hemingses of Monticello: An American Family* (New York: Norton, 2008). Also see Cassandra Pybus, "Thomas Jefferson and Slavery," in *A Companion to Thomas Jefferson*, ed. Francis D. Cogliano (Malden, MA: Wiley-Blackwell, 2012), 271–283.

25. Despite a professed aversion to selling slaves, except as a punishment in extreme cases, in the decade between 1784 and 1794 Jefferson sold eighty-four slaves, mainly to generate income. He earned more than $15,000 from these sales. "Negroes Alienated from 1784 to 1794" in *Thomas Jefferson's Farm Book*, ed. Edwin M. Betts (Princeton, NJ: Princeton University Press, 1953), 25.

26. Ellen W. Randolph Coolidge to Joseph Coolidge, October 24, 1858, *Family Letters*, http://tjrs.monticello.org/letter/1266, accessed August 24, 2018. TJ to Thomas Mann Randolph, April 19, 1792, PTJDE.

27. TJMB, entry for December 1771.

28. TJ to Thomas Mann Randolph, February 18, 1793, PTJDE. Also see TJ to Francis Willis, July 15, 1796, PTJDE.

29. TJ to Samuel Biddle, December 12, 1792, PTJDE.

30. Farm Book, 1774–1824, 77, by Thomas Jefferson [electronic edition]. Thomas Jefferson Papers: An Electronic Archive. Boston, MA: Massachusetts Historical Society, 2003, http://www.thomasjeffersonpapers.org/, accessed August 13, 2018.

31. TJ to John Strode, June 5, 1805, Founders Online, accessed August 14, 2018.

32. Thomas Mann Randolph to TJ, April 12, 1800, PTJDE.

33. TJ to Thomas Mann Randolph, January 23, 1801, PTJDE.

34. Martha Jefferson Randolph and Thomas Mann Randolph to TJ, January 31, 1801, PTJDE.

35. James Oldham to TJ, November 26, 1804, PTJDE.

36. TJ to James Oldham, July 20, 1805, Founders Online, accessed August 24, 2018; James Oldham to TJ, July 23, 1805, Founders Online, accessed August 24, 2018; Gordon-Reed, *Hemingses of Monticello*, 577–583; Stanton, *Those Who Labor for My Happiness*, 178.

37. TJ to John Strode, June 5, 1805, Founders Online, accessed August 13, 2018.

38. PTJ:MB, entry for September 26, 1802, PTJDE. Stanton, *Those Who Labor for My Happiness*, 146–147.

39. Daniel Bradley to TJ, September 7, 1805, Founders Online, accessed August 15, 2018; Daniel Bradley to TJ, October 6, 1805, Founders Online, accessed August 15, 2018; TJ to Daniel Bradley, October 6, 1805, Founders Online, accessed August 15, 2018.

TJ paid George Swink $20 for transporting Hubbard to Charlottesville on December 17, 1805, and a further £35 to Daniel Bradley for the cost of holding Hubbard at the Fairfax County jail on January 19, 1806. See TJMB, and TJ to Daniel Bradley, January 19, 1806, Founders Online, accessed August 15, 2018; TJ to Lewis DeBlois, January 19, 1806, Founders Online, accessed August 15, 2018.

40. Conveyance of James Hubbard to Reuben Perry, February 1811, PTJDE.

41. *Richmond Enquirer*, April 12, 1811; Reuben Perry to TJ, March 29, 1811, PTJDE; TJ to Reuben Perry, May 10, 1811, PTJDE.

42. TJ to Reuben Perry, April 16, 1812, PTJDE; Note on Expenses, May 1, 1812, PTJDE; April 5, 1812, TJMB.

43. TJ to Reuben Perry, April 16, 1812, PTJDE.

44. It is not known what happened to James Hubbard after Reuben Perry took ownership of him. For Hubbard, see Gordon-Reed, *Hemingses of Monticello*, 443–444; Stanton, *Those Who Labor for My Happiness*, 147–153.

45. Ellen W. Randolph Coolidge to Joseph Coolidge, October 24, 1858, *Family Letters*, http://tjrs.monticello.org/letter/1266, accessed August 24, 2018.

46. Cassandra Pybus, "Jefferson's Faulty Math: The Question of Slave Defections in the American Revolution," *William and Mary Quarterly* 62 (2005): 243–264, quotation 245–246. Jefferson estimated he lost thirty slaves to the British; Pybus puts the figure at twenty-three. For Jefferson's various estimates of slaves lost during the revolution, see "Jefferson's Statement of Losses to the British at his Cumberland Plantations in 1781," [January 27, 1783], PTJDE; TJ to William Gordon, July 16, 1788, PTJDE; Other Losses by the British in 1781, Farm Book, 1774–1824, 29, by Thomas Jefferson [electronic edition]. Thomas Jefferson Papers: An Electronic Archive. Boston, MA: Massachusetts Historical Society, 2003, http://www.thomasjeffersonpapers.org/, accessed August 15, 2018.

47. TJ to John Wayles Eppes, June 30, 1820, PTJDE; James A. Bear, ed., *Jefferson at Monticello* (Charlottesville: University of Virginia Press, 1967), 97.

48. Thomas Mann Randolph to TJ, May 30, 1803, PTJDE; TJ to Thomas Mann Randolph, June 8, 1803, PTJDE. Annette Gordon-Reed argues that the sale of Cary was intended to send a message to the other enslaved persons at Monticello, but that historians have misunderstood that message. Rather than threaten the other slaves through Cary's sale, Jefferson sought to reassure them by exiling a dangerous, possibly homicidal man who represented a danger to other enslaved persons on the mountaintop. Colbert was a member of the extended Hemings family, and Cary's banishment, Gordon-Reed suggests, was intended by Jefferson to signal his protection of them. Gordon-Reed, *Hemingses of Monticello*, 579–580.

4. Americans Will Never Be Tax'd without Their Own Consent

Epigraph: PTJDE.

1. Kennedy J. Pendleton, ed. *Journals of the House of Burgesses of Virginia, 1766–1769* (Richmond, VA: Colonial Press, 1906), 189. Washington and Jefferson are listed as Burgesses on 181, the first time their names appear together in a state paper. For the opening of the session, see 187–189. Also see Rutherford Goodwin, *A Brief and True Report Concerning Williamsburg in Virginia* (Williamsburg, VA: Colonial Williamsburg, 1941), 57, 240.

2. Resolutions for an Answer to Governor Botetourt's Speech [May 8, 1769], PTJDE; Pendleton, *Journals of the House of Burgesses of Virginia, 1766–1769*, 189.

3. Francis D. Cogliano, *Revolutionary America, 1763–1815: A Political History*, 3rd ed. (London: Routledge, 2017), 28–29.

4. TJA, 311; TJ to William Wirt, August 14, 1814, PTJDE.

5. Pendleton, *Journals of the House of Burgesses, 1766-1769*, lxvi–lxvii.

6. *Maryland Gazette* (Annapolis), July 4, 1765.

7. GW to Francis Dandridge, September 20, 1765, PGWDE; GW to Robert Cary and Company, September 20, 1765, with enclosures, PGWDE. For Washington's transition from tobacco to wheat, see Bruce A. Ragsdale, "George Washington, the British Tobacco Trade and Economic Opportunity in Prerevolutionary Virginia," *Virginia Magazine of History and Biography* 97 (1989): 132–162.

8. Morgan and Morgan, etc.

9. See Patrick Griffin, *The Townshend Moment: The Making of Empire and Revolution in the Eighteenth Century* (New Haven, CT: Yale University Press, 2017), 125–151.

10. Colin Nicolson, ed., *The Papers of Francis Bernard*, 4 vols. to date (University of Virginia Press, for the Colonial Society of Massachusetts, 2008–), 4:359–362.

11. Pendleton, *Journals of the House of Burgesses, 1766–1769*, 174.

12. GW to George Mason, April 5, 1769, PGWDE.

13. GW to George Mason, April 5, 1769, PGWDE.

14. GW to Robert Cary and Company, May 1, 1764, PGWDE.

15. TJ to Mary Jefferson Eppes, January 7, 1798, PTJDE.

16. GW to George Mason, April 5, 1769, PGWDE.

17. GWD, 2:142; George Mason to GW, April 5, 1769, PGWDE; George Mason to GW, April 28, 1769, PGWDE.

18. Pendleton, *Journals of the House of Burgesses, 1766–1769*, 214–215.

19. Pendleton, *Journals of the House of Burgesses, 1766–1769*, 218.

20. TJMB, entry for May 18, 1769.

21. Virginia Nonimportation Resolutions, 1769, PTJDE. GWD, entries for May 17 and 18, 1769.

22. Virginia Nonimportation Resolutions, 1769, PTJDE.

23. *Virginia Gazette* (Williamsburg), May 25, 1769. GWD, entry for May 19, 1769.

24. TJ to Thomas Adams, June 1, 1771, PTJDE.

25. TJA, 312, TJ to Samuel Adams Wells, May 12, 1819, PTJDE.

26. Mary Beth Norton, *1774: The Long Year of Revolution* (New York: Knopf, 2020), ch. 1.

27. TJA, 312; Resolution of the House of Burgesses Designating a Day of Fasting and Prayer, May 24, 1774, PTJDE; Kennedy J. Pendleton, ed. *Journals of the House of Burgesses of Virginia, 1773–1776* (Richmond, VA: Colonial Press, 1905), 124.

28. TJA, 313; Pendleton, *Journals of the House of Burgesses, 1773–1776*, 132. Association of the Late House of Burgesses, [May 27, 1774], PTJDE; Proceedings of a Meeting of Representatives in Williamsburg, May 20, 1774, PTJDE; From Peyton Randolph to Members of the Late House of Burgesses, May 31, 1774, PTJDE.

29. GW to George William Fairfax, June 10–15, 1774, PGWDE; GWD, entries for May 25, 26, and 27, 1774; *Virginia Gazette*, May 26, 1774. It's not clear whether Jefferson attended the ball and reception in honor of Lady Dunmore, although he did contribute twenty shillings toward the cost of the event. TJMB, entry for May 26, 1774.

30. GW to George William Fairfax, June 10–15, 1774, PGWDE.

31. GWD 3:261–262 (entries for July 17 and 18, 1774); Fairfax County Resolves, PGWDE; GW to Bryan Fairfax, July 20, 1774, PGWDE.

32. Resolutions of the Freeholders of Albemarle County [July 26, 1774], PTJDE. Also see Draft of a Declaration of Rights [ca. July 26, 1774], PTJDE. Jefferson spent twenty-four shillings on six dozen cakes to treat the voters at the election. TJMB, entry for August 16, 1774.

33. TJMB, entry for July 29, 1774, n. 29.

34. TJA, 314.

35. Draft Instructions to the Virginia Delegates in the Continental Congress (MS Text of *A Summary View*) [July 1774] PTJDE; Historical and Bibliographic Notes on *A Summary View of the Rights of British America*, PTJDE.

36. PTJDE. Although Washington and Mason did not go back to the early Middle Ages for precedents, they did make a similar argument concerning emigration. The first Fairfax Resolve reads (in part) as follows:

> [O]ur Ancestors when they left their native Land, and setled in America, brought with them . . . the Civil-Constitution and Form of Government of the Country they came from, and were by Laws of Nature and Nations, entitled to all it's Privileges, Immunities and Advantages; which have descended to Us their posterity, and ought of Right to be fully enjoyed, as if We had still continued within the Realm of England. (PGWDE)

There's an important difference between their interpretations. Mason and Washington argue that the British constitution applied equally in America and Britain; Jefferson argued the rights of Americans, like those of their Saxon antecedents, antedated the British constitution and that Americans possessed natural rights.

37. TJA, 314.

38. GW Cash Accounts, August 1774, PGWDE.

39. Andrew Burnaby, *Travels through North America*, ed. R. R. Wilson (New York: Wessels and Bissell, 1904; repr. of the 3rd ed. 1798), 55–56.

40. Fairfax County Resolves, [July 18, 1774], PGWDE.

41. Virginia Nonimportation Resolutions, 1769, PTJDE.

42. Advertisement for a Runaway Slave [September 7, 1769], PTJDE.

5. An Immense Misfortune to the Whole Empire

Epigraph: PTJDE.

1. GWD entries for October 26–30, 1774.

2. GW to Lord Dunmore, April 3, 1775, PGWDE 10:320–322; GWD, entry for March 7, 1775; GW to William Stevens, March 6, 1775, PGWDE; James Cleveland to GW, May 12, 1775, PGWDE.

3. GWD, entry for November 13, 1774, note; GWD, entry for January 16, 1775, note; GWD, entry for March 16, 1775; GW to William Milnor, January 23, 1775, PGWDE;

Richmond County Independent Company to GW, March 17, 1775, PGWDE; GW to John Augustine Washington, March 25, 1775, PGWDE. Washington resigned his command of the companies when he was appointed commander of the Continental Army in June 1775. The companies never took the field and were absorbed into a new militia system when the Virginia Convention reorganized the defense of the colony in August 1775. GW to the Officers of Five Virginia Independent Companies, June 20, 1775, PGWDE.

4. GW to John Connolly, February 25, 1775, PGWDE. GWD 3:303, 309, entries for January 16, 17, and 18 and February 20, 1775.

5. William Wirt, *Sketches of the Life and Character of Patrick Henry* (Philadelphia: James Webster, 1817), 123.

6. "Edmund Randolph's Essay on the Revolutionary History of Virginia 1774–1782: The History of the Revolution," *Virginia Magazine of History and Biography* 43 (1935): 209–232, quotation 223. The records of the Second Virginia Convention are printed in William J. Van Schreeven, et al., eds., *Revolutionary Virginia: The Road to Independence: A Documentary Record*, 7 vols. (Charlottesville: University of Virginia Press, 1973–1983), 2:347–386.

7. Report of a Committee to Prepare a Plan for a Militia, PTJDE. Also see GWD, entries for March 20–27, 1775, and GW to John Augustine Washington, March 25, 1775, PGWDE, n.2.

8. *Virginia Gazette* (Purdie), April 21, 1775; Prince William Independent Company to GW, April 26, 1775, PGWDE.

9. TJ to William Small, May 7, 1775, PTJDE.

10. GWD, entries for May 4–9, 1775. Curwen quoted 329 (entry for May 9).

11. GW to George William Fairfax, May 31, 1775, PGWDE.

12. Cash Accounts [June 1775], PGWDE.

13. JCC, 2:89–90.

14. GWD, entry for June 15, 1775.

15. JCC 2:91.

16. [In Congress, June and July 1775], *The Adams Papers Digital Edition*, ed. Sara Martin (Charlottesville: University of Virginia Press, Rotunda, 2008–2020).

17. Benjamin Rush to Thomas Ruston, October 29, 1775, in Lyman H. Butterfield, ed., *The Letters of Benjamin Rush*, 2 vols. (Princeton, NJ: Princeton University Press, 1951) 1:92; Silas Deane to Elizabeth Deane, September 10, 1774, Paul Smith, et al., eds., *Letters of Delegates to Congress, 1774–1789*, 26 vols. (Washington, DC: Library of Congress, 1976–2000) 1:61–62.

18. Address to the Continental Congress, [June 16, 1775], PGWDE.

19. Eliphalet Dyer to Joseph Trumbull, June 17, 1775, *Letters of Delegates to Congress*, 1:499–500. John Adams to Elbridge Gerry, June 18, 1775, *Adams Papers Digital Edition*. New Englanders often equated Washington's wealth as evidence of his worthiness to command. On August 31, 1774, John Adams recorded in his diary the rumor that "Coll. Washington made the most eloquent Speech at the Virginia Convention that ever was made. Says he, 'I will raise 1000 Men, subsist them at my own Expence, and march my self at their Head for the Relief of Boston.'" *Adams Papers Digital Edition*. Silas Deane, echoing Adams, commented on Washington's wealth, circulating the same rumor that Washington

had pledged to raise and arm a thousand men in response to the Boston Port Act, noting, "His Fortune is said to be equall to such an undertaking." Silas Deane to Elizabeth Deane, September 10, 1774, *Letters of Delegates to Congress, 1774–1789*, 1:61–62. There is no foundation to this rumor, but it attests to Washington's national reputation both for wealth and militancy as early as the summer of 1774.

20. George W. Corner, ed., *The Autobiography of Benjamin Rush* (Princeton, NJ: Princeton University Press, 1948), 113.

21. See GW to Robert McKenzie, October 9, 1774, PGWDE.

22. Virginia Resolutions on Lord North's Conciliatory Proposal [June 10, 1775], PTJDE; TJA.

23. TJMB, entries for June 11–20, 1775.

24. John Adams to Timothy Pickering, August 6, 1822, Founders Online; Diary and Autobiography of John Adams, *Adams Papers Digital Edition*, entry for October 25, 1775.

25. The Declaration as Adopted by Congress [July 6, 1775], PTJDE. For the complicated history of the evolution of the text with all the various drafts by Jefferson and Dickinson, see Declaration of the Causes and Necessity for Taking Up Arms [June 26–July 6, 1775], PTJDE.

26. TJA, 316–317; Second Petition from Congress to the King [July 8, 1775], PTJDE.

27. Resolutions of Congress on Lord North's Conciliatory Proposal, PTJDE.

28. Agreement with John Randolph, April 11, 1771, PTJDE; TJMB, entry for August 17, 1775, n.

29. TJ to John Randolph, August 25, 1775, PTJDE. Randolph wrote a poignant response to Jefferson:

> Tho we *may politically* differ in Sentiments, yet I see no Reason why <u>privately</u> we may not cherish the same Esteem for each other which formerly I believe Subsisted between us. Should any Coolness happen between us, I'll take Care not to be the first mover of it. We both of us seem to be steering opposite Courses; the Success of either les in the Womb of Time. But whether it falls to my share or not, be assured that I wish you Health and Happiness.

> John Randolph to TJ, August 31, 1775, PTJDE.

30. *By the King, a Proclamation, For suppressing Rebellion and Sedition* (Boston, 1775).

31. Woody Holton, *Liberty Is Sweet: The Hidden History of the American Revolution* (New York: Simon & Schuster, 2021), 202–204.

32. TJ to John Randolph, November 29, 1775, PTJDE.

6. Our Lives, Our Fortunes, Our Sacred Honor

Epigraph: TJW, 1501.

1. GW to Richard Henry Lee, July 10, 1775, PGWDE; *Connecticut Journal, and the New-Haven Post-Boy*, July 5, 1775; Address from the New York Provincial Congress, June 26, 1775, PGWDE; Address to the New York Provincial Congress, June 26, 1775, PGWDE.

2. James Thacher, *A Military Journal During the American Revolution* (Boston: Lord & Richardson, 1823), 37; TJ to Walter Jones, January 2, 1814, PTJDE; Abigail Adams to John Adams, July 16, 1775, *Adams Papers Digital Edition*; Phillis Wheatley to GW, October 26, 1775, enc. PGWDE.

3. General Orders, July 4, 1775, PGWDE.

4. GW to Richard Henry Lee, July 10, 1775, PGWDE; also see GW to John Augustine Washington, July 27, 1775, PGWDE.

5. For the "Troops of the United Colonies," see General Orders, July 4, 1775, PGWDE. GW to John Hancock, January 4, 1776, PGWDE; General Orders, January 1, 1776, n. PGWDE.

6. Rick Atkinson, *The British Are Coming: The War for America, Lexington to Princeton, 1775–1777* (New York: Henry Holt, 2019), chs. 9, 11.

7. Council of War [February 16, 1776], PGWDE. Also see Circular to the General Officers, September 8, 1775, PGWDE; Council of War, January 16, 1776, PGWDE.

8. General Orders, January 1, 1776, PGWDE; Robert Middlekauff, *Washington's Revolution: The Making of America's First Leader* (New York: Alfred A. Knopf, 2015), 86–92; Atkinson, *British Are Coming*, ch. 4. For smallpox, see GW to Joseph Reed, December 15, 1775, PGWDE; Joseph J. Ellis, *His Excellency: George Washington* (New York: Random House, 2004), 86–87; Elizabeth A. Fenn, *Pox Americana: The Great Smallpox Epidemic of 1775–1782* (New York: Hill and Wang, 2002).

9. GW to Thomas Gage, August 19, 1775, PGWDE.

10. GW to Lund Washington, August 20, 1775, PGWDE.

11. TJ to Francis Eppes, November 7, 1775, PTJDE 1:252. For Jefferson's travels from Philadelphia to Monticello, see TJMB entries for December 28, 1775, to January 11, 1776.

12. Refutation of the Argument that the Colonies Were Established at the Expense of the British Nation [after January 19, 1776], PTJDE. Thomas Nelson Jr., who remained in Philadelphia representing Virginia, sent TJ a copy of *Common Sense* on February 4, 1776, Thomas Nelson Jr. to TJ, February 4, 1776, PTJDE.

13. TJ to William Randolph, [June] 1776, PTJDE. Jefferson recorded in his Memorandum Book on March 31, 1776, "My mother died about 8. oclock this morning in the 57th. year of her age. TJMB. Virginia Scharff, *The Women Jefferson Loved* (New York: Harper Collins, 2010), ch. 4, esp. 47–57. For Jefferson's migraine, see Edmund Pendleton to TJ, May 24, 1776, PTJDE.

14. James McClurg to TJ, April 6, 1776, PTJDE; John Page to TJ, April 6, 1776, PTJDE. For TJ's journey to Philadelphia, see TJ to Thomas Nelson, May 16, 1776, PTJDE and TJMB.

15. Resolutions of the Virginia Convention calling for Independence, May 15, 1776, PTJDE.

16. TJ to Thomas Nelson, May 16, 1776, PTJDE. For Jefferson and the Virginia constitution of 1776, see the Virginia Constitution [June 1776], PTJDE, and Francis D. Cogliano, "'The Whole Object of the Present Controversy': The Early Constitutionalism of Paine and Jefferson," in *Transatlantic Revolutionaries: Jefferson and Paine in America, Britain and*

France, ed. Peter S. Onuf and Simon P. Newman (Charlottesville: University of Virginia Press, 2013), 26–48.

17. TJ to Thomas Nelson, May 16, 1776, PTJDE.

18. TJ to William Fleming, July 1, 1776, PTJDE. For dispute over Jefferson's election to another congressional term, see William Fleming to TJ, June 22, 1776, PTJDE; Edmund Randolph to TJ, June 23, 1776, PTJDE; TJ to Edmund Pendleton, c. June 30, 1776, PTJDE.

19. Resolution of Independence, Moved by R. H. Lee for the Virginia Delegation [June 7, 1776], PTJDE.

20. John Adams, Diary and Autobiography of John Adams, Volume 3, Diary, 1782–1804; Autobiography, Part One to October 1776, *Adams Papers Digital Edition.*

21. JA to Timothy Pickering, August 6, 1822, Founders Online, accessed June 28, 2020.

22. The best primary source for the drafting of the Declaration of Independence is Notes of Proceedings in the Continental Congress [June 7–August 1, 1776], PTJDE. Jefferson inserted these notes, which include Jefferson's draft of the declaration, into his 1821 autobiography. Julian P. Boyd, the original editor of the PTJ, believes that Jefferson compiled them between August 1776 and 1783. Other important accounts are John Adams, Diary and Autobiography of John Adams, Volume 3, Diary, 1782–1804; Autobiography, Part One to October 1776, *Adams Papers Digital Edition*; TJ to Samuel Adams Wells, May 12, 1819, PTJDE; JA to Timothy Pickering, August 6, 1822, Founders Online; and TJ to JM, August 30, 1823, Founders Online. The best account of the drafting of the Declaration, which seeks to balance and reconcile the conflicting accounts, is Pauline Maier, *American Scripture: Making the Declaration of Independence* (New York: Knopf, 1997), ch. 3. Also see Gordon S. Wood, *Friends Divided: John Adams and Thomas Jefferson* (New York: Penguin, 2017), ch. 3.

23. Maier, *American Scripture,* 103.

24. Notes of the Proceedings in the Continental Congress [June 7–August 1, 1776], PTJDE.

25. JA, Diary and Autobiography of John Adams, Volume 3, Diary, 1782–1804; Autobiography, Part One to October 1776, *Adams Papers Digital Edition.* Adams repeated this claim in 1822: "The Sub-Committee met; Jefferson proposed to me to make the draught. I said I will not; You shall do it. Oh No! Why will you not? You ought to do it. I will not. Why? Reasons enough. What can be your reasons? Reason 1st. You are a Virginian, and Virginia ought to appear at the head of this business. Reason 2d. I am obnoxious, suspected and unpopular; You are very much otherwise. Reason 3d: You can write ten times better than I can." "Well," said Jefferson, "if you are decided I will do as well as I can." JA to Timothy Pickering, August 6, 1822, Founders Online, accessed June 28, 2020.

26. Quotations from TJ to JM, August 30, 1823, Founders Online, and TJ to Henry Lee, May 8, 1825, Founders Online, accessed June 30, 2020.

27. The Virginia Constitution [June 1776], PTJDE; *Pennsylvania Gazette,* June 12, 1776. For the influence of these two documents on Jefferson, see Maier, *American Scripture,* 125–128.

28. JA, Diary and Autobiography of John Adams, Volume 3, Diary, 1782–1804; Autobiography, Part One to October 1776, *Adams Papers Digital Edition*.

29. First Report of the Committee to Digest the Resolution of the Committee of the Whole Respective Canada &c. [June 17, 1776], PTJDE; Additional Report of the Committee to Digest the Resolutions of the Committee of the Whole Respecting Canada [June 17, 1776], PTJDE; Report of the Committee on the Cedars Cartel [June 17, 1776], PTJDE.

30. TJ to JM, August 30, 1823, Founders Online.

31. Notes of Proceedings in the Continental Congress [June 7–August 1, 1776], PTJDE.

32. Notes of Proceedings in the Continental Congress [June 7–August 1, 1776], PTJDE.

33. TJ to Augustus B. Woodward, April 3, 1825, Founders Online, accessed June 30, 2020; Composition Draft of that Part of the Declaration of Independence Containing Charges Against the Crown, PTJDE; Jefferson's "original Rough draught," PTJDE.

34. TJ to JM, August 30, 1823, Founders Online. Jefferson mentioned the story of Franklin and the hatmaker's sign in passing in this letter. He told a fuller version in Anecdotes of Dr. Franklin [ca. December 4, 1818], PTJDE.

35. TJ to Richard Henry Lee, July 8, 1776, PTJDE. On July 21 Lee responded as Jefferson hoped he would: "I thank you much for your favor and its inclosures by this post, and I wish sincerely, as well for the honor of Congress, as for that of the States, that the Manuscript had not been mangled as it is." Richard Henry Lee to TJ, July 21, 1776, PTJDE.

36. Notes of Proceedings in the Continental Congress [June 7–August 1, 1776], PTJDE.

37. Notes of Proceedings in the Continental Congress [June 7–August 1, 1776], PTJDE.

38. Jefferson's Third Draft, Virginia Constitution, PTJDE.

39. Notes of Proceedings in the Continental Congress [June 7–August 1, 1776], PTJDE.

40. My thinking on the deleted clause in the Declaration has been influenced by Peter S. Onuf, *Jefferson's Empire: The Language of American Nationhood* (Charlottesville: University of Virginia Press, 2000), ch. 5.

7. That Service to the Cause of Liberty

Epigraph: PTJDE.

1. GW to Benjamin Harrison, December 18–30, 1778, PGWDE.

2. General Orders, July 9, 1776, PGWDE; Worthington C. Ford, ed., *Correspondence and Journals of Samuel Blachley Webb*, 3 vols. (New York: Wickersham, 1893), 3:153; General Orders, July 10, 1776, PGWDE.

3. General Orders, July 9, 1776, PGWDE.

4. GW to Lund Washington, December 10–17, 1776, PGWDE. For the New York and New Jersey campaigns of 1776–1777, see David Hackett Fischer, *Washington's Crossing* (New York: Oxford University Press, 2004); and Rick Atkinson, *The British Are Coming:*

The War for America, Lexington to Princeton, 1775–1777 (New York: Henry Holt, 2019), chs. 15–16, 18, 20–22.

5. GW to John Hancock, December 20, 1776, PGWDE. For the development of the Continental Army, see Robert K. Wright, "'Nor Is Their Standing Army to Be Despised': The Emergence of the Continental Army as a Military Institution," in *Arms and Independence: The Military Character of the American Revolution*, ed. Ronald Hoffman and Peter J. Albert (Charlottesville: University of Virginia Press, 1984), 50–74; Charles Royster, *A Revolutionary People at War: The Continental Army and American Character, 1775–1783* (Chapel Hill: University of North Carolina Press, 1979).

6. Ricardo A. Herrera, *Feeding Washington's Army: Surviving the Valley Forge Winter of 1778* (Chapel Hill: University of North Carolina Press, 2022).

7. For the "southern strategy," see Ira D. Gruber, "Britain's Southern Strategy," in *The Revolutionary War in the South: Power, Conflict, and Leadership*, ed. W. Robert Higgins (Durham, NC: Duke University Press, 1979), 205–238.

8. TJA, 317.

9. Bill for the Revision of the Laws [October 15, 1776], PTJDE.

10. The Revisal of the Laws, 1776–1786, PTJDE. John B. Boles, *Jefferson: Architect of American Liberty* (New York: Basic Books, 2017), ch. 6; Malone, *Jefferson and His Time*, 1, chs. 17–21.

11. TJA, 318. Holly Brewer, "Entailing Aristocracy in Colonial Virginia: 'Ancient Feudal Restraints' and Revolutionary Reform," *William and Mary Quarterly* 54 (1997): 307–346; John A. Ragosta, *Religious Freedom: Jefferson's Legacy, America's Creed* (Charlottesville: University of Virginia Press, 2013).

12. See Francis D. Cogliano, "'The Whole Object of the Present Controversy': The Early Constitutionalism of Paine and Jefferson," in *Transatlantic Revolutionaries: Jefferson and Paine in America, Britain and France*, ed. Peter S. Onuf and Simon P. Newman (Charlottesville: University of Virginia Press, 2013), 26–48.

13. For Hamilton, see John D. Barnhart, *Henry Hamilton and George Rogers Clark in the American Revolution* (Crawfordsville, IN: R. E. Banta, 1951); Elizabeth Arthur, "HAMILTON, HENRY," in *Dictionary of Canadian Biography*, vol. 4 (University of Toronto/Université Laval, 2003–), http://www.biographi.ca/en/bio/hamilton_henry_4E.html, accessed July 23, 2020; Bernard Sheehan, "'The Famous Hair Buyer General': Henry Hamilton, George Rogers Clark, and the American Indian," *Indiana Magazine of History* 79 (1983): 1–28.

14. George Germain to Guy Carleton, March 26, 1777, as quoted in Barnhart, *Henry Hamilton and George Rogers Clark*, 29.

15. For the prolonged period of conflict in the Northwest, see Patrick Griffin, *American Leviathan: Empire, Nation, and Revolutionary Frontier* (New York: Hill and Wang, 2007), chs. 4–6.

16. George Rogers Clark to Patrick Henry, February 3, 1779, in James Alton James, ed., *George Rogers Clark Papers, 1771–1781* (Springfield: Illinois State Historical Library, 1912), 97. Historians have questioned whether Hamilton deserves his bloodthirsty reputation. See Sheehan, "'Famous Hair Buyer General'"; N. V. Russell, "The Indian Policy of Henry Hamilton: A Re-valuation," *Canadian Historical Review* 11 (1930): 20–37.

17. TJ to Theodorick Bland, June 8, 1779, PTJDE. Jefferson's language with respect to Native Americans echoed that which he used in the Declaration of Independence, writing that George III used Indigenous soldiers, "the merciless Indian savages, whose known rule of warfare is an undistinguished destruction of all ages, sexes, & conditions of existence," against the colonists.

18. Dodge quoted in Order of the Virginia Council Placing Henry Hamilton in Irons, June 16, 1779, editorial note (p. 295), PTJDE. Also see John Dodge, *A Narrative of the Capture and Treatment of John Dodge, by the English at Detroit* (Philadelphia: T. Bradford, 1779).

19. Order of Virginia Council Placing Henry Hamilton and Others in Irons, June 16, 1779, PTJDE. For Hamilton's journals of the campaigns of 1778–1779, including his time as a prisoner of war, see Barnhart, *Henry Hamilton and George Rogers Clark*, 102–205. Because Hamilton was barred from the use of pen and paper after he was imprisoned in Williamsburg, his journal is incomplete.

20. GW to TJ, July 10, 1779, PTJDE. Also see TJ to GW, June 19, 1779, PTJDE.

21. GW to TJ, August 6, 1779, PTJDE. Also see William Phillips to TJ, July 5, 1779, PTJDE; TJ to GW, July 17, 1779, PTJDE; TJ to William Phillips, July 22, 1779, PTJDE; GW to TJ, September 13, 1779, PTJDE; TJ to GW, October 1, 1779, PTJDE.

22. GW to TJ, September 5, 1780, PTJDE; TJ to GW, September 26, 1780, PTJDE; GW to TJ, October 10, 1780, PTJDE; TJ to GW, October 25, 1780, PTJDE; GW to TJ, November 8, 1780, PTJDE.

23. Johann von Ewald, *Diary of the American War: A Hessian Journal,* ed. Joseph P. Dustin (New Haven, CT: Yale University Press, 1979), 268. For the British invasions of Virginia during Jefferson's gubernatorial term, see Michael Kranish, *Flight from Monticello: Thomas Jefferson at War* (New York: Oxford University Press, 2010); Merrill D. Peterson, *Thomas Jefferson and the New Nation* (New York: Oxford University Press, 1970), 166–240; Malone, *Jefferson and His Time,* 1, chs. 22–25; Francis D. Cogliano, *Emperor of Liberty: Thomas Jefferson's Foreign Policy* (New Haven, CT: Yale University Press, 2014), ch. 1.

24. Jonathan Trumbull Jr., "Minutes of Occurrences Respecting the Siege and Capture of York in Virginia," *Proceedings of the Massachusetts Historical Society,* 1st ser., 14 (1876): 333; GWD, 3:419, entry for September 9, 1781.

25. For the Yorktown campaign, see Robert A. Selig, "Washington, Rochambeau, and the Yorktown Campaign of 1781," in *A Companion to George Washington,* ed. Edward L. Lengel (Malden, MA: Wiley Blackwell, 2012), 266–287; Nathaniel Philbrick, *In the Hurricane's Eye: The Genius of George Washington and the Victory at Yorktown* (New York: Viking, 2018); Robert A. Middlekauff, *Washington's Revolution: The Making of America's First Leader* (New York: Alfred A. Knopf, 2015), ch. 11.

26. TJ to GW, June 19, 1779, PTJDE; GW to TJ, July 10, 1779, PTJDE.

27. GW to TJ, June 8, 1781, PTJDE.

28. Resolution of Thanks to Jefferson by the Virginia General Assembly, December 12, 1781, PTJDE.

29. TJ to GW, October 28, 1781, PTJDE.

30. GW to TJ, November 30, 1781, PTJDE.

31. *Notes on the State of Virginia*, TJW, 253; TJ to the Speaker of the House of Delegates, March 1, 1781, PTJDE.

32. TJ to GW, May 28, 1781, PTJDE.

33. GW to Benjamin Harrison, December 18–30, 1781, PGWDE.

8. *Yr. Most Obedt. & Very Hble. Servt.*

Epigraph: PGWDE.

1. For documents relating to Washington's resignation and Jefferson's response, see George Washington's Resignation as Commander-in-Chief, December 20–23, 1783, PTJDE. For an analysis of the meaning of Washington's resignation, see Craig Bruce Smith, *American Honor: The Creation of the Nation's Ideals during the Revolutionary Era* (Chapel Hill: University of North Carolina Press, 2018). The two best eyewitness accounts, quoted here, are James McHenry to Margaret Caldwell, December 23, 1783; and James Tilton to Gunning Bedford Jr., December 25, 1783, both which appear in Edmund C. Burnett, et al., eds., *Letters of Delegates to Congress, 1774–1789* (Washington, DC: Library of Congress, 1976–2000), 21: 222 [McHenry] and 233–234 [Tilton].

2. James McHenry to Margaret Caldwell, December 23, 1783; *Letters of Delegates to Congress, 1774–1789*, 21: 222.

3. John Trumbull, *Autobiography, Reminiscences and Letters of John Trumbull from 1756 to 1841* (New York: Wiley and Putnam, 1841), 263. The quote attributed to George III about Washington was reported by Rufus King, who spoke to Benjamin West in London on May 3, 1797. According to King, West had told him that the king had praised Washington using the language quoted above. Charles R. King, ed., *The Life and Correspondence of Rufus King*, 6 vols. (New York: G. P. Putnam, 1894–1900), 3:545. The following year West told Joseph Farington, an English landscape painter, that the king had asked him what Washington would do if the Americans won their independence. West told the king Washington would "retire to a private situation." According to West the king replied, "If He did He would be the greatest man in the world." Joseph Farington, *The Farington Diary*, ed. James Greig, 8 vols. (1923–1928) 1:278 (entry for December 28, 1799).

4. TJ to Benjamin Harrison, December 24, 1783, PTJDE.

5. Report of a Committee on the Response by the President of Congress, [December 22, 1783], PTJDE.

6. GW, Farewell Address to the Armies of the United States, November 2, 1783, GWW 543–545.

7. TJ to Benjamin Harrison, November 11, 1783, PTJDE.

8. John Parke Custis to GW, June 10, 1776, PGWDE; GW to Jonathan Trumbull, November 6, 1781, Founders Online, accessed October 7, 2020.

9. TJ to the Marquis de Chastellux, November 26, 1782, PTJDE.

10. Henry S. Randall, *The Life of Thomas Jefferson*, 3 vols. (New York: Derby & Jackson, 1858), 1:382.

11. Lines copied from *Tristram Shandy* by Martha and Thomas Jefferson, PTJDE.

12. TJMB entry for September 6, 1782.

13. Randall, *Life of Jefferson*, 1:382.

14. Edmund Randolph to James Madison, September 20, 1782, Founders Online, accessed September 29, 2019.

15. TJ to Elizabeth Wayles Eppes, October 3, 1782, PTJDE.

16. Randall, *Life of Jefferson*, 1:382.

17. TJ to James Monroe, May 20, 1782, PTJDE.

18. JCC, 25:818.

19. Dr. James Tilton to Gunning Bedford, December 25, 1783. For Jefferson's interactions with George Mann, who hosted the dinner, see TJMB, entry for December 30, 1783, and n. 8.

20. GW to Bushrod Washington, January 15, 1783, Founders Online, accessed September 25, 2022.

21. General Meeting of the Society of Cincinnati [May 4–18, 1784], editorial note, PGWDE. For criticism of the society, see Aedanus Burke, *Considerations on the Society or Order of Cincinnati* (Philadelphia: Robert Bell, 1783).

22. GW to TJ, April 8, 1784, PTJDE.

23. TJ to GW, April 16, 1784, PTJDE; TJ to GW, November 14, 1786, PTJDE.

24. See General Meeting of the Society of Cincinnati [May 4–18, 1784], PGWDE, for Washington's notes on the society as well as extensive documentation relating to the General Meeting in Philadelphia. The branches eventually insisted that the society retain hereditary membership.

25. GW to TJ, March 3, 1783, PTJDE. For an astute analysis of the Washington-Jefferson discussion over the Society of Cincinnati, see Tom Cutterham, *Gentlemen Revolutionaries: Power and Justice in the New American Republic* (Princeton, NJ: Princeton University Press, 2017), 28–35. According to Cutterham, "Before he made up his mind, Washington consulted Thomas Jefferson, someone whom he could trust to give an honest and considered opinion" (28).

26. TJ to GW, March 15, 1784, PTJDE.

27. *Notes on the State of Virginia*, TJW, 123–325, quotation 190.

28. By comparison Jefferson wrote two letters to Washington before he became governor of Virginia in June 1779. During his tenure as governor from June 1779 to June 1781, the two men exchanged eighty-three letters. These entirely concerned the war. Between the end of Jefferson's governorship in June 1781 and his departure for France in July 1784, they exchanged fifteen letters.

29. TJ to GW, December 10, 1784, PTJ 7:566–567; TJ to GW, July 10, 1785, PTJDE. Also see TJ to Benjamin Harrison, January 12, 1785, PTJDE. For Houdon, see Anne L. Poulet, *Jean-Antoine Houdon: Sculptor of the Enlightenment* (Chicago: University of Chicago Press, 2003).

30. TJ to GW, August 14, 1787, PTJDE. Also see TJ to GW, January 4, 1786, PTJDE; GW to TJ, August 1, 1786, PTJDE.

31. For Houdon's visit to Mount Vernon, see TJ to the Governor of Virginia, July 11, 1785, PTJDE; GWD, the entries for October 2, 7, 9, 10, and 19, 1785. Also see GW to Lafayette, November 8, 1785, PGWDE. Also see TJ to the Governor of Virginia, July 11, 1785, PTJDE. TJ to Joseph Delaplaine, May 3, 1814, PTJDE.

32. TJ to Benjamin Harrison, November 11, 1783, PTJDE. Jefferson, still a member of Congress in March 1784, was one of the signers of the deed of cession and then drafted a plan for Congress to govern the newly acquired territory. See the Virginia Cession of Territory Northwest of the Ohio [March 1, 1784], PTJDE; Plan for Government of the Western Territory [February 3–April 23, 1784], PTJDE.

33. Joel Achenbach, *The Grand Idea: George Washington's Potomac and the Race to the West* (New York: Simon & Schuster, 2004); Colin G. Calloway, *The Indian World of George Washington: The First President, the First Americans, and the Birth of the Nation* (New York: Oxford University Press, 2018), 37–40; Charles Royster, *The Fabulous History of the Dismal Swamp Company: A Story of George Washington's Times* (New York: Vintage, 1999); Edward G. Larson, *The Return of George Washington, 1783–1789* (New York: William Morrow, 2014), ch. 3.

34. *Notes on the State of Virginia*, TJW, 290.

35. Plan for Government of the Western Territory [February 3–April 23, 1784], PTJDE. For the role of western land in Jefferson's thinking about political economy, see Drew R. McCoy, *The Elusive Republic: Political Economy in Jeffersonian America* (Chapel Hill: University of North Carolina Press, 1980). For the Northwest Ordinance (and associated acts), see Peter S. Onuf, *Statehood and Union: A History of the Northwest Ordinance* (Bloomington: Indiana University Press, 1987).

36. TJ to GW, March 15, 1784, PTJDE.

37. GW to TJ, March 29, 1784, PTJDE.

38. For Washington's western journey, see GWD entries for September 14–20 and October 4, 1784. Also see Larson, *Return of George Washington*, ch. 2.

39. GW to Benjamin Harrison, October 10, 1784, PGWDE.

40. GW to TJ, February 25, 1785, PTJDE.

41. TJ to GW, July 10, 1785, PTJDE; GW to TJ, September 26, 1785, PTJDE.

9. The Same World Will Scarcely Do for Them and Us

1. Henry Stuart to John Stuart, August 25, 1776, in William L. Saunders, ed., *Colonial Records of North Carolina*, 10 vols. (Raleigh, NC: P. M. Hale, 1886–1890) 10:778, emphasis added. Jeffrey Ostler discusses the use of "Virginians" by Natives in the Ohio Valley to describe avaricious settlers in *Surviving Genocide: Native Nations and the United States from the American Revolution to Bleeding Kansas* (New Haven, CT: Yale University Press, 2019), 11. Also see Jeffrey Ostler, "To Extirpate the Indians": An Indigenous Consciousness of Genocide in the Ohio Valley and Lower Great Lakes, 1750s–1810," *William and Mary Quarterly* 72 (2015): 601–602.

2. Colin G. Calloway, *The Indian World of George Washington: The First President, the First Americans, and the Birth of the Nation* (New York: Oxford University Press, 2018), 20. Figure on the Native population of Virginia on 22, 28 and Ostler, *Surviving Genocide*, 15.

3. GW Diary Entries, March 23, 25, 1748, PGWDE.

4. Calloway, *Indian World of George Washington,* 37–40.

5. Rosemary Zagarri, ed., *Life of George Washington by David Humphreys with George Washington's Remarks* (Athens: University of Georgia Press, 1991), 10; Calloway, *Indian World of George Washington,* 69–70. For Washington's use of the name, see [The Expedition to the Ohio, 1754: Narrative], PGWDE; and GW to Andrew Montour, October 10, 1755, PGWDE.

6. Annette Gordon-Reed and Peter S. Onuf, *"Most Blessed of the Patriarchs": Thomas Jefferson and the Empire of the Imagination* (New York: Norton, 2016), 27–28. Also see Susan Kern, *The Jeffersons at Shadwell* (New Haven, CT: Yale University Press, 2010); Anthony F. C. Wallace, *Jefferson and the Indians: The Tragic Fate of the First Americans* (Cambridge, MA: Harvard University Press, 1999), 21–34.

7. Annette Gordon-Reed and Peter Onuf, two of the most astute of Jefferson's biographers, have observed, "The Jeffersons . . . were frontier people, strivers, and a frontier society is, by definition, an unsettled society, built on improvisation, opportunism, hope, and, almost always, a level of insecurity." *"Most Blessed of the Patriarchs,"* 28.

8. TJ to John Adams, June 11, 1812, PTJDE.

9. TJ to John Adams, June 11, 1812, PTJDE. For Native visits to Shadwell, see Kern, *Jeffersons at Shadwell,* 197–202. For Ostenaco and his visit to Britain, see Kate Fullagar, *The Warrior, the Voyager and the Artist: Three Lives in an Age of Empire* (New Haven, CT: Yale University Press, 2020), chs. 1–4. The scene took place several years before Jefferson crowded into the back of the Virginia capitol to witness Patrick Henry's passionate condemnation of the Stamp Act. Though a poor, and reluctant, speaker himself, Jefferson appreciated oratorical skill in others.

10. *Notes on the State of Virginia,* TJW, 187–189. The precise circumstances surrounding the murder of Logan's family have been the subject of dispute for more than two centuries, as has the provenance of the speech Jefferson immortalized as "Logan's Lament." See Wallace, *Jefferson and the Indians,* 1–20.

11. *Notes on the State of Virginia,* TJW, 187; Adam Hodgson's Account of a Visit to Monticello, [June 17, 1820], PTJ:RS 16:36. For Jefferson's thinking on stadial theory and Native Americans, see Andrew Cayton, "Thomas Jefferson and Native Americans," in Francis D. Cogliano, ed., *A Companion to Thomas Jefferson* (Malden, MA: Wiley-Blackwell, 2012), 237–252, esp. 243–246.

12. Ostler, *Surviving Genocide,* 5.

13. Cayton, "Jefferson and Native Americans," 238–239.

14. See Robert G. Parkinson, *The Common Cause: Creating Race and Nation in the American Revolution* (Chapel Hill: University of North Carolina Press, 2016), 617–260.

15. TJW, 21–22.

16. Calloway, *Indian World of George Washington,* ch. 11; Ostler, *Surviving Genocide,* 69–74; Alan Taylor, *The Divided Ground: Indians, Settlers, and the Northern Borderland of the American Revolution* (New York: Knopf, 2006), ch. 3.

17. GW to John Sullivan, March 6, 1779, PGWDE; John Sullivan to GW, April 16, 1779, PGWDE, see n. 1 for the background to the campaign.

18. Ostler, *Surviving Genocide,* 73.

19. GW to John Sullivan, May 31, 1779, PGWDE.

20. Sayengeraghta, quoted in Ostler, *Surviving Genocide,* 73.

21. John Sullivan to GW, September 28, 1779, PGWDE.

22. GW to John Laurens, September 28, 1779, PGWDE.

23. For the number of refugees at Niagara, see Calloway, *Indian World of George Washington,* 256. For the impact of the campaign on the Haudenosaunee population, see Ostler, *Surviving Genocide,* 76–77. For the Sullivan Campaign generally, see Calloway, *Indian World of George Washington,* ch. 11; Ostler, *Surviving Genocide,* 69–75; Taylor, *Divided Ground,* ch. 3.

24. GW to LaFayette, September 12, 1779, PGWDE. Also see Rachel B, Herrmann, *No Useless Mouth: Waging War and Fighting Hunger in the American Revolution* (Ithaca, NY: Cornell University Press, 2019), ch. 2.

25. Seneca Chiefs to GW, December 1, 1790, PGWDE.

26. Patrick Griffin, *American Leviathan: Empire, Nation, and Revolutionary Frontier* (New York: Hill and Wang, 2007), chs. 5–6, quotation (Republic of Virginia), 143.

27. TJ to George Rogers Clark, January 1, 1780, PTJDE; TJ to GW, February 10, 1780, PTJDE.

28. TJ to William Short, January 3, 1793, PTJDE.

29. TJ to George Rogers Clark, March 19, 1780, PTJDE.

30. John D. Barnhart, ed., *Henry Hamilton and George Rogers Clark in the American Revolution, with the Unpublished Journal of Lieut. Gov. Henry Hamilton* (Crawfordsville, IN: R. E. Banta, 1951), 182–183.

31. Ostler, *Surviving Genocide,* 64–65.

32. GW to Elias Boudinot, June 17, 1783, Founders Online, accessed November 13, 2020.

33. GW to James Duane, September 7, 1783, Founders Online, accessed November 13, 2020. Also see Calloway, *Indian World of George Washington,* 291–294.

34. GW to James Duane, September 7, 1783, Founders Online, accessed November 13, 2020.

35. Plan for the Government of Western Territory, February 3–April 23, 1784, PTJDE. Also see Peter S. Onuf, *Statehood and Union: A History of the Northwest Ordinance* (Bloomington: Indiana University Press, 1987).

36. GW to TJ, April 4, 1791; TJ to GW, April 17, 1791, PTJDE.

37. Colin G. Calloway, *The Victory with No Name: The Native American Defeat of the First American Army* (New York: Oxford University Press, 2015).

38. TJ to William Henry Harrison, February 27, 1803, PTJDE. Ostler, *Surviving Genocide,* ch. 3; Calloway, *Indian World of George Washington,* chs. 14–18.

39. TJ to William Henry Harrison, February 27, 1803, PTJDE.

40. TJ to Andrew Jackson, September 19, 1803, PTJDE.

10. I Like Much the General Idea of Framing a Government

1. GW to TJ, June 2, 1784, PTJDE. Also see TJ to David Humphreys, PTJDE. GW wrote similar letters, as well as a general testimony to Humphreys, the same day. See GW

to Chastellux, GW to Benjamin Franklin, and GW to David Humphreys, all dated June 2, 1784, PGWDE. Washington closed his letter to Franklin with a more formal valediction than he used for Jefferson: "Yr Most Obedt & very Hble Servt."

2. For Jefferson's period in Europe, see Andrew Burstein and Nancy Isenberg, *Madison and Jefferson* (New York: Random House, 2010), ch. 3; William H. Adams, *The Paris Years of Thomas Jefferson* (New Haven, CT: Yale University Press, 1997); Dumas Malone, *Jefferson and the Rights of Man* (*Jefferson and His Time*, vol. 2) (Boston: Little Brown, 1951), chs. 1–12; John B. Boles, *Jefferson: Architect of American Liberty* (New York: Basic Books, 2017), chs. 9–13; Jon Meacham, *Thomas Jefferson: The Art of Power* (New York: Random House, 2012), chs. 18–22.

3. For Jefferson's activities as a diplomat, see Francis D. Cogliano, *Emperor of Liberty: Thomas Jefferson's Foreign Policy* (New Haven, CT: Yale University Press, 2014), ch. 2.

4. TJ to Charles Bellini, September 30, 1785, PTJDE.

5. Annette Gordon-Reed, *The Hemingses of Monticello: An American Family* (New York: Norton, 2008), 253. For the "Head and the Heart" letter, see TJ to Maria Cosway, October 12, 1786, PTJDE. Also see Virginia Scharff, *The Women Jefferson Loved* (New York: Harper Collins, 2010), 206–208.

6. Elizabeth Wayles Eppes to TJ, October 13, 1784, PTJDE; Francis Eppes to TJ, October 14, 1784, PTJDE.

7. Gordon-Reed, *Hemingses of Monticello*.

8. The fullest treatment of the Hemings-Jefferson relationship is Gordon-Reed, *Hemingses of Monticello*. For the way historians have treated their relationship and the controversy it's engendered in some quarters, see Annette Gordon-Reed, *Thomas Jefferson and Sally Hemings: An American Controversy* (Charlottesville: University of Virginia Press, 1997). Also see Andrew Burstein, *Jefferson's Secrets: Death and Desire at Monticello* (New York: Basic Books, 2005); Catherine Kerrison, "Sally Hemings," in Francis D. Cogliano, ed., *A Companion to Thomas Jefferson* (Oxford: Wiley-Blackwell, 2012), 284–300.

9. GW to George William Fairfax, February 27, 1787, PGWDE.

10. Edward G. Lengel, *The First Entrepreneur: How George Washington Built His—and the Nation's—Prosperity* (New York: Da Capo, 2016), chs. 5–6; Bruce A. Ragsdale, *Washington at the Plow: The Founding Farmer and the Question of Slavery* (Cambridge, MA: Belknap Press of Harvard University Press, 2021), ch. 4. See also Dennis J. Pogue, "Entrepreneur," in *A Companion to George Washington*, ed. Edward G. Lengel (Oxford: Wiley-Blackwell, 2012), 70–85.

11. JM to GW, January 9, 1785; Thomas Stone to GW, January 28, 1785, PGWDE. For the documents relating to the conference, see Robert A. Rutland, ed., *The Papers of George Mason, 1725–1792*, 3 vols. (Chapel Hill: University of North Carolina Press, 1970), 2:812–823.

12. GW to JM, November 30, 1785, PGWDE. The best recent biography of Madison is Noah Feldman, *The Three Lives of James Madison: Genius, Partisan, President* (New York: Random House, 2017). For Madison and Washington, see Stuart Leiberger, *Founding Friendship: George Washington, James Madison, and the Creation of the American Republic* (Charlottesville: University of Virginia Press, 1999). For Madison's relationship with Jefferson, see Burstein and Isenburg, *Madison and Jefferson*.

13. John Dickinson to TJ, December 28, 1803, n, PTJDE. The Annapolis Convention, September 1786, *The Papers of James Madison Digital Edition,* ed. J. C. A. Stagg (Charlottesville: University of Virginia Press, Rotunda, 2010). Canonic URL: https://rotunda .upress.virginia.edu/founders/JSMN-01-09-02-0037, accessed December 5, 2020.

14. Statistics from Francis D. Cogliano, *Revolutionary America, 1763–1815: A Political History,* 3rd ed. (New York: Routledge, 2017), 111. For Shays's Rebellion generally, Leonard L. Richards, *Shays's Rebellion: The American Revolution's Final Battle* (Philadelphia: University of Pennsylvania Press, 2002); Terry Bouton, *Taming Democracy: The People, The Founders, and the Troubled Ending of the American Revolution* (New York: Oxford University Press, 2007), ch. 7; and Robert A. Gross, ed., *In Debt to Shays: Bicentennial of an Agrarian Rebellion* (Charlottesville: University of Virginia Press, 1993).

15. For Shays, see Robert A. Gross, "The Uninvited Guest: Daniel Shays and the Constitution," in Gross, *In Debt to Shays,* 1–43, detail about Lafayette's sword, 1.

16. Henry Knox to GW, October 23, 1786, PGWDE.

17. GW to John Jay, August 15, 1786, PGWDE.

18. GW to David Humphreys, December 26, 1786, PGWDE.

19. GW to JM, November 5, 1786, PGWDE.

20. GW, Circular to State Governments, June 8, 1783, GWW, 516–526, quotations, 516–517.

21. GWW, 517–518.

22. GWW, 518–519, 520, 521.

23. GW to James Warren, October 7, 1785, PGWDE.

24. GW to John Jay, May 18, 1786; GW to John Jay, March 10, 1787, PGWDE.

25. See GW Diaries, entries for May 14 and 25, 1787, PGWDE.

26. TJ to John Adams, August 30, 1787, PTJDE.

27. Joseph J. Ellis, *His Excellency: George Washington* (New York: Random House, 2004), 177.

28. GW to Benjamin Harrison, September 24, 1787, PGWDE. For two excellent accounts of the Constitutional Convention, see Feldman, *Three Lives of James Madison,* chs. 4–5; and Michael Klarman, *The Framers' Coup: The Making of the United States Constitution* (New York: Oxford University Press, 2016), chs. 3–4.

29. GW to TJ, September 18, 1787, PTJDE; GW to Lafayette, September 18, 1787, PGWDE. Also see GW to TJ, January 1, 1788, PTJDE.

30. Francis D. Cogliano, "'The Whole Object of the Present Controversy': The Early Constitutionalism of Paine and Jefferson," in *Paine and Jefferson in the Age of Revolutions,* ed. Simon P. Newman and Peters S. Onuf (Charlottesville: University of Virginia Press, 2013), 26–48.

31. TJ to GW, November 14, 1786; TJ to Benjamin Hawkins, August 4, 1787, PTJDE.

32. TJ to JM, January 30, 1787, PTJDE.

33. TJ to William Stephens Smith, November 13, 1787, PTJDE.

34. TJ to Edward Carrington, August 4, 1787; TJ to JM, December 16, 1786. Also see TJ to JM, June 20, 1787, PTJDE.

35. TJ to John Adams, November 13, 1787; TJ to Edward Carrington, December 21, 1787, PTJDE. For a lengthy exchange between Jefferson and Madison on the proposed constitution, see JM to TJ, October 24, 1787, and TJ to JM, December 20, 1787, PTJDE.

36. TJ to GW, May 2, 1788, PTJDE. For Jefferson's criticisms of the Constitution, see (in addition to the letters cited in n. 35 above) TJ to William Stephens Smith, February 2, 1788; TJ to Edward Carrington, May 27, 1788; TJ to William Carmichael, June 3, 1788; TJ to Edward Rutledge, July 18, 1788; TJ to JM, July 31, 1788, PTJDE. In his letter to William Carmichael on June 3, 1788, Jefferson wrote, "There is no doubt that Genl. Washington will accept the presidentship, tho' he is silent on the subject."

37. TJ to JM, December 20, 1787, PTJDE.

38. TJ to GW, December 4, 1788, PTJDE.

39. TJ to David Humphreys, March 18, 1789, PTJDE.

11. I Will Converse with You on the Subject

Epigraph: PTJDE.

1. For Washington's election and inauguration, see Gordon S. Wood, *Empire of Liberty: A History of the Early American Republic, 1789–1815* (New York: Oxford University Press, 2009), ch. 2. For Washington's cabinet and his use of the cabinet to govern, see Lindsay M. Chervinsky, *The Cabinet: George Washington and the Creation of an American Institution* (Cambridge, MA: Belknap Press of Harvard University Press, 2020).

2. Notes of a Conversation with George Washington, August 6, 1793; JM to TJ, May 27, 1789; TJ to JM, August 28, 1789, PTJDE; Senate Executive Journal, 1st Cong., 1st Sess., 1:32–33.

3. TJ to William Short, December 14, 1789; TJ to GW, December 15, 1789, PTJDE.

4. GW to TJ, January 21, 1790; TJ to GW, February 14, 1790, PTJDE. For Madison's role as an intermediary, see Andrew Burstein and Nancy Isenberg, *Madison and Jefferson* (New York: Random House, 2010), 202–204. Marriage Settlement for Martha Jefferson, February 21, 1790, PTJDE.

5. See GW Diaries, PGWDE, entries for March 23 and 26, 1790, and June 30, 1790. Editorial Notes: Plans and Estimates for the Diplomatic Establishment; Plans Presented to Washington, March 26, 1790; Plans presented to the Conference Committee, June 21, 1790; Observations on the Diplomatic Establishment, July 17, 1790; Estimates of Funds Required for the Diplomatic Establishment, 1790–1791, PTJDE. Lindsay Chervinsky discusses this episode at length and argues that this early, successful collaboration between Washington and Jefferson helped assert presidential control over foreign policy. Chervinsky, *Cabinet*, 171–176, esp. 176.

6. For examples of Jefferson offering Washington advice, see TJ to GW, October 23, 1791, and TJ to GW, November 1, 1792. Also see TJ to GW, December 16, 1791; GW to TJ, December 18, 1791; GW to TJ, March 12, 1792; GW to TJ, July 7, 1792, PTJDE.

7. GW to TJ, August 21, 1791, PTJDE. Also see GW to TJ, January 16, 1792, PTJDE.

8. JM to TJ, February 14, 1790, PTJDE.

9. Ron Chernow, *Alexander Hamilton* (New York: Penguin, 2004); Stanley Elkins and Eric McKitrick, *The Age of Federalism: The Early American Republic, 1788–1800* (New York: Oxford University Press, 1993), ch. 2.

10. Report of the Secretary of the Treasury on the Public Credit, January 14, 1790, *The Documentary History of the First Federal Congress of the United States, March 4, 1789–March 3, 1791: Digital Edition*, ed. Charlene Bangs Bickford, Kenneth R. Bowling, William C. diGiacomantonio, and Helen E. Veit (Charlottesville: University of Virginia Press, 2019); Elkins and McKitrick, *Age of Federalism*, 92–114; Francis D. Cogliano, *Revolutionary America, 1763–1815: A Political History*, 3rd ed. (New York: Routledge, 2017), 147–149.

11. *Notes on the State of Virginia*, TJW, 291. For Jefferson's vision of political economy, see Drew McCoy, *The Elusive Republic: Political Economy in Jeffersonian America* (Chapel Hill: University of North Carolina Press, 1980); and Francis D. Cogliano, *Emperor of Liberty: Thomas Jefferson's Foreign Policy* (New Haven, CT: Yale University Press, 2014), 45–51.

12. Jefferson's Account of the Bargain on the Assumption and Residence Bills, [1792?], PTJDE. See Julian P. Boyd's lengthy editorial note (and accompanying documents), Opinions on the Constitutionality of the Residence Bill, PTJDE. Boyd estimates that Jefferson's encounter with Hamilton occurred on June 14 and the dinner with Madison and Hamilton took place the following day, June 15, 1790. Stanley Elkins and Erick McKitrick estimate the dinner took place on June 20. Elkins and McKitrick, *Age of Federalism*, 157, n47. Also see Jacob E. Cooke, "The Compromise of 1790," *William and Mary Quarterly* 27 (1970): 523–545; and Kenneth R. Bowling (with a rebuttal by Jacob E. Cooke), "Dinner at Jefferson's: A Note on Jacob E. Cooke's 'The Compromise of 1790,'" *William and Mary Quarterly* 28 (1971): 629–648. Jefferson described his accommodation at 57 Maiden Lane as "indifferent" in a letter to his daughter, Martha, soon after he rented it. TJ to Martha Jefferson Randolph, April 4, 1790, PTJDE. St. John de Crèvecoeur wrote that Jefferson "Lived in a Mean House in Maiden Lane and not approving much of the Stiff Style and Etiquette of New York he gave up all his Time to the Establishment of his new department, foreign affairs and Home." Crèvecoeur to William Short, c. July 15, 1790, as quoted in the editorial note following Jefferson to Thomas Mann Randolph, March 18, 1790, PTJDE.

13. Annette Gordon-Reed, *The Hemingses of Monticello: An American Family* (New York: Norton, 2008), 445–454.

14. Jefferson's Account of the Bargain on the Assumption and Residence Bills [1792?], PTJDE.

15. See Elkins and McKitrick, *Age of Federalism*, 155–161, for the origins and significance of the compromise.

16. Cogliano, *Revolutionary America*, 148–150.

17. TJ to GW, September 9, 1792, PTJDE; Jefferson's Introduction to the "Anas," February 4, 1818, PTJDE.

18. For the most comprehensive summary of the matter, see the editorial note and relevant documents collected under the heading "Fixing the Seat of Government," in volume 20 PTJ, available in PTJDE. GW to TJ, November 30, 1791; GW [TJ] to Pierre Charles L'Enfant, December 1, 1791; TJ to GW, December 11, 1791; GW to TJ, January 18, 1792;

TJ to Pierre Charles L'Enfant, February 27, 1792, PTJDE. Also see Saul K. Padover, ed., *Thomas Jefferson and the National Capital: Containing Notes and Correspondence exchanged between Jefferson, Washington, L'Enfant, Ellicott, Hallett, Thornton, Latrobe, the Commissioners and Others Relating to . . . the City of Washington, 1783–1818* (Washington, DC: Government Printing Office, 1946); Elkins and McKitrick, *Age of Federalism*, ch. 4; C. M. Harris, "Washington's Gamble, L'Enfant's Dream: Politics, Design and the Founding of the National Capital," *William and Mary Quarterly* 56 (1999): 527–564.

19. Pierre L'Enfant to GW, September 11, 1789, PGWDE.

20. TJ to George Gilmer, June 27, 1790, PTJDE; Wood, *Empire of Liberty*, 79–80.

21. They were not necessarily the same as the Federalists of 1787–1788 who supported the drafting and ratification of the Constitution. Jefferson and Madison, for example, supported the Constitution but came to oppose many tenets of Federalism during the 1790s.

22. TJ to Philip Freneau, February 28, 1791, PTJDE. For the newspaper war, see Elkins and McKitrick, *Age of Federalism*, 282–292; and Jeffrey L. Pasley, *"The Tyranny of Printers": Newspaper Politics in the Early American Republic* (Charlottesville: University of Virginia Press, 2001).

23. Memoranda of Conversations with the President, March 1, 1792, PTJDE. Jefferson believed that Washington intended to retire in 1793 because, a year earlier, he had written in response to a proposal by the government of Pennsylvania to improve the federal facilities in the city, including the building of a residence for the president, with an eye to persuading the government to making Philadelphia the permanent capital of the nation, that "the most superb edifices may be erected, and I shall wish their inhabitants much happiness, and that too very disinterestedly, as I shall never be of the number myself." GW to TJ, April 1, 1791, PTJDE.

24. Memoranda of Conversations with the President, March 1, 1792, PTJDE. For Jefferson's plan to reform the post office, see Plan for Expediting Postal Service [March 4, 1792], PTJDE. Washington kept the post office within the Treasury Department.

25. TJ to GW, May 23, 1792, PTJDE.

26. Notes of Conversation with George Washington, July 10, 1792, PTJDE.

27. Notes of Conversation with George Washington, July 10, 1792, PTJDE.

28. GW to Alexander Hamilton, July 29, 1792, PGWDE; Alexander Hamilton to GW, August 18, 1792, *The Papers of Alexander Hamilton Digital Edition*, ed. Harold C. Syrett (Charlottesville: University of Virginia Press, Rotunda, 2011); GW to TJ, August 23, 1792 (quoted), PTJDE; GW to Alexander Hamilton, August 26, 1792, PGWDE.

29. An American Numbers I, II, III [August 4, 11, and 18, 1792], *Papers of Alexander Hamilton Digital Edition*; TJ to GW, September 9, 1792, PTJDE.

30. TJA, 371.

31. GW to Gouverneur Morris, October 13, 1789, PGWDE; TJ to William Short, January 3, 1793, PTJDE.

32. TJ to C. W. F. Dumas, March 24, 1793, PTJDE. Cogliano, *Emperor of Liberty*, ch. 3.

33. GW to the Cabinet with Enclosure: Questions on Neutrality and the Alliance with France, April 18, 1793, PTJDE; Notes on Washington's Questions on Neutrality and the Alliance with France, [May 6, 1793], PTJDE.

34. TJ to JM, June 23, 1793, PTJDE; Neutrality Proclamation [April 22, 1793], PGWDE. Elkins and McKitrick, *Age of Federalism*, 336–341.

35. Jefferson's Opinion on the Treaties with France, April 28, 1793, PTJDE.

36. Alexander Hamilton and Henry Knox to GW, May 2, 1793, PGWDE; TJ to James Monroe, May 5, 1793, PTJDE.

37. Gouverneur Morris to GW, December 28, 1792, PGWDE. Harry Ammon, *The Genêt Mission* (New York: Norton, 1973).

38. "Instructions to Genêt," in Frederick Jackson Turner, ed., *Correspondence of the French Ministers to the United States, 1791–1797, Annual Report of the American Historical Association doe 1903* (Washington, DC: Government Printing Office, 1904), 210–211.

39. *Aurora* (Philadelphia), May 14, 17, and 20, 1793.

40. TJ to JM, May 19, 1793 (quotation); Edmond Charles Genêt to TJ, May 22, 1793; Genêt to TJ, May 23, 1793; Genêt to TJ, 1793; TJ to Genêt, June 11, 1793, PTJDE.

41. TJ to GW, June 6, 1793, PTJDE.

42. GW to TJ, July 11, 1793; Notes of a Cabinet Meeting on Edmond Charles Genêt, July 23, 1793; GW to TJ, July 25, 1793; Memorandum of a Conversation with Edmond Charles Genêt, July 26, 1793; Notes of a Cabinet Meeting on Edmond Charles Genêt, August 1, 1793; Notes of a Cabinet Meeting on Edmond Charles Genêt, August 2, 1793; TJ to Gouverneur Morris, August 16, 1793, PTJDE. For Genêt and the cabinet's response to him, see Cogliano, *Emperor of Liberty*, 110–114.

43. TJ to GW, July 31, 1793; Notes of a Conversation with George Washington, August 6, 1793, PTJDE.

44. Notes of a Conversation with George Washington, August 6, 1793, PTJDE.

45. TJ to GW, December 31, 1793; GW to TJ, January 1, 1794, PTJDE.

12. The Sincerity of a Friendship

Epigraph: PTJDE.

1. GW to TJ, April 24, 1794; TJ to GW, May 14, 1794, PTJDE.

2. Stanley Elkins and Eric McKitrick, *The Age of Federalism: The Early American Republic, 1788–1800* (New York: Oxford University Press, 1993), 388–396. TJ to GW, May 14, 1794, PTJDE.

3. Proclamation on Violent Opposition to the Excise Tax, February 24, 1794; Proclamation Calling Out the Militia to Occupy the Western Counties of Pennsylvania, August 7, 1794, PGWDE. William Bradford quotation: Gordon S. Wood, *Empire of Liberty: A History of the Early Republic, 1789–1815* (New York: Oxford University Press, 2009), 157.

4. For the Whiskey Rebellion, see Thomas P. Slaughter, *The Whiskey Rebellion: Frontier Epilogue to the American Revolution* (New York: Oxford University Press, 1986); and William Hogeland, *The Whiskey Rebellion: George Washington, Alexander Hamilton, and the Frontier Rebels Who Challenged America's Newfound Sovereignty* (New York: Scribner's, 2006).

5. GW to the US Senate and House of Representatives, November 19, 1794; GW to Burgess Ball, September 25, 1794, PGWDE.

6. TJ to JM, December 28, 1794, PTJDE.

7. GW to Henry Lee, August 26, 1794, PGWDE. Washington appointed Lee, a former comrade from the Continental Army, to command the army that suppressed the Whiskey Rebellion.

8. TJ to James Monroe, May 26, 1795, PTJDE.

9. Malone, *Jefferson and His Time*, 3:191; Henry Lee to GW, August 17, 1794; GW to Henry Lee, August 26, 1794, PGWDE; TJ to James Monroe, May 26, 1795, PTJDE.

10. Elkins and McKitrick, *Age of Federalism*, ch. 9.

11. *American Mercury* (Hartford, CT), August 31, 1795.

12. GW to Alexander Hamilton, July 29, 1795, PGWDE. For the debate over the treaty, see Todd Estes, *The Jay Treaty Debate, Public Opinion, and the Evolution of Early American Political Culture* (Amherst, MA: University of Massachusetts Press, 2006).

13. GW to Alexander Hamilton, July 29, 1795, PGWDE; TJ to Thomas Mann Randolph, August 11, 1795; TJ to Mann Page, August 30, 1795, PTJDE.

14. GW to the US Senate and House of Representatives, March 1, 1796, PGWDE.

15. TJ to James Monroe, September 6, 1795, PTJDE.

16. "Paulding," *Aurora* (Philadelphia), June 9, 1796. Also see James D. Tagg, "Benjamin Franklin Bache's Attack on George Washington," *Pennsylvania Magazine of History and Biography* 100:191–230; and Lindsay M. Chervinsky, *The Cabinet: George Washington and the Creation of an American Institution* (Cambridge, MA: Belknap Press of Harvard University Press, 2020), 276–279, as well as Jeffrey L. Pasley, *"The Tyranny of Printers": Newspaper Politics in the Early American Republic* (Charlottesville: University of Virginia Press, 2001). "Paulding" reproduced the questions in GW to the Cabinet, April 18, 1793, PGWDE.

17. TJ to GW, June 19, 1796, PTJDE.

18. TJ to GW, June 19, 1796, PTJDE.

19. GW to TJ, July 6, 1796, PTJDE.

20. Alexis Coe helpfully sums up Washington's various ailments in *You Never Forget Your First: A Biography of George Washington* (Penguin: New York, 2020), xxi–xxii, xxx–xxxi.

21. Farewell Address, September 19, 1796, PGWDE.

22. TJ to JM, December 17, 1796, PTJDE.

23. Jeffrey L. Pasley, *The First Presidential Contest: 1796 and the Founding of American Democracy* (Lawrence: University Press of Kansas, 2013).

24. TJ to JM, January 8, 1797, PTJDE.

25. Henrietta Liston, Journals: Description of the resignation of General Washington as President, of visits to him at Mount Vernon, and of his death, March 5, 1797, MS.5698, p. 4. National Library of Scotland, Edinburgh.

26. Malone, *Jefferson and the Ordeal of Liberty*, 295. Liston, Journals, March 5, 1797, MS.5698, p. 1; John Adams to Abigail Adams, March 5, 1797, *The Adams Papers Digital Edition*, ed. Sara Martin (Charlottesville: University of Virginia Press, Rotunda, 2008–2021).

27. TJ, Notes on Conversations with John Adams and George Washington [after October 13, 1797], PTJDE. The dating on Jefferson's notes is somewhat confusing. He seems

to have written his recollections of Adams's inauguration, including the dinner with Washington, on May 10 and then returned to them in October. GWD, entry for March 6, 1797, PGWDE.

28. Merrill D. Peterson, *The Jefferson Image in the American Mind* (New York: Oxford University Press, 1960), 118.

29. Extract and Commentary Printed in the New York *Minerva* [May 2, 1797], PTJDE.

30. Extract and Commentary Printed in the New York *Minerva* [May 2, 1797], PTJDE.

31. The tangled history of the letter and its publication is helpfully delineated in the editorial note under the heading "Jefferson's Letter to Philip Mazzei" in the PTJDE.

32. John Langhorne to GW, September 27, 1797; GW to John Langhorne, October 15, 1797, John Nicholas to GW, November 18, 1797, PGWDE; Malone, *Jefferson and His Time*, 3:308–311.

33. GW to John Nicholas, March 8, 1798.

34. Liston, Journals, March 5, 1797, MS.5698, p. 4.

35. Liston, Journals, n.d. "Written fourteen months after," MS.5698, p. 5; Henrietta Liston, Journals, North America 1800, Journey to the Natural Bridge in Virginia, MS.5701, p. 18.

13. Cruel War against Human Nature Itself

Epigraphs: PGWDE.

1. Phillis Wheatley, *Poems on Various Subjects, Religious and Moral* (London: Archibald Bell, 1773). Also see David Waldstreicher, *The Odyssey of Phillis Wheatley: A Poet's Journey through Slavery and Independence* (New York: Farrar, Straus & Giroux, 2023); Vincent Carretta, *Phillis Wheatley: Biography of a Genius in Bondage* (Athens: University of Georgia Press, 2011); and Henry Louis Gates Jr., *The Trials of Phillis Wheatley: America's First Black Poet and Her Encounters with the Founding Fathers* (New York: Civitas, 2003).

2. Phillis Wheatley to GW, October 26, 1775, enc PGWDE.

3. GW to Phillis Wheatley, February 28, 1776, PGWDE.

4. *Notes on the State of Virginia*, TJW, 267.

5. *Notes on the State of Virginia*, TJW, 270.

6. *Notes on the State of Virginia*, TJW, 289.

7. My thinking with respect to Washington and slavery owes much to Mary V. Thompson, *"The Only Unavoidable Subject of Regret": George Washington, Slavery, and the Enslaved Community at Mount Vernon* (Charlottesville: University of Virginia Press, 2019); Dorothy Twohig, "That Species of Property: Washington's Role in the Controversy over Slavery," in *George Washington Reconsidered*, ed. Don Higginbotham (Charlottesville: University of Virginia Press, 2001), 114–139; Philip D. Morgan, "'To Get Quit of Negroes': George Washington and Slavery," *Journal of American Studies* 39 (2005): 403–429; Kenneth Morgan, "George Washington and the Problem of Slavery," *Journal of American Studies* 34 (2000): 279–301; L. Scott Philyaw, "Washington and Slavery," in *A Companion to George Washington*, ed. Edward G. Lengel (Malden, MA: Wiley-Blackwell, 2012), 104–120.

8. Bruce A. Ragsdale, *Washington at the Plow: The Founding Farmer and the Question of Slavery* (Cambridge, MA: Belknap Press of Harvard University Press, 2021); Bruce A. Ragsdale, "George Washington, the British Tobacco Trade, and Economic Opportunity in Prerevolutionary Virginia," *Virginia Magazine of History and Biography* 97 (1989): 132–162; Morgan, "'To Get Quit of Negroes,'" 412–413.

9. GW to, July 10 [11], 1775, PGWDE.

10. Council of War, Cambridge, October 8, 1775, PGWDE.

11. *Virginia Gazette*, November 25, 1775; GW to Joseph Reed, December 15, 1775, PGWDE; GW to Richard Henry Lee, December 26, 1775, PGWDE; Commission to Robert Breck, January 24, 1776, PGWDE; General Orders, February 21, 1776, PGWDE. James Corbett David, *Dunmore's New World: The Extraordinary Life of a Royal Governor in Revolutionary America—with Jacobites, Counterfeiters, Land Schemes, Shipwrecks, Scalping, Indian Politics, Runaway Slaves, and Two Illegal Royal Weddings* (Charlottesville: University of Virginia Press, 2013).

12. See James Varnum to GW, January 2, 1778, PGWDE; Nicholas Cooke to GW, February 23, 1778, PGWDE.

13. GW to Continental Congress Camp Committee, January 29, 1778, PGWDE.

14. John Laurens to Henry Laurens, February 2, 1778, David R. Chestnutt, ed., *The Papers of Henry Laurens*, 16 vols. (Columbia: University of South Carolina Press, 1968–2002), 12:392.

15. GW to Henry Laurens, March 20, 1779, PGWDE.

16. GW to Lund Washington, August 15, 1778, PGWDE.

17. GW to Lund Washington, February 22–[26], 1779, n. 3, PGWDE. Also see Lund Washington to GW, April 8, 1778, PGWDE; Lund Washington to GW, September 2, 1778, PGWDE.

18. Marquis de Lafayette to GW, February 5, 1783, Founders Online, accessed October 8, 2018.

19. GW to the Marquis de Lafayette, April 5, 1783, Founders Online, accessed October 8, 2018.

20. William Gordon to GW, August 30, 1784, PGWDE.

21. GW to Robert Morris, April 12, 1786, PGWDE.

22. GW to John Francis Mercer, September 9, 1786, PGWDE.

23. GW to Robert Morris, April 12, 1786, PGWDE.

24. See Francois Furstenberg, "Atlantic Slavery, Atlantic Freedom: George Washington, Slavery and Transatlantic Abolition Networks," *WMQ* 68 (2011): 247–286.

25. Morgan, "'To Get Quit of Negroes,'" 422–423.

26. GW to Lawrence Lewis, August 4, 1797, PGWDE.

27. GW to Arthur Young, December 12, 1793, PGWDE.

28. GW Last Will and Testament, July 9, 1799, PGWDE.

29. GW Last Will and Testament, July 9, 1799, PGWDE.

30. GW Last Will and Testament, July 9, 1799, PGWDE.

31. GW Last Will and Testament, July 9, 1799, n. 3, PGWDE.

32. TJ to Edward Coles, August 25, 1814, PTJDE. In his autobiography Jefferson recalled, "I made one effort in that body for the permission of the emancipation of slaves,

which was rejected: and indeed, during the regal government, nothing liberal could expect success." TJA, 310. Paul Finkelman is skeptical about Jefferson's involvement in the 1769 debate over manumission; Paul Finkleman, "Jefferson and Slavery: 'Treason against the Hopes of the World,'" in *Jeffersonian Legacies*, ed. Peter S. Onuf (Charlottesville: University of Virginia Press, 1993), 181–221, esp. 188–189. The only evidence to support Jefferson's claim that he supported Bland's motion comes from his letter to Coles and his 1821 autobiography. There is no record in the journal of the House of Burgesses, but the House did not usually record unsuccessful motions.

33. TJ, *Summary View of the Rights of British America* (Williamsburg, 1774), repr. in TJW, 103–122, quotation 115–116.

34. Pauline Maier, *American Scripture: Making the Declaration of Independence* (New York: Knopf, 1997).

35. My thinking on the deleted clause in the Declaration has been influenced by Peter S. Onuf, *Jefferson's Empire: The Language of American Nationhood* (Charlottesville: University of Virginia Press, 2000), 147–188.

36. TJ to John Vaughn, September 16, 1825, Founders Online, accessed October 16, 2018.

37. Philip Mazzei, *My Life and Wanderings*, ed. Margherita Marchione, trans. S. Eugene Scalia (Morristown, NJ: American Institute of Italian Studies, 1980), 223. Mazzei's memoir was originally published in Italian in Switzerland, *Memorie della vita e delle peregrinazioni del fiorentino, Filippo Mazzei*, 2 vols. (Lugano: Tipografia della Svizzera Italiana, 1845).

38. TJA, 327.

39. Revisal of the Laws, 1776–1786, A Bill Concerning Slaves (Bill number 51), PTJDE.

40. For the adoption of the Bill Concerning Slaves in December 1785, see *Journal of the House of Delegates of Virginia, 1785* (Richmond, VA: Thomas White, 1828), 12–15, 54, 64, 71, 78, 79, 133; and TJA, 328. For the 1782 manumission law, which superseded key elements of Jefferson's 1779 bill, see An Act to Authorize the Manumission of Slaves, in William Waller Hening, ed., *Statutes at Large Being a Collection of All the Laws of Virginia from the First Session of the Legislature, in the Year 1619*, 13 vols. (Richmond, VA: R. & W. G. Bartow, 1819–1823), 11:39.

41. Jefferson's Draft Constitution for Virginia, Proposed Revision of the Virginia Constitution [May–June 1783], PTJDE.

42. Revised Report of the Committee, March 22, 1784, PTJDE; see Editorial Note: Plan for the Government of the Western Territory, PTJDE; Peter S. Onuf, *Statehood and Union: A History of the Northwest Ordinance* (Bloomington: Indiana University Press, 1987).

43. *Notes on the State of Virginia*, TJW, 264.

44. See, for example, TJ to Rufus King, July 13, 1802, PTJDE; TJ to Albert Gallatin, December 26, 1820, PTJDE.

45. *Notes on the State of Virginia*, TJW, 264.

46. *Notes on the State of Virginia*, TJW, 270. For the passage on racial difference, see 264–270.

47. TJ to John Holmes, April 22, 1820, PTJDE.

48. TJ to Albert Gallatin, December 26, 1820, PTJDE.

49. [TJ], Notes on Arthur Young's Letter to George Washington, June 18, 1792, PTJDE; GW to Arthur Young, June 18–21, 1792, PGWDE. Washington wrote in response to Arthur Young's letter of January 18, 1792. Young published an edited version of his correspondence with Washington after Washington's death. See Arthur Young, *Letters from His Excellency General Washington to Arthur Young, Esq. F. R. S.* (London, 1801).

50. TJ to Edward Coles, August 25, 1814, PTJDE.

51. GW to David Stuart, March 28, 1790, PGWDE.

52. Jefferson's "original Rough draught" of the Declaration of Independence, PTJDE; *Notes on the State of Virginia*, TJW, 264.

53. GWD, entry for March 16, 1790.

54. GW to David Stuart, March 28, 1790, PGWDE. Washington later wrote to Stuart: "The introduction of the (Quaker) Memorial, respecting Slavery, was to be sure, not only an ill-judged piece of business, but occasioned a great waste of time. The final decision thereon, however, was as favourable as the proprietors of that species of property could well have expected considering the great dereliction of Slavery in a large part of this Union." GW to David Stuart, June 15, 1790, PGWDE. Also see GW to the Society of Quakers, October 13, 1789, n. 1, PGWDE; Warner Mifflin to GW, March 12, 1790, PGWDE.

Epilogue

Epigraphs: PTJDE. Ogden had sent Jefferson a copy of his eulogy for Washington, *Two Discourses, Occasioned by the Death of General George Washington, at Mount-Vernon, December 14, 1799* (Newark, NJ, 1800).

1. Henrietta Liston, Journals, MS.5698 Description of the resignation of General Washington as President, of visits to him at Mount Vernon, and of his death, National Library of Scotland, Edinburgh, entry for November 29, 1799, 7.

2. Liston, Journals, MS.5698, 9–10. Henry Lee, *Funeral Oration on the Death of George Washington* (Boston, 1800).

3. Robert Troup to Rufus King, January 1, 1800, Charles R. King, ed., *The Life and Correspondence of Rufus King*, 6 vols. (New York: G. P. Putnam's Sons, 1894–1900), 3:171. For Jefferson's trip to Philadelphia in December 1799, see TJ to Mary Jefferson Eppes, January 17, 1800, PTJDE.

4. TJ to Samuel Miller, February 25, 1800, PTJDE. Also see Samuel Miller to TJ, February 13, 1800; and Samuel Miller, *A Sermon, Delivered December 29, 1799, Occasioned by the Death of General George Washington* (New York, 1800).

5. TJ to Mary Jefferson Eppes, January 3, 1801, PTJDE. Also see TJMB, entry for January 3, 1801.

6. William Watson Andrews, ed., *The Correspondence and Miscellanies of John Cotton Smith* (New York: Harper and Brothers, 1847), 224–225; William P. Cutler and Julia P. Cutler, eds., *Life, Journals and Correspondence of Rev. Manasseh Cutler, L.L.D*, 2 vols. (Cincinnati, OH: Robert Clarke and Company, 1888), 2:55–57.

7. Andrews, *Correspondence and Miscellanies of John Cotton Smith,* 224.

8. TJ, First Inaugural Address, March 4, 1801, PTJDE.

9. TJ, First Inaugural Address, March 4, 1801, PTJDE.

10. TJ to Joel Barlow, May 3, 1802, PTJDE.

11. John Marshall, *The Life of George Washington,* 5 vols. (Philadelphia: C. P. Wayne, 1804–1807); 5:33, 353–355.

12. Joanne B. Freeman, *Affairs of Honor: National Politics in the New Republic* (New Haven, CT: Yale University Press, 2001), 63. For circulation figures on *The Life of Washington,* see Francis D. Cogliano, *Thomas Jefferson: Reputation and Legacy* (Charlottesville: University of Virginia Press, 2006), 52.

13. TJ to Joel Barlow, April 16, 1811, PTJDE; Notes on the Fifth Volume of John Marshall's *Life of George Washington* [c. February 4, 1818], PTJDE.

14. Introduction to the Anas, February 4, 1818, PTJDE. For a discussion of the provenance and compilation of the Anas, see PTJ 22:33–38, and PTJ:RS 12:416.

15. Introduction to the Anas, February 4, 1818, PTJDE.

16. Introduction to the Anas, February 4, 1818, PTJDE.

17. Notes of a Conversation with George Washington, October 1, 1792, PTJDE.

18. Memoranda of Conversations with the President, March 1, 1792, PTJDE.

19. Walter Jones to TJ, November 25, 1813, PTJDE.

20. TJ to Walter Jones, January 2, 1814, PTJDE.

21. TJ to Spencer Roane, September 6, 1819, PTJDE.

22. TJ to Roger C. Weightman, June 24, 1826, TJW, 1516.

Acknowledgments

George Washington described friendship as "a plant of slow growth," which must "withstand the shocks of adversity before it is entitled to the appellation." In writing this book, I have relied on the support and wise counsel of many friends and colleagues. I fear they may have experienced "shocks of adversity" as they helped me. It gives me great pleasure to acknowledge their assistance and support.

I was working on this book for a long time when I encountered a conceptual block that seemed to doom the entire project. One sunny morning during a conference in Santiago, Chile, I went to a café with Annette Gordon-Reed, Patrick Griffin, and Peter Onuf. After I told them I was considering giving up the project, we spent two hours dissecting and reassembling it. They talked me through my writer's block and helped me to understand what I was trying to achieve. Afterward, I had the clarity I needed to finish the book. It was an impromptu seminar with some of the smartest and most generous scholars I know. I'm fortunate to have such kind and patient friends.

This project would not have been possible without institutional support from the University of Edinburgh, particularly the School of History, Classics, and Archaeology. It has been a privilege to have spent most of my career at the University of Edinburgh. I am especially grateful to Edinburgh colleagues and friends: Douglas Cairns, Ewen Cameron, Enda Delaney, Fabian Hilfrich, Scott McQuarrie, Liz Reilly, and David Silkenat. My graduate students shared their enthusiasm and insights with me. Thanks to Benjamin Anderson, Krysten Blackstone, Kate Clarke, Devin Grier, James Mackay, Paul McFarlane, Robbie McNiven, and Miles Stanley for asking tough questions and sharpening my thinking. Chris Bates had a

fellowship at Monticello at the same time as me, and we enjoyed numerous mutually enlightening conversations on Jefferson and his world.

I benefited immensely from several fellowships at Monticello's International
Center for Jefferson Studies while I wrote this book. These were arranged by its
then-director Andrew Jackson O'Shaughnessy. Andrew read an early version of
my manuscript and offered helpful suggestions. At Monticello, I enjoyed the company and advice of numerous friends and colleagues with whom I discussed this
project, including the following: Anna Berkes, Andrew Davenport, and Caitlin
Lawrence, Jeff Looney, Fraser Neiman, John Ragosta, Liz Ragosta, Tasha Stanton,
Susan Stein, Endrina Tay, and Gaye Wilson. I was awarded a research fellowship
at the George Washington Presidential Library at Mount Vernon. Unfortunately,
I was unable to take up that fellowship because of the COVID-19 pandemic, but
I'm grateful to Doug Bradburn and Kevin Butterfield, who made Mount Vernon's
electronic resources available to me. Doug has been especially enthusiastic about
this project.

Eliga Gould, Patrick Griffin, and Peter Onuf read the manuscript in its entirety
(more than once in Peter's case) and provided detailed criticism and helpful feedback. In so doing they set the standard for scholarly collegiality. Numerous historians (and friends) offered their advice and support while I was working on this
book. My thanks go to Andy Burstein, Lindsay Chervinsky, Christa Dierksheide,
Matthew Dziennik, Joanne Freeman, Nick Guyatt, Nancy Isenberg, Jim McLure,
Virginia Scharff, Hannah Spahn, and Maurizio Valsania. Sadly, Richard Bernstein,
a wonderful historian, generous scholar, and valued friend, passed away while this
book was in production. I hope he would have liked it.

Chris Rogers at Dunow, Carlson & Lerner Literary Agency was an early and
enthusiastic supporter of this project. Chris helped to shape the book through his
wise counsel and helped to place it at Harvard University Press, where Kathleen
McDermott has been a wonderful editor to work with. Kathleen provided encouragement and assistance, suggesting illustrations as well as possible titles for this
book. She has been the most supportive editor with whom I have yet worked.
Though not my editor, Nadine Zimmerli gave me the insight and advice of a top
editor and the encouragement of a friend. Whitney Pippin was indefatigable when
it came to tracking down image rights and high-resolution files. Aaron Wistar at
Harvard helped to make sure that the illustrations were publishable. I'm grateful
to Armin Mattes for preparing the index.

Numerous friends, in Scotland and beyond, helped me in ways large and small.
The Blether Group—Douglas Cairns, Andrew Dorward, Peter Dorward, Gavin
Francis, Allan Little, and John Scally, with whom I discussed this project and
much else—have been great companions on this journey. I owe thanks, too, to
Simon and Nikki Fennell, Joe Pilkington, Margaret Reis, Brendan and Isabel

MacNeill, Pete and Cary Harris, Jane Gray, Tommy Hepburn, and Rhona Hughes. Mark Kinghorn died all too young while I was working on this book. He was skeptical about the need for books about dead presidents but encouraged me nonetheless. He was a steadfast friend with an unerring moral compass and a brilliant sense of humor. I miss him.

This book is dedicated to my wonderful siblings: Beth Cogliano, Andrea Katter, Sally Giangrande, and David Cogliano, to whose number must be added the in-laws: Chuck Katter, John Giangrande, and Lisa Cogliano. They know how our grandmother described us. She was (mostly) right.

My greatest debt, as ever, is to my family: Mimi, Edward, and Sofia. Mimi lived with this book for longer than either of us expected—she was locked down with it in 2020—and balanced encouragement and skepticism as appropriate. If Edward, the project manager, had his way, I would have finished this book years ago. At a crucial moment while I was completing my manuscript, I spent a weekend showing Sofia around Monticello. Her tough questions and sharp humor were exactly what I needed, as always. Rob and Emmi have recently joined our family and have only known me while I was working on this. Fear not, books are like London buses: no sooner do you finish one than another one comes along.

Index

Abingdon plantation, VA, 146
abolition, 63, 117, 262–265, 269–270
Act of Union, 87
Adams, Abigail, 104; and TJ, 186
Adams, John, 94–97, 99–100, 104, 167, 170,
     311n19; and Declaration of Independence,
     111–116; autobiography of, 95; as minister to
     GB, 186, 197, 202; as president, 248–249, 251,
     280, 283; relationship with GW, 249;
     relationship with TJ, 247, 249, 280–281
Adams, Samuel, 111
Africa, 17, 272; West, 255
African Americans. *See under* enslaved persons
     and slavery; United States, free Black people
     in
agriculture, 145, 219, 243; American, 233–234,
     275; commercial, 214; economy, 305n36;
     encouragement of, 285; GW's interest in, 20,
     211, 281; Native Americans and, 182;
     plantation, 52; study of, 57; TJ's interest in,
     211, 281
Albemarle County, VA, 51, 61, 85, 251; militia of,
     19
Alexandria, VA, 30, 92, 161, 215
Algonquin, 15
Allegheny River, 174
Ambler, Jacquelin, 44
American Mercury, 239
American Revolution, 5, 7, 35, 235; and
     Continental Army, 123; historians of, 263;
     legacy of, 195, 231, 253, 288; and Native
     Americans, 170; principles of, 6, 264;
promise of, 192; relation to French
     Revolution, 224; and slavery, 55, 70–71, 257;
     study of, 9; as Virginia Revolution, 110; and
     War of Independence, 125, 139–141
anarchy, 4, 224, 286; Jacobin, 294
Anglican Church: disestablishment of, 125–126,
     270
Anglo-Cherokee War, 167
animals: blackfish, 2; game, 182; horses, 10, 25,
     35, 72, 93, 99, 104, 260, 280, 283; parrot, 34;
     sea bass, 2; sheep, 62; whip-poor-will, 2
Annapolis, MD, 36, 99, 142, 144, 145; Congress
     at, 148, 151, 158
Annapolis Convention, 191–192; Hamilton at, 212
Antigua, 254
Appalachian Mountains, 171, 180, 235
aristocracy, 201, 230; British, 21; of merit,
     126–127; Scottish, 71, 84; and Society of
     Cincinnati, 151–153, 200; VA elites as, 20, 29;
     of wealth, 126–127
Aristotle, 113
army: British, 19, 25, 78, 97, 101, 121–124, 128,
     129, 135–137, 172, 262; and civilian authority,
     133–134; French, 137; standing, 7–8, 106,
     122–124, 139, 140
Arnold, Benedict, 135
Articles of Confederation, 111, 205; crisis of,
     191–199, 200, 202
asylum, 229
Atlantic Ocean, 14, 16, 25, 54, 71, 187, 208, 218,
     264; British, 78; and slave trade, 269, 276, 278
Aurora, 240–242